THE ILLUSTRATED
HISTORY OF
SURGERY

THE ILLUSTRATED
HISTORY OF SURGERY

KNUT HÆGER

Revised and updated by Sir Roy Calne FRS

PROFESSOR OF SURGERY, ADDENBROOKE'S HOSPITAL, CAMBRIDGE

HAROLD
S
STARKE
PUBLISHERS

FITZROY DEARBORN
PUBLISHERS

First published in the United Kingdom, 1989,
and reprinted 1990
Second edition published in 2000
by Harold Starke Publishers Ltd
203 Bunyan Court, Barbican
London EC2Y 8DH and
Pixey Green, Stradbroke, Eye
Suffolk IP21 5NG

Published for the library market in
the United States of America by
Fitzroy Dearborn Publishers
919 North Michigan Avenue
Chicago, Illinois 60611

A Cataloging-in-Publication record is available
from the Library of Congress

ISBN 1-57958-319-9 Fitzroy Dearborn

Printed in Spain

THE ILLUSTRATED
HISTORY OF SURGERY
has been produced by AB Nordbok,
Gothenburg, Sweden

Editor and translator: Jon van Leuven

Consultant: Professor Yngve Edlund

Designer: Mats Persson

Artwork: Lennart Molin

Coordinator: Kerstin Gunnarsson

Contents

Editor's foreword

This well-established and beautifully illustrated book has been updated with a short section on recent advances in surgery, especially minimal invasive surgery and transplantation. It has been a pleasure to edit the previous text, which has been only slightly altered for the sake of accuracy and clarity.

Roy Calne

Preface

Surgery has played a central role in health and healing throughout the ages. Its development can be traced ever more clearly as a result of worldwide research in medical and social history. What emerges is an extraordinary tale that should be narrated in several dimensions. Not just a chronicle of facts or a survey of civilizations, this book is an account of surgical progress for the specialist and layman alike.

The ideas and methods of surgery as a profession are fascinating from many points of view. They have often come from, or passed to, further fields of knowledge. Equally important is an understanding of the people and events "behind the surgical mask". Here, the focus is on surgeons and patients as individuals—frequently remarkable in themselves—and as actors in the drama of their times, with personal touches inside as well as outside the operating theatre.

No story of a subject so vast as surgery can be complete. Exactly who made a discovery, or what chiefly gave rise to it, is commonly controversial. The literature on surgery is not widely available, and includes translations which may differ slightly from the original sources. Nor has medicine been consistently documented with pictures, and many amazing scenes must be left to our imagination. Nevertheless, a wealth of creative activity and human experience characterizes the surgeon's art.

CHAPTER 1

The beginnings of medicine

Surgery is an art of working with the hands. Its name derives from the Latin word *chirurgia*, which in turn comes from the Greek *cheiros* (hand) and *ergon* (work). As a branch of medicine, surgery deals with injuries, deformations and unhealthy physical changes of kinds that require manual treatment, with or without instruments. A well-known description of its concerns was recorded by the sixteenth-century French surgeon Ambroise Paré:

"There are five duties in surgery: to remove what is superfluous, to restore what has been dislocated, to separate what has grown together, to reunite what has been divided and to redress the defects of nature."

Prehistoric and primitive healing

Surgery is as old as mankind. Its age can thus be reckoned to around half a million years, from the time when Java Man, *Pithecanthropus erectus*, evolved on earth. Bone tumours have been identified in Java Man. This condition, probably along with several others, is in fact older than

MEDICAL practice in many parts of the world has very old traditions: this operation, resembling Stone Age trepanations, was depicted in the highlands of Peru as late as 1923. The medicine-man, or shaman, treated a melancholic woman by placing hot oil in a cut on her scalp. He chewed coca leaves and used the juice to anaesthetize the wound.

human beings. It has been found in dinosaurs, which lived some 150 million years ago.

We may assume that the earliest surgery was devoted to tending wounds. Archaeology can tell us little about how it was practised during prehistoric times. However, it is likely to have been done in more or less the same way as among primitive folk today. A common trait of most primitive tribes is the instinct to cover wounds with leaves and other parts of plants. Filling them with spider-webs is a further popular method of treatment. In many places, the belief that spider-webs help to stop bleeding arose very early and continued for a long time. Shakespeare refers to this in *A Midsummer Night's Dream* (Act III/1):

"I shall desire you of more acquaintance, Good Master Cobweb:

If I cut my finger I shall make bold with you..."

Indeed, little boxes containing spider-webs belonged to every soldier's field-equipment at the Battle of Crécy in 1346! Primitive peoples know of other blood-stanching methods as well. The North American Indians once had a special powder which was prepared from certain herbs. Various peoples have also understood how to use heat for stanching. Their procedures are numerous—hot stones, the glowing-red needles and shells of Indians and, of course, the simplest of all, direct burning with a torch or firewood. From these,

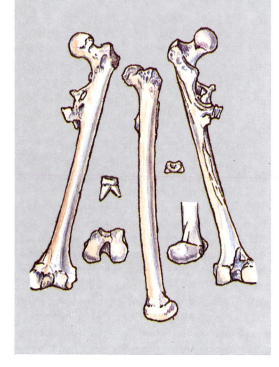

ONE of the oldest known human diseases is tumour growth on bones (exostosis), as in Java Man at least 500,000 years ago. His thigh-bone, found in 1891 by a Dutch doctor, was illustrated in this view from three sides.

more sophisticated techniques were developed. Centuries ago, Tibetan monks poured a mixture of sulphur and saltpetre onto wounds, and set it alight. Such a precedent for blood-stanching with amputations survived well into the eighteenth century, when gunpowder was set off on stumps (see Chapter 8).

Wounds have not only been bandaged with fresh leaves. The ancient Egyptians recommended raw meat, while eaglet-down and sand were used in America, and animal excrement has been laid directly on wounds for centuries throughout the world. The latter, to be sure, is hardly a safe method, since tetanus bacilli thrive in fresh excrement. But it is far from certain that tetanus existed in prehistoric times. Bacteria may undergo peculiar mutations and alter their disease-causing properties.

Nor is there any reason to doubt that our distant ancestors realized the value of draining a wound. The need to create an outlet where pus has collected is an old rule. How this can be done with primitive means is shown by the Dakota Indians. They sharpened a feather-quill and mounted it on an animal's bladder. The quill was stuck into the afflicted area, and the pus was sucked up into the bladder. The Indians did not stop at that: they left some hollow quills in the wound, allowing a free outlet for fluid and pus. The same principle is still followed today, the difference being that we use rubber tubes.

Early man was also aware of the benefit of closing large wounds. Here, too, we must depend on the evidence of primitive folk, although bone needles of the Old Stone Age have been discovered which could have been used for wound sutures. The Masai tribes in Africa exhibit a clever technique. At a secure distance from each edge of the wound, they employ a sharp awl to make a path for a long acacia thorn; it is then stuck through both edges, and its ends are united with a thread of twined plant fibres. Yet the prize for inventiveness must be awarded to tribes in India and South America, where the surgeon sewed a wound by bringing its edges together while his assistant allowed a termite or beetle to bite across them. When the insect had taken a good bite, its neck was twisted quickly. The jaws, stiffened in death, made a perfect wound-clamp! This principle continues with the *agraffe* which, however, is fortunately manufactured nowadays of stainless steel or silver.

Medicine was highly developed among the Aztecs of Mexico. As early as five hundred years ago, they treated superficial contusions and haemorrhoids with a wound salve which was not unlike modern ones. They were also adept in the use of herbs, and we know that they exploited pain-killing drugs as well as a kind of crude narcotic. Most remarkable, from a surgical viewpoint, is the following advice for treatment of a broken bone:

"First the broken bone should be splinted, extended, and fitted together...and if this is not effective, an incision should be made, the bone ends exposed, and a branch of fir-wood inserted in the marrow cavity..."

This method, now called marrow-pinning, was not rediscovered until the twentieth century!

Bone fractures must have been among the commonest problem of Stone Age folk. Hunting and fishing tribes on the move are slowed down by invalids who cannot keep the pace or, perhaps, travel at all. Bones have been found with healed fractures which indicate that some kind of splinting was used. Setting a broken bone to immobilize it is fairly obvious, since the victim otherwise feels pain.

Simple splints have often been made from suitable tree-branches, but there have been triumphant innovations even in this area. The American Indians were experts at binding broken bones with long strips of bark. Other peoples used soft clay, which dried like a sheath around the injured member – a forerunner to plaster casts.

While Stone Age man had little idea of how to relocate a broken bone in its normal position, the results of extremity surgery were by no means poor. The scientist Karl Jaeger has investigated bone remains that were broken during life, and found that the healing was satisfactory in more than half of the cases. This record was surpassed only at the beginning of the last century.

It is not impossible that ingenious prehistoric physicians learned adequate manipulations for curing dislocations and sprains. Many such conditions are treated manually even by modern surgeons, sometimes without any anaesthesia. A good example is "Kocher's manoeuvre", which is applied when the upper armbone has moved out of its joint on the shoulder-blade. Hippocrates' method of reducing a dislocated shoulder is to put the surgeon's foot gently in the axilla and apply traction on the arm, until the head of the humerus slips back into the glenoid fossa. But primitive folk have used orthopaedic manipulation techniques for much more serious conditions. The English priest William Ellis, who voyaged

THE Aztecs inherited much learning from older native cultures, but they had to fight many diseases and wars in the environment of central Mexico. On the one hand, their obsidian knives were as sharp as a modern scalpel, and were used without hesitation. They made such a virtue of cleanliness that their superficial operations were probably more successful than those in Europe until our century. On the other hand, Aztec thinking was dominated by abstract religion and placed little value on human life, or on the profession of healing. It was believed that the gods had to be kept alive by continual offerings of blood and hearts from sacrificed people, as illustrated here.

among the South Sea islands in the early nineteenth century, told of a young man who suddenly contracted acute back pain by carrying a heavy stone. He was laid face-down on the grass, and one comrade pulled upward on his shoulders while another pulled hard on his legs. A leader of the team sat on the patient's back and pressed with every ounce of weight on the spot where the injury seemed to be. Apparently the operation succeeded, as the young man returned to work after just a few hours—with what we may suppose was a dampened enthusiasm for lifting the heaviest stones.

Trepanation

Among the medical feats of our ancestors, the most remarkable is trepanation, or skull-boring. Skulls with holes bored in them have been found by archaeologists from as far back as 4900 BC. The oldest of these occur in the Alsace region. Hundreds of skulls with traces of trepanation are known all over Europe—in Denmark, Sweden, Poland, France, Spain, and the British Isles. A Swedish physician, Professor Folke Henschen, reports that Soviet archaeologists, along the Dnieper River in the 1960s, found crania with oval left-side trepanation holes of 16–18 mm (0.6–0.7 in) diameter. These were thought to date from the Mesolithic, or Middle Stone Age. If so, we must raise the age of this practice to some 12,000 years.

The amazing thing about such crania is that evidence exists for the patients' having survived the operation. Holes in bone are healed by new formation of bone tissue, and the sharp edges of bored or hacked holes become rounded off by so-called callus tissue. This proof of healing is more the rule than the exception. In one study of skull material from the Yantyo tribe in Peru, a researcher found callus tissue in 250 out of 400 crania. Verifications in Europe are fewer, but even here it has been confirmed that most of the patients survived. Further proof of this—and reason for believing in the method—is the discovery of skulls which were trepanned more than once. The record seems to be held by an

Inca at Cuzco with seven bore-holes, at least some of which were made on separate occasions.

Nowadays, trepanation is performed to relieve acute pressure on the brain. The usual cause is internal bleeding after a blow on the head. In this case, the operation has a rational justification. The Stone Age finds, and customs of primitive peoples, indicate that our ancestors also used trepanation for such injuries. However, the great majority of skulls show that the operation was done on an intact cranium with no previous signs of violence. Here it must have been intended to relieve an apparent excess of pressure, which is easy to imagine in the event of, for example, migraine or sudden headaches of other kinds.

Magic has obviously played a role as well. The belief that an evil spirit lives in the head and must be let out is very old. But the possibility of repeatedly letting out such spirits has, so far as we know, never existed. Werner von Heidenstam's fine description of a Stone Age leader in *The Swedes and their Chieftains* (1908) must, sadly, be ascribed to fantasy:

> "On their bare heads, a small lid was attached over a round hole, which had been bored right in the crown-bone. Such a hole was held in great reverence, and belonged only to the most eminent. Through it, evil vapours were able to escape, and the sunlight could enter to absorb their spirits after death."

There were at least four different methods of trepanning. The crudest was simply to scrape a hole in the skull-cap by means of a piece of flint or a polished mussel-shell. A second method was to make a circular cut in the bone with a flint or obsidian knife, and to deepen it until the hard brain-membrane was reached. Alternatively, and doubtless worse for the patient, a hammer and chisel were used to cut four grooves in a rectangle, then lift out the square piece at their centre.

Most elegant, though, was the procedure which gave this operation its name. With a drill-

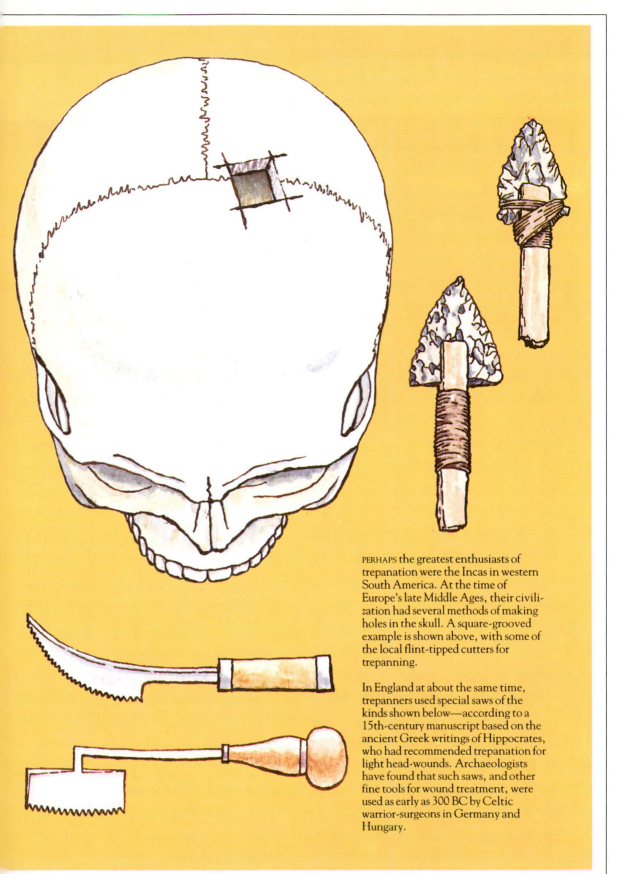

PERHAPS the greatest enthusiasts of trepanation were the Incas in western South America. At the time of Europe's late Middle Ages, their civilization had several methods of making holes in the skull. A square-grooved example is shown above, with some of the local flint-tipped cutters for trepanning.

In England at about the same time, trepanners used special saws of the kinds shown below—according to a 15th-century manuscript based on the ancient Greek writings of Hippocrates, who had recommended trepanation for light head-wounds. Archaeologists have found that such saws, and other fine tools for wound treatment, were used as early as 300 BC by Celtic warrior-surgeons in Germany and Hungary.

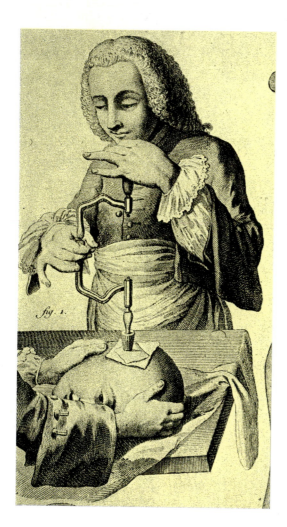

fig. 1.

INSTRUMENTS for trepanation were perfected even during the Enlightenment, as illustrated by Denis Diderot's famous scientific *Encyclopédie* (1772).

bore, called *trypanon* in Greek, a wreath of tiny holes was made. These could be united easily with a chisel or knife. Such an operation took little time even with primitive tools. An adept French surgeon named J. Lucas-Championnière (1843–1913), experimenting with instruments of flint, needed only 35 minutes to complete the operation. During the nineteenth century, a scientist travelling in the South Pacific saw a medicine-man do it in half an hour. His patient woke up after several days of unconsciousness and regained perfect health!

The medicine-men or shamans who dealt with trepanations stood high in society. They could also earn a fortune from the practice. Not only may we assume that they were well rewarded by every cured patient and his family. In addition, they conducted a lively trade with the pieces of bone which they extracted from people's skulls. Such amulets were greatly prized for magical protection from illness and accidents. Researchers have even wondered whether the demand for skull-bone contributed to the prescription of trepanations. There are actual records of amulets measuring about 8–9 cm (3.1–3.5 in). No medical reason can exist for making such enormous holes, and it is very unlikely that the patients survived the serious risk of infection with meningitis.

The first anaesthetics

Our ancestors probably had a greater tolerance of pain than we do. Yet they naturally looked for ways of stopping pain, both in treating illness and as an anaesthetic in operations. Perhaps the earliest pain-killer was alcohol, which was discovered long ago and is produced by nearly all peoples in one form or another. Nor is there a lack of descriptions as to how trepanations began, in many tribes, with the patients as well as the surgeon getting themselves drunk.

The oldest known pain-relieving drugs are

Trepanation in Sweden, 1761

The greatest Swedish surgeon of the eighteenth century was Olof af Acrel, chief physician at the Seraphim Hospital. He described the purpose of trepanation as follows:

"Trepanation of the skull is intended to release what has forced its way out of the blood-vessels, or to lift up and remove what, having been forced in, causes meningitis (irritation of the brain-membrane)—or to both of these ends together."

MANY plants have long been used as folk remedies, and some still have medical value as drugs. Most of them maybe taken either internally or externally but need careful preparation and are dangerous if overdosed. Widely known examples: (*a*) Asiatic hemp, *Cannabis sativa*, yielding hashish, for narcosis; (*b*) common juniper, *Juniperus communis*, a diuretic and disinfectant; (*c*) grapewine, *Vitis vinifera*, yielding wine, a general anaesthetic; (*d*) monkshood or aconite, *Aconitum napellus*, for rheumatism and fever; (*e*) opium poppy, *Papaver somniferum*, yielding opium as well as morphine and codeine —all narcotics; (*f*) peppermint, *Mentha piperita*, for digestive complaints and inflammations; (*g*) coca, *Erythroxylon coca*, containing cocaine, a local anaesthetic.

opium from China, hashish or Indian hemp, and mandragora which is extracted from the mandrake plant. Opium was familiar to the Chinese several thousand years ago, although not at first as a pain-killer. This delay was probably due to a peculiar difference between races of people when it comes to the pharmacological effects of opium. White people tend to feel the drug's sleep-inducing and analgesic, pain-stopping effects, whereas the Chinese and other Asiatic peoples react to it more often with euphoria and hallucinations. A Chinese who chews or smokes opium may soon find himself surrounded by beautiful maidens in Paradise.

It is likely that the analgesic properties of opium were exploited quite early in Europe. Here the drug seems to have occurred at least by 700 BC, when the epic poet Homer composed the *Iliad* and *Odyssey*. That the old Greek word *nepenthe* referred to opium is now generally agreed. A drug employed by the lovely heroine Helen can hardly have been anything else, as depicted in the *Odyssey*:

"Into the bowl where the wine was blended, she dropped a drug which had the power to blunt anger and anxiety, eliminating painful memories. None who drank of this wine could shed a tear the whole day long, even to weep for a lost father or mother, or if he had to witness a brother's execution by the sword. It was a pain-relieving drug, one of many that the daughter of Zeus had received from the Egyptian Polydamna, wife of Thon."

Homeric poetry originated a few centuries previously, in the Late Bronze Age of Greece and Cyprus, where archaeologists have found other possible evidence for opium—notably interest in poppies and pipes—though in religious, not specifically medical, contexts.

The leading ancient authority on medicines, Dioscorides Pedanios, gave prescriptions for the preparation of mandragora, and described its use in surgery: "Boil the roots in a third part of wine; preserve the resultant juice. Of this, administer a *kyathos* (about 4.6 cc) to induce insensibility before cutting or cauterizing (burning with a hot iron)." The use of mandragora in Roman medicine is attested by Apuleius, around AD 200: if someone was to have a limb amputated, he drank half an ounce of the root with wine, and then "slept until his limb had been removed without pain."

We can only guess that our earliest forefathers employed such decoctions internally for general anaesthesia. However, the facts are clearer as to local anaesthesia, which is thousands of years old, at least in South America. The Indians of Peru, Bolivia, and the Amazon valley were well acquainted with the pharmacological effects of coca leaves, which they chewed for pleasure and intoxication. When an Inca priest trepanned, he sat down on top of the patient, holding the head tightly between his knees. While cutting the opening, he fortified himself by chewing coca, and relieved the patient by spitting into the wound. The anaesthetist R. Woolmer has concluded that this method does have some local numbing effect.

A common symptom in various painful conditions is local swelling. Primitive folk have found it easy to believe that an evil spirit lived in a swollen spot, which would disappear if the spirit were released. Nor was this an unfounded opinion! They could hardly have failed to see how aches and pains vanish when a swelling goes down, the pus runs out of a broken boil, or a collection of blood disperses. Therefore, to dispel a pain-causing demon was the sensible way of curing such ailments.

The simplest method consists of sucking out the evil spirit. It is still practised by aboriginal inhabitants of Mexico and Australia. They suck sores, animal bites, and insect stings, so energetically that they leave blue marks around the source of pain. A refinement is "cupping", or sucking through an animal horn. Another is known as scarification: the intact skin over the swelling is scraped roughly with a shell, flint piece, or polished fishbone. In many places, the use of blood-sucking leeches was also learned,

THE Sumerians were recording medical prescriptions by 2200 BC, as proved by this clay tablet from the city of Nippur in Iraq (*left*). One of their main cure-alls was beer. A few centuries later, the Babylonians still diagnosed patients by religious means, referring to a clay model of a normal sheep's liver (*above*) on which instructions were written.

and it lasted well into the twentieth century.

Blood-letting, too, is an age-old procedure. This treatment, eventually applied to almost every infirmity (even bleeding itself!), was specifically used for relieving local pain. Veins were cut at a point near the injury or swelling. There could be refinements, as the English medical historian Harvey Graham illustrates:

"The technique befits a warrior people. From a close distance, the surgeon shoots a little arrow into the patient; he holds it near the tip, so that it does not penetrate too deeply. If the arrow hits a vein and blood flows freely, all is good and well. If it misses, the operator tries again—presumably in an eloquent silence, which shows the unfortunate surgeon that the good old tale of the evil spirit who snatched away the vein has been told too many times..."

A distinctive form of blood-letting was practised by the Incas of Peru. Their treatment for headache employed a piece of flint, mounted on a wooden shaft. It was forcefully applied between the patient's eyes, until a suitable flow of blood resulted. One wonders whether this operation was a last-ditch effort before considering trepanation.

Doctors in Mesopotamia

The Garden of Eden, or Paradise, has usually been connected with the location of Anah and Hit, or the Hairlah Oasis in Mesopotamia, between the rivers Euphrates and Tigris. It was in this region that the "cradle of civilization" emerged. Around 4000 BC, a powerful folk whom we call the Sumerians appeared in the fertile valley. They possessed the world's oldest written language, later known as cuneiform. After ruling for two thousand years, they were succeeded by Semitic peoples such as the Amorites, who established a capital at Babylon in about 1800 BC. The Babylonians' greatest king was Hammurabi. In turn, they bowed to the Assyrians, who made Nineveh a cultural centre and reached a climax of glory under the emperors Assurbanipal and Nebuchadnezzar in the sixth and fifth centuries BC. The latter, of course, was responsible for conquering the Jews and leading them into Babylonian Captivity.

Medicine was highly respected in these cultures. One proof is that, of 30,000 cuneiform tablets which have been discovered, no less than 800 deal with medicine. On one of them is the world's first prescription! We also know the name of Urlugaledin, who lived in about 2300 BC and was among the earliest surgeons on earth. His seal, displaying two knives, together with gods and plants of healing, can be seen today in the Louvre Museum in Paris.

People in that Land of Two Rivers explained illness as a divine punishment, carried out by demons. A doctor's first task was to identify the kind of demon afflicting a patient, rather like a modern microbiologist looking for bacteria to diagnose an infection. It was no easy task, since the catalogue of diseases listed some 6,000 evil spirits. However, there were several diagnostic aids. An important one was hepatoscopy—learning signs of illness, or the future, by inspecting the liver of a sacrificed animal. Clay models of normal livers were kept in the temples for such divination. This large, blood-rich organ was regarded as the body's main part, producing the liquid of life in which the soul resided.

Astrology was also important. The Babylonians and Assyrians were clever astronomers. From the familiar positions of the heavenly spheres, they could read both the diagnosis and prognosis of an illness. An even stronger basis for judgement was the study of birds in flight. When a bird was released from its cage in the temple, the priests watched whether it flew to the right or left. The former direction gave rise to optimism, while the latter meant disaster. This is the origin of our own superstition that left is inferior to right—and of the dual significance, left and unlucky, in the word "sinister".

The treatment was an odd mixture of rites,

herbs and physical therapy. After having elaborately combined the diagnostic methods to establish the nature of the illness demon, an effort was made to drive it out. This involved prayers, charms and sacrifices, especially to the god who was supposed to be angry at the patient. An abundance of healing plants, and a form of psychotherapy, were additional aids.

Such procedures could be quite complicated. The Spanish-American medical historian F. Marti-Ibañez has described a case of illness in the penis, in a patient who was thought to have been cursed by a foe. A clay model of the organ was shaped, dried in the sun, and wrapped in meat and animal fat, to resemble a pie. It was then inscribed with the patient's name, and eaten by a cat. The cat was believed to be a magical creature which could not only remove the illness in this way, but also transfer it to the enemy!

Despite all the sorcery and superstition in Babylonian and Assyrian medicine, their practitioners eventually learned a great deal. In 1951, after many years of patient research, the French scholar Labat published a translation of several cuneiform texts which display a level of knowledge that is often surprising. They contain, for example, a clinical description of tuberculosis, showing acute powers of observation:

"The patient coughs continually. What he coughs up is thick and frequently bloody. His breathing sounds like a flute. His hand is cold, his feet are warm. He sweats easily, and his heart activity is disturbed."

The comparison with a flute may refer to the whistling sound that characterizes a consumptive patient in the terminal stages. It may also reveal that the Babylonian doctors used some kind of stethoscope, or simply laid their ear to the patient's chest. A flute-like sound can be heard even in early stages of lung tuberculosis, and is now called *sibilanta rhonci*. The cold hands are another well-known sign of lung tuberculosis—familiar to Giuseppe Giacosa and Luigi Illica,

HAMMURABI was shown receiving his laws from the sun-god, at the top of the stone on which the laws were inscribed in about 1750 BC. Surgery was only one of many activities covered by his great code.

gical instruments of bronze and obsidian have been found: scalpels, saws and even specially constructed trepans. Probably even as early as 4,000 years ago, the Mesopotamian doctors could perform such comprehensive operations as herniotomy and bladder-stone removal.

The most important medical legacy of Babylonian culture, however, is the world's oldest legislation for the medical profession—indeed, mankind's oldest regulation for any profession. Hammurabi was one of Babylon's cleverest kings, particularly as a lawgiver. His decrees were inscribed permanently in black diorite stone, and no doubt originally decorated some hall of justice in the city. But the stone dealing with medicine, about two metres high, was discovered at Susa, in what is now Iran, where it was presumably carried by the Assyrian conquerors. Today it stands in the Louvre.

Hammurabi's law covers mainly the economic relationship between doctor and patient:

> "If a doctor has treated a man for a serious injury and cures him, or opens a swelling with a knife and saves the patient's eye, he is to receive ten shekels of gold. If the patient is a free man, the payment is five shekels. If he is a slave, the owner will pay two shekels."

There are also laws for punishment of negligent doctors:

> "If a doctor inflicts a serious wound with his operation knife on a free man's slave and kills him, the doctor must replace the slave with another. If a doctor has treated a free man but caused a serious injury from which the man dies, or if he has opened an abscess and the man goes blind, the man is to cut off his hands."

Considering this sort of justice, which was established by 1650 BC, it is small wonder that the doctors of that age preferred to minimize their risks by concentrating on internal medicine...

Yet the doctor's art was evidently not well-

the librettists of Puccini. In *La Bohème*, Rodolphe sings: "Your tiny hand is frozen..." to the consumptive Mimi.

The Mesopotamians' attitude toward the origin and treatment of diseases made it natural that internal medicine was the leading specialty. In practice, these doctors were the priests. Surgeons could not be dispensed with, but were otherwise viewed as a pariah caste—a prejudice that survived in places until long into the nineteenth century. But this did not lessen the surgeons' skill. At Nineveh, well-balanced sur-

developed everywhere in Babylonia. The great "father of history", Herodotus of Halicarnassus, travelled in the country between the Tigris and Euphrates rivers around 440 BC, and wrote:

"Another sensible custom is as follows. The sick are carried out to the market-place, since there are no doctors. Then the inhabitants go to the sick man and offer advice, if they have had a similar ailment or seen anyone else with it. Thus they counsel and exhort him to use the means by which they or others have been cured. It is not permitted to pass by the sick man in silence: one must at least ask what ails him. The dead are buried in honey, and the mourning ceremonies are the same as in Egypt."

Egyptian medicine

Egypt's ancient period of greatness lasted over three thousand years. It began around 3200 BC, when the first pharaoh conquered upper and lower Egypt, and built his capital at Memphis. At about the same time, the first calendar was invented, and hieroglyphic writing came into use. During the first dynasties, nearly 500 years long, the first treatise on surgery was also written. This has been dated to about 2700 BC, and its author was no less than Imhotep, the pharaoh's grand vizier (or prime minister). He is among the earliest doctors known to us by name.

Imhotep was both a spiritual leader and a practical genius. At once an astronomer, philosopher, high priest and architect, he built—among other things—the famous step pyramid of Sakkara. But to the people he was, first and foremost, a doctor. His status and reputation

were so great that he was eventually declared to be a god and was worshipped for hundreds of years. This god, often called Ptah, resembled the Greek god Asclepius in many ways. Medicine was a large part of the cultural exchange which certainly went on between Egypt and Greece.

IMHOTEP'S bronze statue expresses his godlike, benevolent role in the eyes of generations of ancient Egyptians. It was because his many talents made him the empire's chief "magician" that his name and medical work were remembered so well.

Many bronze statuettes of Imhotep have survived. He was usually portrayed with a papyrus roll on his knee, although scholars believe that this indicated his plans for buildings rather than his medical writings. Sadly, none of the latter are preserved. Their existence is proved only by, for example, citations in writings from the time of Christ.

In addition, we know the names of some other doctors who were active at the pharaonic court during the so-called Old Kingdom, from about 2500 to 2100 BC. King Sahure was served by one Sachmet—a name that also belonged to a goddess whose priests were renowned doctors. A doctor named Nesmenau functioned as a kind of general director for all medical work, suggesting that there was some organization of the profession as early as 4,000 years ago. The same period, too, has yielded the world's oldest known depiction of a surgical operation, specifically a circumcision. This portrayal is cut into a door-post of a royal tomb at Memphis. In age, however, it must give precedence to that of a veterinary operation at Meir, showing the birth of a calf, in a relief dated to 3000 BC.

Medical papyri

The Egyptians learned early to write on papyrus. Quite a number of examples have been preserved in the country's dry climate. As many as nine rolls with medical content are now known and interpreted. Most famous is the *Papyrus Ebers*, named for the German professor Georg Ebers (1837–98).

Ebers was obsessed with ancient Egypt, and made countless trips to the Middle East. During one of them, he was approached by an Arab who wanted to sell a papyrus that had supposedly been found between the legs of a mummy. Ebers bought it for a song, and it turned out to be a unique collection of prescriptions. With the help of some notes on the back side, it has been dated rather exactly to 1550 BC.

The Papyrus Ebers is just over 20 metres long, and in very good condition. A copy of it was published by Ebers some years after his discovery, but its interpretation had to wait until 1890, when his compatriot Joachim produced a German translation. What is probably the conclusive study, by a Norwegian district doctor, Bendix Ebbell, appeared only in 1937. He considered this paypyrus to be "Egypt's most significant medical document", which few would deny. It consists mainly of prescriptions and a textbook in internal medicine. There are instructions on how to drive out stomach ailments—for instance, drinking a decoction of cumin, goose-fat and milk, or a mixture of milk, sycamore fruit and honey. Milk was prescribed frequently, perhaps due to its rarity and expensiveness. Indeed, the still rarer human milk was thought to have a special healing effect.

The Egyptians also knew how to brew beer, another drink that was rated highly in medicine. There were numerous varieties—sweet, bitter, yeast—and each was recommended for a particular purpose. In that dry land, even water was such a treasure that it attained the status of a healing substance, though not in the form of the impure Nile River water. More exclusive were the "Water-of-heavenly-rain", "Water-of-birdponds", and the most effective of all: "Water-in-which-the-male-member-has-been-washed"…

Every treatment had to be followed by prayers and incantations to an appropriate god. The most popular deities were Ra, Isis and Horus. There was probably little other than magic, too, behind such special remedies as a drink prepared from the testicles of a black ass; or a mixture of extracts from the vulva, penis, and a black lizard (to cure baldness!); or a hair-dye prepared from flatworms, scrapings of an ass's hoof, and extract from a bitch's genitals. The Papyrus Ebers is full of cosmetic recipes, and the advanced status of cosmetics in Egypt can easily be seen from the decorative scenes in temples.

Surgery did not receive much attention in the Papyrus Ebers. The first chapter, on the human body's structure, was relevant but could not have been very helpful for operations. Its anatomical views are surprisingly inadequate, in particular

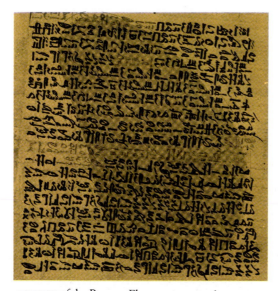

A SECTION of the Papyrus Ebers, written in the Egyptian hieratic script about 1550 BC. The work gave some 700 magical and medicinal remedies, besides describing the system of blood circulation.

when one recalls that Egyptian doctors must have learned a great deal through their preparation of mummies, when the contents of the chest and abdominal cavity were removed in a single piece. There are even two contradictory descriptions of the heart and its vessels in the Papyrus Ebers. One of them shows a basic misunderstanding of the heart's connections with other organs, and maintains that the heart vessels carry air, urine and semen, as well as blood! The heart's central role was recognized, but was exaggerated to include functions that, as we now know, belong to the brain: the powers of thought, memory and consciousness.

The instructions for surgical treatment were almost entirely concerned with "minisurgery". For bites by crocodiles—or people—a dressing of raw meat was prescribed. Several remedies existed for burns, such as an application of frogs boiled in oil, or of fermenting goat-dung. A number of salves were guaranteed to be useful in the extraction of splinters. There were salves also for smelly wounds, their most valuable ingredients being ostrich eggs and turtle shells.

Actual surgery was recommended only for superficial swellings, but the fact that they could not all be treated in the same way was clearly recognized. "Fat-swellings" (which presumably also included diseases of the sebaceous glands) were treated by excision. However, bitter experience had taught that certain skin tumours should be avoided:

"If you find the god Xensus' great swelling on an extremity, it is odious and may produce much pus; something like wind is formed in it, and causes irritation. The swelling calls loudly to you: Is it not like the most repulsive of all pus-sores? It spots the skin and creates figures. All the limbs come to resemble that which is first afflicted. Then you should say: It is the god Xensus' swelling! Do not touch it!"

One may well speculate over this surgical caution. On some occasion, probably, a boil was cut rather half-heartedly, resulting in general blood-poisoning, or in a postoperative inflammation that "spotted the skin and created figures". Another possibility is that a pigmental tumour, or malignant melanoma, was removed with too little margin, leading to a general spread of the disease.

The Papyrus Ebers also contains a chapter on women's ailments and obstetrics. As Harvey Graham drily and understandably remarks, the patients would have been better off without a word of it. Among its frequently fantastic pieces of advice are the smearing of peppermint on the buttocks to speed up a difficult birth, and the smearing of a paste—made from honey, dates, onions, and acanthus fruit—in the vulva to bring about an abortion. None of these prescriptions can have had the effects intended…

Of almost equal importance is a papyrus roll which was found in 1862 at Thebes. Its discoverer, a young Egyptologist named Edwin Smith, was perhaps the first American to learn the an-

From the Papyrus Ebers

Remedy for night-blindness: the liver of an ox, fried and mashed, should be taken; it is truly remarkable!
(Note: this advice was perfectly reasonable, since night-blindness is caused by a lack of vitamin A, which is abundant in liver. The remedy was forgotten, to be rediscovered only in the twentieth century.)
Remedy for crying: fly-dirt from a wall should be blended, strained, and taken for four days; it works immediately.

In regard to crying, this is a thing done by children.
Initial remedy for avoiding a miscarriage, that which floods a woman with blood: wait for her menstruation to begin, and rub it into her stomach and thighs; she will suffer no miscarriage.
Remedy for dispelling malignant ulcers on the palate: cow's milk, fresh dates, and manna should be placed in dew overnight; rinse the mouth for nine days.

From the Edwin Smith Papyrus

First examination: *If you visit a man with a deep wound on the head, you must palpate (feel) it, even if he trembles awfully. Ask him to lift his head, and learn if it hurts when he opens his mouth, and if his heart beats weakly. Observe, too, whether he has saliva round his mouth and if it dribbles or not; and whether he bleeds from the nose or ears, and is stiff in the neck and cannot move his head so as to see his shoulders or chest.*

First diagnosis: *You must look at him and say, "He who has a deep wound on the head, with injury to the skull-bone, bites his jaws together and bleeds from the nose and ears, and suffers from a stiff neck. I shall fight this torment."*

First treatment: *As soon as you see him spasmodically bite his jaws together, make him warm so that he feels better and opens his mouth. Hold it open by means of lint, lard and honey, until the crisis reaches a climax.*

Second examination: *If you later find the patient to have a fever because of his skull injury, lay your hand on him. If you then find that his forehead is clammy with sweat, his neck sinews are tense, his face red, his breath smells like sheep-urine, his mouth is closed, his eyebrows drawn-out, and he looks as if he has wept, you must look at him and say:*

Second diagnosis: *"He who has a deep wound in the head with skull injuries, cannot open his mouth and is stiff in the neck, is incurable."*

Third examination: *Yet you find that this man has grown pale and shows signs of exhaustion.*

Third treatment: *You must hold his mouth open with a piece of wood wrapped in linen, and give him a fruit drink. He must sit upright between two supports of bricks, until the symptom has passed.*

cient Egyptian language. Smith never published his find; it was left in 1906 to the New York Historical Society, and was interpreted by the theologian James Henry Breasted in Chicago. The roll is 4.68 metres (15.4 feet) long, beautifully printed on both sides with about 500 lines. It has been dated to around 1600 BC, and is thus of the same age as the Papyrus Ebers.

The *Edwin Smith Papyrus* describes forty-eight cases of surgery. Its preserved portion is obviously just an introduction to a longer work. At the beginning is a report on twenty-seven skull injuries, disproportionate to the following account of twenty-one neck and chest injuries. A remarkably high level of knowledge is evident. The surgeon—or surgeons—who wrote it were less reliant on divine assistance than on what they could see and feel. The importance of a correct diagnosis, and of an exact prognosis before starting treatment, is emphasized time and again.

The rate and quality of the pulse were known to be valuable indications, and it was recommended that the depth and extent of a wound should be observed carefully. Also familiar was the fact that a brain injury could cause loss of speech (aphasia) and paralysis (pares). Possibly the best example of the Egyptian surgeons' accuracy and experience was their ability to distinguish tubercular abscesses from septic ones due to bacteria. Tuberculosis as such had not been discovered, but the doctors were aware of the danger in opening that type of pus formation. This is not done today, either, insofar as tubercular abscesses still occur.

A disjointed jawbone was restored in proper position by the same method that is used in modern surgery. Greek medicine inherited this technique, as is illustrated by a fine painting on a vase. Broken bones were splinted with pieces of wood, or with bandages rolled in glue. The ancient Egyptians were equipped with good surgical instruments, many of which had doubtless been developed in connection with mummification. They were made of flint at first, and later of bronze, with wooden handles.

Hygiene was valued greatly by the Egyptians, a fact which aided surgery and contributed to its high quality. Besides the well-developed sense of personal cleanliness, there were laws as to inspecting meat and other food. The aversion to dirt was even exaggerated, notably by the priests who adopted it in magical rites. Regular enemas and ritual washings, several times daily, were prescribed for temple servants. To avoid bringing dirt into the sanctuaries, the priests had to be both completely head-shaven and circumcised.

Egyptian medicine was a peculiar blend of superstition, ceremony and rational thinking. Not least from the papyri of Ebers and Smith, it is clear that empirical experience of earlier illnesses played an important role. A good summary has been given by Acke Renander: "If the ailment had a palpable and natural cause, one went to a doctor; if it seemed more complicated or quite mysterious, the priest or exorcist had to step in. These 'specialists' may be imagined to have referred cases to each other, just as modern specialists do."

In a sense, this specialization was elaborated

A Doctor's Certificate

Certifications of health are based on old customs. At Hermopolis in Egypt, two papyrus leaves have been found, bearing the same text: "I, the doctor, have observed a swelling that bleeds on the left eyebrow, a scratched skin on the left side of the nose, and a swelling on the testicle or scrotum; and I, the police constable, certify that I have come with him and seen the afflictions… In conformity with this, we submit the certification to Your Graciousness for perusal, and will testify to it if desired…"

(From the Ciba Journal, *No. 11, 1947.)*

THIS early Egyptian scene of circumcision suggests both clear teaching and "mass production". Dating from about 2200 BC, it was found in the Sakkara cemetery at the city of Memphis—where the great doctor Imhotep himself had lived.

to absurd lengths. Particularly around a Pharaoh and his court, virtually every organ or sickness gradually acquired its own specialist. Pharaoh Senusret had a doctor for his right eye and another for his left eye! We also know of a doctor who ranked as "keeper of the royal anus". Such overspecialization may have hastened a decline in the standards of medicine, which at any rate was not very vigorous during the last thousand years of the Egyptian empire, until the Persian wars and the conquest by Alexander the Great in 332 BC.

Circumcision

Circumcision of males is a process by which the outer portion of the penis' foreskin is cut away. This operation is still practised ritually among Orthodox Jews and Muslims, as well as many other peoples—the Copts, Bantu, Australian aborigines, and various tribes in South America and the South Pacific. But the English anthropologist Grafton Elliot Smith showed that circumcision occurred in Egypt at least 4,000 years ago, at the same time as the carving of the relief at Memphis, mentioned above.

Egyptian ritual circumcision was probably at first a privilege of the priesthood, yet it was later extended to the Pharaohs and their families. At Karnak, a scene of circumcision is thought to portray one of the sons of the great Ramses II. As so often happens, the court imitated its leader and, from the higher dignitaries, the custom was spread to circumcision of common men. The ultimate result was that nobody who had not been circumcised could enter a holy temple. The Greek philosopher Pythagoras (c. 580-500 BC) told that he had to let himself be circumcised during a trip to Egypt, in order to see how the Egyptian sanctuaries looked from the inside!

From Egypt, circumcision was introduced to neighbouring regions. The Jews may have learned it during their Egyptian bondage, and made it part of their religion, attaching shame to the lack of it. Thus it played a role in the tale of Abraham in Genesis, written by 800 BC. The Lord's command of circumcision on the eighth day after birth, in fact, seems unique to Judaism. Almost all other peoples who practise it do the operation at the beginning of puberty as an initiation to manhood.

The origins of circumcision have been much debated. It probably arose from a desire to increase fertility, and not only for the circumcised man, but also for the fruit of the soil. There may have been a belief that the penis was inhabited by powers which produced life. This is suggested by peoples who strew the cut-off foreskin on their fields, or bury it in the earth. Evidence of a connection with harvests is also found in Nicaragua, where blood from the operation is mixed with maize to be eaten during the ceremony.

However, the dominant idea in Egypt was presumably cleanliness. Especially if the foreskin is tight, it makes the tip of the penis hard to clean thoroughly—and, as we have seen, impurity of whatever kind was unthinkable in the houses of Egyptian gods. The custom of circumcision is, of course, a reasonable way of preventing infections under the foreskin, known as balanitis, and the recurrence of these is treated even today by circumcision. The same blend of mysticism and hygiene was adopted later by Muhammad: for the devout Muslim, uncircumcised people are impure.

Circumcision was also long applied to prisoners of war by their victors. The original motive was perhaps even more extreme—that enemies should be totally castrated in order to defile

THAT a surgical operation can long remain a religious and social event, as well as a source of fine art, is seen in this engraving of circumcision by Crispin de Passe (1599).

them, as well as to stop their breeding. Many peoples, like the Philistines, seem not to have practised circumcision, and therefore risked the treatment if captured in these lands. A horde of foreign invaders, recorded in Egyptian art near the end of the Bronze Age, evidently added insult to injury by being uncircumcised, and were duly castrated.

The early circumcisions probably involved a short lengthwise cut on the upper side of the penis. This corresponds to the simpler form of operation which is carried out today, when the foreskin is constricted on small boys (a dorsal slit). It may have been a demand for fertility-inducing preparations during periods of bad harvest that led to the later popularity of real circumcision. In this operation, the foreskin is entirely removed.

In 1868, a French military doctor watched a circumcision ceremony of an Arab tribe in Algeria. It doubtless followed ancient customs. The surgeon, his assistants, and the patients were all attired in gold silk. The boys had to sit on basins of sand that had been illuminated by the full moon during the night. Holding the penis with a compress so that only the foreskin was exposed, the surgeon cut it quickly. His technique was the same as ours, except that the edges of the wound were not sewn. A bandage was applied with a powder of dried juniper berries, which must have been at least somewhat blood-stanching. During the whole ceremony, the tribal women were locked in a nearby house where they threw a riotous party with cymbals and drums. Finally all the cut-off foreskins were collected and buried with traditional pomp.

Circumcision of girls has been conducted by similar methods. Muhammad said that the operation was necessary for men, but glorious in the case of women! Here it amounts to cutting away the labia, and may include the clitoris, thus removing the woman's most important organ for sexual pleasure. The motive for this brutal treatment was that such a woman would not be prone to infidelity.

Surgery has often been employed for other measures of sexual protection. Many peoples have regarded women as goods of trade, whose value depended greatly on virginity. Fathers and slave-owners were therefore anxious to guard the sexual parts of young girls against inappropriate contact. The most common technique, so-called "infibulation", was by sewing a ring into the vaginal opening, large enough for passage of body fluids, but too small for undesired intrusions. The ring was removed with a new operation when the girl became marriageable or saleable. Infibulation was also used by travelling men on their wives to ensure fidelity, a predecessor of the medieval "chastity belt" with its artistic decoration.

Moses Wasn't Circumcised!

About 1280 BC, the Captivity of the Jews in Egypt came to an end. It was perhaps there that they learned the custom of circumcision. Remarkably, their leader Moses, who had been a favourite of the Pharaoh and could enter the temples, was never himself circumcised. Even when his own son underwent the operation, he did not perform the operation personally, as was the tradition, but left the ceremony to his wife Zipporah.

What the Bible says about Circumcision

When Abraham was ninety-nine years old, the Lord appeared to him and said: "This is the covenant between Me and you and your seed, which you must obey: all males among you shall be circumcised on the foreskin... Down the generations, each of your boys shall be circumcised when eight days old, even the native servants and those bought from abroad...and thus shall my covenant be displayed as eternal on your flesh. But an uncircumcised male...shall be eliminated from your kind; he has broken my covenant."

(Genesis 17: 1-2, 10-14)

At that time the Lord said to Joshua: "Make knives of stone and circumcise the children of Israel once again." Then Joshua did so, and circumcised them on the Height of the Foreskin.

(Joshua 5: 2-3)

Chinese surgery

Medicine among the Chinese is founded on a different way of thinking from that in the West. Diseases are interpreted as a breakdown in the universe's harmony and the five basic elements' balance. These elements are earth, water, fire, wood and metal. They both create and destroy one another. Everything that happens is controlled by two forces, Yang and Yin. Within the human body, the two normally hold each other in balance; but if either becomes predominant, an illness results, its nature depending on which force dominates and which organ is overpowered. For example, Yang works externally and is seen in perspiration; so if the body's pores are closed and the perspiration is hindered, sores and swellings may arise.

The ancient Chinese considered a dead body to be sacrosanct. Their doctors were not allowed to dissect any human corpses, and thus learned nothing about internal anatomy. They had obscure ideas of five solid, formative organs—the heart, liver, spleen, lungs and kidneys—and five hollow, decomposing organs: the gall bladder, stomach, small intestine, large intestine, and urinary bladder. Another supposed organ, the "San chiao", has no equivalent in reality. It was also known as "the three burning places" and, understandably enough, the medical writers were hard put to locate it.

The source for such knowledge was the famous book *Nei Ching*, credited to none less than "the golden emperor" Huang Ti, who lived around 2600 BC. Actually the book was written 1,500 years later, but its age was increased to give it greater authority! At any rate, when knowledge is so vague about the internal organs of a patient, capable surgery is difficult – and the level of Chinese surgery was predictably low. The main treatments were

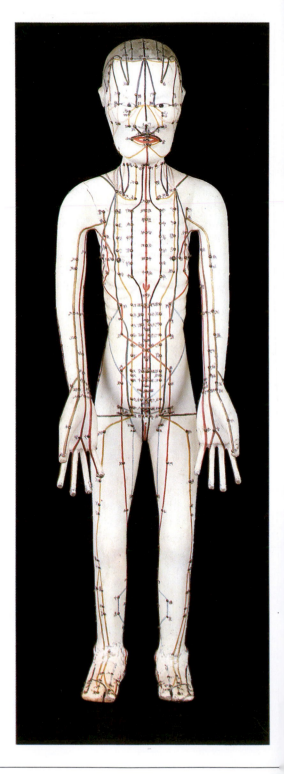

THE Chinese methods of acupuncture were taken to Japan and demonstrated with dolls like this one, made of papier-mâché about a century ago. Its 660 points were also used for moxibustion therapy.

minor superficial ones, including massage, acupuncture and moxibustion (herbal cauterization).

Massage developed into a fine art in China. It was subsequently taken over by the Japanese, who advanced it further and are still ranked among the world's leading medical masseurs. In acupuncture, the aim is to restore the balance between Yang and Yin. This is done by inserting thin needles at one or more of 365 (or up to 660, according to certain schools) exactly defined points, which are located along twelve meridians. Each meridian is related to an inner organ. A number of these points have counterparts in Western medicine, such as McBurney's point in the lower right abdominal wall, which is often a site of pain during appendicitis. Similar are a point on the neck which all good masseurs treat for headache, and a point on the right shoulderblade to which gallstone pain often spreads.

Moxibustion is a pain-alleviating measure. A small cone of combustible plant material (ordinary wormwood is most popular) is laid on the skin, according to a precise system like that of meridians in acupuncture. The cone is set alight, causing a painful burn-blister. Naturally it works at least for a while—the acute artificial pain suppresses the pain of the original ailment. This principle has often been used later in applying so-called derivants, such as Spanish fly and blistering plaster.

Medicines fascinated the Chinese, who had a rich pharmaceutical range. Octopus ink was mixed with vinegar to cure heart diseases. Warm urine from boys was prescribed for throat and lung illness, and elephant skin was used to cure persistent sores. There were pulverized seahorses for goitre, and snake-meat for the eyes. Among the herbal drugs, opium was actually employed only for diarrhoea—the Orientals respond much less than do white people to this drug's anaesthetic effect, as mentioned already. More remarkable was the local treatment of sores and boils with a strong poison, aconitin, from the monks-hood plant. With bad luck, this can be absorbed

Vaccination with Moxa

Species of Artemisia plants, such as moxa, were normally used in the Far East for cauterization. But Sun Sse-Miao, who lived in the seventh century AD, related that Chinese officials travelling abroad protected themselves from epidemic diseases by applying moxa on one thigh, at point 36 in the stomach's meridian. He confirmed that this was a sure safeguard against miasma, malaria and poisons.

The Idiot's Heart

The Chinese believed the heart to be the body's main organ. The body, in turn, was a miniature copy of the universe. So the heart was an emperor who ruled the body, and its pericardium was his palace, walled in by the chest. Highly gifted Chinese were thought to have seven heart chambers, and a talented man five, while an average Chinese made do with only two. As for an idiot, he had just one little chamber.

(From Bengt I. Lindskog, The Heart in Medical History.)

Chinese Self-Restraint

While this Kuan Yün was still struggling on earth, he found himself one day at the house of Hua To, seeking liberation from a poison which an enemy arrow had dug deeply into his upper arm. Hua To wanted to benumb him before performing the operation, but this Kuan Yün refused with a laugh. Undaunted, he held forth his arm and, while the doctors treated the malignant wound and cut away the diseased flesh, Kuan Yün calmly played a game of chess with one of his friends.
(H. Wallnöfer and A. von Rottauscher, Medicine in the Chinese Empire.)

through skin and membranes, killing the patient quickly!

Additional plants used in medicine were angelica, burdock, dragonhead, mugwort, senna, clematis, daphne, cardamum, and crown-imperial, many of which have a rational basis still recognized in our day. Alder buckthorn, rhubarb, castor oil, and senna were purgatives that we also use; pomegranate was effective against diarrhoea, and gentian bitter calms a disturbed acid stomach.

According to legend, the Chinese were the first to use narcosis in their operations. The following event is said to have taken place around 300 BC:

"One day the two men Lu and Chao called on him. He gave them a benumbing drink, and they fell unconscious for three days. Pien Ch'iao performed a gastrostomy and examined the heart. After having removed some organs and replaced others, he gave them a wonder-working drug, and both men went home cured."

The duration of narcosis, and fantastic ignorance of the patients' anatomy, in this document show that it cannot be taken seriously. Gastrostomy means that the stomach is opened, which certainly does not permit a profitable examination of the heart. Besides, it is rather implausible that organs could have been replaced three hundred years before Christ; even now we have only begun to achieve such feats.

The truth is probably that Chinese surgeons were limited to the simplest superficial operations. They treated—not necessarily with the knife—plain boils and furuncles, and they cut out small external tumours. The court's demand for eunuchs also meant that surgeons knew the art of castration, and in such operations the testicles were carefully preserved, so as to follow their owners into the grave.

The only prominent surgeon produced by ancient China was Hua To, who lived in the second century. In contrast to the legendary Pien Ch'iao, he can perhaps be called the discoverer of narcosis. It is said that he gave his patients a well-weighed mixture of hashish and wine, enabling him to carry out the most arduous operations without pain. Records state that Hua To opened the abdomen, but the evidence is sparse and we know neither the symptoms nor which operation was involved. The reason is that Hua To ordered the destruction of all his notes after he died, and his widow loyally obeyed.

Hua To's most famous patient was the warlord Kuan Yün, and this proved to be his own undoing. The general's bitterest enemy, Tsao Tsao, also came to Hua To with a bad headache. The surgeon decided to trepan, but just as he was about to begin, the patient suddenly got the idea that Hua To had been bribed by Kuan Yün to murder him. On this mere suspicion, Hua To was executed on the spot. If such things were done today, the insurance lawyers would have a difficult time distinguishing between malpractice and homicide!

Indian surgery

Two thousand years before Christ, the Hindus settled in the plains along the river Indus. During the following centuries, they developed a great civilization, which is familiar to us through abundant literature. Their earliest writings—the *Rig Veda*, *Yahur Veda* and *Sama Veda*—consist largely of eloquent praise to the gods, but there are several chapters on medicine in the latest book, *Atharva Veda*. Around 800 BC, in an addition to it, whose name *Ayur Veda* meant "Teaching for a Long Life", the authors dealt with problems of natural science.

The Vedic books contain little rational medicine. Illnesses were often described with amazing confidence, but were thought, here again, to be the work of demons. As in Mesopotamian medicine, one had to establish the demon's identity before starting a successful treatment. It is first in the Ayur Veda that therapy based on natural science can be glimpsed. This manuscript,

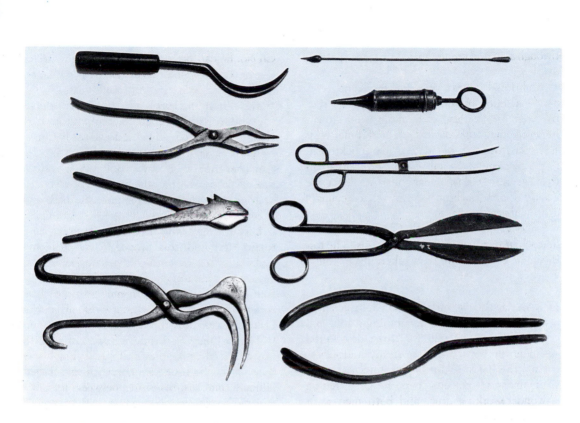

ANCIENT Hindu surgical instruments were highly specialized for operations like lithotomy and skin grafting. Many of these types have continued in use in India and are still studied today.

too, is the background to one of the best of all surgical books known to us, *Susruta Samhita*.

Susruta was the author of *Samhita*, but whether the name meant a person or a group of writers is uncertain. The book may be due to a school which was founded by a doctor called Susruta. It could well be that a doctor of that name lived at some time, and his birthplace has even been proposed as Benares, the holy city by the river Ganges. Still more curiously, in spite of much research, the date when the book was compiled has never been established, and theories vary from about 800 BC to AD 400! But the latter is certainly a limit, since in 1890 a British officer in Turkestan discovered a Buddhist manuscript from the fifth century AD which mentions Susruta's book.

Even if we date Susruta somewhat after the birth of Christ, his surgery was extraordinarily advanced. Broken bones were healed by splinting, fistulas were cauterized, wounds were sewn, and unhealthy collections of fluid were drained. These methods are not so surprising in themselves, but they were carried out with exquisite techniques and, as we shall see, far more difficult treatments were also given. In the book is a catalogue of no less than 121 different instruments: knives, scissors, needles, probes, lancets, trochars, catheters, tweezers, tongs—even magnets for removing metal objects. Pictures of them show the consummate beauty of functionality: the Hindu surgeons had soon found the right forms, many of which still exist today. The instruments were made of permanent metal, and were stored in fine hardwood boxes.

PLASTIC surgery on the nose, called rhinoplasty, is at least 2,000 years old in India. It amazed even English colonists, who saw this illustration in the "Gentleman's Magazine of Calcutta" in 1794.

Among the operations pioneered by the Hindus were primarily those of plastic surgery. Already as children, the Hindus had their ears pierced to hold amulets against evil powers. The operation was not carried out by trained surgeons, but by amateurs—and the result could often be terrible. Especially if the holes became infected, the ears might grow very deformed. The *Samhita* contains all of fifteen methods for repairing such damage. Even more advanced were the techniques for replacing cut-off noses,

which were a common punishment for theft. The underlying idea was to warn the public of a noseless person's long-fingered habits.

One elegant method was to cut a piece of skin from the patient's forehead, looking rather like an ace of spades. The stalk remained at the top of the nose, and the piece was swung down to be sewn over the hole in the face. Before it healed, it thus obtained nourishment through the blood vessels in the stalk. Exactly the same approach is the basis of modern use of skin flaps. To keep the air passage free while the transplant healed, finely polished wooden tubes were inserted, and the new nostrils developed around these.

In the time of Susruta, cremation was obligatory for everyone who died over two years of age. Thus, children's bodies were the only source available to Hindu doctors for study of the body's structure. This explains, for instance, why it was believed that the body contained three hundred bones: in children, not all bone joints are connected! On the whole, even the best surgeons were wondrously ignorant in anatomy. So it is all the more remarkable that they could actually conduct successful operations for ileus. There are claims that portions of the bowel were removed and the healthy parts sewn together again. Anaesthesia was given entirely by alcoholic intoxication, which is curious since the Hindus were otherwise forbidden to drink liquor. The ban against eating beef, too, could be suspended by a surgeon: it was said that the sick and weak should fortify themselves with an animal diet. These violations of holy Brahmin rules bear witness to the very strong status of the physicians.

Bladder stones are now a fairly unusual ailment in the civilized world, while—for still unknown reasons—they occur frequently among primitive peoples. We are also aware that a stone in the kidney was a common condition in former times. It was sometimes so common that special stone-cutters could live on the proceeds of removing stones, shifting from market to market: this is seen even today in India. The surgeons use a technique which was described by

Susruta. One inserts a finger into the rectum, where the stone can be felt through the wall between intestine and kidney. Then one presses the stone down toward the perineum, and cuts in toward the hard resistance. When the stone becomes visible, it is extracted with a bent scoop. The wound is left open, and normally heals with no complications.

Gynaecology and obstetrics were included in Susruta's surgery. For example, eight pathological foetal positions were known, and there were various methods of turning the foetus to a proper position. But these were used only when the baby was already dead and the mother's life had to be saved. If she died during the birth, one applied the operation which came to be known as a Caesarean (see Chapter 4).

The Indian doctors were skilful at treating cataracts. We find in Susruta, moreover, the first known description of the operation's technique:

"The doctor chooses a bright morning and sits on a bench at knee height. Opposite is the patient who, after washing and eating, sits tied to the ground. The doctor palpates the impurity in the eye, then the patient stares at his nose while an assistant holds his head firmly. The surgeon holds a lancet with index finger, long finger and thumb, then draws it toward the pupil's edge, half a fingerwidth from the black and one-fourth fingerwidth from the outer eye corner, and next he draws it upward. He cuts in the left eye with his right hand, and in the right with his left. If he has cut properly, a sound is heard, and a drop of water comes out."

A modification of this technique can still be used for cataracts. The point is to move aside or extract the blurred lens, so that the path of light from cornea to retina becomes free.

When describing his operations, Susruta always emphasized the importance of complete cleanliness and careful preparation. In this he was long before his time. But just as important as

a suitable operation area was that the surgeons themselves should be knowledgeable and well-prepared for the operation. Instead of relying on their book-learning, they had to perfect their technical skill systematically. Incisions were trained on pickles, gourds and watermelons; operations on vitreous organs were tried on water-sacks and animal bladders; blood-letting was rehearsed on hollow lotus-stalks. Bandage application was rehearsed on puppets of natural size, and the prospective surgeon had to practise suture techniques on pieces of cloth and leather.

Not everything in Susruta's work was original, and much may have been learned from older doctors, as well as from contemporary surgeons in the West. Yet it is indisputable that Susruta has had an enormous influence on the surgeons of later times.

Susruta's Ideal Surgeon

"He shall belong to one of the three highest castes and be of good family. He shall be inquisitive, strong, energetic, self-controlled, and of good character, with intelligence and a good memory, courage and spiritual purity. He shall have thin lips, teeth, and tongue, a straight nose, honest and clever eyes, and a friendly mouth… A man with the opposite qualities must not be admitted to the holy realm of medicine…"

Elephant Surgery

The elephant was a sacred animal to the Hindus, as well as a useful one. The Indian veterinarians had access to a huge textbook of elephant medicine (Hasty Ayurveda), which contained 7,600 verses and 46 prose chapters, including a section on surgery. "As a companion in battle, the worthy beast had the same value as the heroic soldier," according to Henry Zimmer, one of our leading authorities on ancient Indian culture.

CHAPTER 2

The rise of Western surgery

European civilization began to emerge five thousand years ago in the Balkan peninsula and, particularly, on the isles and coasts of the Aegean Sea. Almost from the start, it was stimulated by contacts with many other cultures, especially in the east. The peoples of Greece and Asia Minor were already establishing relations with Egypt. Tribes of Indo-European folk—the linguistic ancestors of historic Greeks themselves—wandered down from northerly regions and settled. During the Bronze Age, new links with the Far East would be made possible by caravans from Mesopotamia, Persia, and India.

Perhaps the most prosperous of these peoples lived on Crete, the long thin island that lies like a giant wavebreaker in the southern Aegean. Unusually free from foreign interference, the Cretans developed a remarkable culture between 2500 and 1200 BC, which we now call "Minoan" after a mythical king Minos. Archaeological research continues to reveal a great deal about this gifted, happy and healthy nation.

THE great Achilles bandaging a wound on his cousin Patroclus, during the Trojan War. This may have occurred as early as 1250 BC, but was narrated by Homer around 700 BC. Greek doctors were not yet true professionals: Patroclus himself learned the healing art from Achilles, and both men were warriors—like the contemporary Celtic surgeons in central Europe. However, when the above scene was painted on a Classical Greek bowl after 500 BC, medicine had become a distinctive occupation.

As to the treatment of injuries and illnesses, we know only that they had a religious attitude toward the human body and were familiar with medicinal plants. But much more can be seen of their sanitation techniques.

Minoan water supplies, sewage removal, and bathing installations reached a level of refinement that was not to be reached by many Westerners until three thousand years later. Personal hygiene also stood in high repute among the Minoans, whose products included soap. To the body's purity they added its strengthening by elaborate athletic activities. One popular game was apparently to leap over running bulls, and such risky acrobatics by both men and women have been partly documented in excavations.

The Minoans were thus pioneers in "body culture", and passed some of it on to the Greek-speaking folk of the adjacent mainland. These robust "Mycenaeans" seem to have worshipped a god of healing, whose fame spread as far as the Hittites of Asia Minor, firm believers in magical cures. Even a set of surgical instruments was recently found in a tomb, and might have belonged to a local doctor around 1400 BC. This heritage was taken over by the historic Greeks of the Iron Age, and laid a foundation for their interest in medicine.

Traditional Greek surgery

The oldest sources of knowledge about Greek medicine are the Homeric poems, the *Iliad* and *Odyssey*. Scholars now agree that they were composed around 700 BC, but were based on events and customs as much as five or six centu-

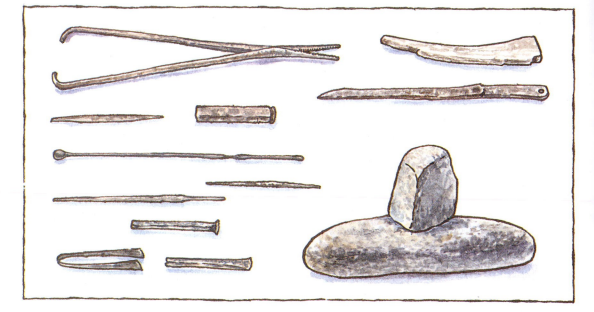

AMONG the oldest medical equipment yet identified by archaeologists is a set of instruments found in 1971, in a Mycenaean tomb at Nauplion in Greece, dated to about 1400 BC in the Late Bronze Age. Shown here are a stone grinder, possibly for preparing herbal remedies, and some of the copper tools: from top to bottom, a pair of scissors (over 30 cm long) with toothed jaws, long blades, various probes, needles, chisels and tongs. The tomb also contained a couple of small balls, perhaps for divining a patient's future. It might even have been the grave of Palamides, a doctor and inventor whom later Greek myths connected with this place.

arrow, evidently in the waist. Agamemnon, the Mycenaean king in command of the Greeks at Troy, ordered the herald Talthybios to summon a doctor, Makaon, who was the very son of the healing-god:

"So he spoke, and the herald obeyed his message quickly, and went to the bronze-clad Achaean army looking around for Makaon, and espied him standing surrounded by ranks of well-armed warriors who had followed him there from horse-rich Trike. The herald drew near with winged words:
"Hurry, son of Asklepios! King Agamemnon calls you to help Menelaus, the warring son of Atreus, who's been hit by a clever archer's arrow, a Trojan or Lycian, winning praise that gives us pain."

ries earlier. Most importantly from our point of view, the detailed descriptions of life in the *Iliad* have been proved to coincide rather well with the archaeological finds from those periods. We may conclude that its information on medicine and surgery, too, gave a fairly correct picture of the times.

The *Iliad* presents one of the world's first literary accounts of a battle-wound. None other than King Menelaus, the beautiful Helen's forsaken husband, was the victim. He was hit by an

Makaon went with the herald to Menelaus, who lay on the ground, abandoned by all the Greek chiefs. The doctor drew out the arrow—

"and when he drew it out, its sharp barbs broke. He loosed the shining belt and the mail-coat below, and last the girdle, bronzed

A typical ancient votive gift was this stone plaque, showing a leg with varicose (dilated) veins. It was placed, around 300 BC near the Acropolis of Athens, in the shrine of a doctor named Amynos, who was apparently worshipped for his talents.

by wondrous smiths. But seeing the wound where the painful arrow entered, he sucked out the blood, then skilfully smoothed on salve which Cheiron once had kindly given his father."

Aside from the fact that it would have been better to undress the patient before removing the arrow, this treatment must have worked, since we read that Menelaus went away alive. Makaon "sucked out" the wound—that is, he presumably cleaned it somehow—and then laid on a healing salve, which was an heirloom in the physician's own family. The character named Cheiron was a centaur, or man-horse, who had brought up the god Asklepios and taught him the art of healing. We shall never know what the salve contained, nor are there any other clues about wound-healing salves from the days of the Trojan War.

Menelaus was lucky, because his bronze-clad girdle weakened the force of the shot, or because he was treated by the army's best doctor. Mortality from battle-wounds was very high according to the *Iliad*. A calculation of all the wounds named in the poem has shown a total of 147 cases: 106 spear-thrusts, 17 sword-chops, 12 arrow-shots, and 12 sling-shots. Of those wounded by a spear, four in five died; of the sling victims, about two in three; of the sword victims, every one; and of the arrow victims, nearly half. So Menelaus was among seven who survived.

Evidently, Asklepios was already established in Homeric times as the god of medicine. In Greek mythology, he was the son of Apollo and the nymph Koronis, but the centaur Cheiron brought him up. Asklepios became such a good doctor that Hades, the god of the underworld,

Greek Health Resorts

The temples of Asklepios were usually located in beautiful and wholesome surroundings. With time, they developed into centres of recreation and pleasure, even for people who were not ill. The life-style at these holy places has been compared with that of spas and mineral wells, thousands of years later. Among other activities, theatre performances were given for the patients and their attendants. No fewer than 20,000 could sit in the famous amphitheatre at Epidauros—a place where the Greeks had begun to worship, and perhaps to heal, as early as 1600 BC back in the Bronze Age during Mycenaean times.

became angry at the declining death-rate and complained to Zeus, who found the complaint justified and killed Asklepios with a lightning-bolt.

After that, Asklepios was worshipped as the doctors' divinity. His tale is certainly similar to the deification of Imhotep by the Egyptians. In addition, Asklepios and his family contributed much to medical terminology. The Latin form of his name, Aesculapius, gave rise to the term *aesculap* for a physician. His daughter Hygieia became the goddess of health care, and explains our word "hygiene". Another daughter, called Panakeia, was the special protectress of healing plants. Ever since then, people have been searching for a "panacea" which would cure all illnesses.

The cult of Asklepios reached its zenith around 500 BC, when more than three hundred temples to the god existed in the Hellenic world—notably in Athens, Pergamon, and Epidauros. Their priests were known as "asklepiads", and developed into a corps of physicians. To be treated in a temple, the patient usually came with a votive gift, often a portrait showing his illness in stone or precious metal. This was set up at Asklepios' statue, and the priest gave the patient some sleep-inducing drug. He then slept for a night by the god's altar, followed by elaborate washing and other ceremonies. Once the patient began to emerge from his trance, a priest in the shape of the god appeared to him. Thus, upon leaving, he was sure that the god had paid him a personal visit. Such treatment can naturally produce improvement by autosuggestion, but it can hardly cure ailments which call for cutting or cauterizing. The only kinds of active therapy which we know that the asklepiads conducted were incisions of abscesses and boils.

At the same time as the cult of Asklepios was blossoming, though, a much more scientifically oriented medical philosophy began to emerge. Anaximenes of Miletos, who lived about 585–525 BC, taught that air was the principal element and the source of all life. Alkmaion of

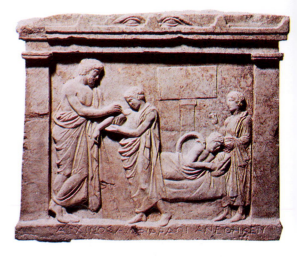

THE god Asklepios treats one patient, and is awaited by another. This "clinic" scene, from around 350 BC, was given by a man named Archinos to a holy place at Oropos, near Athens.

Croton, around 520 BC, denied the old doctrine of disease as possession by demons. He thought that illness was an upset balance between the opposites of wet and dry, hot and cold, bitter and sweet—a philosophy which strikingly reminds us of the Chinese. Alkmaion was a pioneer of dissection, and found that the arteries were empty, whereas the veins were full of blood. This observation is correct after death, although it led to the long-existing misconception that the arteries carried nothing but air. He, too, was the first to recognize that the brain played a central role in a person's life. Still more significant was Empedocles (495–435 BC), who maintained that there were four basic elements: fire, water, earth, and air. It may be hard to believe today, yet this view contained the foundations of modern chemistry and biology.

The natural-scientific way of thought caught on especially among the non-priestly assistants of the asklepiads. Their enormous intake of patients gave them great experience of practical medicine. Gradually they took over from their superiors who, because of more theoretical education, clung to the theurgical idea that illness was a divine punishment. It was probably from the secularized asklepiads that the first medical schools arose.

The initial school of importance was founded around 700 BC at Cnidos in Asia Minor. The Cnidians totally abandoned theurgical medicine and based their diagnoses on bedside observation. For them, a tumour was just a malignant growth, not a visitation from some infuriated god. While little is known of such early medical schools, there are hints—not necessarily reliable—that "small surgery" was performed, and that doctors were bold enough to attempt operations inside the abdominal cavity.

The Hippocratic age

About a hundred years later, the Cnidian school acquired a competitor on the nearby Aegean island of Cos. Its eventual leader was Hippocrates, a Greek doctor who has been honoured as the "father of medicine". He was born there in 460 BC and, according to legend, was introduced to medicine by his own father. After deepening his wisdom with long journeys in Egypt, Macedonia, and the lands around the Black Sea, he settled at Larissa in central Greece, where he died in 377 BC. Hippocrates' time coincided with the Hellenistic "golden age" of men like Pericles in politics, Socrates and Protagoras in philosophy, Herodotus and Thucydides in history, and Aeschylus, Sophocles and Euripides in dramatic art.

That a clever doctor named Hippocrates was active at the school of Cos, at least for a while, is scarcely doubted. But it is uncertain whether a single person wrote the seventy-two medical works which, by order of the later pharaoh Ptolemaios Soter, were collected under the title *Corpus Hippocraticum*. Most likely they derived from a circle of doctors on Cos, either during or shortly after Hippocrates' lifetime. There is, however, reason to believe that some of these books were written by Hippocrates himself.

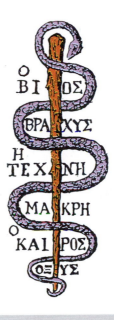

The Doctor's Emblem

Ever since Asklepios' time, the medical profession has used a staff entwined by a snake as its special symbol. This is commonly called the Aesculapian staff, after the god's Latin name. Modern scholars, however, doubt that the symbol originated in Greece. It probably derived from the Jews' imprisonment in Egypt and their desert wanderings.

People in that region suffered from a type of worm known as Dracunculus medinensis. (These worms grow under the skin, particularly in the lower extremities. When they push out through the skin, blisters and infected sores often arise. Their toxins can also produce general reactions such as hives, nausea, vomiting and fever.) But a way was found to get rid of the worms, which could be up to half a metre long. They were carefully rolled up on a little peg. This may be why the Jews considered the snake a sign of victory. The brazen serpent which God commanded Moses to make (Numbers 21) might have been a Dracunculus worm!

Aphorisms of Hippocrates

Life is short, art is long, the right opportunity is fleeting, experience is deplorable, and judgement is hard.

If an operation is considered necessary, one should act at the beginning. Once the illness has reached a peak, it is best left alone.

If two ailments occur at the same time in different places, the weaker is obscured by the stronger.

What cannot be cured with medicaments is cured by the knife, what the knife cannot cure is cured with the searing-iron, and whatever this cannot cure must be considered incurable.

It is best not to treat hidden tumours. Such patients, if treated, soon go under, but otherwise they can live long.

Do not disturb a patient during or just after a crisis; attempt no experiments with laxatives or fluid-removing medicines.

Even if they regard their illnesses as serious, many patients regain health simply through satisfaction with an understanding doctor.

Very fat people tend to die sooner than those who are thin.

From Hippocrates' Writings:
On Surgery

Surgery is concerned with the patient, operator, assistants, and instruments; the light, of what sort and where; how the patient and instruments should be placed; the time, method, and place.

The operator must sit or stand in a well-lighted place that is comfortable for both him and the patient.

The nails should be cut to the fingertips. A surgeon must learn to use his fingers through assiduous practice. The index finger and thumb are especially important. They must be trained in all kinds of work, individually as well as together: they should function well, elegantly, rapidly, easily, cleanly and immediately.

On Treating Injuries

Only wine should be used to moisten a wound, unless it is on a joint. Sparse food, and no drink but water, are important with all injuries —and more so with fresh wounds than old, with wounds that have somehow become or risk becoming inflamed, with joint injuries, or when cramps may occur, but also with abdominal wounds and, most of all, with injuries of the head or thighbone or any other bone.

An upright body position is harmful with wounds, especially on the leg. The patient must neither stand nor walk, and not even be allowed to sit. Rest and quiet help most. Fresh wounds and their surrounding parts are least likely to inflame if one can bring about pus formation as soon as possible. Do not let pus

HIPPOCRATES was portrayed as a thinker in late antiquity (*opposite*), and even twelfth-century Byzantine Greeks wrote his oath in the form of a cross (*above*) relating it to Christian ideas.

collect in a wound's opening. If pus cannot be brought forth, keep the wound dry with some medium that is not too strong. For if the wound dries out too much, fever results, as shown by chilling and cramps.

If the wound is caused by a cut or impact of a sharp weapon, some means is needed to stop the bleeding quickly, as well as preventing pus formation and drying up the wound. If the wound is lacerated or mutilated by the weapon, it must be treated in a way which makes pus form as soon as possible.

The Hippocratic Oath

Probably a mixture of principles dating from both before and after Hippocrates' time, the Oath has been given in many versions, but essentially as follows:

"I swear by Apollo the Healer, by Asklepios, Hygieia and Panacea, and by all other gods and goddesses, to keep this oath to the best of my ability and judgement. I will honour him who taught me this art as highly as my parents, and share my goods with him if he be in need. I will regard his children as my own brethren, and teach them this art for no fee or obligation if they wish to learn it. I will impart this art by every means to my sons and those of my teacher, and to disciples who have sworn to the rules of the profession, but to them alone. I will prescribe regimen for the good of my patients as far as my ability and judgement allow, and not for their harm. I will give no deadly drug or any such counsel to anyone, even if asked, nor will I help women to procure abortion. I shall lead my life and ply my art in purity and piety. Stones I will not remove, but leave them to those who deal with them. I will enter every house to benefit the sick, refraining from all wrongdoing or corruption, and from any act of seduction of male or female, bound or free. Whatever I see or hear, in practising my profession or apart from it, and which ought not to be spread about, I will hold secret and never reveal. If I keep my oath faithfully, may I enjoy my life and practise my art, respected by all men and at all times. But should I violate it, may the opposite be my lot."

A Great Clinician's View of Hippocrates

Sir Thomas Clifford Allbutt, professor of medicine at Cambridge University, expressed a widespread verdict: "Who was this Hippocrates, this extraordinary man? He seems to have been one of the mighty personalities, like Moses, Thales, Pythagoras, Socrates, Paul, Francis of Assisi, Luther, Lincoln. Even had he never written a line, the force of his personality would have made him immortal."

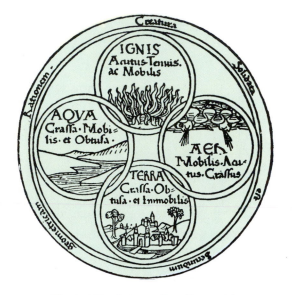

THE Classical Greek theory that all materials were made up of four "elements" persisted among philosophers—and doctors—as late as the sixteenth century when this manuscript picture was drawn.

The Hippocratic writings repudiated the old theurgical and philosophical medicine. Observation at the bedside and ideas of the new natural science formed their background, as in the Cnidian school. Medicine was refashioned into a systematic science in Hippocrates' time, even if grave relapses were to occur afterward. The traditional internal medicine was combined with surgery, which had already gained a more rational basis. Indeed, the books on surgery in the *Corpus Hippocraticum* are regarded as its best sections, and as the very ones which were written by Hippocrates in person.

In the collection's surgical part, at least some of the anatomy is correct, and rather thoroughly discussed—especially that which was essential to proper care of bone fractures and disjointings. In the part on internal medicine, though, the anatomy is only scantily surveyed. This in itself is logical, since Hippocratic medicine was built not on anatomy, but on Empedocles' doctrine of the four elements. The teachings about fire, water, earth and air were turned into a concept of four body fluids: warm dry blood, cold dry yellow bile, warm wet black bile, and cold wet mucus. Sickness was an imbalance between the fluids—a disharmony caused by influence from the environment, seasons, weather, diet and nutrition. Treatment was thus an effort to restore the balance.

The Hippocratic physicians always worked on the same pattern. First they described the symptoms and the results of examination in detail. Inspection, auscultation, and palpation were used, and the smell and taste of secreted body fluids were studied. Hippocrates described the typical auscultation finds for lung inflammation, the signs of fluid around the lungs, and observations of "dry" lung inflammation. His writings contain illuminating, perceptive reports on mumps, tuberculosis and joint inflammations.

The diagnosis was followed by prognosis. What course could the illness be expected to take? How long might the patient live? If treatment was thought worthwhile, general rules were first given about rest, diet, proper climate, and so forth. Then came specific measures against the actual illness, including operations. Fresh air, light in the home and sickroom, cleanliness and a sound diet were among the favourite themes of Hippocrates. He often recommended bathing, massage, and moderate exercise, although he opposed arduous bodily movement. A wide range of healing plants was known to him, many being considered sensible even today. But on the whole he was rather cautious with medicaments, even if he did admit that extreme conditions called for extreme methods.

A number of Hippocrates' surgical methods can still be called valid. Pus collection around the lungs (*empyema pleurae*) is a good example. It was treated, and usually cured, by making a small opening in the chest wall, and inserting a tube for drainage of the pus. Fractures in which the bone ends had slipped past each other were restored to correct position by traction and alignment.

A Roman method of repairing a bone fracture or dislocation was to stretch the limb with a weight—as shown here on an arm, fifteen hundred years later—or with a traction apparatus.

Some of his methods were fairly ingenious. For a broken upper armbone, with shortening of the arm, the patient was hung by his armpit over a trapeze-like structure. The broken arm was bent at the elbow joint into a horizontal position, and an assistant supported the wrist. Then a weight was hung in a silken bandage as close to the elbow bend as possible. With this downward pull, the surgeon could easily manipulate the broken bone ends into contact with each other. For a broken thighbone, the bone ends were restored in position by a similarly clever method of extension. If we did not have access to anaesthetics and muscle-relaxing drugs today, we would probably be using Hippocrates' methods, since nobody has come up with better ones.

Hippocrates was a brilliant clinical observer, as his descriptions of illnesses show. Perhaps the best example, though, is his account of the appearance of a very sick individual in the condi-

tion now called surgical shock. We rightly still use the expression *facies hippocratica* for these symptoms:

"With acute ailments, the patient's face should first be inspected, as to whether it resembles a healthy person's or, even better, that person as he usually looks. The contrary is bad, and worst are the following: a protrusive nose, hollow eyes, sunken temples, cold ears that are drawn in with the lobes turned outward, the forehead's skin rough and tense like parchment, and the whole face greenish or black or blue-grey or leaden."

The greatness of Hippocrates lies on a level beyond diagnosis, prognosis or treatment. He laid the basis for modern medical ethics. This is manifested in his oft-quoted phrase, "The most important thing is to avoid injuring"—and primarily in the oath which is credited to him. Still currently used in many medical colleges, Hippocrates' oath shows that present-day issues such as abortion and euthanasia were also relevant twenty-five centuries ago. Its words about the doctor's duty of confidentiality have almost the same formulation in the legal codes of most civilized countries. Yet Hippocrates' main legacy was the credo which he himself never violated: to be a good doctor, one must first of all be a good human being.

The Hellenistic doctors

Hippocrates' medical experience and ethics long remained unknown to the rest of the ancient world. When his writings were published at last in Alexandria, they had not been outdated. The only problem was that the pioneers of medicine were, by then, too fascinated with new discoveries to remember or heed Hippocrates' basic truths. For the time being, bedside observation and surgical techniques had to take second place to physiology and the dawn of pathological anatomy.

THE inexpert treatment of a woman giving birth in ancient Greece is well expressed by the assistants on this plaque, from Oropos around 350 BC.

Instead, the greatest influence on the next century's medicine came from Aristotle (384–322 BC). The son of a Macedonian physician, born at Stagira in Thrace, he became a disciple of Plato at the age of seventeen. On the latter's death in 347 BC, Aristotle left Athens to spend the next twelve years travelling. When his pupil Alexander the Great became a king, he soon returned and founded his famous Lyceum. The philosophy taught there received the name of the Peripatetic School, from the garden colonnade or *peripatos* where teachers and students carried on their discussions.

Aristotle was a creative thinker in fields as varied as ethics, logic, psychology, poetry and politics. Although he was one of the most interesting figures in antiquity, we may focus on his success in natural science. His writings on zoology and anatomy described nearly five hundred species of animals. Rich in details and biologically accurate, they show that he often conducted dissections, a method which he bequeathed to the Alexandrian doctors. As the father of comparative anatomy, Aristotle has no rival.

He had certainly learned a great deal of medicine from his father, but was too absorbed in research and teaching to have time for practical healing. Still, his view of nature and anatomical findings would dominate medical thinking and methods for five hundred years, until the time of Galen. One of Aristotle's principles was the idea that nature is practical—an idea largely but, of course, not universally true. This was to result in errors, and not least among doctors. Moreover, he built upon the theory of four elements, advanced by Empedocles and by Hippocrates' son-in-law Polybos. The doctrine of four fluids, or "humoral pathology", was also to persist in the following centuries.

The Peripatetic School had several prominent doctors, among them Diocles of Karystos, Praxagoras of Cos, and Theophrastos of Eresos. Each of them made permanent contributions. Perhaps the most important was Praxagoras' teaching about the pulse, although it was misguided, since he believed that the arteries transported air. Blood did issue from an artery which was cut during life—but he explained that the blood was simply sucked out, due to nature's fear of empty space, the *horror vacui*! And with the doctrine of four humours as a background, it is to be expected that the Peripatetics had little use for surgery, which presupposes a solid substance to work with.

In 333 BC, Alexander the Great defeated Darius III, the great Persian king, at Issos in Asia Minor. This opened the way to Egypt, which was taken easily enough. The next year, Alexandria was added. Soon the city developed into a trading centre, and dethroned Athens as the cultural focus of the Greek empire. "Elements from the east and west merged under Greek sovereignty into a unified world medicine," as is stated pompously but correctly by German historians. Excellent conditions for medical research were created in Alexandria through libraries, institutions, and the favour of the Egyptian vassal kings. These conditions were exploited as well. In the third century BC, the so-called Alexandrian School reached its apogee. Two scientists rose above all others: Herophilos and Erasistratos.

Herophilos of Chalcedon, born at some time in the late fourth century, became a disciple of Praxagoras, whose work in physiology and anatomy he continued. He is said to have been the first performer of public dissections, which the Ptolemaic rulers encouraged. One of the latter was so interested that he himself not only dissected corpses, but placed condemned criminals at the disposal of the scientists. There are good reasons for supposing that people were actually vivisected!

The main achievement of Herophilos lay in anatomy of the nervous system, known today as

The Doctrine of Four Humours

It was Polybos, the son-in-law of Hippocrates, who developed this theory in his work On Human Nature. *The word "humour" meant moisture in Latin, and the idea of a few basic kinds of body fluids lasted into the Middle Ages. But in Greek, the four humours were* cholera, phlegma, melancholia, *and* haima. *These names passed into many languages, being associated respectively with yellow bile, phlegm or mucus, black bile, and blood. The choleric temperament is fiery, the phlegmatic is cold, the melancholic is gloomy, and— based on the Latin word for blood—the sanguine is buoyant.*

On Aristotle

There must have been a particularly lucky constellation of the planets when the great man from Stagira was born. In the first part of the Inferno, *Virgil leads Dante to an elect gathering who sat on the stars upon green meadows, the family of philosophers who devoutly gazed at "the master among those who knew"—*il maestro di color che sanno. *No one has ever held sway over such an intellectual empire: logic, metaphysics, rhetoric, psychology, ethics, poetry, politics, and the natural sciences—a creator in them all and a master of them all. There is no equal to his career in the history of human intelligence. As a founder of comparative anatomy, systematic zoology, embryology, teratology, botany and philosophy, his writings are of eternal interest. They represent a superb collection of facts about the structure and function of the individual body parts. It is a miracle that a single man, even with a school of apprentices, could achieve so much!*

Sir William Osler

neuroanatomy. He established that the brain was the centre of the mental functions, and described parts such as the "writing pen" (*calamus scriptorius*) and "Herophilos' wine-press" (*torcular Herophili*). In addition, he distinguished between sensory and motor nerves, showing that all nerves are connected with the central nervous system. Another area of concern to him was the liver. He gave the lasting name "duodenum" to a part of the small intestine, and proved that the veins from the intestine end in the liver.

Erasistratos of Keos, who lived from 304 to about 250 BC, studied much the same organs as did Herophilos—the brain and the biliary system. He discovered the large bile duct (*ductus choledochus*), which collects the bile from the liver and leads it to the duodenum. Moreover, he pursued Herophilos' finding of the liver's blood supply, and traced the portal vein system. He managed to show that the fine liver veins run parallel with the bile capillaries, a beautiful piece of miniature dissection. This became the key to understanding how the liver functions, and thus the starting point for biliary surgery, though the latter was still very far away.

To that extent, the schools of Herophilos and Erasistratos agreed with each other, but they came into conflict elsewhere. Erasistratos could not accept humoral pathology, which Herophilos blindly believed in. According to Erasistratos, illness was caused mechanically, by the blood streaming into an organ and making it plethoric—overfull. This, he thought, hindered the air (*pneuma*) in entering the arteries, leading to the organ's decline. Apart from the preliminary stage of plethora, his idea is correct for some ailments, such as gangrene and softening of the brain. In any case, the mechanistic view of illness gave rise to a "solidary pathology", which opposed the old humoral pathology.

These schools' representatives became ever more dogmatic and unrealistic. Wandering into theoretical subtleties, they lost interest in practical medicine and surgery. The reaction came in about 180 BC, when the teachings of both Herophilists and Erasistrateans were rejected. Unfortunately, to some degree, the baby was thrown out with the bath-water: their important discoveries were forgotten. The new fundamental philosophy became empiricism: "only experience makes a physician".

The main champion of empiricism was Glaukios of Tarentium, who lived in the first century before Christ. He recognized, as the only reliable basis for medical practice, a triad of factors: personal experience, the results of older colleagues, and—if one had no experience—logical analogies. Empiricism moved the fundamental branches of medical science, anatomy and physiology and pathology, into the background. On the other hand, it improved the description of illnesses and the technique of surgery. The empiricists conducted lithotomy and cataract operations with clear success.

Empiricism's golden age can also be called the birthday of remedial medicine, or pharmacology. This concurrence had peculiar causes. The rulers of the time lived in constant fear of being poisoned, yet they made sure that their court druggists kept a supply of poisons for use on obnoxious opponents. Nicomedes of Bithynia, and Attalos III of Pergamon, were skilled poison-mixers, and tested their concoctions on criminals in prison. The most renowned of these royal pharmacologists was Mithradates of Pontus. Having gained fame for inventing a universal antidote, known as *teriak* and containing fifty-four ingredients, he was not content to test it on prisoners, but took it himself in increasing doses, so as to become immune from all kinds of poison. It got him as far as the age of 57, when his son staged a revolution and he had himself stabbed by a slave.

AENEAS, the Trojan and later Roman hero, receives surgery for a leg wound before leaving Troy with his family, in this fresco from the city of Pompeii (destroyed AD 79).

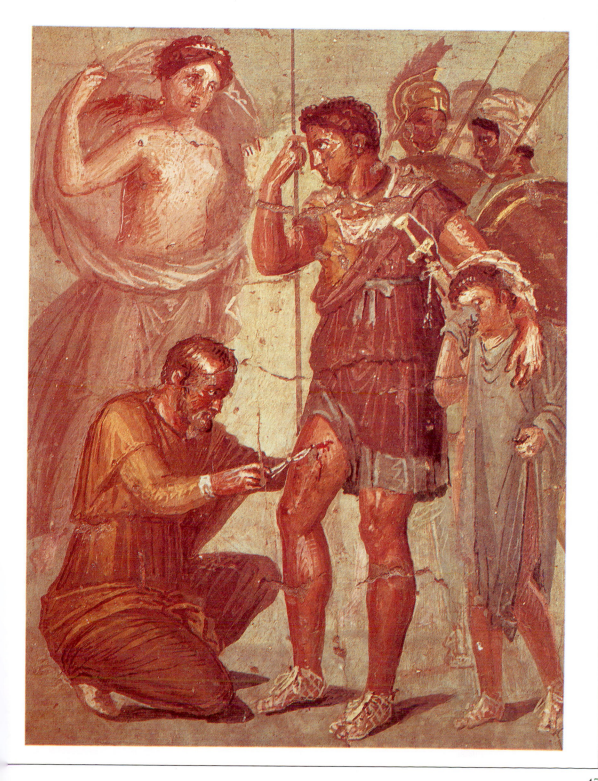

A more scientific spirit was shown by Dioscorides Pedanios, from Cilicia, who has been regarded as the first true pharmacologist. As a surgeon in the Roman army, he had an opportunity to see most of the known world. During his journeys, he tirelessly assembled lore about plants for healing. His work *De materia medica* was published in five volumes. It remained the standard treatise on remedial medicine for more than a thousand years.

Surgery in Roman times

Before Rome conquered Greece in 146 BC—the same year when Carthage was destroyed—medicine and surgery had a low status in Italy. The healing which was practised, on the whole, resembled that of Babylonia and Assyria. Oddly enough, the only notable exception was dentistry. Egyptians, Greeks and Phoenicians had long used gold wire to repair loose teeth, but the Etruscan folk in central Italy developed this technique into a master craft. Etruscan graves have yielded tooth prostheses of both fixed and loose kinds, in which real or artificial teeth were held together with gold bands, melted over the tooth crowns. Tooth prostheses of gold were probably a status symbol in Etruria, and in Guerini's *History of Dentistry* we read:

> "Since the gold that was used in the construction covered a large part of the crowns, it was clearly not meant to be hidden; on the contrary, it was quite conspicuous. One must therefore assume that the possession of false teeth and other signs of dental repair was nothing to be ashamed of. It was a luxury article, a sort of refinement available only to the rich."

The later Romans learned dental prosthetics from these earlier practitioners. Horace wrote, for example, of how two witches ran so fast that one of them dropped her false teeth. And Martial praised the beauty of a certain Laecanias' snow-white teeth, hastening to add that they

had been bought. Such ancient odontology is confirmed by discoveries of the first dental mirrors. Apart from this, however, healing played no prominent role in Rome before the Caesars.

One reason for the doctor's low standing was that most of the representatives of this profession were Greeks, a people whom the Romans despised—possibly in awareness of their own cultural inferiority. It is also possible that immigrant Greek doctors were ignorant and unhelpful: Pliny recorded that they failed to win the confidence of patients. For a Roman citizen, or *civis romanus*, it was unthinkable to engage in anything as low as a doctor's work. When the need for physicians grew and the Greek immigrants had to be supplemented, this was done by relying on slaves or other imports. A notable instance was Luke the Evangelist, who accompanied Paul to Rome.

Individual doctors did raise themselves above the majority. Asklepiades of Bithynia arrived in Rome around 90 BC, and soon became a lionized society-doctor, perhaps chiefly because his treatment involved—as has been written by Acke Renander—"bathing, massage, walking,

EVEN in pre-Roman times, ailing women in Italy often sought divine help by dedicating models of the uterus in sanctuaries. This clay example shows what may be a Fallopian tube at its side. Such anatomical knowledge could have been acquired from Caesarean and other operations as well as from autopsies.

hydrotherapy and a diet of wine: prescriptions which suited the Romans perfectly." Asklepiades had no use for Hippocratic medicine, which he called "a meditation on death". He based his healing on a rather fuzzy idea of stopping up the body's pores, almost a variant of Erasistratus' solidary pathology.

This teaching left a single memorial. It employed the concept of "bulk" (in Greek, *onkos*) for diseased organs, and the term "oncology" for the science of tumours has recently been revived. At the opposite end of the descriptive scale, we might place one of the few surgeons whose name is known to us from the days of Rome before Christ. He was really called Archagathos, but seems to have been no great asset to the profession. Pliny relates that his methods were so brutal as to earn him the nickname Carnifex—the executioner!

Even if Roman citizens thought themselves too fine to practise healing, they did not shrink from observing and writing about it. In the year AD 30 in the reign of Tiberius, one of the most extraordinary texts of antiquity was published in Rome. The author was Aulus Cornelius Celsus, an upper-class literary man who lived there at least temporarily. Of his numerous scientific works, the only one to survive is *De Re Medica Libri Octo*, or "Eight Books on Medicine". The last two books dealt with surgery, and give us a well-written and exhaustive picture of the surgical art at the time of Christ. The signs of inflammation—heat, redness, swelling, pain and loss of function—have long been known to medical students as "the signs of Celsus".

Celsus begins his chapters on surgery with a short history. He mentions some earlier surgeons, "recently and most notably Tryphon the Elder, Euelpistus, and Meges who, as his writings show, was the best-educated of these, all of whom have introduced diverse improvements and contributed quite a lot to the progress of this science." Sadly, we are not told which progress he means. But the passage clearly has one important implication: that surgery was by then regarded as a science, not

Asklepiades' Motto

Tuto, cito, jucunde—*sure, speedy, and pleasant.*

Pliny: the Blessings of Urine

Gaius Plinius Secundus the Elder (23–79 AD) came from northern Italy and served for many years as a cavalry officer in Germany, concluding his brilliant official career as admiral in the Roman fleet. He died of asphyxia in the eruption of Vesuvius, when Herculaneum and Pompeii were destroyed. Pliny's hobby had been to write down everything he heard. His Naturalis Historia is very unreliable, but still shows what he—and other Roman citizens of high standing—could be brought to believe. In the chapter "On Urine" he says:

"The ashes of burnt oyster shells, mixed with old urine, yield a remedy against all sorts of running sores and skin rashes on children. Corrosive sores, burns, anal trouble, cracked skin, and scorpion bites are also treated with urine. The greatest midwives have asserted that no better washing-medium exists for skin diseases. With an addition of soda, urine cures head wounds, dandruff, and spreading sores, particularly on the genitals. Every individual benefits most from his own urine, if I may say so. A dog-bite should immediately be washed with urine, or else pierced with a sea-urchin whose spines are moistened by a sponge or cloth drenched in urine. Ash kneaded in urine is used to treat the bites of snakes and mad dogs…"

as a handicraft. For Celsus, it was inseparable from the two other branches of medicine—dietetics and pharmacotherapy. Indeed, he may have granted surgery a status of *primus inter pares*, the first among equals:

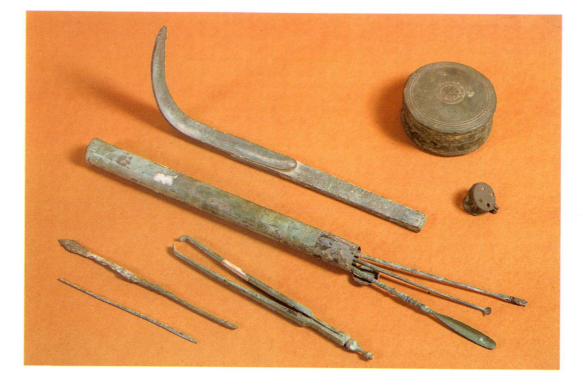

ROMAN surgical instruments were usually made of copper alloy, often by fine craftsmen. Many were copied in later times, but those shown here are genuine, having been found in a surgeon's tomb. From top: medicine box, strainer and scraper (known as a strigil); instrument case containing a probe with threaded end (for cleaning or medicating), a small spoon (ligula) and a long spatula; tweezers or forceps, a lancet or scalpel, and a needle.

"And even in the cases where we count most on medicaments, it is evident not only that they often fail to restore health, but that health often returns without them. Whereas in the surgical branch of medicine, one can see that every successful cure, however supported to some degree by the other branches, is due primarily to the manual treatment."

Celsus' work on surgery has a vast breadth. It discusses joint dislocations, pus formation, fistu-las, shot wounds, eye and ear ailments, dropsy, abdominal injuries, ruptures, varicose veins, illnesses of the urinary tract, consolidated and crooked fingers. The whole eighth chapter deals with bone fractures and limb injuries. He goes beyond surgical technique, presenting the different conditions in stringent detail, and frequently adding clues for the judgement of prognosis. His medical insights are so good that many readers have suspected him to be actually a trained physician.

Much of the practical advice is clever and quite applicable today. For example, with an arrow-wound, the surgeon should consider the location of the tip and barbs, then determine which way the arrow can be extracted in order to minimize further injury. Celsus recommends a special extracting instrument that was originally launched by Diokles of Karystos—a sort of curving, grooved scoop, which could be brought round the arrow-tip to ease it out elegantly. Wounds were usually sewn with sutures, and bleeding vessels were burnt with a cauterizing-iron if the blood did not stop with a pressure bandage. Moreover, Celsus often implies that it was bleeding which scared people. This is, of course, understandable—vessel ligature had not yet been invented.

A nice instance of Celsus' documentary skill is his description of the operational technique in lithotomy. We abridge it slightly:

"On a high chair sits a very strong and intelligent man, who holds the patient, leaning backward and turned away, resting with bottom on his knees. He draws the lower legs backward and lets the patient pull his own knees apart as far as possible. If the patient is relatively large, two strong people sit on two joined stools, and tie together both the stools and their adjacent legs so that these cannot be separated, and then the patient is placed on both their knees in the stated manner.

"When the doctor has carefully cut his nails and lubricated his left hand, he inserts two of its fingers, first one and then the other, slowly into the patient's rectum, while applying the right hand's fingers to the lower abdomen, also with caution to avoid harming the bladder in case the fingers should meet the stone too strongly from both sides… it is usual that lesions of the bladder cause convulsions which may be fatal.

"The stone is first sought in the bladder neck and, if found there, it can be brought out with little trouble. If the stone is not there or has receded, the left hand's fingers are pushed up towards the upper part of the bladder, followed by the right hand. The stone cannot avoid being found with the hands, and is then brought down, with ever more caution as it is smaller and smoother, so that it does not slip away.

"Once the stone has descended, a crescent-shaped incision should be made in the skin near the anus, going into the bladder neck, with its corners slightly oriented toward the posterior pelvic bone. Then a transverse cut is

Celsus on Cancer

Malignant cancerous diseases were familiar to Celsus. He was resigned: "Certain doctors use corrosive substances. Others burn, and still others wield the knife. The corrosive substances have never done anyone any good. Through burning, the tumour is activated and grows faster until the patient dies. If cut out, it comes back after the scar is formed, and the patient dies also. To distinguish a benign tumour from a malignant one is almost impossible. All we can do is to wait and see."

Smoking Out Hysteria

Soranos was opposed to an old method of curing hysteria in women. The treatment probably originated in the power of words over thoughts. For the word "hysteria" was taken from the Greek hyster, *meaning the uterus, and people believed that the mental disturbance came from this organ! The old therapy was to burn sweet-smelling herbs and let the smoke rise into the afflicted woman's vagina.*

The Ideal Surgeon According to Celsus

A surgeon ought to be in early manhood, or at any rate not much older; have a swift and steady, never-faltering hand, and no less skill in the left hand than the right; have sharp and clear eyesight; appear undistressed, and compassionate inasmuch as he wishes to heal those whom he treats, but does not allow their cries to hurry him more than the circumstances require, or to cut less than is necessary, and permits the patient's groaning to make not the slightest impression on him in anything he does.

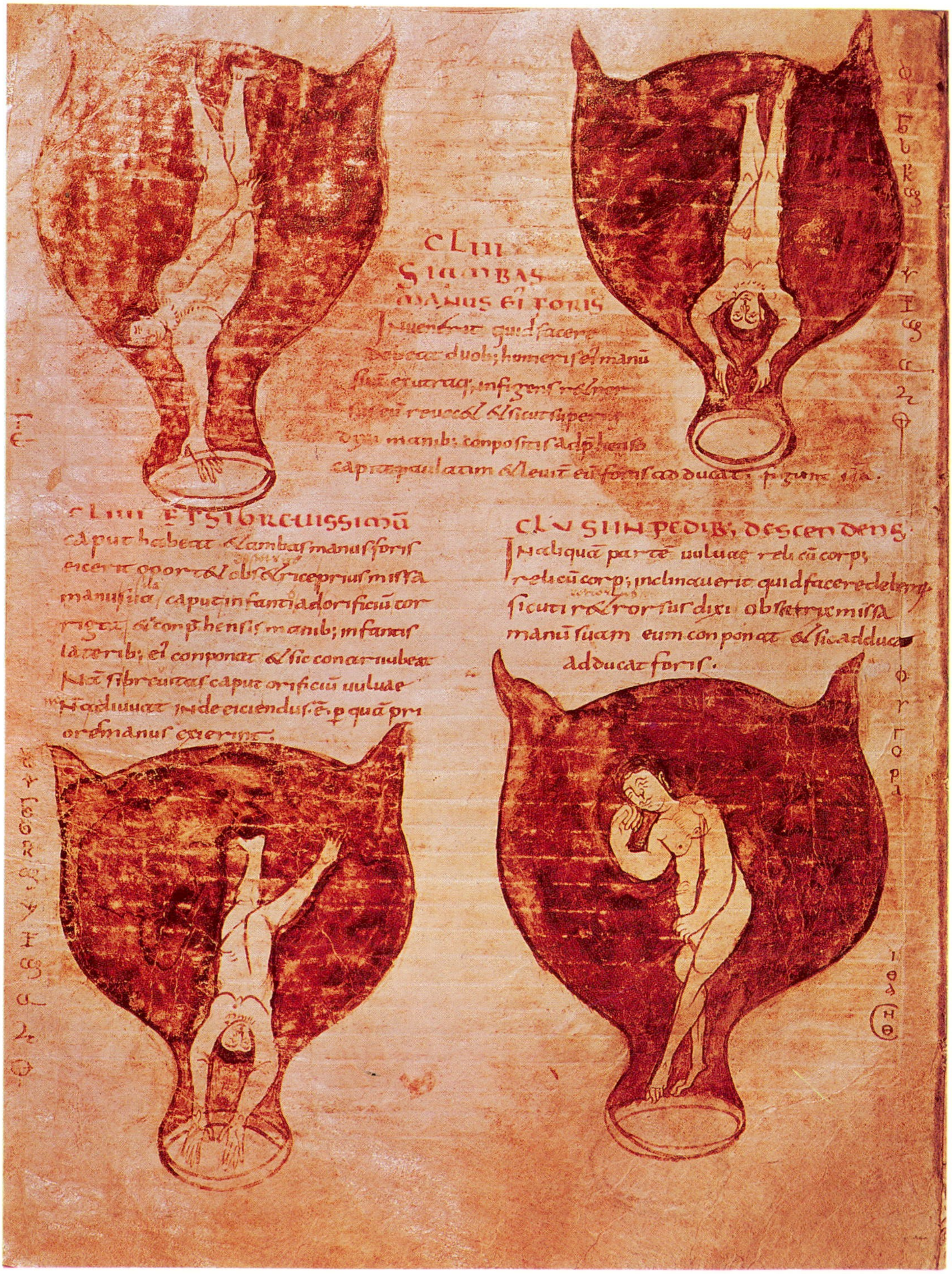

made to open the bladder neck. This will expose the stone. If it is small, it can be pulled out with the bare fingers by working it sideways. But if it is bigger, a specially constructed hook must be got round it. This has a thin end with a crescent-shaped, bent plate having blunt teeth, and is smooth on its outside. When the stone is definitely held securely, one makes a threefold movement at almost the same time, to each side and then outwards, but slowly and so that the stone is at first pulled only a little. Then, raising the hook's outer end to make it lie better inside, one can more easily draw out the stone."

This was the standard technique. The complete version included much detailed advice, and Celsus went on to tell what was done in case of complications or abnormal circumstances. Among other methods of extracting the bladder stone, he cited the method of "lithotripsy", invented by Ammonius. With a special instrument, the stone was crushed, inside the bladder or its neck, so that the small particles could pass out spontaneously.

Further methods that were well-developed in Roman times may be illustrated by the operations of plastic surgery. Celsus gave a method for covering a defect in the lower lip, with a displacement transplant from the surrounding skin—and even a technique of discharge incision was known. He described methods of tapping morbid pus accumulations, and devoted a long section to wounds in the abdomen. But perhaps the culmination of his operational teaching was reached with "strumectomy", the cutting away of struma (scrofula):

"Directly over the swelling one makes a cut next to the sac, then uses one's finger to separate the diseased hollow formation from the healthy

DIFFERENT positions of a foetus were among the many aspects of obstetrics discussed by Soranus of Ephesus in his book *Gynaikeia*. This imaginative illustration is from a ninth-century Latin copy.

tissues, and takes it out in a single piece together with its envelope."

A long time was to pass before such operations were ventured again.

The best physician who was active in surgery during the early Imperial period was a Greek immigrant, Soranus of Ephesus (AD 98–138). He concentrated chiefly on children and obstetrics, introducing the Roman birth-chair. In the absence of modern aids, it is most suitable for the woman to bear her child sitting rather than lying, since the abdominal pressure is utilized better. Soranus was also the first to succeed with the transverse foetal position, a frightful complication which endangers the mother and, without proper care, almost always results in stillbirth. Soranus performed the manoeuvre which was later called "turning the foot"—he eased a hand into the uterus and pulled down one of the foetus' legs, so that the child would be born feet-first, which gives some chance of success. This also suggests that he knew of treatments such as membrane explosion and widening of the outer cervical mouth, which are employed to speed up a sluggish delivery.

The first nursing care

A related medical feature of those times is best understood in the light of its ancestry. The earliest written record of nurses is a limestone inscription from about 1250 BC, when Ramses II ruled Egypt. Certain women were said to be free of work duties at the construction of temples in the Valley of the Kings: they could stay home to tend sick members of their families. This, of course, was not a matter of professional nurses, but it is not impossible that such people existed in ancient Egypt. The many priests, who also sometimes cared for the sick, were aided in the temples by women who often possessed high status and, probably, fulfilled various tasks of the same kind.

Nursing as a profession, however, arose in India. It was rooted in the monastic system which Buddha founded, around 500 BC. The

Hindu medical texts frequently mention the role of nurses. They describe the qualities needed by a nurse: she should be clean, intelligent, knowledgeable and full of sympathy for the patient. The *Kasyapa* emphasizes that she must not be squeamish, and must be able to control her temperament. In *Susruta Samhita*, absolute loyalty to the doctor and his orders is stressed. All these requirements are identical to those laid down by Florence Nightingale, two and a half millennia afterward!

To be sure, *Susruta Samhita* is sceptical of female nurses. But we know that they worked in

eighteen hospitals which were built, around 225 BC, by the great Hindu ruler Asoka. One of his larger enterprises was the colonization of Sri Lanka and its conversion to Buddhism. Among his successors on the island was Dutugamunu, a legendary king who built several hospitals. It is likely that the world's first nursing school was associated with at least some of them.

The ancient Greeks, in their wisdom, refused to accept women as workers of full value. Consequently, there were no female nurses in Greek sick-care. The entire *Corpus Hippocraticum* contains not a hint of women as assistants! When bedside care was needed, young physicians were employed:

"Leave one of your apprentices with the responsibility for carrying out your instructions and for administering the treatment. Choose

THE early Christian hospitals of Rome were comparable in spirit—though not in organization—to later Italian ones like this, portrayed around 1500 in a medical manuscript.

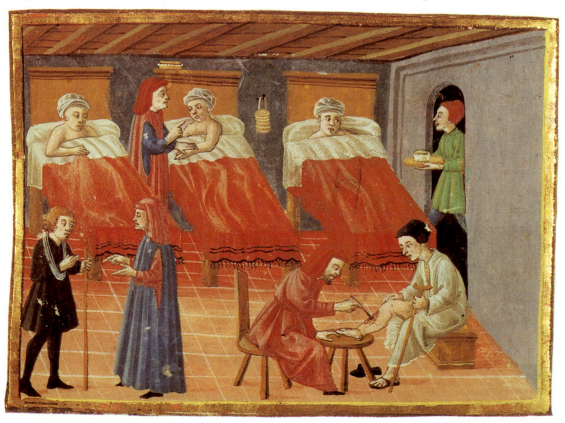

one who has already been initiated into the mysteries of the art, so that he can add what is essential and give secure treatment. He can also note the signs which appear between your own visits. Never let a layman take care of the sick, else his errors may rebound upon you…"

The only acceptable women were thus the *omphalotomai*, literally the "umbilical-cord cutters": in other words, midwives. Yet to take part in childbirth was not a profession—it fell to the old women in the family and neighbourhood.

The spread of Christianity affected the nursing profession in two ways. Naturally, the Christian idea of love supported the women who wanted to engage in self-sacrificing care of the sick. On the other hand, the old-fashioned Christian attitude involved a retreat from the rational physiological medicine that had broken through in Greece and at Alexandria. People believed ever more fatalistically in divine providence, and treatment became a process of praying—and encouraging the patient to pray—to God and the appropriate saints.

But there were remarkable exceptions. Outside Caesarea in Cappadocia, a social institution was established in the year 370, called "Basileas" after its creator, the city's bishop. It included hospitals, leper houses, homes for the elderly and the insane, as well as residences for doctors and other personnel, in addition to a nursing home run by the bishop's pious sister Macrina. This surely served as both a residence and a place of education. We do not know what was taught here, in the oldest Christian nursing school. One must assume that it had less to do with rational physical care, than with knowledge of how to prepare a sick person for death.

From the medical viewpoint, things were better in Rome a few decades later, at what is called the world's oldest Christian hospital. In general, Roman women differed in status from their Greek sisters. They were respected, and could come or go as they pleased, being shielded by their *stola matronalis*, the mantle which they wore after marrying. At the oldest Christian

Saint Basil

Also called Basileus the Great, he was born about 330 in Caesarea in Cappadocia, and became bishop of his home city in 370. Basil founded the monasticism of the Eastern Roman church, with an outward-looking, socially active organization of cloisters which remains the basis for the orders of Greek Orthodox monks. He was an opponent of the Arians in theology, even under threat of exile or death, until he died in 379. His liturgical order is still used by the Greek and Roman churches for ten days every year.

On Nurses

Susruta Samhita:
He alone is suited for nursing who has a cool head and agreeable behaviour, never speaks badly of anyone, is strong, pays attention to the needs of the sick, and follows the doctor's instructions with tireless strictness.

Euripides' Hippolytus:
It is better to be sick than to be a nurse. Sickness poses only one problem for the patient, but for the nurse it involves both mental agony and hard physical work.

Theodor Billroth, in a letter to Johannes Brahms (1874):
To tend such a luckless patient with so little hope of success is one of the heaviest burdens that can be laid on a human being. Only women with their eternal patience can bear it for any length of time.

Stephen Paget, Confessio Medici:
"Talk about Job's patience!" said a nurse. "Job never had night duty…"

Sir William Osler, Aequanimitas:
The well-trained nurse has become one of mankind's blessings, next to the doctor and the priest—and no less significant than either of them.

church in Rome, women went into sick-care more or less professionally. These were called *diakonissae*, after the Greek word for service or care. The step towards organized sick-care, though, was taken only near the end of the fourth century when Marcella, a rich Roman widow, fitted out her magnificent home as a cloister for nursing nuns.

Closer to the modern meaning was a hospital founded in 390 by the beautiful Fabiola. With two unhappy marriages behind her, she converted to Christianity and devoted the rest of her life to charity. She, too, was very wealthy, and went out among the sick and poor of Rome, re-housing some of them in her palace. Fabiola did not shrink from the most filthy, revolting work in sick-care. Her teacher was none other than Hieronymus, who lived from about 340 to 419, subsequently became a saint, and is known for his translation of the Bible's verses from Hebrew and Greek into Latin as the famous *Versio Vulgata*. Hieronymus wrote of Fabiola's work:

"There she assembled all the sick from streets and highways, and personally tended the unhappy and impoverished victims of hunger and disease. I have often seen her washing wounds which others—even men—could hardly bear to look at. There are many who cannot overcome their natural revulsion for such awful sights, and who do their work of love through other people; they give money instead of their own labour. I do not condemn them, but if I had a hundred tongues, I would still be unable to count all the patients who received comfort and care from Fabiola...

"She founded a hospital and gathered there the sufferers from the streets, and gave them all the attention of a nurse. Need I describe the many woes which can befall a human being: the cut-off noses, lost eyes, mangled feet, leprous arms, swollen bellies, withered thighs, the ailing flesh that is filled up by hungry worms? How often she carried home, on her own shoulders, the dirty and poor who were plagued by epilepsy! How she washed

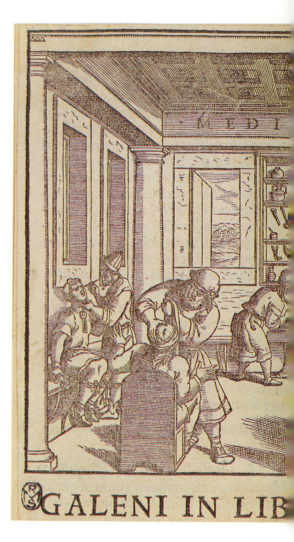

the pus from sores which others could not even behold! She fed the patients with her own hand, and even when a man was nothing but a panting corpse, she cooled his lips with drops of water."

The genius of Galen

With Hippocrates, Galen stands out as the supreme figure in ancient medicine. His views dominated European medicine—for better or worse—through almost fifteen hundred years. It was left to Andreas Vesalius in 1543 to correct Galen's anatomical mistakes, and his erroneous physiology could not be dispensed with until Harvey's discovery of the circulation of the blood in 1628.

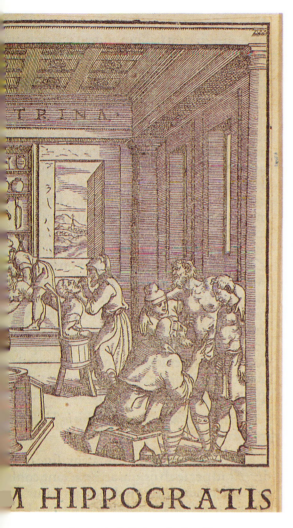

A very active surgical clinic as depicted in Galen's writings when they were republished at Venice in 1576.

Galen was born in Pergamon in AD 130. The city was still solidly under Greek influence and, incidentally, had one of the biggest temples to Asklepios. His father was a timid architect, his mother a shrew, bad-tempered and malicious. Her temperament was passed on to her son, who did not exactly live up to his name: Galen meant "serene".

The father was anxious to procure the best possible education for his son, and had the means to do so. Galen went to school in Perga-

mon and, in order to gain objectivity about the teachings of the time, he had to attend the lectures of four philosophers, each of a different school. When he was seventeen, his father had a dream that Galen would become a great doctor, and sent him to Straconicus and Satyrus, who both belonged to the Hippocratic school. They taught him all they could, and he travelled to medical schools in Smyrna, Corinth, and Alexandria. In 158, he returned to Pergamon and was made physician to the gladiators. This service was useful: he saw many kinds of injury and learned a great deal of practical surgery.

Four years later, he set off for Rome. Once again, he devoted his talents to the gladiators and won a great reputation for his skill. Nor was Galen slow to blow his own trumpet: he lectured, took an active part in public debates, and gave physiological demonstrations. During this period, he embarked on medical authorship, producing more than four hundred works. His reputation grew, and he became the personal physician of the emperor Marcus Aurelius. For some reason he refused to follow the emperor into the field, his official excuse being that he could serve better by tutoring his master's son.

It was Galen's misfortune that autopsies were forbidden in Rome. Apart from one occasion, when he found a corpse left by a bandit and managed to rescue the skeleton after birds had finished off the soft parts, he was actually never allowed to see what the inside of a human being looked like. He based his anatomy on the dissection of animals, which naturally led to mistakes. For instance, he thought that the heart had two chambers, with numerous connections between them, through small pores in the dividing wall. The brain was a large clot of phlegm, from which the psychic "pneuma" was forced out into the nerves by a rhythmical pump. And the reason for the length of the small intestine was to let its owner off having to eat all the time... His physiology, in turn, was distorted by the misinterpretation and incorrect observation of anatomy. Nevertheless, there is no doubt that he enriched medical science in many areas.

Among his true observations was that the individual's voice is lost when both of the recurrent laryngeal nerves are cut—a lesson which every surgeon keeps in mind when operating for goitre. He showed that the urine travelled from the kidneys to the bladder via the ureters—a fact which we would now regard as inescapable, but which was actually controversial in Galen's time. Little thought had been given to digestion before then, and his own reasoning was certainly wrong, but his theories laid the foundations for the physiology of digestion. One of his more fanciful notions was the "first cooking" of food in the stomach, with heat supplied by the surrounding liver, spleen and heart. The "second cooking" took place in the mesenteric veins, and the third in the liver, where the digested food (*chylus*) turned into blood!

Galen's achievements were greater in pathology and internal medicine than in surgery. Yet this does not mean that the old gladiators' surgeon failed to bestrew his books with surgical notes and recommendations. Most significant in this respect is his book on pathological swellings. It covers not only what we would call a swelling today, but also what was known in general about tumours at that time. Galen has exercised a negative influence on the development of surgery, mainly because he believed that suppuration was essential to the healing of a wound.

The Romans set great store by Galen, not for his speculations on theoretical medicine but for his practical skill. "It is through my achievements in the art of medicine and not through sophistical arguments that I have made myself known, first to the leading citizens of Rome and next to her emperors," as he himself wrote. He was clearly a very efficient surgeon, too. We know that his operations included the removal of nasal polyps and varicose veins, plastic surgery for harelip, and even intestinal and abdominal wall suture after injuries that penetrated the abdomen—which were common in the gladiatorial games at the amphitheatre.

Galen trepanned skulls and covered the post-operative wounds with pigeon's blood, although he admitted that the result was as good without this special remedy, as he had seen when no pigeons were available. Further, his operation for coughs can only be described as irrational—he cut off the palate's uvula! One might say that this harmless but senseless procedure was probably one of the main sources of Galen's accumulated wealth: it was, inexplicably, a highly popular treatment in Rome. It has been compared by Harvey Graham to the passion for tonsillectomy which arose in our century among the less scrupulous ear-nose-throat specialists.

In 180, Galen's friend and benefactor Marcus Aurelius died, and shortly afterwards a great deal of Galen's library and personal manuscripts was destroyed in a fire. Galen continued to work, and to serve the emperor's worthless adopted son and successor, Commodus. But his practical activities seem to have declined progressively. Around 193, he returned to his home city of Pergamon, where he died in 199 or 200. He had never acquired a wife, children, or any disciple who could carry on his labours. His importance, though, has been brilliantly summarized by Leo Zimmerman and Ilza Veith:

"Galen's everlasting monuments were the remarkable scientific discoveries and the wealth of writings which he left behind. In the following centuries, his work became sanctified to such a degree that any adverse opinions were regarded as something like heresy. Reverence for him after his death actually outgrew that which he had received in his lifetime. Scientific progress was seriously impeded, because all medical thought had to fit into Galen's system. When free thinking at last became possible, Galen was unjustly blamed for this blind dependence, and his historical role was suppressed. Only in recent years, as a result of objective studies, has his true role in medical development been established."

GALEN learns from Hippocrates: a representation of science in a fresco painting, around 1250, in the cathedral of Anagni in central Italy.

Aretaios the Cappadocian

Had Aretaios become as famous as Galen, the art of medicine would probably have reached a much higher level during the Middle Ages. His few surviving books display an amazingly firm grasp of medical theory, extraordinary powers of observation, and sound treatment. But unlike Galen, Aretaios was a very modest man. He wrote nothing about himself, and we do not even know where he practised medicine.

The only certainty is that he came from Cappadocia (in what is now central Turkey) and practised at some period in the first centuries after Christ. He must have been born in AD 50 at the earliest, and worked during the fourth century at the latest. It is thought that he was trained in Alexandria, for autopsies and dissections were then allowed only at that Egyptian academic centre, and Aretaios surely had to see many of them in order to acquire his great knowledge of the structure of the human body.

Spending little effort on theoretical reflections, Aretaios went straight to practical medicine. From allusions in his preserved writings, we can infer that he wrote at least six books on medical topics—perhaps in an attempt to create a universal encyclopedia of the medical art. Among the lost volumes were at least one on surgery and another on women's ailments. What remain are two books on the symptoms and treatment of acute and chronic diseases. These give us a good look at the views of an intelligent, informed and observant doctor on the illnesses

Galen: On an Imperial Patient

"*Something really amazing happened when the emperor (Marcus Aurelius) himself was my patient. Both he and the doctors in his company, during a trip abroad, thought he had caught an illness which would cause fever. But the second day, and the third day's morning by its third hour, proved everybody wrong. On the previous day, at the first hour, he had as usual taken a drink of bitter aloe, and then a little teriak.*

"*After that, he had eaten at about the sixth hour, bathed at sunset, and taken a light supper. All night long, he felt colic-like pains, with emptying of the bowels, which made him feverish. The doctors about him ordered, therefore, that he should lie still, and at the ninth hour they prescribed liquid food. Next I, too, was called to the palace for the night.*

"*Just when the lamps were lit, a messenger came and brought me to the Emperor as he had bidden. Three doctors had watched over him since dawn, and two of them felt his pulse, and all three thought that a fever attack was coming. I stood alongside, but said nothing. The Emperor looked first at me and asked why I did not feel his pulse as the other two had. I answered: 'These two colleagues of mine have already done so and, as they have followed you on the journey, they presumably know what your normal pulse is, so they can judge its present state better.'*

"*When I said this, he bade me, too, feel his pulse. My impression was that—considering his age and body constitution—the pulse was far from indicating a fever attack, but that his stomach was stuffed with the food he had eaten, and that the food had become a slimy excrement. The Emperor praised my diagnosis and said, three times in a row: 'That is it. It is just as you say. I have eaten too much cold food.'*

AN engraving of Galen as he was imagined in the sixteenth century. According to the French text, it was believed that he had lived for 140 years.

"*He then asked what measures should be taken. I replied that I knew of a similar case, saying: 'If you were any plain citizen of this country, I would as usual prescribe wine with a little pepper. But to a royal patient as in this case, doctors usually recommend milder treatment. It is enough for a woollen cover to be put on your stomach, impregnated with warm spiced salve.' The Emperor said that, on other such occasions, he always laid warm spikenard salve, wrapped in purple-coloured wool, on his stomach.*

"*Then he ordered Pitholaus to do this, and let me go. When the cover had been laid on and his feet were rubbed warm, he called for Sabine wine, strewed pepper in it, and drank. Afterwards, he told Pitholaus that he had 'a doctor who was a truly extraordinary person'. And as you know, he still continues to say of*

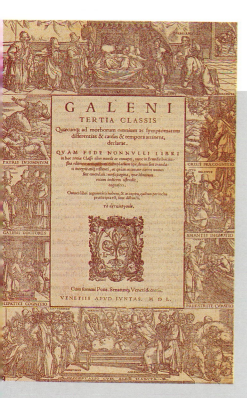

THIS frontispiece to an edition of Galen's works (Venice, 1565) shows many of the legendary events in his life, including his cure of an emperor.

...me that I am 'the greatest of physicians and an exception among philosophers'. For he already had experience of so many who were not only profit-seeking, but also quarrelsome, haughty, selfish and mean."

A Profitable Profession

The Roman doctors lived well during the golden days of the Caesars. In 117, Hadrian decreed that all doctors would be freed from municipal tax and could avoid both military service and the duty to hold public offices. This immunity was extended by Constantine, who abolished taxes on all the buildings owned by a doctor at his place of residence. These reforms had not yet been initiated when Pliny the Elder observed that "the art of medicine is the most lucrative of all".

From the Works of Galen

De cognosis curandisque animi morbis, VI:
Hunger is no reason for our greedily filling our bellies to excess, nor does it justify thirsting until the jug is emptied in one gulp. We must be careful to eat less than our guests, to refrain from delicacies, and to eat sound food in moderate portions.

De humoribus:
Confidence and hope do more good than medicines. The doctor is nature's assistant.

Definitiones medicae, XXXV:
Surgery is the unceasing movement of steady, experienced hands.

No False Modesty in Galen

"*I have done as much for medicine as Trajan did for the Roman Empire, and when he built bridges and roads through Italy. It is I, and I alone, who have revealed the true path of medicine. It must be admitted that Hippocrates already staked out this path, but he did not go as far as one could have wished; his writings have faults and lack essential distinctions, his knowledge of certain topics is insufficient, and he is often unclear as the old tend to be. In sum: he prepared the way, but I have made it passable.*"

A Healthy Anagram

A Viennese monk called Abraham of Santa Clara (1644-1709) tried to inspire the sick-care of his day with the following words:
"*The most famous doctor was named Galenus. If one juggles the letters, one gets Angelus, meaning an angel—and that is what every doctor ought to be.*"

and injuries which come within the surgical field.

Aretaios' work *On the Causes and Symptoms of Acute Diseases* is evidence of his truly remarkable capacity for observation. It covers many illnesses which have never since been described better or more lucidly. An example is the world's first description of tetanus:

"Tetanus consists of extremely painful spasms, which are a peril to life and very difficult to relieve. The attack begins in the jaw muscles and tendons, but spreads to the whole body, because all the bodily parts suffer in sympathy with the one first affected.

"There are three types of spasms. Either the body is stretched, or it is bent either backward or forward. With stretching, the disease is called *tetanus*: the subject is so rigid that he cannot turn or bend. The spasms are named according to the tension and the position of the forward or backward arching. When the posterior nerves are affected and the patient arches backward, we call the condition *opisthotonus*; when the anterior nerves are affected and the arching is forward, the condition is called *emprosthotonus*. *Tonus* applies to both the nerves and the tension.

"There are countless reasons for these diseases. They arise mainly with punctures of skin, muscles or nerves, whereupon most patients die, since traumatic tetanus is fatal. Women who miscarry sometimes contract tetanus and they, too, seldom survive...

"In general, it can be said that the disease progresses with painful flexion of the tendons in the back, and of the muscles in the jaws and chest. The lower jaw is pressed so hard against the upper jaw that the two cannot easily be separated, either by lever or wedge. Yet if one succeeds in forcing the mouth open and dropping in liquid, it cannot be swallowed—and will either trickle out, or be retained in the mouth, or be pressed up into the nose, because the throat is constricted and the tonsils are hard and distended, thus preventing what is drunk from passing down. The face is

flecked red, the eyes staring and needing great effort to turn; breathing is short and difficult; the arms and legs lie outstretched, with muscular contractions; the features are distorted in various ways, with twitching of the cheeks and lips, a quivering chin and chattering teeth..."

Aretaios continues his description, and none of it contains a line which would be out of place in a modern surgical textbook. His book on treatment mentions that the patient should be carefully warmed with ointments, bladders of oil, or bags of fine salt; he also specifies asafetida, castoreum and myrrh. But he is well aware that their effects are only symptomatic:

"The affliction is inhuman and, to anyone seeing such patients, it is a lamentable and painful sight. Nothing can cure their suffering. The distortion makes them unrecognizable, even to their closest friends. An otherwise impious wish of the relatives now becomes charitable, namely that the patient's life may depart, releasing him from both the agony and the wretched disease. Nor can the attending physician save his life, for to straighten the limbs it would be necessary to sever and rupture the living person. Once the patient has been attacked, the doctor stands powerless and can only pity, which causes great anguish."

Aretaios' symptomatology includes brilliant descriptions of pleurisy, cholera, epilepsy and diabetes—the last of which was named by him. Of particular interest to surgery are his ideas about ileus. This disease, he believed, could be caused by "tainted, varying and unusual foods, or diverse indigestions, but above all by ileus-inducing drinks such as the black juice of the cuttlefish". He also guessed that the hasty consumption of cold drinks might play a part, which is not true. On the other hand, he correctly described in detail the ileus which occurs in association with obstructed hernia.

According to modern terminology, ileus means acute intestinal obstruction, and surgical treatment is the only choice. Aretaios' explanation of the disease prevented him from realizing that an operation was necessary. His view of the outcome was, quite rightly, pessimistic—and it was to persist for a long time: in the seventeenth century, the ailment was known as *miserere*, a word taken from the funeral service! All that could be done was to alleviate the symptoms. Blood was let, until the patient nearly fainted, to allay the pain; soporifics were administered, and efforts were made to relieve the tension in the intestine by giving emetics and enemas containing cumin, rue, terebinth, honey, hyssop and colocynth (bitter-apple).

In the two surviving books, Aretaios consistently shows very little interest in surgery, but he undeniably made a considerable contribution to the history of surgery with his descriptions of diseases. We can only regret the lost chance to read what this observant physician had to say in his textbook on surgery.

Byzantine surgery

When Theodosius the Great died in 395, his huge Roman Empire was divided. The Western Empire, still centred on Rome, was constantly beset by invading neighbours and wracked by internal conflicts. Constantinople, the ancient Byzantium, became the capital of the Eastern Empire, which was generally left in peace. Its culture, including medicine, could thus develop undisturbed during the first centuries of the Middle Ages.

Byzantine medicine was inherited from the Greeks. One task assumed by its representatives was to assemble the finest scholarship of Greece as well as of those Greeks who lived in Rome. The first great compiler of such an encyclopedia was Oribasius (325–403), personal physician to Julian the Apostate. His *Synagoge*, in no less than seventy volumes, contained all that was best in Greek and Roman medicine.

Alexander of Tralles (525–605), brother to the architect of the capital city's cathedral Hagia Sophia, was a devoted follower of Galen, and worked as both an encyclopedist and a practising physician. The most noteworthy of his own observations were excellent descriptions of the worm diseases. He was also the first European to recommend the ancient Chinese laxative *rha barbaricon*—rhubarb. This was at least a rational remedy, but the good Alexander was addicted to somewhat capricious ideas, for instance when he prescribed live green beetles. Henbane, according to him, could be administered effectively only if held between the left thumb and index finger, while the moon had to be in either Pisces or Aquarius...

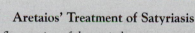

Aretaios' Treatment of Satyriasis

Inflammation of the genital nerves causes erection of the penis, with desire for intercourse and pain in performing the sexual act. Spasmodic tensions arise, difficult to alleviate, and no means of coitus can palliate the evil. The mind runs wild, as is shown especially by their shameless and frank manner of talking about their lusts, since their unbridled desire for coitus makes them impudent...

The genitals, waist, perineum, and testicles are wrapped in unwashed sheep-wool, soaked in rose-oil and wine; the body parts in question are bathed in this, so that no heat develops in the wool... One should also apply poultices, using bread with the juice of plantain, nightshade, chicory and poppy leaf... Leeches are also particularly suitable for extracting blood from the inner parts... Wine and meat are avoided until the patient has mostly recovered, because wine excites the nerves, relaxes the soul, revives voluptuousness, creates sperm, and stimulates the sexual urge.

Emphasis on surgery was stronger in the case of Aetius of Amida, during the seventh century. One of his main works was *De vasorum dilatatione* ("On the Dilation of the Vessels"). This is supposedly based on a study by Philagrios of Thessalonika, an otherwise unknown Greek. The book, now in the Vatican Library, deals with what we call aneurysms, the pulsating swellings of arteries which may either be caused by trauma or arise spontaneously, usually as a result of arteriosclerosis. Among his prescriptions was the following:

"An aneurysm located in the bend of the elbow is treated thus. First we carefully trace the artery leading to it, from armpit to elbow, along the inside of the upper arm. Then we make an incision on the inside of the arm, three or four finger-breadths below the armpit, where the artery is felt most easily. We gradually expose the blood-vessel and, when it can be lifted free with a hook, we tie it off with two firm ligatures and divide it between them. We fill the wound with incense and lint dressing, then apply a bandage. Next we open the aneurysm itself and no longer need fear bleeding. We remove the blood clots present, and seek the artery which brought the blood. Once found, it is lifted free with the hook, and tied as before. By again filling the wound with incense, we stimulate good suppuration."

As the last sentence shows, Aetius supported the theory that no wound heals well unless it forms pus. By "incense" he meant a mixture of dried herbs, which was a splendid method of infecting the wound!

Aetius was a practical surgeon and gave much sensible advice. His devices for providing a good operational field and keeping the patient quiet during uterine operations are well-known. The unfortunate woman was placed on the operating table with her knees bent, thighs against the stomach, and legs as wide apart as possible. A rope was tied round one ankle, passed round the

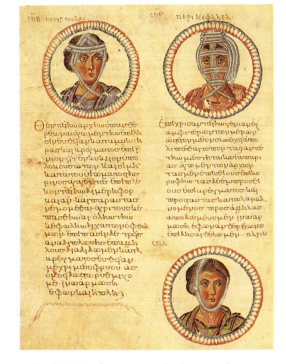

THE book *On Bandages*, written by Soranus of Ephesus in the second century AD, continued to be read by the Byzantine Greeks, as this page from an early tenth-century copy shows. Its text described in detail how to wind strips of cloth into well-fitting bandages for various head-wounds.

knee on the same side, round the back of the neck down to the knee on the other side, and finally to that ankle—a position which, though scarcely comfortable or aesthetic, was extremely practical for surgery. Aetius was a pioneer of gynaecological surgery, and devoted 112 chapters of his great textbook to it. Perhaps his chief practical contribution was a "vaginal speculum" with which the surgeon could open up the vagina for internal inspection.

In general, Aetius was a rational surgeon, but he could not quite shake off the old belief in the intervention of higher powers. For example, when explaining how to remove a fishbone from the throat, he first advised the surgeon to address

THE Byzantine way of reducing a dislocated jaw was one of many illustrations in an eleventh-century manuscript by Apollonios of Kition, a city in Cyprus. His text commented on the book about treatment of joints which had supposedly been written by Hippocrates 1500 years earlier.

the bone respectfully and kindly, to come forth "as Lazarus emerged from the grave and Jonah from the belly of the whale". Only if this failed should action be taken, either by trying to lodge the bone in a sponge soaked with resin, or by grasping it directly with pincers. But it was crucial that this be done in the name of St. Blaise!

Here we may pause for a glimpse at the hagiolatry which, especially in this early part of the Middle Ages, was so intimately linked with medicine and surgery. The St. Blaise in question was really the patron of veterinaries, but he also helped people if they had some foreign body lodged inside them. His fame had begun when he succeeded in extracting a bone from the throat of a woman who was nearly choking to death. Blaise was an Armenian bishop of the fourth century, and his love of animals became his downfall. The governor, Agricola, was supposed to procure wild beasts for the gladiatorial games in Rome. Blaise opposed this—both in order to spare the animals, and to save the Christians whom they were meant to tear apart in the Coliseum. So he fell out of favour and suffered a refined death, being skinned alive with wool-combs before he was beheaded.

Blaise belonged to an elite of the saintly corps, known as the Fourteen Helpers. Among them were several notable specialists. St. Christopher—today a patron of motorists—could be summoned to deal with epilepsy. St. Erasmus warded off seasickness and stomach aches. St. Anthony gave protection against erysipelas, also called St. Anthony's Fire, a disease which was dreaded and often fatal until the era of penicillin. St. Margaret of Antioch was the patron of women in childbirth. Once, when out walking, she met a dragon which was rude enough to swallow her whole. Margaret had the presence of mind to make the sign of the Cross in her uncomfortable straits within the dragon's stomach. The sign materialized into a real cross, and grew until the dragon burst with a thud, releasing Margaret herself!

The most renowned of all medically inclined saints must have been St. Cosmas and St. Damian, the Arab twin brothers who were converted to Christianity. They became the special patrons of surgery, due to their miraculous operations. On one occasion, they amputated a cancerous leg and replaced it with another, taken from a Moor who had just died. This dramatic cure was meat and drink for artists, and has been portrayed many times, as by Andrea Mantegna and in the *Antiphonarium SS Cosmae et Damiani*, now in London.

The last of the classical Byzantine doctors was Paul of Aegina (607–690). He was a close contemporary of Heraclius I, the emperor under whom the Eastern Roman Empire began to decline. We know little about Paul, except that he

studied in Alexandria and was greatly respected by his colleagues. He intended to produce a book which would combine the best of Greek and Roman medicine, since he was familiar with the greatest authors:

> "particularly with Oribasius, who has given us the most important of all that concerns health. I have collected the best of them and tried not to leave anyone out. Oribasius' books certainly hold the entire art of medicine, but their size makes them difficult for ordinary people to obtain…"

Paul succeeded in his project, with an *Abridgement of Medicine in Seven Books* which long remained a "bible" especially of surgeons. They were translated into Arabic and thus laid the foundations for the Arabian age of medicine. Paul's sixth book, dealing with surgery, was taken over almost word for word by the leading Arab writers, such as Albucasis.

Despite his intentions, we do not find unadulterated classical Greek medicine or surgery in Paul. Older methods had crept back in for two or three centuries, involving superstition and irrational hagiolatry as well as crude surgery. The cauterizing-iron became the most popular instrument; wounds were treated openly by stimulating suppuration; bleeding and cupping were commonplace. In hernia operations, it was thought necessary to remove the testicle on the same side, a step which is almost never needed and which earlier surgeons had been able to avoid. All this was a feature of the times, and Paul recorded it. Yet he himself was a technically adept surgeon, and his writings contain

COSMAS and Damian, the twin physicians from Cilicia (in southern Turkey) during the third century, were well-established as saints when Ambrosius Francken the Elder, around 1600, painted them as though about to perform a leg transplant on an amputee in a hospital in the Netherlands.

clear, precise descriptions of operations, like this one for struma (goitre):

"Struma…which are soft on palpation can be operated as follows. Those which are superficial and close to the skin are laid bare with a single incision and freed from the surrounding tissue. The skin flaps are held apart with hooks, as already described in the angiological (blood-vessel) operations, and the tumour is removed step by step. A larger one is transfixed with hooks, pulled forward and dissected from the skin in the same way, but we must also free it completely from the surrounding tissues and be especially careful to avoid the carotid arteries and the *nerves recurrentes*. If the operation is impeded by a bleeding vessel, we can close it off with a ligature or, if it is large, tie and divide it. When the base of the struma disappears into some narrow place, we can simply cut it off, but must verify with the middle finger that no other struma tissue is left behind. Yet if we suspect that there may be some large blood vessel under the lowest part of the tumour, we need not cut it off, and can strangle it with a ligature, so that it later drops off spontaneously…"

Whether the "struma" in all of Paul's cases had the same meaning as today, the enlargement of the thyroid gland, is not certain. Paul mentioned, in fact, that such *choreas* or *scrofulae* may be located on the lower sides of the neck. It is then very probable that he was discussing enlarged lymph nodes—perhaps the tubercular nodes later called *scrofulae*. Interestingly, Paul knew that one need not remove portions of the glands which are difficult to reach, indicating that he had found an opportunity in autopsies to study the field of operations which concerned him.

After Paul, the last of the four great Byzantine encyclopedists, it is no exaggeration to say that nothing new happened in surgery for the next thousand years.

Incense as a Medicament

Incense was a mixture of aromatic herbs, which were generally allowed to burn slowly, giving off smoke. It was especially popular in the Orient, where great store was set by the very finest-smelling concoctions. The practice of burning herbs to purify sanctuaries began as early as the Bronze Age, and was continued notably by the Jews as "a sweet savour unto the Lord" (Leviticus 1, 17). After the great victories of Xerxes and Alexander, incense was burned as an offering of thanks.

Hippocrates prescribed incense cures, in particular for women's diseases. The sick were made to sit astride the smouldering herbs, so that the smoke rose into the vagina. The ingredients were very diverse, and suggest that the "savour" was not always appealing—hartshorn, unripe olives, cow dung, dried cypress, goat horn, gall, and frankincense. A specialty was oisype, soiled goat wool from the anal tract: "evil-smelling substances are used to smoke the womb, but sweet-smelling ones for the nose."

The incense used by Aetius was presumably based on mixtures advised by Dioscurides and the later Romans. Among its ingredients were galbanum (gum resin), sulphur, calmus, bayberry, and castoreum—the stinking extract of the beaver's dried scrotum.

In monasteries, incense was used chiefly to ward off witches. There it included stinking asafetida, master-wort to expel sweat, fennel to promote bleeding, sandarac to relieve flatulence, antipruritic sassafras, throat-constricting mezereum, nose-stinging dittany, valerian which smelled of cats and was also called witch-weed, amber made from lynx's urine, black Jew's-pitch, red coral and, finally—to complete the number twelve of the Apostles—the true incense resin, frankincense.

CHAPTER 3

Medieval medicine

The dark Middle Ages... a period of decline and stagnation... Das Abendland... surgery in eclipse... centuries of ignorance... These are some examples of how historians have characterized the medical arts in medieval times, from the fall of the Roman Empire until the Renaissance. As a whole, the picture is right, even though there were rays of illumination—from Arab medicine, among certain Western surgeons, and in the growth of hospitals.

It is not easy to determine the causes of this stagnation, not to say regression, in medicine. One of them was the almost unbelievable influence of Galen, whose erroneous views of anatomy and physiology made, unfortunately, a far greater impression than did sound advice and experience. Another factor was the Church. When Europe fell apart, the Church remained as the only fixed point amid general feelings of insecurity. The clerical organization became ever stronger, yet in order to retain its power over souls, it had to crush all opposition and doubt about its dogma. Among the

sceptics, of course, were the natural scientists and the physicians. Innovative thinking was definitely not encouraged, and at worst it was condemned as heresy.

The result was a return to religious medicine. Illness came to be regarded as a punishment from heaven, and treatment was fatalistic. An operation could hardly be worthwhile if the cure still depended on God's will! Secondary details were the strict ban on autopsies and the virtually nonexistent hygiene. No doctor had the chance to learn correct anatomy, and those who suffered most from this problem—as well from the poor personal cleanliness and the insanitary housing—were the surgeons.

Medieval medicine is usually divided into three periods: monastery medicine, the Arab doctors and the Scholastic doctors. The monasteries became natural places of collection for the sick and weak. It was equally natural that their therapy often amounted only to faith-healing, by means of prayers, penance, supplication to suitable saints, and contact with sacred relics. Medicine was practised by priests and monks without any insight into human anatomy and physiology.

To be sure, since free-thinking doctors existed in spite of religion's power over minds, and since many of them knew the old Greek and Latin writings in translation, a more rational medicine eventually began to develop. But this tendency was stopped almost as soon as it arose. The ecclesiastical council of Clermont in 1150 directly forbade priests and monks to concern

A physician combines the old method of trepanation with the renewed interest in human dissection, characterizing the changes in surgery during the late Middle Ages. This was one of the illustrations of study and treatment in a book on anatomy (1345) by Guido of Vigevano, a town in northern Italy.

THE INTERIOR of the *Hôtel Dieu* in Paris was shown in this fifteenth-century engraving, on a charter of religious favours granted to the hospital's patrons. Patients, prayers, and corpses being sewn into shrouds were all part of the scene.

themselves with any medicine. The institution which had achieved greatest progress was Benedict of Nursia's beautiful monastery on Monte Cassino.

The first hospitals

One virtue of monastery medicine was that it stimulated the development of hospitals. This went far beyond the individual establishments for sick-care which, as we have seen, existed previously. Perhaps the oldest were founded in Sri Lanka around 500 BC, and India certainly had effective hospitals in about 260 BC. At Rome in the fourth century AD, Marcella and Fabiola had rebuilt their palaces into sick-wards, and the widespread Roman army camps had "valetudinaries" for sick and wounded soldiers. No less renowned a Christian hospital was that of the powerful bishop Basileus at Caesarea in Asia Minor from AD 370.

But the first places resembling what we now call hospitals in Western Europe seem to have been two *Hôtels-Dieu* in France. The oldest was initiated about 542 in Lyons, by the Frankish king Childebert I, and the next arose a century later in Paris under that city's bishop. Subsequently, at a respectable distance from the urban limits, hospitals for lepers were built. Their care, however, was overshadowed by the need to isolate the sick. They were called "leprosories" after the Latin name of the disease, but also "lazarettes" after its protective patron, Saint Lazarus.

In England, hospital construction did not get under way until after the Norman Invasion by William the Conqueror in 1066. Saint Cross in Winchester and Saint Bartholomew's in London were both founded in 1123, while Saint Thomas's Hospital in London opened in 1215. The two latter institutions are still in service at the same places. As for the famous "Bart's", an odd story surrounds its origin. Rahere, a courtier of King Henry I, became ill during a journey to Italy, but Saint Bartholomew appeared and helped him. In gratitude, Rahere promised to build a church for the saint when he reached home, and not only did so, but erected a big hospital next to it as well. The beautiful St. Bartholomew's-the-Great is, apart from Tower Chapel, the only extant Norman church in London, and its principal relic is Rahere's tomb. The hospital is celebrated for many great doctors, including William Harvey, the discoverer of blood circulation, and the surgeons Thomas Vicary, Percivall Pott and John Abernethy.

Far across the medieval world, Baghdad had more than sixty hospitals already in the mid-twelfth century. However, the finest of all such institutions in the Middle Ages may have been the Al-Mansur in Cairo. Founded in 1283, it was a gigantic building with separate departments for patients with different diseases—the first time we hear of division into specialties. There was a dietary kitchen, an out-patient clinic, an orphanage, a vast library and huge lecture-halls. Special convalescent wards existed, where the sick could stay as long as they wished, and those who left were given a sum of money for a fresh start in life. This could be afforded: the hospital enjoyed boundless income from donations.

The Arab doctors

On 16 July 622, Muhammad travelled from Mecca to Medina, where he gathered a following that became the core of Islam. This trip, the Hegira, marked the beginning of the Muslim calendar. Muhammad's teachings were spread

A Medieval Hospital

When the Hundred Years' War between France and England groaned to its end, Europe was wracked by misery. Hungry, freezing, ailing people stumbled from town to town in hope of begging bread for a day and warmth for a night. They scarcely dared to think about any sort of organized sick-care. It was in these conditions that the Duke of Burgundy's chancellor, Nicolas Rolin, and his wife Guigone de Salins decided to build a "God's Inn" for the poor and ill. They chose the city of Beaune, since it lay at an important intersection of the great east-west route between France and Germany with the highway north from the Mediterranean coast.

On New Year's Day, 1452, the Hôtel-Dieu de Beaune stood ready for its first patient. The lovely buildings in Flemish style have survived as a ward, the world's oldest hospital with original premises. The large hall, or Grande Chambre des Pauvres, measuring 72 by 14 metres, is crowned with a magnificent boat-shaped roof, supported by 11 strong beams painted blue and red with sculptural decoration. It looks just the same today as five hundred years ago. Along the walls are draped partitions to separate the patients, each with a chair and small table, a tin pot and bowl, and a copper basin.

Six nuns served as nurses in the hospital when it was founded. There are now many more, but they wear the same costume as their predecessors. The Hôtel-Dieu de Beaune has been expanded several times, and functions as a fully modern hospital at present.

from Medina by force of arms and, after his death in 632, an enormous Arab expansion continued not only in order to expand the new faith, but also to relieve thirst and hunger in the original Arab countries. After conquering Syria and Egypt, the Arabs came west along the North

African coast, crossed the Strait of Gibraltar, and took Spain. They were not stopped before reaching well into France, and in the east they pushed as far as the Indus River.

The Muslims were tolerant towards their subjects' religion and culture, even if they taxed the unfaithful more stiffly than themselves. They realized that conquered peoples were more advanced in many respects in art and science, and they were clever enough to learn. The library at Alexandria had, of course, been largely destroyed, but they tried to utilize what was left of it. Arab doctors were raised in the Alexandrian tradition, and the more readily because these nomadic tribes, so long divided, had never before possessed the means or possibility to concern themselves with physicians at all.

Perhaps more important than Alexandria as a cultural centre was Gondeshapur in Persia. During the fifth century, Bishop Nestorius of Constantinople had come into theological conflict with his colleague Cyril in Alexandria (over the weighty question of whether the Virgin Mary ought to be called Christ's mother or God's). Both gentlemen are said to have been arrogant, cruel, high-handed despots. Nestorius lost, and was excommunicated at a synod. He and his clique fled, first to Edessa in Mesopotamia, and then to Gondeshapur where they were protected by the blessed king Chosroe.

The Nestorians built a famous school at Gondeshapur, which became the starting-point for genuine Islamic medicine. Their service lay in working frantically to translate Greek writings into Arabic. This colossal academic labour took up virtually all of their initial two centuries. With few exceptions, they engaged in no practical medicine, and surgery stagnated. Yet the first great Arab doctor was to be a Nestorian. Hunayn ibn Ishaq (808–873), also known as Johannitius, began his education at Gondeshapur. His teacher Johannes Mesue the Elder thought him untalented, so he went off in a fury to Greece and studied for two years. Returning to Baghdad, he soon published brilliant translations of, among others, Hippocrates. Mesue

then admitted the mistake and became reconciled with him.

Hunayn was so adept that he caught the notice of the Caliph, who had many enemies and ordered him to brew a poison for one of them. He refused, and was tossed into a dungeon. Once freed, he received a new offer—either a princely reward, or an execution. He replied: "I have already told the Ruler of the Faithful that my art must be used only for the good of people." Such integrity impressed Caliph Al-Mamum, who adopted Hunayn as a personal physician. In this post, which evidently also made him chief of the whole empire's medical corps, Hunayn achieved a great deal. He established a board of translators in Baghdad, headed by his old foe Mesue, and from it developed the first medical school of the Islamic world proper. Remarkably, too, Baghdad witnessed the creation of a board of censors, who ensured that no doctor went without the necessary training.

The Arab school mainly boasted doctors who were hardly interested in surgery. Indirectly, however, they were to have great significance for medicine as a whole. A generation after Hunayn, there came Abu Bakr Muhammad ibn Zakaria (852–925), known as Rhazes after his birthplace Ray in Persia, not far from Teheran. Rhazes was also the Caliph's personal physician, as well as the director of the biggest hospital in Baghdad, which he helped to establish. Legend tells that he chose the healthiest site for the hospital by hanging up animal cadavers at four points in the city, and seeing which of them rotted most slowly.

Rhazes wrote masterly descriptions of diseases, notably measles and smallpox. Surgery concerned him little, but he was no stranger to it. He operated, for example, on caries—by the undeniably extreme method of removing the afflicted bone entirely. There are also accounts of how this very experienced and wise man cured patients through his sensitive psychology. A woman at the Caliph's court complained of paralysis in both arms; Rhazes was summoned. Bending down, he swiftly pulled up her skirts.

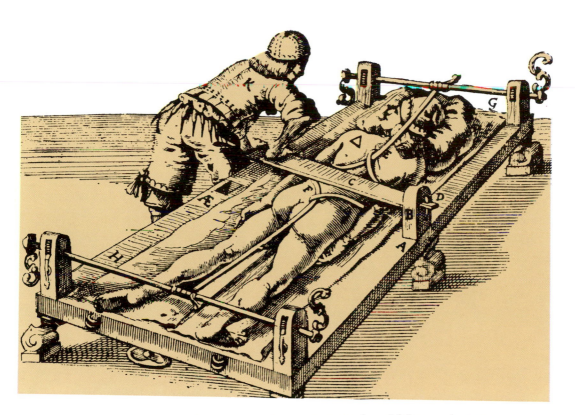

CORRECTION of spinal deformities by extension and pressure was one of Avicenna's methods which remained in use for centuries. This refined apparatus was shown in the famous surgical textbook by Johann Scultetus (1679).

With equal speed, the woman bent over and pushed them back down with her arms. The "paralysis" was thus shown to be a hysterical condition!

The work that proved most useful for future doctors, though, was *Kanon*, written by another of the Caliph's physicians: Ali ibn Sina, later called Avicenna (981–1038). In this enormous book, Avicenna tried to systematize everything that was known about medicine and surgery. Unfortunately, he regarded surgery as little more than a necessary evil. It was to be a longlasting attitude, which led the Arab world—and subsequently western Europe—to consider surgeons a lower caste than the doctors of internal medicine with their more philosophical orientation. But Avicenna's view was fairly natural, judging by the surgical methods he recommended. Almost the sole treatment which he advised for surgical illnesses was the cauterizing-iron.

Being the Caliph's Grand Vizier too, Avicenna prematurely burned himself out with work, wine, women and song. His tomb is in Hamadan, where faithful Muslims still travel in hopes of medical miracles. There were also eminent doctors in the Arabs' western caliphate,

such as Avenzoar (1113–1162) and his disciple Averroes (1126–1198), who was called "the most learned man in Spain". In that land, too, lived the Islamic world's only significant surgeon, Albucasis.

Abul Qasim, known as Albucasis, was born in 936 at Cordoba, and probably died in 1013. (The sources are very confused about these dates—some of them put him nearly a century later.) His book *Altasrif*, or "Collection", is dominated by surgery, although mostly as a translation and expansion of the writings of Paul of Aegina. The book had little importance for the Arab colleagues of Albucasis, yet it was often cited in the western world. For example, around two hundred quotations appeared in the works of the French doctor Guy de Chauliac (1300–1380?), whom we shall meet soon. And in Italy, Fabricius ab Aquapendente (1537–1619) maintained that his three great mentors were Celsus, Paul and Albucasis.

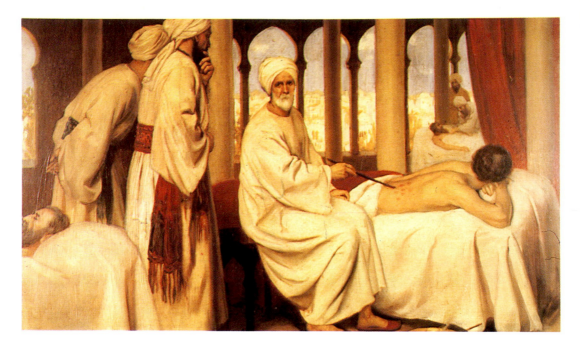

ALBUCASIS cauterizes a patient at Cordoba, as depicted by contemporary sources and, in this painting, by Ernest Board around 1912.

An interesting part of the surgical chapters in *Altasrif* consists of illustrations of surgical instruments, explained by the text. From these and the rest of Albucasis' work, we can see that he was a manually adept surgeon, and advanced the art of his teacher Paul. Cauterization no longer prevailed. Albucasis gave instructions for bandaging, as with wine-moistened compresses (the word "alcohol" itself was taken from Arabic to the West via medicine). He adopted the old Etruscan method of fastening loose teeth with gold wire, and he offered clever advice for the treatment of fractures and dislocations. His operational techniques for lithotomy and lithotripsy (removing and breaking down bladder stones) were also rich in detail.

Albucasis could not, however, forget the idea that cauterization was beneficial. Like Avicenna, he used the cauterizing-iron for almost any ailment: epilepsy, stroke, toothache, melancholy and ischias, to name a few. In spite of his fine instruments, Albucasis made an all too great legacy of the cauterizing-iron to his successors. And, paradoxically, he still emphasized the need to know anatomy:

"He who neglects anatomy will wrong and kill his patients... I have seen an uninformed doctor cut over scrofula on the neck, open the carotid arteries, and cause such bleeding that the patient perished in his hands. I have seen another doctor remove a bladder stone from a very old man: the stone was large and, when he extracted it, a piece of the bladder wall followed, so that the man died on the third day. I myself had requested the removal, but the stone's size and the man's condition led me to refuse. And I have seen how a doctor, who was in fact employed by the ruler, treated a Negro with an open lower-leg fracture.

"In his folly, the doctor laid a very tight bandage of compresses and splints, without leaving drainage for the wound. He left the patient alone for several days and forbade removal of the bandage. Finally both the foot and leg had swollen and the patient was dying. Once summoned, I immediately took off the bandage, whereupon the patient recovered and the pain ceased."

The Salerno school

On the bay of Paestum, south of Naples, lies beautiful Salerno. Already in Roman imperial times, the city was renowned for its healthy climate, and developed into an illustrious place of rest and cure, visited by the Caesars themselves and by foreign princes and rich folk from all over the Mediterranean.

Legend tells that a medical school was established at Salerno by four doctors of different origins: a Greek, a Roman, a Jew and a Saracen. Even if the tale is not taken literally, there may be something in it. This area was a Greek-speaking enclave within the Roman state, many Jewish colonists lived near by, and numerous Arabs had moved to the west coast of Italy after the conquest of Sicily.

Just when the medical school was founded is uncertain. Yet already in the ninth century, it was so highly regarded as to attract students from far away. Unlike other universities and colleges, it was a purely secular institution, outside the Church's sphere. This fact possibly contributed to its great quality in medicine: for reasons which we have mentioned, the Church hardly served as a promoter of healthy culture in such respects.

The Salerno school was at its zenith from around 1000 until the thirteenth century. It received much help from the country's rulers. In 1140, Roger II of Sicily introduced a degree and a corresponding certificate for doctors, probably the first in the world. His grandson Frederick II, who became Holy Roman Emperor, even decreed that the doctors of Salerno should have exclusive rights to the practice of medicine in his empire. Still more important, however, was Frederick's establishment of an examination procedure with fixed standards of knowledge,

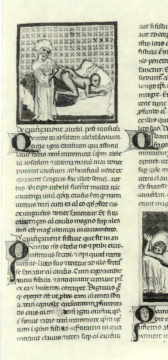

ALBUCASIS' use of the cauterizing-iron was demonstrated on this page from a fourteenth-century manuscript of his book about surgery.

which ranked medicine together with surgery.

This was a rehabilitation for surgery, as it had been reduced to a despised handicraft under the Arab domination. But such a backward attitude had not been due only to the Arabs' notorious lack of interest. In Europe, the priests had been explicitly frightened away from dealing with surgical therapy. According to canon law, a priest automatically lost his job if he caused another person's death, which included fatality during surgical treatment!

During its first centuries, the Salerno school built upon practical experience and oral tradition. A man arrived in the eleventh century who was to play a significant part in Salerno's development into the leading European centre of

Albucasis' Treatment for Arterial Bleeding

In such a case, put your index finger quickly on the point of bleeding and press until the flow stops. Heat up cauterizing-irons with olive-shaped tips. Choose one of them, depending on the vessel's size, and place it on the vessel as soon as your finger is removed, holding it there until the bleeding stops.

Be careful, when you burn, not to damage the nearby nerves, since you may then cause a further ailment in the patient.

Remember that an arterial bleeding, especially from a large vessel, can be stopped by only four means: burning, as described already; parting of the artery—if it has not been completely lost—since the ends of a parted artery will actually close up and arrest the bleeding; by a strong ligature; and by applying remedies that can stop bleeding together with a pressure bandage.

But those who try to arrest serious bleeding with bandages, compresses, caustic soda or any other method will seldom if ever succeed.

Unguentum Aegypticum

Egyptian unguent was a corrosive substance used to clean fetid granulations from wounds. The prescription came from either Mesue or Rhazes. This brownish, viscous paste was made from verdigris (basic copper acetate), vinegar and honey. When the mixture was cooked, the copper salt was reduced by the sugar to metallic copper, yielding the brown colour. The word "Aegypticum" was corrupted in Sweden to "Egyptiack", then to "Gypsjack" and finally to "Gips-Jakob". Under this name, it was used on animal wounds as late as the twentieth century.

Medicine in the Devil's Bible

When the field marshal Hans Christoffer Königsmarck stormed Prague in 1648 with a small Swedish force, the loot was tremendous. Among the most valuable items taken to Sweden was the Gigas Librorum ("Giant of Books"), famous even then, and generally called the "Devil's Bible" because of an impressive picture in it (shown above). The work is now in the Royal Library at Stockholm.

Surprisingly, besides the usual Biblical text, it contains long sections on history, a calendar, a list of saints and—medical writings! Research has now proved that the latter were introduced with a section by none other than Hunayn ibn Ishaq. Accompanying this are perhaps the most important of Hunayn's own works, his ten treatises on the eye. The translation from Arabic in this case is believed to have been made by Constantine Africanus himself.

A Caliph and his Physician

The following anecdote was related by the historian Arthur Christensen in his book Already Hippocrates: "What do you know about medicine?" asked Harun al Rashid of his doctor Djabril, who replied: "I know how to cool what is hot and to warm what is cold, to wet what is dry and to dry what is wet." Then the Caliph said, smiling, "That is all one can ask of the healing art!"

Ahead of His Time

Moses Maimonides (1135-1204) was a famous physician and philosopher, whose medical writings are surprisingly modern. He supported them by daring to disavow the deep belief in astrology among his own Jewish people: "Notice your faith in astrology and the planets' influence on human destiny. You should give up such notions. Clear your minds as one washes dirty clothes! Experienced scientists refuse to allow any truth in this knowledge. Its claims can be disproved by irrefutable evidence on rational grounds."

Treatment for Swallowing a Leech

A young man, vomiting blood, went to Rhazes. His story revealed that, during a recent trip, he had drunk water from a pond with still water. Rhazes called for water full of algae, and forced the patient to drink a great quantity of it. When he protested that he could drink no more, his servant was ordered by Rhazes to sit on his stomach, hold open his mouth, and pour the rest of the smelly sludge into him. Finally the young man vomited violently and up came a leech that had caused the original symptom! This tale, if true, exhibits both the diagnostic talents of Rhazes and his drastic methods of treatment.

The Ancestry of the Lie-Detector?

A mysterious illness had afflicted a young man. He was downcast and apathetic, beyond help. Avicenna sat down with him, took his pulse and asked questions. Several cities in the vicinity were mentioned, and one of them caused the man's pulse to speed up suddenly. More questions followed, and when a particular street was named, the pulse quickened again. A list of people who lived on the street was obtained, and the patient's pulse sped up further at the mention of a certain girl. She was sent for—and the young man became well! In relating this anecdote, the historian Harvey Graham remarked that the same principle is used by the modern lie-detector, which registers a suspect's blood pressure and pulse during interrogation.

From the Sayings of Avicenna

An ignorant doctor is the myrmidon of death.

THE *Domus Sanitatis*, "house of health": a view of Salerno's medical school, engraved in 1522 at Pavia.

medical education. Constantine, called "Africanus", was born at Carthage about 1020. Long journeys in the Orient enabled him to learn Arabic and study its literature. He collected all the medical books he could find and brought them home. For some weird reason—it has been claimed that he was accused of dealing in black magic—he had to leave Carthage and he settled in Salerno.

Constantine may have practised medicine in Salerno, or at least taught at the college. Here, at all events, he began his main work of translation. In 1076, he took up residence at Benedict of Nursia's lovely mountain cloister, whose tradition of monastery medicine was by then five hundred years old. He remained a monk at Monte Cassino until his death in 1087. Through his continued translations of Greek and Arabic texts into Latin, he shaped the core of the Salerno school's message. Arab medical knowledge was thus spread to the West, and its communication of ancient Greek learning allowed the latter to undergo a Renaissance. Not by chance, the only educational centre that could compete with Salerno was Montpellier in France, not far from the border of the Arabs' western caliphate.

Conspicuous among Constantine's translations is the "royal book" *Al-Malaki* by Ali Abba, in twenty volumes. A handbook covering all medicine, it was called *Pantekne* or "the whole art" by Constantine himself. Also remarkable is how he brought back, in Latin guise, Hippocrates and Galen who had been long since forgotten in Italy. Constantine is estimated to have translated or edited a total of some thirty medical treatises. His work was continued a century later when Rhazes, Avicenna and Albucasis became available in Latin, thanks to a school of translation at Toledo led by Gerhard of Cremona (1114–1187).

The doctors and teachers of the Salerno school were inspired by the new-won knowledge to produce their own writings. At first, these were mostly about internal medicine and medical ethics, in the Arab tradition. A certain Archimatteus offered good advice: the physician should not look too long at a patient's wife, daughter, or servant-girl, as this repelled God's grace and hardly encouraged sympathy for the patient...

The most popular of the diagnostic methods was uroscopy. Its basic assumption was that a doctor could establish the nature of an illness by observing the patient's urine, sometimes even without seeing the patient. This method had been been practised since antiquity, but was quite meaningless, except perhaps when the patient exhibited macroscopic hematuria—in other words, had blood in the urine. In Salerno, the teachings about the appearance of urine went to absurd lengths. As the historian Werner Möller has said:

"Uroscopy judged the quality and quantity of the urine, with regard to its concentration (distinguished in five degrees), its colour (in twenty different nuances), its smell and transparency, the occurrence of foam or sediment, admixture of mucus and blood, and so forth. The entire artificial, complicated doctrine was given its final form during the thirteenth century, when it became a cunning system of unrealistic, fantastic subtleties."

Of all the Salerno school's writings, the most famous was the anonymous *Regimen Sanitatis Salernitanum*, probably published in the mid-thirteenth century. It was less a medical text than a popular collection of health rules, composed in verse for easier memorization. But far more important were the surgical books produced in Salerno. These rested largely on per-

THE ancient method of diagnosing illnesses by inspecting samples of urine was still standard in medieval times, as this anonymous chart shows. Its symmetrical design expressed the old belief that even diseases belonged to the world's divine order.

sonal experience. The doctors still did not dare to go so far as dissecting human bodies, but they acquired useful knowledge by studying the anatomy of pigs, which resulted for example in the *Anatomica Porci* by Cophos. Nor were they

From the *Regimen Sanitatis Salernitatum*

Sensus et ars medici curant, non verba sophistae— hic aegrum relevat curis, verbis necat iste.

In other words, it is the doctor's art and good sense that heal, not the sophist's words—the former helps a patient with cures, while the latter kills him with talk.

so proud as to ignore the findings of cataract-curers, hernia-carvers and lithotomists, who met scorn elsewhere. When the latter's manual skill and undeniable clinical competence were combined with the lessons from Greece and Arabia, a sound surgery was developed. Salerno became the cradle of modern Western surgery.

The oldest surgical text of Salerno was discovered in a library of the principality and bishopric of Bamberg, and is the Bamberg Manuscript. Only a fragment survives. It probably had several authors, who followed Paul of Aegina and Albucasis—while adding practical hints from their own experience, particularly for operations. The manuscript also contains an interesting comment on a "sleep-inducing sponge", which might be an ancestor of the anaesthetic mask!

This document is dated to the mid-twelfth century. A few decades later, Salerno acquired its first great surgeon, Ruggiero Frugardi, usually called Roger of Salerno. He and his students put together *Chirurgia magistri Rogeri*, which has been described as the first known independent surgical work in the Western world. It became familiar all over Europe and laid the basis for education in surgery, as taught for example by Wilhelm de Congenis at Montpellier. Once Roger's apprentice Roland published an addition to it, the book spread even farther.

The Salerno doctors' wisest contribution to surgery was surely their teaching on the care of skull wounds. They maintained that any skull trauma could be complicated by intracranial bleeding. And they emphasized that an open wound associated with violence to the head should be examined for possible fractures. Loose fragments and impressed bits of bone should be removed. On the other hand, they warned against the bad habit of trepanning for every skull wound. Surgeons who did so "received the stern but fair verdict of being stolid idiots", to cite Werner Möller. According to him, documents also say that, if trepanation had to be done, one should avoid the cold or the full moon, and the operator should ensure that his hands and bandages were clean—"a modest beginning for asepsis".

It was still believed that wounds could only heal properly after the formation of pus (*per intentio secundam*). Nevertheless, the doctors threw themselves wholeheartedly into rather advanced surgery. There are reports, for example, of so serious a matter as an open wound on the chest wall, where a part of the lung became attached and gangrened. It was treated by extirpating that part. Roger described a method of operating on struma, and emphasized that the capsule should come out completely to prevent a relapse. He continued:

"Yet if the struma is very large, and the patient old and weak, it is best in our opinion not to use this treatment. These large struma have, as a rule, many lobes which are difficult to dissect away properly, and we refuse to burn them for fear of damaging arteries or nerves. But if such patients must be treated with surgery, we tie them to the table and hold them down firmly, so that we can see exactly what we are doing…"

Roger and his school were cautious in other respects, too. He had enough experience of battle wounds to warn his colleagues against trying to remove deeply imbedded arrowheads and spearheads—for he had witnessed more harm from such manoeuvres than the weapons themselves caused! Similarly, if a wound went to the heart, lungs, liver or diaphragm, it was wisest to forget any sort of operation. Totally sacrosanct were kidney wounds, which he simply recommended to the grace and goodness of God.

Salerno's successors

In 1215, Pope Innocent III issued his *Ecclesia Abhorret a Sanguine* ("The Church Abhors Bloodshed"), which should have put an end to all surgical activity—as indeed it aimed to do. Remarkably, surgery advanced in spite of it, even in Italy, the heartland of Catholicism.

NOT too much love-making, reading in bed, straining at stool, or drinking! The Salerno School's *Regimen* contained about 350 rules of health, illustrated in this way by its later editions.

After Roger and his apprentices, the Salerno school declined. Medical leadership moved northward, notably to Bologna, which had a large university. Its medical faculty was founded by Ugo di Borgognoni (ca. 1160–1257), sometimes called Ugo or Hugo of Lucca. He is known not from surviving works of his own, but through his disciple—who may have been his son—Theoderic (1205–96). Their main doctrine was centuries ahead of its time. They denied that wounds must heal by the aforementioned principle of *per intentio secundam*:

"It is not necessary, as Roger and Roland have written and many of their disciples hold, and as all present surgeons maintain, that pus be formed in wounds. No mistake can be greater! Such a procedure is quite against nature, prolongs illness, and hinders healing and the consolidation of the wound."

This short passage, from Theoderic's *Chirurgia* (1267), is one of the most heretical in the entire history of medicine. The notion of *pus bonum et laudabile* ("good and praiseworthy pus") was a pillar of early surgery. It had been preached and applied by the Classical Greeks, by Galen and by the Arabs. As the historian Harvey Graham remarks, "Theoderic must have been as original a thinker as Lord Lister, but he lived six hundred years too early." Unfortunately, Theoderic's doctrine of wounds drowned in a muddle of reasoning about humoral dyscrasia (constitutional disease), and its clear lines were obscured by incomprehensible theory. Nor did it win support, and the only man who dared to repeat it during the next few centuries was the French doctor Henri de Mondeville.

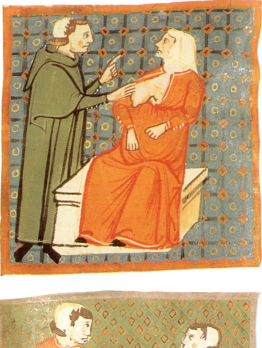

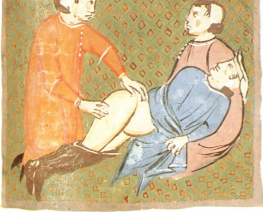

EXAMINATIONS of the breast and rectum were among the procedures depicted in Theoderic's book on surgery.

Theoderic himself shrank from pursuing his thesis. He was afraid to sew up even small wounds. They should heal by themselves under a bandage, and he recommended suture only if the wound edges seemed too far apart to let the wound grow together. His greatness is, in any case, undeniable: "In truth, nothing is more important than cleaning a wound!"

Guglielmo da Saliceto (1210–1280?), often known to us as William, came from a small village near Piacenza in Lombardy. He acquired a fine education with training in both medicine and surgery. Much experience came to him as a doctor in several Bolognese campaigns during the Crusades in Syria and Egypt. Then he became a respected teacher of surgery at the faculty in Bologna, and ended his days as the city physician of Verona. His *Cyrurgia* was actually a kind of surgical testament, written for his son. But many doctors were to count themselves lucky that it also went beyond the family. William's book became, along with that by Roger of Salerno, the most important surgical text during the Renaissance.

William was a humble man: "All is owed to Nature—the doctor is merely her servant." He insisted that it was absurd to distinguish between medicine and surgery—the surgeon was just a doctor who treated with his hands! His good education in both fields supported him, for an even larger work on internal medicine preceded his book on surgery.

More than anyone else, William preferred the knife to the cauterizing-iron. Presumably he knew of Theoderic's doctrine about wound-healing *per intentio primam*, but he did not say so. At any rate, he was restrained and fairly rational in caring for wounds. The bandage should be simple, with egg-white and rose-water; and he rejected the often pungent, sticky salves which had been popular and were usually meant just to cause pus formation. Wound suture was more attractive to William than to Theoderic, and he actually suggested that nerves and sinews be sewn. A novel and revealing fact in *Cyrurgia* shows how little was known about even the simplest physiology: William taught that an arterial wound could be diagnosed by the pulse-like bleeding!

William also called it totally needless to extirpate the testicle in a hernia operation. "Don't

Medical Faculties

The earliest educational institutions were allied to cathedrals or rich monasteries. Led by priests, an organization was created for instruction in the seven free arts: grammar, dialectics, rhetoric, arithmetic, geometry, music, and astronomy. Many places also offered instruction in healing remedies, the embryo of later medical faculties.

The first such institutions, scolae, were mostly cathedral schools or "trivial" schools (referring to the three subjects mentioned first above). In the twelfth century, the term studium generale was introduced, and the subsequent studium universale initiated the universities. These were recognized officially in 1233 by Pope Gregory IX.

Even long before then, many of them were known all over Europe, and each had developed its own specialties. Montpellier and Cambridge were among the most ancient and prominent.

The oldest medical school which counts as a medical faculty was that of Salerno, founded in the late 800s or early 900s. Those of Padua and Bologna came soon afterward in Italy, followed somewhat later in France by Montpellier and Paris. During the 1200s, Paris prevailed as the world's centre of education. Almost contemporary there were Roger Bacon (known as doctor mirabilis), Thomas Aquinas (doctor angelicus), and the German Dominican monk Albertus Magnus (doctor universalis).

But the leader in medicine was Montpellier, perhaps mainly due to its unauthoritarian freethinking, which certainly was (and would be) a drag on the heels of the Paris faculties. In addition, Montpellier was favoured by its location, near Italy as well as the Arabs in Spain. Whereas Salerno lacked proper hospitals, Montpellier could profit from several wealthy monasteries, whose monks were interested and knowledgeable in sick-care.

The church authorities set aside their bias against sick-care in this case, perhaps out of pecuniary interest. In 1220, the medical school at Montpellier was inspected by Cardinal Konrad, who acclaimed its good reputation and announced that the pope "would, as a proof of his grace, devote special attention to the formulation of the college's statutes".

The medical faculty at Montpellier was officially founded in 1289, through the new university statute of Pope Nicholas IV. Further tokens of grace came from the papal seat in 1350, when John XXII ordered—among other things—that his verger would carry a silver vessel in celebrations "as an emblem of the glory that shone from the school at Montpellier". More important to medical progress was the Duke of Anjou's permission for the faculty members to dissect one corpse every year! Once given this licence, the students could easily dig up recent burials in the cemetery by night and drag them to the dissection room...

Medieval Social Medicine

As early as the thirteenth century in many Spanish cities, the local administration appointed a doctor for a particular area. Besides caring for the sick in a hospital, he was to carry out investigative health care by visiting all of his charges at regular intervals. He had a yearly salary, but could take no sick-care fee for a patient's first three visits each month, and according to West Gothic law there was never any fee if the patient died!

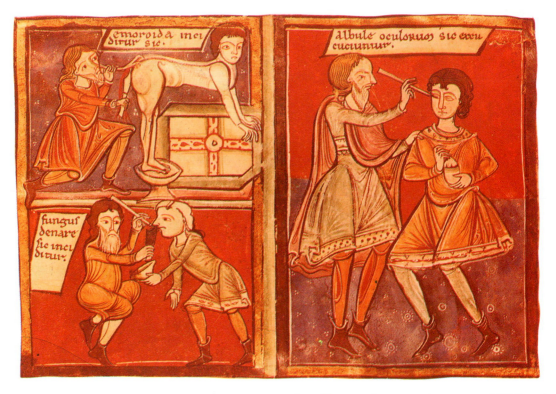

THREE kinds of operations practised by Roger of Salerno—on haemorrhoids, nasal polyps and corneas—appeared in this contemporary illustration.

dream of removing it, as some stupid and ignorant doctors do!" And in cancer surgery, he saw clearly that radical measures were essential:

"The disease can only be properly cured by amputating the organ, since, as I have said, its roots are anchored in the veins that surround it, full of melancholic blood. For a fundamental cure, these veins must be sheared and the roots somehow removed. This cannot be done without completely extracting the diseased body part—there is no other way to get rid of the disease."

In addition, the general section of William's surgical textbook gave some advice for the surgeon's conduct. Some of it throws light on the ethics of the medical guild: "a wise surgeon should refrain from stealing when he treats a patient" and "one should not make use of assistants who have a notoriously bad character"...

Three great Frenchmen

The founder of surgery in France was the dynamic Guido Lanfranchi (d. 1315), better known as simply Lanfranc. A Milanese, he was educated by William of Saliceto, but had to leave Italy in a hurry when he happened to be on the wrong side in one of the fights between the Guelfs and Ghibellines. Lanfranc settled at Lyons in 1290 and, five years later, moved to Paris. There, his academic career was cut short before it even began—he was married, while all professors were supposed to live in celibacy! However, he was received gladly by the independent college of Saint-Côme, which also made him more comfortable. For the teachers at the medical faculty had to live on straw-covered floors in the artists' house, where the rats outnumbered the students. The university was too poor to provide furniture.

Lanfranc shared his educator's view that medicine and surgery were inseparable. "Good Lord," he wrote, "why should there be such a great difference between an internal doctor and a surgeon? Keep well in mind that nobody can become a good internist without any knowledge of surgery, and conversely: nobody can become a good surgeon who knows nothing about medicine."

His books, *Chirurgia Parva* and *Chirurgia Magna*, became widespread and much-used. Generally, Lanfranc was a conservative, though able to be constructive and creative. Among other things, he was the first to use a silver tube in the windpipe for free breathing. The patient had a false passage between the oesophagus and trachea, and so was in danger of suffocation when eating or drinking.

Lanfranc's greatest contribution to practical surgery was his chapter on brain injuries. It gave the first good description of symptoms and signs of a concussion. He also recommended percussion of the skull: if there was no fracture, one heard a sound like an uncracked bell! He refined the method by tying a waxed string to one of the patient's teeth and holding it taut. By plucking on it like a string-instrument, he produced different tones, depending on whether or not the skull was cracked.

A man of high morals and deep humanistic education, Lanfranc demanded the same qualifications of his disciples. The ideal surgeon, according to his introductory chapter, was a gifted man, versed in philosophy and logic—able to read the Scriptures critically, with enough experience in grammar to express opinions, and enough in rhetoric to submit them for discussion. When dealing with a patient, the surgeon should be honest, humble and heartwarming. Lanfranc evidently felt a need to put

LANFRANC.
Professeur en Chirurgie à Paris, au treizieme Siecle.

A sculpture of Lanfranc by A. Humblot, perhaps based on earlier woodcuts, was portrayed in this engraving by S. Ravenet around 1749.

Lanfranc's Superman

What a surgeon needs are a restrained and modest disposition, well-formed fingers and a strong constitution. He must not tremble, and must keep his limbs in shape. He should be intelligent, simple, meek and courageous, but not foolhardy. He ought to be familiar with the natural sciences, as well as philosophy and logic. To formulate himself properly, and support his views with good reasons, is essential.

A fourteenth-century manuscript picture of
Henri de Mondeville lecturing to his students,
who were apparently allowed to ask questions.

this in print. He had little affection for his contemporary colleagues in Paris, who seem to have
been an unusually qualified bunch of illiterates
and clumsy mechanics.

Lanfranc ended his repressed, yet brilliant,
career by becoming the personal physician of
Philip the Fair. His successor in this post was one
of France's greatest surgeons ever—Henri de
Mondeville. Born in 1260, Henri came from
Normandy, attended the universities of Montpellier and Paris, then studied surgery with
Theoderic in Bologna. Henri's main achievement was undoubtedly that he understood the
truth of Theoderic's doctrine about the care and
hygiene of wounds, and was the only man to
carry it further.

After returning from Italy, Henri worked as a
teacher of anatomy and surgery in Montpellier,
until—like all leading French doctors—he was
irresistibly attracted to Paris. As one of the four
physicians to Philip the Fair, he survived that
king and held the same post under the next,
Louis the Quarrelsome. Henri was both clever
and wise, an outstanding surgeon and careful of
his profession's dignity. Somewhere between
1306 and 1320, he wrote *Chirurgie*, which was
not only the first surgical textbook by a native
Frenchman: it made France the world leader in
the field.

Chirurgie was forthright, sharp-tongued and
outspoken, just like its author. He had no patience with ignorant colleagues, nor did he
shrink from lecturing the pillars of society if need
be, including bishops and the king. Henri was
aware of his own significance and his art's:

"It would be vain for a surgeon of our day to
know his art, science and operations, if he
does not also have the adroitness and knowledge of how to make it pay for him. There
are actually rich people so petty, greedy and
narrow-minded that they pay very little or
nothing. They think it enough to give the
surgeon twelve *deniers* or two *sous* per day, as
if he were a bricklayer, furrier or shoeshiner.
It does not cross their minds that wealth is

worthless without health, and that no poverty can be compared with illness...

"The law says, too, that the human body comes before everything else. It follows that a surgeon should not tolerate the offer of a paltry or nonexistent fee, when he has saved an arm or hand...

"Surgeons, if you have operated conscientiously, whether for an adequate salary from the rich or for nothing from the poor, you need fear neither fire, rain nor storms. You do not have to take up religion, go on pilgrimages, or anything of the sort—because you have saved your souls through your science. You can live without want and die in your homes; you can live in peace and joy, glad that your pay will be plenty in Heaven."

Henri, then, was anxious that his colleagues should get a good reward from those who could afford it. But he was equally averse to demanding anything from those who clung to the dark side of life. For everyone's sake, a doctor ought to be available and fully devoted to giving his patient all the necessary care, not forgetting the little things that could make life more bearable. "He must comfort the patient with friendly words, and satisfy desires if they do not interfere with treating the illness." Henri also offered practical advice in medical ethics: "Never dine with a patient if he owes you money—take a meal at some inn, or else he'll deduct the cost of his hospitality from your bill..."

Chirurgie was initially planned to appear in five volumes. But it was never finished, partly due to the author's enormous burden of work, and partly because he himself was ill with asthma and tuberculosis. The first volume, based on Avicenna and dealing with anatomy, is of little interest. The second volume, definitely the most important, concerns wounds and healing them. This was where he expressed his absolute faith in Theoderic's view—that a wound heals faster and better without pus formation. Henri's ethical thoughts, collected in twenty-six notes, formed the introduction to the same book.

The Surgeon's Emergency-Bag

According to Guy de Chauliac, this should contain "five salves: basilica to make pus ripen, apostle's salve to purify, golden salve to make tissues grow, white salve to heal, and dialtea for sweetening. His bag should also hold five instruments: tweezers, probe, razor, lances and needles. A surgeon thus equipped can successfully perform the stated operations on the human body, as long as he has a good knowledge of the prescriptions for cures."

Since ancient times, basilica (unguentum basilicum, also called regium or royal salve) was famous "for cooking out or ripening fluids". It usually had from four to seven ingredients, including turpentine, frankincense, myrrh and pitch. Apostle's salve originated not from Jesus' disciples, but probably in the eleventh century, and had twelve components such as lead plaster, various resins, and verdigris. The three other salves in Guy's emergency-bag cannot be identified today.

Mondeville as Psychotherapist

Keep up your patient's spirits with violin music and a ten-stringed psalter, with false letters about the deaths of his enemies, or—if he is a spiritual man—by telling him that he's been made a bishop!

Guy de Chauliac's Bibliography

The amazingly broad reading done by Guy in medical literature was reflected in his 3,299 references to other works. More than a hundred authorities were mentioned. Galen topped the list with 890 quotations, followed by Avicenna with 661, Albucasis with 173, Rhazes with 161, Haly Abbas with 149, and Hippocrates with 120.

A surgeon extracts a sword from a man's thigh in the fourteenth century: from Guy de Chauliac's *Grande Chirurgie*. Such an "operation" was little more than first-aid, but an illustration helped to persuade students that it could be done at all.

Henri's position was that every wound should be healed in a clean condition. Foreign objects must be removed instantly, bleeding stopped, and the wound be closed if at all technically possible. For bandages, he recommended compresses drenched in hot wine. The patient had to rest and take nourishing food and wine.

The third volume, on surgery of the soft parts, is by no means as acute in tone or as original as the second. Yet its introduction is noteworthy, being one of the many proofs of Henri's fearlessness. He criticizes both the king and the government, for having exploited Henri as a doctor in the army when he could have been more useful elsewhere, and for failing to help his views to spread among ignorant colleagues: "...without being vain, ambitious or greedy, and without

wishing to conquer the world, but in order to be satisfied with what is necessary for life, I regard our surgery, so essential to mankind, as inadequately disseminated..."

The fourth volume was to be about fractures and dislocations, but Henri never even began it. He placed greater weight on a *materia medica*, in which he argued against Galen and, indeed, had the temerity to write that "God surely didn't use up all genius on Galen"—an almost heretical remark at the beginning of the fourteenth century. But matters were not as bad as they seem from an isolated quotation. Henri admitted many of Galen's teachings and followed him in numerous passages, while warning that "we now know things which were unknown in Galen's time, and it is our duty to clarify them in our writings."

Henri de Mondeville was, sadly, all too correct that his views did not reach far in the medical world. The opposite is true of the third great medieval French surgeon, Guy de Chauliac, whose *La Grande Chirurgie* was accepted for centuries as an unquestionable authority. It has been said that, except for that of Hippocrates, there has not been a single textbook in surgery that can take precedence or even be compared to this one.

Guy de Chauliac was born some time in the late thirteenth century, a farmer's son in Auvergne. He became a canon, then studied medicine and surgery at the universities in Toulouse, Montpellier and Paris. Guy always emphasized the value of anatomy, a subject on which he concentrated under Mundinus in Bologna. When finished with his education, he settled in Avignon and became physician to three popes during their "Babylonian captivity" in the city—Clement VI, Innocent VI and Urban V. He lived in the right place at the right time, for Avignon had a well-stocked library which gave him access to new translations of medical literature, both the Greek and the Greek-based Arab.

Guy's huge seven-part work, *La Grande Chirurgie* (*Chirurgia Magna*) or what he called

Inventarium seu Collectorium Cyrurgie, dealt with swellings and tumours, sores and ulcers (Guy distinguished between *vulnus*, a wound due to injury, and *ulcus*, a wound due to disease), as well as fractures, antidotes and drugs. One volume covered "all conditions of illness which, by nature, are not boils, ulcers or bone diseases". To give an idea of the book's size, it contains 3,299 quotations from earlier authors!

Guy considered Galen as the best of all mentors, just ahead of Hippocrates and the great Arabs: Rhazes, Albucasis, Haly Abbas, Avicenna. He knew, to be sure, of Theoderic and Henri de Mondeville. It is usually said that Guy was to blame for the fact that these two doctors' approach to wound-healing did not catch on. He was in principle an adherent of the *pus bonum et laudabile* school—but perhaps less dogmatically than that school has claimed. One passage in the third part of *Chirurgia Magna* is significant in this connection:

"In the first place, foreign objects should be removed, if any exist between the severed tissues; secondly, the latter must be rejoined; thirdly, they must be kept together and united as one; fourthly, the organ's substance must be supervised and preserved. But in the fifth place, complications have to be combated."

This is actually more consistent with modern wound treatment and the principle of healing *per primam*, than with the idea of stimulating pus in the wound at any price!

Another passage from Guy sums up in a nutshell the fourteenth-century surgeon's outlook on his science. He writes that, in his time, there were five medical sects with different orientations. The first was represented by Roger of Salerno, the latter's apprentice Roland, and the "four masters" of their school in Salerno. They stimulated pus formation in all wounds and boils without distinction, by using poultices and proclaiming that "runniness is good, but rawness is evil". The second school was Theoderic's, which treated wounds with wine and held that "dryness is nearly healthy, but moistness is not". The third, belonging to William of Saliceto and including Lanfranc, aimed to mediate between the first two with a rule that "the only way to cure is to do so without perfidy or pain". The fourth orientation was said to be embraced by almost all German soldiers: they treated wounds with sorcery, healing beverages, oil, wool and cabbage leaves. The fifth concerned women and many ignorant people (*mulierum et multarum idiotarum*), who appealed to the saints and observed that the Lord takes what He gives—*sit nomen domini benedictum, Amen*. Granted that Guy was a factual author, less pungent in style

Bad News for Hernia Patients

Guy de Chauliac had very definite instructions for care of patients with hernia, which he regarded as a potentially quite dangerous ailment:

"The doctor should prescribe laxatives and blood-letting to produce regular bowel movement. The patient should avoid beans, fresh fruit, whole-grain baked bread, port wine, fish, cheese and radishes. New wine and pure water are not allowed. Great exertion (including copulation) is forbidden, and the intestines must be kept loose with enemas, laxatives and suppositories. The food should be spiced with sage, and every meal should include a sugar-coated pill of coriander and nasturtium. Once this regimen has begun, the doctor should try to reduce the hernia, manually or letting the patient hang by his legs. Then a special plaster is laid over the hernia gate, and strengthened with a band that can secure the reduction. The patient should stay in bed for fifty days, while the plaster is moved every ninth day."

Guy emphasized that the sole basis for this treatment was sheer hope!

than Henri de Mondeville, this passage suggests that he had an indulgent sense of humour.

To posterity, it was perhaps mainly in the lesser tasks that Guy displayed his wisdom as a surgeon and doctor. He built a bedframe which helped the patient to rise or turn, and had a removable bed base for answering the call of nature. He also recommended several ways to splint a fracture, making the wound more accessible for changing bandages. The splints were often strengthened with bandages soaked in egg-white, resulting in something like a plaster cast. His splinting method even found a novel use, for fractures of the leg-bone shaft. Earlier, following Albucasis, the broken bone's heel had been fixed to the seat so that the underbone served as a splint, which must have caused the patient much pain and difficulty. But most importantly, Guy tied weights to the underbone, laid across a pulley at the foot of the bed. This was the first extension treatment since the time when such an idea occurred to Hippocrates.

Guy de Chauliac's methods dominated surgery in France, and to some degree in England, for two hundred years. It would take a Vesalius and a Paré to revise them.

The medieval English

Britain's natural science, and thus its medicine, were born in the middle of the thirteenth century with Roger Bacon (1214–92?). He was a universal genius, deserving of his honorary title *doctor mirabilis*. Among Bacon's scientific discoveries were a magnifying glass and the definitions of reflection and refraction in his studies of optics; he also came close to inventing gunpowder. More importantly in the long run, he stressed the significance of mathematics—and the decisive role of experimentation in natural science, where logic was not enough. English scientists have always followed Bacon: healthy scepticism, and faith in the clarity of experiments, belong to the nation's character, not least in medicine and surgery.

Bacon wrote generally about human sources of error—"the example of frail and worthless authority, the old tradition, the attitude of ignorant masses, and the effort to hide the unscientific beneath the cloak of wisdom". His *Tractatus de erroribus medicorum* listed thirty-six radical mistakes in medicine. He was to play a direct role not in surgical practice, but in the overall development of surgical science. It is one of history's whims that the ideas of Bacon were revived three centuries later, although from another point of view, by his namesake Francis Bacon—the Baron Verulam and statesman at the court of Queen Elizabeth I.

English medicine in the 1300s was dominated by three doctors, all named John. Two of them had very little to do with surgery, although John of Gaddesden dabbled in dentistry and chiropody: that is, bunion-cutting. John of Mirfield was primarily a chaplain at Saint Bartholomew's Hospital in London, but also librarian and—without any normal medical education—an amateur doctor. His chief contribution was a collection, *Breviarium Bartholomei*, of original works by the authorities of that age, such as Galen and Guy de Chauliac. It was interlarded with his own notes, mainly about therapy and prognosis, which today seem hazardous—for instance, that if tears run from a sick man's right eye, he will die.

In the history of surgery, John of Mirfield is worth mentioning for a passage in his second large book, *Florarium Bartholomei*. Most of it was a theological discussion, but he objects:

"If I am not mistaken, physicians long ago practised surgery. Nowadays there is a clear distinction between physicians and surgeons. I fear it has arisen through pride, as physicians loathe working with their hands—though I suspect that this is because they do not know how to operate. Such an unhappy development has made people believe that an individual cannot practise both disciplines. But the well-informed realize that no one can become a good doctor by neglecting all

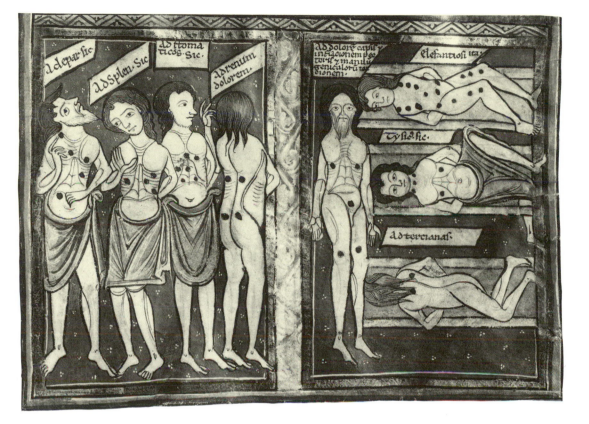

CAUTERIZATION points recommended for various diseases by the *Libri Quattuor Medicinae* (ca. 1200).

surgery and, on the other hand, that a surgeon is worthless if he is ignorant of medicine."

We are reminded, for example, of Lanfranc; the message did no harm when repeated in England. But the contempt for surgeons lasted, perhaps, longer there than anywhere else. It is significant that British physicians in general are addressed as "Doctor", while surgeons and orthopaedists are still called "Mister". Ironically, the latter has now become an honorary title, jealously guarded by operating specialists!

The surgeon in the John-triad was John of Arderne. Where he got his education is a mys-

tery, but he was certainly a field surgeon in the Hundred Years' War under the Dukes of Lancaster. He was present at the Siege of Algiers, where gunpowder was used for the first time in European military history. In 1349, he came home from the wars and settled at Newark in Nottinghamshire. Later he moved to London and joined the guild of military doctors. Familiar with highly placed men from his campaigns, he acquired a status that matched his own lofty self-esteem.

John asserted his worth as a surgeon—today he would have been very strict with the title "Mister"—and called himself *chirurgus inter medicus*. Relevant, too, was his financial sense: for a fistula operation, which was his specialty, he charged a hundred shillings cash, plus a hundred for every year the patient lived. These stupefying sums (100 shillings then would be

91

(LEFT) A portrait of John of Arderne, from a fifteenth-century manuscript of his book on fistulas. (*Right*) A page from Arderne's writings on surgery, illustrating skeletal structure and treatment for urinary stones.

over a thousand pounds now) were extracted from the rich. The poor were let off with the cash fee, "for never in my life took I less than an hundred shillings for cure of that sickness…"

Of the many books which flowed from John's pen, *Treatment of Anal Fistulas* is the most famous and contributed most to surgery. His technique was elementary but radical. The patient lay in the position for a lithotomy. With a probe, four ligatures were taken up through the fistula, and their ends, drawn down through the anus, were knotted hard to stop the bleeding. Next, John pushed one grooved instrument through the fistula into the rectum, where it contacted another one. He then made a bold cut with his scalpel to remove the whole intervening segment, and stopped the bleeding between the

ligatures with a hot sponge. The wound was cared for by cleaning—John had learned Lanfranc's methods in France—and the patient's stool was kept loose with daily enemas to prevent trauma. The same principles are employed today and, except for improvements in detail, no surgeon need be ashamed of closely following John's rules.

John of Arderne never used salves in wounds as, for example, Guy de Chauliac prescribed, because he was well aware that they did more harm than good. His favourite application to wounds was fine flour in egg-white, and seldom for more than three days at that. But he was not entirely rational. He still confidently recommended superstitious treatments, although possibly due less to his own faith than to the need of strengthening the patient's. Thus, epileptics were advised to write—with their blood on a piece of parchment—the names of the Three Wise Men, and to soothe the latter's souls by reading three Pater Nosters and three Ave Marias daily for three months. On the whole, however, John clung to reality. He relied far less on astrology than did most of his colleagues.

There are reasons for regarding John of Arderne as not only England's first important surgeon, but also the world's first proctologist—a specialist in diseases of the rectum. Apart from the operation for anal fistulas, he repeatedly noted the dangers of an ulcer in the rectum, which could easily be palpated by finger. What he meant was rectal cancer, though he called it an "owl boil", since owls also lurk in the dark! He correctly described the clinical development of such cancer, and was the first to establish the classic diagnostic triad: blood, mucus, and constriction. But the therapy was gloomy. All that could be given were ordinary enemas with a bran decoction. Operation was out of the question: "do not be deceived, it will only make a fool of you..."

Leading English surgeons of the fourteenth century organized themselves into "The Guild of Surgeons Within the City of London", which gained official sanction in 1368. This was a clumsy attempt to separate the surgeons from the barbers, as the two spheres of interest overlapped. But it was far from successful. Not only did the surgeons have too much pride for shaving and delousing their fellow human beings. There were also economic factors, and an honourable contest went on as to who should perform the simpler, yet profitable, operations such as cutting boils, blood-letting, and removing small tumours. In the army of Henry V at Agincourt (1415), surgeons and barbers worked side by side, with mutual irritation and envy. Almost two hundred years were to pass before Henry VIII put some order into their relationship.

A Case of Tetanus

John of Arderne was an observant clinician. His writings include a well-described case of what was evidently tetanus. One may wonder whether the disease arose from the original injury or from the treatment. This comprised, among other things, hairs from a hare, which could very well have been infected with tetanus bacillae. John says:

"A gardener who worked with vines cut his hand on the Friday after Saint Thomas of Canterbury's Day. His thumb was cut nearly off, and could be folded up next to the underarm, bleeding profusely. The treatment was as follows. First the thumb was put back in place and sewn on. The bleeding was curtailed with Lanfranc's red powder and hare bristles. On the third day, the bandage was removed, and the bleeding had stopped. Then medicaments were applied which bring forth blood, and we changed the bandage daily. The wound began to clean itself, and the pus came out. But on the fourth, blood emerged at around midnight, and the patient lost nearly

two pounds. The bleeding was stopped and a new bandage applied. On the eleventh day, even more blood emerged than the first time. We stopped it again, but in the morning, the patient suffered bad cramps in the jaws and arm, unable to feed himself or open his mouth. On the fifteenth day, he bled uncontrollably. The cramps continued and, on the twentieth day, he died."

The incubation time and the lockjaw indicate tetanus. What the red powder was, we can only guess: it might have been pimpinella, which was mentioned for example by the Swedish author Arvidh Månsson in A Very Useful Herb-Book: "Pimpinella draweth out Iron and Thorns easily from wounds with no pain, if one lays a little Leaf around the wound; thus in Latin it is called Sanguisorba, meaning Blood-sucker or Blood-drinker." Another possibility is peony, which has been used since ancient times—its seeds, surprisingly, were recommended by Pliny himself against tetanus!

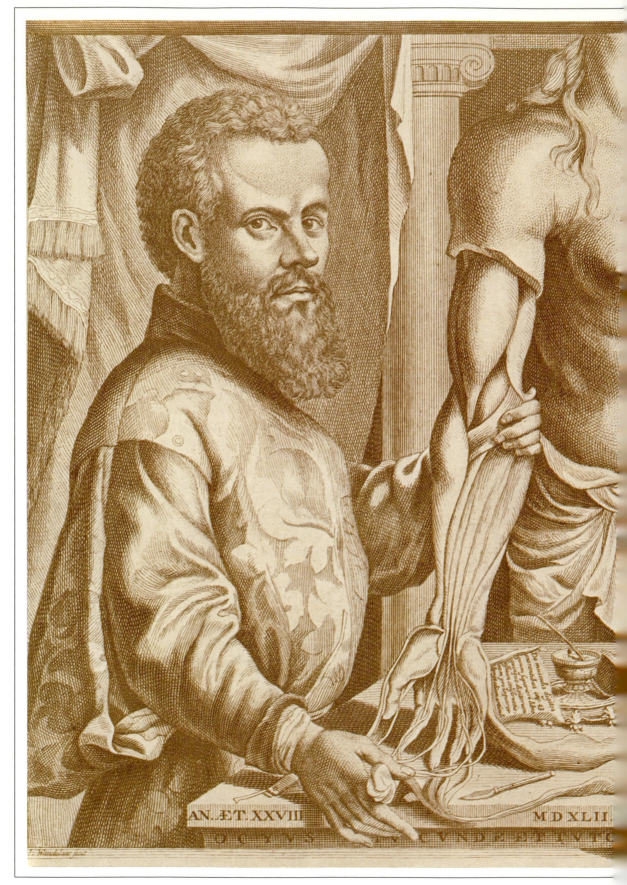

AN. ÆT. XXVII · MDXLII

CHAPTER 4

Surgery in the Renaissance

From the fifteenth century onward, historians speak of "the new age". It is a well-chosen term: people in Europe acquired a fresh view of many aspects of life. The renewal occurred not least in the natural sciences, and perhaps especially in medicine. Criticism and revision were hallmarks of the time. Old texts were supervised by a circle of authors, whom we generally call the "philological school". Some of these were Niccolo Leoniceno (1428–1524), an amazingly erudite man who successively became professor of medicine at Padua, Bologna and Ferrara; Thomas Linacre (1460–1524), the first personal physician of Henry VIII; and Valerius Cordis (1515–44), who published a new edition of Dioscorides, so improved and expanded that it amounted to the first modern pharmacopoeia, or book of remedies.

The birth of a new surgery

A herald of developments in surgery was the Florentine doctor Antonio Benivieni (1440?–1502). He was educated at Pisa and Siena, but returned to his beautiful home town and practised surgery until he died. He grew mightily rich on his art, and was so respected that he was elected to the city's highest offices.

Throughout his surgical career, Benivieni kept careful notes. Since he followed up his cases

ANDREAS Vesalius at the age of twenty-eight when about to publish his great work on human anatomy.

with autopsies, the notes proved extremely valuable when found after his death, and were published in 1507 by his friend Rosati under the title *De Abditis Morborum Causis* ("The Hidden Causes of Illnesses"). Certain turns of phrase in the manuscript give us to understand that Benivieni had won permission for autopsies from both the Pope and the victims' relatives—when he failed to do so in one fascinating case, his displeasure was obvious! At any rate, the autopsies sufficed to yield many new results in pathology, of direct benefit to surgeons. An English successor called Benivieni "the founder of pathological anatomy" and another summarized his work as "the beginning of the end for the old humoral tradition".

Some of Benivieni's accounts are remarkable. One of his relatives had poor digestion and vomited after every meal. The patient was treated "with all manner of cures for stomach trouble", to no avail. He wasted away "to little more than skin and bone". Autopsy revealed that the lower stomach orifice was constricted and hardened, so that nothing could pass through it. This is a typical stomach cancer, but the peculiar thing is that Benivieni did not claim—as he often did—to have made the diagnosis while the man was alive. Evidently doctors were not yet able to interpret these almost characteristic symptoms of stomach cancer—an obvious sign of the period's ignorance, particularly in anatomy.

Among the ailments reported by Benivieni were gallstones, cancer of the large intestine with ileus, various kinds of hernia, and two cases

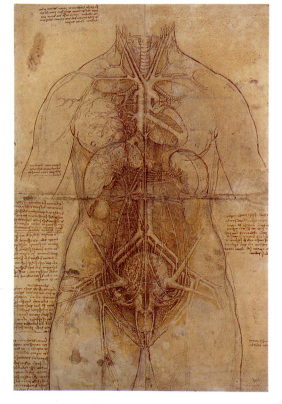

FEMALE organs and arteries: one of the many observant anatomical drawings by Leonardo da Vinci. They had no influence on medical science, but his methods were the Renaissance's finest. Aiming to create an encyclopedia of all such knowledge, he laid a basis for modern scientific illustration.

universities of Padua and Bologna, had got to know their prominent medical faculties. This new right was confirmed by Clement VII, whose pontificate saw the rise of Rome as a centre for anatomy. During the early sixteenth century, there was apparently no longer any obstacle to either dissection or autopsy. When Emperor Charles V asked the faculty at Salamanca, he heard that dissection was permitted by edict of the Catholic Church.

A further stimulus existed for the study of the human body's structure. Artists had become eager to show people as they looked in reality, rejecting the stylized Gothic portraiture of the fifteenth century. The first artist to dissect a human body was Donatello or else Pollaiuolo. They were followed by the greatest painters and sculptors of the age: Verrocchio, Leonardo, Michelangelo, Albrecht Dürer, Titian. We know that the young Michelangelo requested the right to dissect bodies from the hospital chapel of a monastery in Florence, as part of his fee for decorations there.

From a medical standpoint, Leonardo da Vinci (1452–1519) was the most significant of Renaissance artists. He studied anatomy with scientific interest and, just before his death, confessed that he had personally dissected more than a hundred bodies! Among the works he left to history were 779 anatomical drawings. An example of his observational powers and accuracy is a precise drawing of transverse veins in the lower leg, kept at the archive of Windsor Castle. It was to be 450 years before surgeons understood the role of these veins—they are decisive for the commonest type of leg wound.

The leading universities had more or less energetically acquired permission for dissections as early as the fifteenth century. At Bologna, it was allowed to investigate two bodies per year, although they had to be obtained from several kilometres outside the city! Padua obeyed Venice, which had an unbiased government and officially sanctioned dissection in 1429, so that a traveller could tell of fourteen bodies being dissected during 1444. The beautiful theatre of

of a hip disease which was presumably tuberculosis. Beyond the realm of surgery, he gave a good description of syphilis (*morbus gallicus*), "a new illness which swept over Italy and almost all of Europe in the year 1496". Benivieni's clinical report must have been one of the first ever made of this illness, which had recently been brought home to Cadiz by the sailors of Columbus.

The church's ban on opening a dead man's body was thus showing a few gaps. Sixtus IV (1414–84) became the first Pope to approve, perhaps since he himself, as a student at the

anatomy, built in 1446, enabled Vesalius to teach, Realdo Colombo to describe pulmonary blood circulation, and William Harvey to take part in dissections. Even earlier at Montpellier, in 1376, Louis of Anjou gave his university the right to dissect an executed criminal every year.

The Renaissance's first great anatomist was Jacob Sylvius (1478–1555) in Paris. Personally he was despised, as can be seen from the adjectives used by his chroniclers: intolerant, avaricious, coarse, impetuous, vindictive, pompous. His greed was especially grotesque, and inspired the inscription on his gravestone:

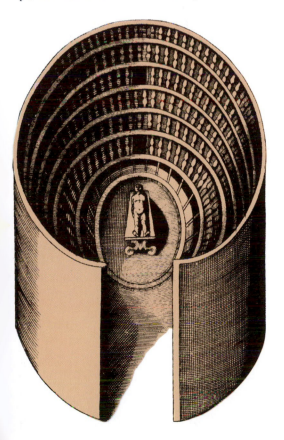

A view of the anatomical theatre at Padua in the mid-seventeenth century, after its use by pioneers such as Fabricius and Harvey.

"Here lies Sylvius, who never did a thing without a fee.
Even in death, he grieves that you read this inscription free."

Sylvius was an incurable believer in Galen, whose anatomy he accepted without reservation. Nor was he upset when his students demonstrated clear differences between Galen's texts and real corpses: his standard reply was that man had evidently changed during the previous 1,400 years! Thus, his significance lay not in anatomical discoveries, but in his zeal as a teacher—although not without economic motives, since he had five hundred paying students at lectures. And his chief apprentice was Andreas Vesalius.

Once, in the United States, where such information finds a ready audience, there was a

Another Sylvius

Jacob Sylvius should not be confused with a far greater anatomist, François Sylvius (1614-1672). No less than thirteen anatomical parts have been named after the latter. The best-known is probably the aquaeductus cerebri Sylvii, mesencephalic duct. It has often been attributed wrongly to the former Sylvius, according to the cataloguer of these names, Carl-Herman Hjortsjö.

Vesalius' Penance

It was long wondered why Andreas Vesalius set out for Jerusalem. But a letter has been found, written in 1563 by one Herbert Languer. It says that Vesalius had obtained permission to dissect a Spanish nobleman who had died in his care. When he opened the chest, he found that the heart was beating! The parents learned of this, accused him of murder, and even brought in the Inquisition. It is said that the King intervened and had the punishment changed to a journey of penitence to the Holy Land.

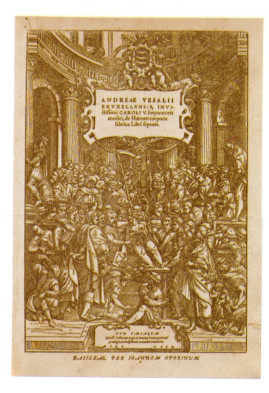

questionnaire asking many medical authorities to list the ten greatest achievements in the field. Nearly all of them included Andreas Vesalius' magnificent textbook of anatomy from 1543. It need hardly be added that this book entirely re-formed surgery. For the first time, a surgeon could know what he was really dealing with.

Vesalius was born in Brussels, on New Year's Eve of 1514, under fortunate astrological circumstances—so good, in fact, that his mother preserved the placenta, which she believed to have magical powers! He first studied at the University of Louvain and learned Hebrew, Arabic, Greek and Latin: the latter was to prove useful in his reading of old medical texts. But his main interest was the human body's structure. He borrowed books by Albertus Magnus and Michael Scatus at the library, yet they did not satisfy him. He wanted to see for himself how it looked.

Moving to Paris, he became a student of Jacob Sylvius, whose fanatical faith in Galen he was one of the first to oppose. Sylvius ended by "playing second fiddle" to Vesalius, hated him throughout life and called him crazy, untruthful, shameless and despicable. He received no more sympathy from the university's other teacher in human anatomy, Gunther of Andernacht, who knew only what could be read in the classics and, according to Vesalius, had never used a knife except at the dinner table. Vesalius, therefore, got little out of Paris. He realized that man was probably built in a different way than people had imagined. Upon his return to Louvain, he started an institute of anatomy, and began his secret dissections on the bodies of newly hanged criminals. Then he introduced the practice of displaying the body's organs in an auditorium when dissecting.

In 1537, Vesalius became a doctor at Padua and was instantly made a professor of anatomy in that university. His continual dissections showed eventually that Galen was quite un-reliable about anatomy. The next years were occupied by work on his monumental study of the subject, *De Humani Corporis Fabrica Libri Septem*. Printed at Basel in 1543, it contained extraordinarily beautiful illustrations by Jan Stephan van Calcar, the favourite disciple of Titian (who himself was long thought to have created them). The book led to a violent academic quarrel between Vesalius and almost the whole medical world, with Sylvius at its head.

Subsequently, Vesalius served as the personal physician of Charles V. Once the emperor retired to a monastery, Vesalius was taken over by Philip II and moved to Madrid. He was only fifty years old when, during a pilgrimage to Jerusalem, he died on the Greek island of Zante (now Zakynthos). But his famous book survived,

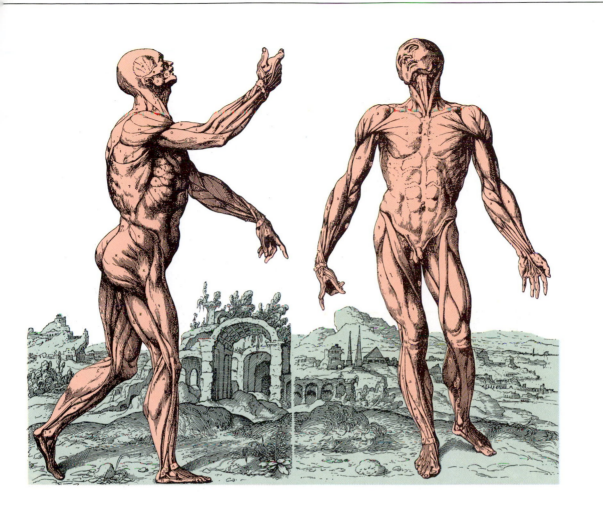

Verdicts on Anatomy

Andreas Vesalius:
Doctors speak of nothing more frequently than the plexus reticularis. *They have never seen one, for it hardly exists in the body—yet they describe one, since it is in Galen. I can hardly believe that I was so stupid as to believe in Galen and the writings of other anatomists.*

Jean Fernel:
Anatomy is for physiology what geography is for the historian: it describes the scene of action.

Inscription on the Theatrum Anatomicum in Paris:
Hic locus est, ubi mors gaudet succurrere vitae. (*Here is the place where death enjoys helping life.*)

Oliver Wendell Holmes:
This, gentlemen, is tuberositas ossis ischii (*a swelling on the seat bone*), *meant for man to sit upon while he gazes at Creation!*

Sir William Osler:
Anatomy brought life and freedom to the medical art. For three centuries the greatest names in medicine were those of anatomists.

Mark Twain:
Surgeons and anatomists never see beautiful women in their whole lives. They see only an awful collection of bones with Latin names and a network of nerves and inflamed tissues…

and is so accurate that it can still be used to teach anatomy. What later specialists have corrected are mostly details.

From barbers to Paracelsus

In England, people never accepted John of Mirfield's claim that surgeons were the equals of doctors. The surgeons' association, founded in the fourteenth century, gradually declined. Doctors of internal medicine, often called "herbalists" because their therapy mainly used healing plants, kept up a conflict with surgeons which culminated a few years after Henry VIII's coronation in 1509. It became a bitter fight about a new regulation on the right to practise medicine professionally. This licence had been given to the Bishop of London or the Dean of Saint Paul's Cathedral! The herbalists won—and partly through their own clumsiness, surgeons sank even lower in status. They had to swallow the insult of being covered by a rule which equated them with bakers, brewers and public notaries.

The internists gained strength by forming an association which eventually became the Royal College of Physicians. Surgeons could do nothing but affiliate themselves with their old adversaries, the barbers. However, this was to prove very advantageous, for the barbers had also played their cards well. In 1540, Parliament approved the Barber-Surgeons' Company, which was to have four masters—two barbers, two surgeons. Among other things, they were supposed to make sure that everybody stuck to his own specialty. The first master surgeon was

(*OPPOSITE*) A sixteenth-century caricature of barber-surgeons at work, combining ordinary haircuts with various medical tasks.
(*Right*) A contemporary portrait of Paracelsus, the great opponent of quack doctors.

FAMOSO·DOCTOR   PARESELSV·

Thomas Vicary, "sergeant-chyrurgeon to King Henry VIII". His practical ability was shown, for example, by his success in curing the king's troublesome leg wound. At the Royal College of Surgeons in London, there is a huge painting by Hans Holbein the Younger, immortalizing Henry's bestowal of the charter for the surgeons' guild upon the kneeling Vicary.

Vicary and his colleague William Clowes did a great deal to improve the reputation of surgery. They lectured, and supervised the training of apprentices—it was usual for a surgeon to study by serving for a few years in the practice of a respected colleague. Vicary and Clowes were naturally anxious to watch out for untrained charlatans, although this was apparently difficult except in counties where a surgeon happened to be the judge! Still, the latter office indicates that surgeons had become so highly esteemed as to be considered for such a post. Thomas Vicary also contributed a book, *Profitable Treatise of the Anatomie of Man's Body*, which was full of mistakes—being based on Galen—but "no worse than others after it", as the historian Graham remarks.

Progress was clearer on the Continent. One of the great medical innovators of all time was Philippus Aureolus Theophrastus Bombastus von Hohenheim (1493–1541). He is also among the most controversial of doctors, and has been portrayed as another ignorant quack. Yet the famous medical historian Henry Sigerist ranked him with the mightiest personalities of the Renaissance, despite some very stiff competition—Henry VIII and Francis I and Charles V, Luther and Zwingli and Calvin, Cosimo de' Medici and Machiavelli and Cesare Borgia, and many artistic geniuses were his contemporaries. In any case, he had no false modesty either: he called himself Paracelsus, meaning the equal of the Roman physician Celsus.

Paracelsus was born at Einsiedeln in Switzerland. We know little about his early education, and it is not certain that he had a right to the doctor's title which he gladly used—no proof has been found that he studied at any university. But he did learn chemistry at the mines in Villach, and in the new laboratories of the Tyrol, where metallurgy was taught. He also spent several years travelling to nearly every country in Europe, including Scandinavia where he probably accompanied the staff of King Christian II at the "Stockholm Bloodbath" in 1520.

A man of boundless curiosity, Paracelsus must have learned more practical medicine from his many conversations with doctors, nurses, pharmacists, monks, bathers and alchemists, than could be got at most universities. With time, his thirst for knowledge became a rootless, almost manic wanderlust, although it may have been

PRACTICAL training of Renaissance physicians in a hospital, including leg amputation, was depicted in a book on surgery by Paracelsus (Frankfurt, 1565).

due to his need of finding work in new places. He could never stay long in the same spot. To be sure, his initial journeying ended at Basel, where he was made professor of medicine, as well as city doctor, in 1527. Yet he began his academic career by declaring war on the old authorities, and burned their works in public! When he went so far as to lecture in German rather than Latin, he was declared unfit for the job, and lost it eighteen months later.

For the rest of his life, Paracelsus was on the move. His only fixed point was Strasbourg where, for a period as short as it was odd, he bought citizenship and joined the local surgeons' guild. Otherwise he lived from hand to mouth, drifting from city to city, working as a doctor— and writing frantically. He never ceased to take the field against whatever he thought foolish and antiquated.

The writings of Paracelsus covered all the medicine of his day. Consistent with his personality, he produced no single great book. His main message was that not even the most respected books should be depended on. A doctor ought to rely on experience and on what nature taught. Strangely enough, his practical medicine often contradicted this view: as the historians Zimmerman and Veith say, "the system he offered was built primarily on chemistry, yet with a liberal dose of cosmology and astrology". Rejecting the doctrine of four humours, he believed in an invisible material called *arcanum* and in a visible material consisting of salt, sulphur and mercury.

His colleagues detested him, no doubt since he spread a low opinion of them:

"They still circle around the medical art as a cat walks around hot porridge... Because I saw that medicine could yield nothing but corpses, death, murder, deformity, decay—and that it lacked any foundation—I was forced to seek the truth in other ways... Not one of you will remain even in the farthest corner where the very dogs are too fine to urinate on you... I tell you, one hair on my neck knows more than all you authors, and my shoe-buckles contain more wisdom than both Galen and Avicenna..."

Worst of all he hated those who robbed their patients with the many panaceas of the age:

"The apothecaries are my enemies since I refuse to empty their jars. My prescriptions are simple and have no need of forty or fifty ingredients. I aim not to make apothecaries rich, but to cure patients."

In one case he found a simple, unmixed remedy which did good, namely the opium extract called laudanum, which he reintroduced as a pain-killing drug.

Paracelsus did his own surgery and was proud of it. He often described himself as "doctor in both arts", meaning medicine and surgery. Yet he probably kept to uncomplicated wounds, as might be guessed from the only one of his books printed during his lifetime: *Grosse Wundarzney*. It was published at Ulm in 1536, and many times afterward. Paracelsus regarded surgery as no less worthy than medicine, and thereby raised the status of his colleagues.

Natural comparisons were the basis of Paracelsus' surgery. When an egg hatches, or an apple skin breaks, the contents rot. For the same reason, air does harm when it reaches tissue

From the Annals of the Barber-Surgeons' Company

The chief of the King's barbers was ordered to be present for the court's Saturday bath, whenever "it pleased the King to wash his head, legs and feet". Nonetheless, members of the guild were expressly forbidden "to shave, wash the beard, or polish any man with any instrument, or to clean anyone's teeth on a Sunday". Other rules forbade any apprentice in surgery to wear a beard, which meant anything that "has grown more than fifteen days".

From the Writings of Paracelsus

Just as God has created all illnesses, he has created a specific remedy for each of them. They exist everywhere in nature, for the whole world is a pharmacy and God is the highest pharmacist.

He who is happy always gets well.

How can one expect to cure ailments in Germany with drugs that God lets grow on the banks of the Nile?

All medicaments are poison and nothing else. Only the right dosage makes them stop being poison.

Knowledge of nature is the precondition for medical science.

Medicine is not just a science, but an art.

A doctor's personality can act more powerfully on a patient than do all the remedies he prescribes.

If a doctor wants to understand the real meaning of health, he has to know that there are more than a hundred, indeed more than a thousand, stomachs. Assemble a thousand people, and every one of them has a digestion unlike anyone else's.

The doctor is only nature's servant, not its overlord.

under the skin. Therefore wounds should be covered as quickly as possible. Oddly, he disdained suture, but he was the first in a long time to agree with Henri de Mondeville that a wound must be kept clean.

The breakthrough of Caesareans

Another great advance had a history that went back long before the Renaissance, and began far from Europe. About 2,500 years ago, in the village of Kapilavastu on the Himalaya slopes, a strange birth took place. Legend tells that a god, disguised as a white elephant, entered the womb of the princess Maya. In due course he emerged as a baby boy, who was named Siddhartha. This was the child destined to receive the honorary title Buddha—the enlightened one. Such a tale is remarkable in itself, but it had more to say about the birth.

According to the text, "when the time came, the future Buddha was born for the world's salvation, out of his mother's right side with no anguish or pain". Susruta, the later commentator, thought that the birth did not sully Buddha with water, blood or mucus. He was not surprised at the unnatural means of birth; no doubt he was quite familiar with the Caesarean section, and took it for granted that the world's saviour had come to life in such a way. Nor should the report that the baby emerged from the mother's right side have surprised him. This technique was, in fact, to be revived in nineteenth-century Germany, although it proved to have no advantage over the method of transverse section over the pubic bone joint.

The Caesarean operation, then, was known to old Hindu surgeons, at least for removing mature foetuses from dead women. Its history is even older than that. We may overlook all the more or less miraculous deliveries in mythology, and not only that of Buddha's mother. The Greeks believed that the goddess Athena—fully equipped with her shield, helmet and spear— sprang from Zeus' head once when it ached and,

to cure it, his brother Hephaistos struck it with an axe. They also told how Dionysos was delivered by Caesarean two months ahead of time, and was incubated in Zeus' thigh until the ninth month. Asklepios, the Greek god of medicine, was cut out of his own mother's dead body after she had fallen victim to a lovers' quarrel on Mount Olympus. We can, however, credit the annals of the early Roman king Numa Pompilius (715-673 BC), who enacted a law that, if a pregnant woman died, the baby was to be removed by incision: *si mater praegnans mortua sit fructus quam primam caute extrahitur.*

If the earliest Caesareans were performed on dead women, could it be that a mature foetus was believed to survive the mother naturally? There are, indeed, descriptions of spontaneous deliveries from dead women, the baby being forced out through the birth canal by gas pressure. The annals of the Spanish Inquisition contain a note on such deliveries. In 1551, a pregnant woman was hanged and, four hours later, her child tumbled down onto the gallows. Some years afterward, a baby's corpse was found in a grave alongside a woman who definitely had been buried there alone. In 1820, the city administration of Cologne ruled that a dead pregnant woman's mouth should be plugged up immediately, to prevent the baby's suffocation—a weird proof of monumental ignorance! As late as the mid-twentieth century, visitors to the city of Queretaro in Mexico could see an entire museum display of women who had become mothers in the adjacent cemetery.

How the name "Caesarean operation" arose has been variously explained. Scipio Africanus (235-183 BC), a famous Roman general, was supposedly born in such a manner. He earned the nickname "Elephant", or caesar in the language of the Carthaginians, after winning a war against their general Hannibal, who had invaded Italy with elephants. The correct term should therefore have been "elephant operation". But scholars deny this romantic interpretation—as well as a derivation from the great Gaius Julius Caesar, whose family name became

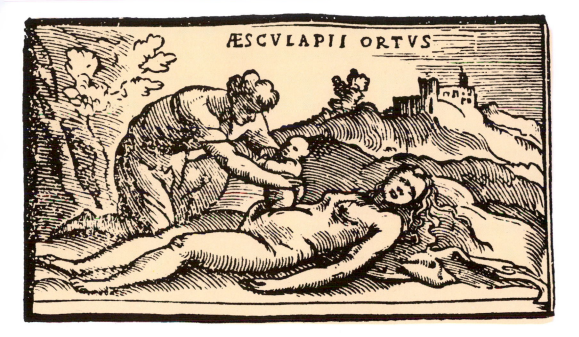

ÆSCVLAPII ORTVS

THE mythical birth of Asklepios—saved by his father, the god Apollo—as shown in a medical book at Basel in 1549.

a title for leaders of state. He was born in the same way, although not from a dead woman, as his mother Aurelia enjoyed a long and luxurious life. At any rate, our linguists have a reasonable explanation. The operation's Latin name, *sectio caesarea*, is just a distortion of the phrase *a matris utero caesus*, meaning "cut from the mother's womb".

Childbirth in antiquity was conducted without any narcosis or other anaesthesia, but these had been thought of. A renowned birth occurred in Persia during the eleventh century, and one of the national epics related how the hero Rustem came into the world:

"King Sal's wife became pregnant, but the child was so big that she could not deliver it and was about to die. Then the Great Spirit came to the king and advised him to give her hyoscyamus. She fell into a numb trance, and they cut open her womb, and freed her from a large strong son, who was named Rustem. Next they sewed up the wound, and the Great Spirit laid his wing over it, and healed it instantly. Something was held to the mother's nose, and it had such a smell that she awoke."

This story is quite credible. Apart from the Great Spirit's role, nothing about it is medically implausible. Hyoscyamus is a herb we call henbane, which stops pain and cramps. But the queen must have been lucky, for the narcosis range—between effectiveness and death—is very narrow with henbane. Smelling salts are also old: the first of them were made from deer-horn salt and ammonia.

The Caesarean section on dead pregnant women was later supported by the Catholic Church's doctrine of preserving life from its very conception, which has continued in the Papal opposition to birth control. Priests were threatened with excommunication if they buried such women before this operation, in which they also had to take part. After the operation, they were rewarded: a Holy Synod in Lyons established a "salary" of forty days' pardon from sins after assisting in the operation. Moreover, the survival rate of babies delivered by Caesarean from dead women was amazingly high. A report in the seventeenth century stated that twenty out of thirty-two were live births.

It was the Renaissance which produced the great reformer of Caesarean sections—a monk from Venice named Scipio Mercurio. Born in Rome in 1540, he studied medicine in Bologna and Padua, where he learned Vesalius' anatomy among other things. His teacher, Arantius, was especially interested in pelvic constriction. To study its variations, both of them dissected the bodies of pregnant women. And, in 1596, a textbook in obstetrics was published in Venice, La Commare o Riccoglitrice, which would last through twenty editions until 1713. Its most famous chapter is about the Caesarean operation, described in detail—from getting four assistants to hold the woman down, to closing the womb and belly-wound with bandages of sour wine, dried roses, balsam and healing herbs.

Yet the first successful, and documented, Caesarean section on a living woman was performed by neither a doctor nor a nurse, but a gelder—a castrater of animals. Around the year 1500, in the German village of Sigershaufen, the wife of Jacob Nufer was having serious difficulty in giving birth. He went to all thirteen midwives in the district, and then to all the available bladder-stone experts, but none could help her. At last the desperate Jacob, who had some idea of sexual anatomy from his own profession, took a knife and cut out the baby. How he sewed up the uterus and abdominal wall is not recorded, but the mother survived and went on to bear her husband several more children by the natural route.

Mortality of the mother in a Caesarean section remained common through the centuries, and people were terrified of it. No such operation was performed between 1787 and 1876 in Paris, according to the city's official history. Elsewhere, one survey by Karl Kayser, a Danish doctor and statistician, showed that 62 % of the women who underwent a Caesarean in 1841 died of bleeding or infection. Even this figure was relatively low. In England, it varied between 86 % and 100 %. There were periods when not a single patient survived in either Paris or Vienna.

The obstetricians tried to avoid going through the abdominal cavity, since most of the deaths involved peritonitis. An alternative was to reach the uterus by cutting through the groin. It was called "Buddha birth", after the Hindu legend. In 1805, a cervical Caesarean section was introduced by a skilful German obstetrician, Friedrich Osiander (1759–1822). This method had already been discussed, but probably never tried, by Robert Wallace in 1769. Here, the uterus is reached through its neck, the cervix, extending into the birth canal.

Finally, in 1828, the English obstetrician and physiologist James Blundell—successful with blood transfusions for women in childbed—suggested that a Caesarean faced less risk, at least from bleeding, if the uterus were removed after taking out the baby. Such a technique was developed by an Italian named Edoardo Porro (1842–1902), but he did not apply it. The first to successfully perform what we now call the Caesarean section, following Porro, was to be Horatio Storer of Boston in 1869.

The Renaissance's greatest surgeon

As we have seen, surgery had a low reputation during the first decades of the sixteenth century. Paracelsus helped it little by championing its equal status with internal medicine. The only practitioners of surgery with some real claim to being educated were the kind of barber-surgeons who had earned official sanction in England. Another category were the travelling characters who gave treatment such as wart-cutting and blood-letting at markets. Interested mainly in money, they had the advantage of being able to get away before any complications set in. This category also included, to a degree, the more or less specialized tooth-extractors, who were accustomed to wielding their skills while on-lookers joked with their unfortunate patients.

The man who was to renew and reform surgery came from the barber-surgeons' ranks. Ambroise Paré, born in 1510 at Laval in northern France, would live to be eighty. This is all the more amazing because he was a personal physician to

five French kings, in an age when each king's courtiers were normally purged by the next, and when horrors such as Saint Bartholomew's Night and the Huguenot Wars took place. But Paré was considered much too valuable. It is said that the king himself once hid Paré in his own bed!

Paré began as a journeyman with a barber-

Leaders and Caesarians

Many important people have been born by Caesarian. This was a tradition for rulers of the old kingdom of Navarre in northern Spain. Their princesses must have needed a good deal of courage to play such a part willingly. However, the custom might have been viewed as a method of selecting women from whom bravery and tenacity could be inherited.

The great Genoese admiral Andrea Doria was born in the same way, as was the Scottish national hero Robert Bruce. In the latter's country, too, according to Shakespeare in Macbeth, *the usurper of the throne had no need to fear anyone born of woman—and his enemy proved to be Macduff, who was not born naturally but cut prematurely from the womb.*

When Henry VIII's third wife, Jane Seymour, approached her time, the king is said to have told her doctors that the child should be saved at all costs. An heir was absolutely essential, whereas wives could always be replaced—as he so often demonstrated. This is supposedly why Edward VI was born by Caesarian. His mother was, in fact, already ill and died just after the delivery. In this case, a Caesarian would presumably be justified even today. But it is not certain how the operation was performed, and some think that the whole story was falsified in order to discredit Henry.

Remarkable Caesarians

In 1784 the Edinburgh obstetrician John Aitkin advanced a peculiar theory. He believed that fresh air must be very harmful to the abdominal organs, so it was essential to avoid letting air into the abdominal cavity during a Caesarian operation. His clever idea was to keep the patient in a bathtub and do the operation under water...

A year later, in the London Medical Journal, *one Doctor Cowley described how he had seen a negress cut open her own belly with a long sharp knife, produce a child, and be sewn up by a veterinarian. She lived happily ever after.*

There are many examples of pregnant women gored by bulls and cows which split their bellies open. Often both the mother and child survived this "accidental" Caesarian.

Perhaps the most wondrous instance of what might be called a Caesarian is a soldier's wife who followed him into the field. She was fetching water in a river when a cannonball literally divided her in two, and a baby fell out into the water. It was salvaged by some troopers—who had to become nursemaids in a hurry—and survived.

AMBROISE Paré at age 72.

keeping the surgeons busy. At that time I was quite inexperienced and had never seen shot wounds treated. Certainly I had read in Jean de Vigo's general work on wounds that the properties of gunpowder made shot wounds poisonous, and that they should be treated with seething elder-oil and a little theriaca (an antidote).

"To avoid doing anything crazy, and knowing that this treatment would be very painful to the victims, I decided to wait until I had seen what the other surgeons did. They actually made the oil as hot as possible and dabbed it on the wound. I then took heart and did the same. But my oil ran out and I had to apply a healing salve made of eggwhite, rose-oil and turpentine.

"The next night I slept badly, plagued by the thought that I would find the men dead whose wounds I had failed to burn, so I got up early to visit them. To my great surprise, those treated with salve felt little pain, showed no inflammation or swelling, and had passed the night rather calmly—while the ones on whom seething oil had been used lay in high fever with aches, swelling and inflammation around the wound.

"At this, I resolved never again to cruelly burn poor people who had suffered shot wounds."

The background was that all authorities of the age considered shot wounds poisonous, and had no other means of saving the patients than to burn them with boiling oil. It was due to his observational ability, as well as because his oil happened to run out, that Paré discovered the oil treatment to be not only needless but directly injurious.

In 1541, Paré passed his examination and joined the college of barber-surgeons. He also married. Sylvius urged him to write a dissertation on shot wounds, and it became a classic when printed in 1545. Besides reporting his findings on wound treatment, Paré presented new methods of locating the shot that remained

surgeon, and took lessons for some years at the Hôtel-Dieu hospital in Paris. There, he was able not only to see many living patients, but also to take part in dissections—which did not usually belong to the education of the nonacademic surgeons. After that, he joined the army as what would best be called a sort of field-surgeon. His whole life was to swing between military surgery and civilian practice in Paris, where he attained a lofty position with the titles of "First Surgeon" and "Councillor of the King".

His field campaigns started at the age of 26, when French troops marched into the Cisalpine plain of northern Italy. This war inspired Paré's first great contribution, which he dramatically described:

"When the castle's garrison saw our men rush forward in a rage, they did all they could to defend themselves. Thus many of our soldiers were killed and wounded by lance and shot,

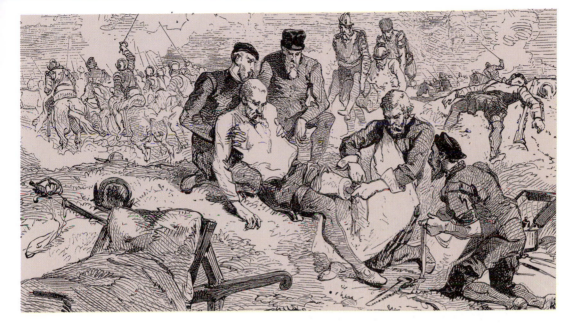

PARÉ applies his ligature on the battlefield:
a nineteenth-century picture.

in a wound. They were based on logical and intelligent interpretation of the signs of the shot's direction of entry.

Paré returned in 1549 from his second field campaign, and began his second book. It dealt mainly with anatomy, building on Vesalius, whom he deeply revered. But it also contained some sections on obstetrics, in which he revived the forgotten technique of "turning the foot" of a foetus in the transverse position, once described by Soranus of Ephesus.

Paré's reputation was now so great that he was made a member of the respected College of Saint Côme. This was something exceptional for a surgeon who had no formal education. Moreover, the college was so extravagant as to exempt him from the rather high membership fee. Paré gave his inaugural lecture in French, instead of the usual Latin, and was duly mocked by the envious. Yet Paré was no stranger to Latin. His close reading of Vesalius was documented in a larger edition of his anatomy

book, elaborated for surgeons: *Anatomie Universelle du Corps Humain*, published in 1561. It had the enormous significance of making Vesalius well-known among surgeons.

Many other areas were enriched by Paré. He reintroduced ligature of bleeding vessels, as a

From the Writings of Ambroise Paré

I bandaged him, but God cured him.

It is better to prescribe a dubious drug than to leave the patient without help.

You say that tying up the blood vessels after an amputation is a new method, and should therefore not be used. That is a bad argument for a doctor.

Always give the patient hope, even when death is near.

(To a quack:) Dare you teach me surgery? You haven't even finished your studies! Surgery is learned by eye and hand. You, little master, know only how it feels to sleep in a chair!

ILLUSTRATIONS from Paré's writings on surgery: techniques for bladder-stone operation, artificial limbs, and suturing a facial wound.

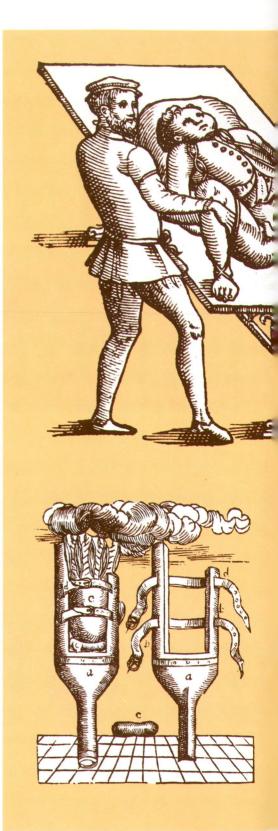

routine method in wound treatment and for amputations. This was a result of his opposition to the cauterizing-iron, until then almost the sole means of stopping blood. He also invented new surgical instruments, designed prostheses for limbs—and a loose nose—and he improved the hernia band, which had never been of much use before.

At the same time, Paré waged war against obsolete methods. He seems to have taken extreme pleasure in condemning the "hobby-horses" of academic doctors, such as mummy-powder and pulverized unicorn-horn. Similarly, he devoted a separate chapter to bezoar stones. These concretions, found for example inside cows' stomachs or goats' gall bladders, were very dear and were believed to have magic medical effects. King Charles IX, the proud owner of one, naturally became angry when Paré called it worthless. So an experiment was set up. A cook, who had stolen two silver plates from his master and was condemned to be strangled in public, received the choice of swallowing a poison along with a bezoar stone, which was thought to be the perfect antidote. It took the poor fellow seven hours to die... The only thing that King Charles reputedly learned from the experiment was that this particular bezoar was a forgery!

Paré's *magnum opus* was published in 1585, when he was aged seventy-five. The *Oeuvres* (Works) were written in French. Once again, this was found shocking by the medical faculty in Paris, true to its habit of small-mindedness. It cited an old law that no medical works could be published without its permission. Paré wrote a denial of the faculty's authority, declaring surgery independent of official whims. As his biographer Janet Doe says:

"In this *apologia pro vita sua*, he depicted arguments, history, and his own methods in con-

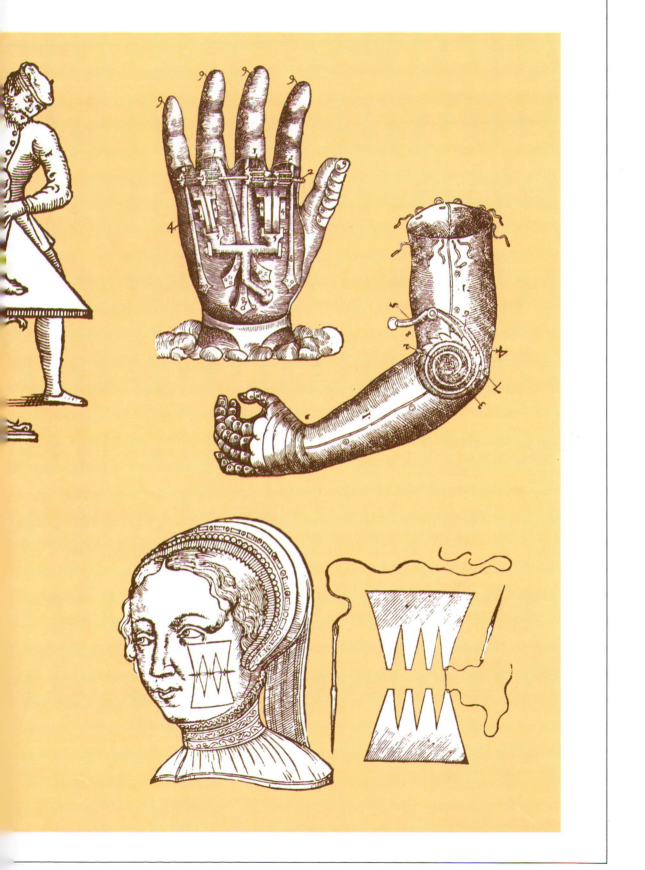

trast to those of his opponents; he described his life with insight, modesty and simplicity—the self-portrait of a master."

Paré exercised vast influence through his personality and writings. His integrity, judgement, technical skill and moral courage made him one of the outstanding surgeons of all times.

The specialists of Italy and Germany

The fifteenth century provided many opportunities for plastic surgery of the face. Among the commonest reasons was congenital syphilis, which causes, for example, a typical and ugly "saddle nose". Further cases of facial repair came from the many local wars in Italy, and the still more numerous duels between hot-tempered noblemen.

As early as the fifteenth century, the unusual specialty of repairing noses and ears was practised by two members of the Branca family at Catania in Sicily. We do not know if they were inspired by the old Hindu "rhinoplasty", but this is hardly likely, since their technique was quite different. It was probably the son, Antonio Branca, who developed the method of skin pedicles from the arm to the head, which became the hallmark of Italian plastic surgery during the sixteenth century.

Branca's operational methods were inherited by other families—Norcini, Pavoni, Vianeo. The last of these provided the training for the "father of plastic surgery", Gasparo Tagliacozzi (1546–99). He eventually became professor of medicine and anatomy at Bologna, where his statue can still be seen, holding a nose in his hand! It is said that he once had more than forty patients lying in his hospital for nose repair.

In 1597, Tagliacozzi published *De Chirurgia Curtorum Per Insitionem* in two volumes. His treatment of nose defects was usually done in six sessions over two months. The method was the same as Branca's: a skin pedicle from the inner upper arm was swung up and fixed to the nose. The arm was tied, by an ingenious leather band,

TAGLIACOZZI'S representation in 1597 of the nose operation which we often call "Italian" or "tagliacotian" rhinoplasty.

with the hand to the top of the head. Tagliacozzi also developed a technique for restoring a defective outer ear, taking the necessary skin from behind it.

This surgeon became famous all over Europe, and his clinic drew patients from near and far. Indeed, he had the honour of being mentioned in the world's first "humour magazine", *Hudibras*, published by the mischievous Samuel Butler. Worse, however, was that the bigots of the Church regarded any improvement in man's appearance as a blasphemy against the Creator. These antiprogressives persecuted Tagliacozzi even after his death. He was originally buried in the cloister of St. John the Baptist in Bologna, but his adversaries managed to convince the nuns that he was haunting the place, and his body was reinterred in unconsecrated ground.

Tagliacozzi's work was continued by his disciple Cortesi in Bologna. For some reason, plastic surgery declined. Neither in Italy nor in the rest of Europe do we hear of any reconstructive surgery for the next couple of centuries. In France, nose plastics were actually forbidden.

In central Europe, academic education had remained poor during late medieval times, while one university after the other was blossoming in Italy, France and England. Before 1400, there were only the Charles University in Prague, the University of Vienna, and the Rupprecht-Karl University in Heidelberg. None of them did any medical research. As a whole, German medicine and surgery lay in a backwater. Time would be needed to bring home the rebirth of such arts from abroad. And in the case of surgery, one reason for this is clear: the German surgeons belonged, more than elsewhere, to a genuine handicraft tradition. It was thought no more suitable for a surgeon to study books than for a carpenter or tinker.

Yet these craftsmen were no mean surgeons. They were even noticeably better at one thing than their learned foreign colleagues—taking care of wounds. For they, too, had a rich supply in the constant wars between small states. In keeping with German logic and orderliness, their empiricism developed into the best battle surgery of the age. It also characterized the oldest German surgical literature. This consisted almost exclusively of little books in the native language, resembling handbooks for field-surgeons. Words like *Wundarzney*, suiting a wound-doctor's manual, occurred in nearly all such books' titles at the time, as already illustrated by Paracelsus.

The oldest of these spokesmen for battle surgery was Heinrich von Pfolspeundt, whose *Buch der Bundth-Ertznei* appeared in 1460. Its title meant something like "wound-bandaging", but it covered much more than that. Heinrich wrote

that he had learned the profession from "German and Italian masters" (typically using guild terminology!) and had gained experience in many wars as a member of the German Order during its campaigns in Poland. His book is most notable for its insistence on cleanliness: hand-washing and clean bandages were, for him, as important as the Pater Nosters and Ave Marias which were chanted at the beginning of treatment to promote healing. He was well ahead of the majority of his colleagues abroad, who still practised the doctrine of *pus bonum*.

Heinrich lived before Tagliacozzi, but he must have learned plastic surgery from his Italian master, who presumably studied with the Branca family. Even the latter's secrecy with their art was inherited by their apprentices two or three generations later:

> "How to make a new nose for someone if it has been lopped off and the dogs have eaten it: This calls for a masterwork. If anyone comes to you with a cut-off nose, let nobody watch, and make him swear to tell nobody how you cured him. Then give him your estimate. If he wants to risk the treatment and can stand the pain, tell him how you will go about it with a knife and bandage, and how long he

---

Surgeons and Wicked Women

According to Heinrich von Pfolspeundt, "the surgeon should make sure that he is not drunk when treating his patients. For otherwise he may neglect them, and will be guilty and punished by God. If he has eaten onions or beans, or spent the previous night with an impure lady, he should be careful not to breathe on any wounds... A wound should be bound with clean white bandages, else there may be harmful effects. He should wash his hands before treating anyone."

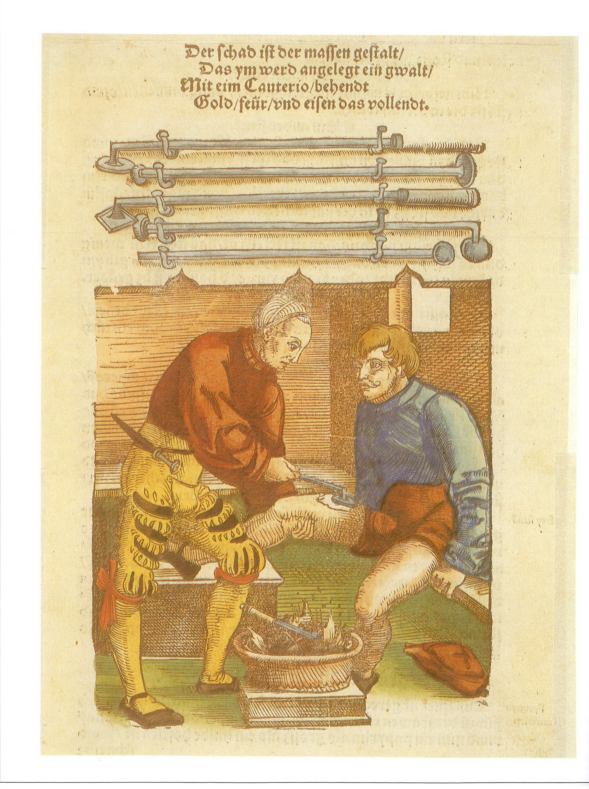

Der schad ist der massen gestalt/
Das ym werd angelegt ein gwalt/
Mit eim Cauterio/behendt
Gold/feür/vnd eisen das vollendt.

CAUTERIZING-IRONS and their use on a wound, according to an early sixteenth-century German woodcut, which appeared in Gersdorff's fieldbook on surgery.

must lie… and the room he lies in must be locked so that only you and your assistant can enter…"

Heinrich proceeds to give a clear, detailed description of the same technique which Tagliacozzi used. He says: "it unquestionably works, it has been proven." He also lists instructions for operating on a hare-lip.

About a generation after Heinrich came a more literate man, Hieronymus Brunschwig. He claimed to have read 3,000 books, which may be doubted since the art of printing books was not many decades old. Yet his *Handbuch von Wundarznei* built upon personal experience as well. Moreover, its wealth of beautiful illustrations helped to portray not only surgery, but also other aspects of society, in the late fifteenth century: it provides, for example, a good view of clothing and living conditions, furniture and household equipment. The book dealt mainly with wound treatment and is not very remarkable in surgical terms. However, it had one distinction—being the first to discuss treatment of shot wounds from firearms. Already here we meet the idea that such wounds were poisoned by gunpowder.

The most famous of all the early German manuals was *Feldbuch der Wundarzney*, a title showing directly that it was written for field-surgeons. Its author, Hans von Gersdorff, is as obscure as his two predecessors; we do not know when he lived, but the book appeared in 1517, placing him in the same generation as Brunschwig. It, too, contained exquisite engravings which offered side-glances at cultural history. Gersdorff's overriding interest was in surgical instruments, and he put a lot into developing new ones. Some of them were rather monstrous. His apparatus for lifting up impressed bone frag-

ments is reminiscent of "art for art's sake"— the same result presumably could have been achieved with simple elevators.

Still, Gersdorff surely did much good. Among other things, he performed at least two hundred amputations and was an authority on the subject. Here he made two improvements: giving the patient opium before the operation, and stopping the bleeding by enclosing the stump in a pressure bandage which he made from an ox bladder. Nor did he underestimate his own ability. At more than one place in the book, we find advertisement verses such as this:

"When I've been hit in hip or thigh
and wounded so that death is nigh
I hope that God will stand by me
and grant me Gersdorff's surgery."

In the same category of surgical books we may count *Armamentarium Chirurgicum*, by Johann Scultetus. Actually named Schultes, he was born in 1595, studied medicine in Padua— under, among others, Fabricius ab Aquapendente—and graduated in 1621. Gaining experience in the Thirty Years' War, he became the city physician of his birthplace Ulm, and died in 1645. A nephew later published the book, which was his only important contribution to medicine.

Scultetus presented many illustrations of the accepted techniques for various kinds of operation and bandaging. He did not have very many new ideas of his own, but he seems to have been the first to use the abdominal bandage which we often call the "Finnish roller"—a rectangular piece of linen with several broad flaps along its short sides. This type of bandaging cloth is superb as a support for the abdomen after operations, since it covers the wound while also, due to its steadiness, easing both the pain and the patient's breathing. Even so, it is only a small symbol of the manifold legacy which, as we have seen, the Renaissance began to create for modern surgery.

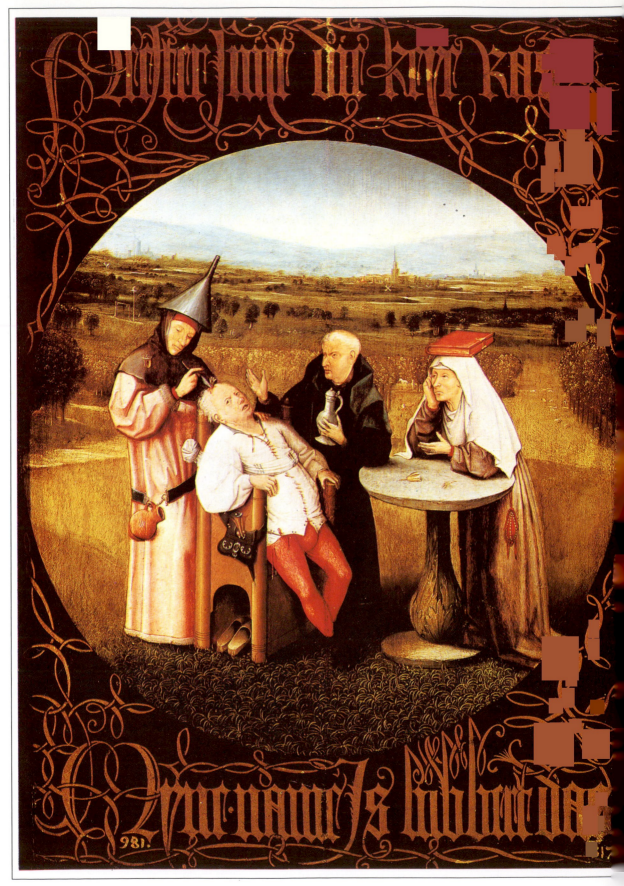

981.

Medicine becomes a science

Medical knowledge was being stimulated enormously by Andreas Vesalius' description of the true structure of the human body. Now the secrets of anatomy began to be revealed in ever greater detail. With this growing awareness of how the organs are formed and interconnected came, too, a heightened interest in their functions. Physiology, which had slept almost undisturbed since the days of Herophilos and Erasistratos, awakened to new life. The "theoretical" disciplines naturally acquired deep importance for both internal medicine and surgery, as we are about to see.

The circulation of blood

Vesalius' successor at Padua, Realdo Colombo (1516–59), besides teaching some anatomy to Michelangelo, amplified his studies in the subject with vivisection of dogs. In a book, *De Re Anatomica*, he presented the theory that blood was oxygenated in the lungs, and showed that there were no openings in the heart's dividing wall between its auricles and ventricles—contrary to what Galen had claimed. With this advance, it could not be long before blood circulation was finally understood.

HIERONYMUS Bosch's late fifteenth-century painting of the "cure of folly", a popular operation on supposed stones in the head to prevent madness, was a reminder of the persistent opposition to medical progress in many parts of Europe.

Colombo was not the first to get on the right track. Worth remembering is a Spanish priest and doctor, Miguel Serveto (1511–53), called Michael Servetus. He had to flee his country because of theological conflicts, and found shelter as a secretary of the archbishop of Vienna, where he completed his book *Christianismi Restitutio*. Discussing the doctrine of the Holy Trinity, he felt obliged to consider blood as the soul of the flesh (*anima ipsa est sanguis*). In one section, he wondered whether the blood was transferred from the lung artery to lung veins, during a passage through the lungs "while it is worked upon and keeps a light red colour". There is little chance that Colombo read this volume, which was otherwise purely religious. But the priests read it all the more eagerly, indignant over its heretical theology. They burned Serveto at the stake in Geneva, using very green wood to prolong his pain!

Another occupant of Padua's famous professorial chair in anatomy was Gerolamo Fabricio (1537–1619), better known as Fabricius ab Aquapendente. His main discovery was that of valves in the veins, which allow blood to flow centrally even from parts of the body below the heart. This was to directly inspire his student, William Harvey, to solve the problem of blood circulation. Fabricius was also a significant comparative anatomist: for example, a part of the cloacal wall in poultry is still termed the *bursa Fabricii*.

Italy had no shortage of great anatomists at that time. The name of Gabriello Falloppio (1523–62) is associated, among other things,

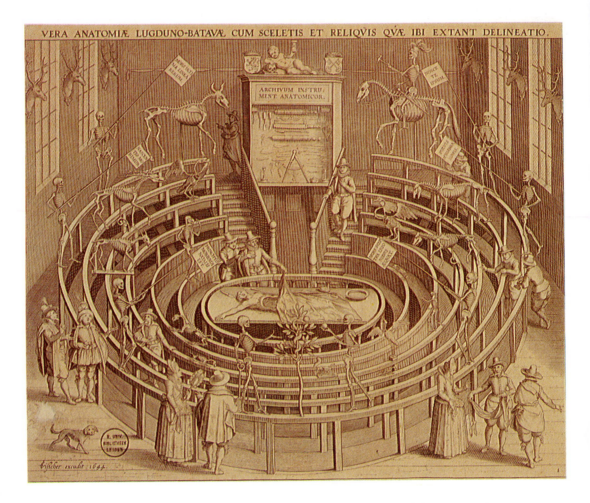

VERA ANATOMIÆ LUGDUNO-BATAVÆ CUM SCELETIS ET RELIQVIS QVÆ IBI EXTANT DELINEATIO.

with the female Fallopian tubes. Several ana-tomical parts are named after Bartolommeo Eustachio (1524–74), who rediscovered what is now called the Eustachian tube—two thousand years after it was described by Alkmaion, also in Italy (see Chapter 2)! Leonardo Botallo (1530–1600) is commemorated by the *ductus Botalli* between the aorta and the pulmonary artery of a baby, which normally closes once the lungs are in use. This little passage was to acquire a special place in the history of surgery four centuries later. It was with a successful operation on an open *ductus Botalli* that Robert Gross of Boston, in 1939, inaugurated the surgery of congenital heart defects.

THE famous anatomical theatre at Leyden University in the early seventeenth century, when even "high society" attended lectures about the structure of human beings—and evidently of animals too.

Botallo played, in addition, an active role in the contemporary controversies about surgery. He was, to be sure, an eager advocate of blood-letting, which could hardly have helped, for instance, in the healing of shot wounds. Yet during the so-called "gunpowder feud", he strongly rejected the theory that gunshot wounds must be poisoned. This theory was later put to rest by his pupil Bartolommeo Maggi

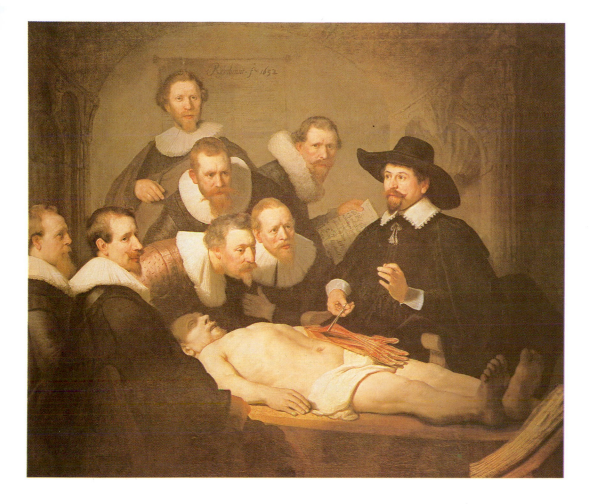

NICOLAUS Tulp, the learned demonstrator in Rembrandt's well-known picture (1632), was a leading physician and anatomist—as well as medical author and, eventually, city mayor—in Amsterdam.

(1516–52). Fortunately, these men's ideas are better known than their dates—one of which must be wrong. Some researchers even believe that 1530 was Botallo's graduation year, as if he were nearly a hundred years old when he died.

Of the earlier anatomists outside Italy, perhaps most prominent was Pieter Paauw (1564–1617) of Leyden. Rather than making original discoveries in medicine, he founded the city's anatomical theatre, as well as its famous botanical garden where, over a century later, Carl Linnaeus was to describe the classification of plants. This marked the beginning of Leyden's renown as a centre of medical education, in many periods the greatest in Europe. Among Paauw's pupils was Nicolaus Tulp (1593–1674), the subject of an immortal painting by Rembrandt, "Doctor Tulp's Anatomy Lesson". Interestingly, this scene portrayed the correct position of the hand in reaction to the nerve being demonstrated—Rembrandt was very fussy about details!

It was in England, however, that blood circulation met a real master in William Harvey

(1578–1657). One of many sons in a prominent merchant's family of Folkstone, he received the best possible education at Canterbury and Cambridge, becoming a Bachelor of Arts at the age of nineteen. Soon he went to Padua and, as we have seen, he studied under Fabricius who was then at the height of his glory. In 1602, Harvey became a doctor of medicine in Padua as well as in Cambridge.

Harvey's clinical arena was to be St. Bartholomew's Hospital in London, where he worked from 1609 to 1643—while Royalists were being purged *en masse* in the political sphere. At the same time he gave anatomical demonstrations and lectures at the Medical Society's new house in Paternoster Row. The first sign of his relative-

WILLIAM Harvey, whose experiments concerned blood circulation and reproduction in animals such as deer, was shown explaining them to King Charles I in this painting by Robert Hannah, about 1640.

ly heretical ideas about blood circulation came in 1616. To paraphrase:

"It is clear from the heart's structure that the blood passes continually through the lungs to the aorta, just as if it were driven by two water-pumps. By applying a ligature, we can show that the direction of blood flow is from the arteries to the veins. Therefore, the blood must move in a constant circle and is driven by the heart's power. The question is whether this is for the purpose of nourishment, or of preserving the blood and limbs by transporting heat, so that the blood which is cooled in the extremities is warmed up again in the heart."

These thoughts were developed by 1628, when one of the most important books in world medicine appeared: *Exercitatio Anatomica de Motu Cordis et Sanguinis in Animalibus* ("An Anatomical Treatise on Heart and Blood Movement in Animals"). The reason for this delay in publication was presumably Harvey's fear of revealing his shocking ideas. Significantly, he had his book printed not in England but at an obscure press in Germany, which used poor paper and made countless errors. Harvey immediately witnessed the impact—his practice declined "and people maintained that he was out of his mind".

Harvey's book describes ingeniously simple experiments and the conclusions that can be drawn from them. If an extremity is tied off, one finds an enlargement of the arteries above that point, and of the veins below it. This is enough to prove that the arteries lead blood outward from the heart, and the veins inward. Even more simply, he had a strong man, with clearly visible veins, embrace a cylinder. It was then easy to observe how the blood runs between the valves in the veins toward the heart. His summary of such tests and results shifted the very foundations of medicine:

"Since everything, both arguments and what can be seen with the naked eye, shows that the blood passes through the heart and lungs by means of the heart's force and is sent out to all parts of the body where it enters the veins and the pores of the flesh, and then goes from smaller veins to larger ones, and from them to the great *venae cavae* and the right auricle—and in such a quantity, in arteries as well as veins, that it cannot be supplied by the body's intake, and is more abundant than what is

Harvey Looks Back

When I took up vivisection as a way of studying the heart's movements and purpose, and tried to unravel these by simple inspection, not through what others had written, I found the task so full of toils and difficulties that I was almost tempted to think like Fracastorius: that the heart's movements could be understood only by God.

A Contemporary Portrait of Harvey

According to John Aubrey, a famous gossip and antiquary, Harvey was "very choleric, like all his brothers. In his younger days, he always carried a dagger, and was inclined to draw it at the slightest provocation.

"He was not tall, but rather short with a round face and olive-coloured skin; small eyes, round and black, full of life; and his hair was black as a raven, but turned totally white twenty years before he died.

"I have heard him say that, when his book on blood circulation came out, his practice suffered and people called him mad, and all doctors opposed his views and envied him, and many wrote against him, such as Doctor Primige and Doctor Paracisanus. But finally, after some twenty to thirty years, his work was recognized by the world's universities and, as Hobbes says in De Corpore, he is perhaps the only man who has seen his doctrine accepted during his lifetime."

I See It, But Don't Believe It!

Harvey demonstrated blood circulation for his colleague Caspar Hofmann in Altdorf, the Swiss town where William Tell is said to have shot the apple off his son's head. The doctor's comment, of course, was: Video, sed non credo!

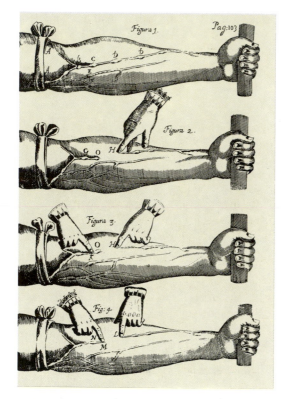

HARVEY'S ingenious observations and reasoning about the direction of blood flow were described with illustrations like this in his book of 1628.

needed for sustenance—the conclusion is absolutely unavoidable that the blood in an animal flows circularly in constant motion."

This long sentence is actually much longer in the original. All that was required to establish the circular flow beyond doubt was to explain how the blood got from the arteries to the veins. This triumph was reserved not for Harvey, but for Marcello Malpighi (1628–94) who described the capillaries and published their discovery in *De Pulmonis Observationis* (1661).

William Harvey was the physician at the courts of both James I and Charles I. Highly esteemed for his cleverness, he was also Charles' personal friend and hunting partner. When this

king fell, Harvey did too, withdrawing into seclusion under the Protectorate. But he was still honoured by the Puritans, serving as Rector of Merton College in Oxford and as President of the Royal College of Physicians. His contribution was summed up by another leader in medicine, Sir William Osler:

"It marks the transition from old tradition to modern thought. We are no longer satisfied with bare observations. Here, for the first time, is an experimental solution of physiological problems, carried out by a man who could evaluate his findings without overvaluing them and had the ability to let his conclusions follow naturally from the results. An age of audiences, who merely listened with attention, turned into an age of the eye, in which people were only satisfied with what they could see. But now came the age of the hand—the thinking, advising, planning hand that is the tool of the brain. And this age was introduced by a modest monograph of seventy-two pages, *which lays the basis for all experimental medicine!*"

The new English school

While royal favour shone upon the Barber-Surgeons' Company, the surgeon's social status rose, although hardly as high as that of his internist colleagues. Simultaneously, he became ever more skilful. The path had been paved by Thomas Vicary, who died at the pinnacle of Henry VIII's power. There followed a long line of well-read, inventive and technically superb practitioners.

William Clowes (1540–1604), one of the personal physicians to Queen Elizabeth I, was the greatest surgeon in Elizabethan England. He acquired his training in Leicester's army in Holland, was with Warwick at Le Havre, then joined the navy and served as a ship's doctor against the "Invincible Armada". Clowes took part in the debate about gunpowder as a poison. He did not think that a shot wound was necessarily poisoned, but noted that nothing ruled out poison being smeared on a bullet before it was fired. The soldiers readily believed this, since shot wounds were commonly followed by infection. It violated a "gentleman's agreement", and more than one innocent prisoner of war was executed for having poisoned ammunition!

Clowes worked at St. Bartholomew's which, among other things, had become a hospital for treatment of syphilis, a disease that was raging like fire across London. He wrote a little book about it, but far more important was his *Prooved Practice for all Young Chirurgians*, a collection of examples from his own experience. One case illustrates his diagnostic cunning. A soldier had received a bullet, not yet located, in the muscles near the hip. Around the bullet, an abscess formed and was emptying through a long fistula. Clowes fed a tube through the fistula passage, and poured silver and alum into it, which he knew would cause irritation. After a day, the patient complained of pain. Clowes could feel a swelling—the abscess had come to life. He cut into the swelling, found the bullet and drained the pus cavity, so that the fistula soon healed.

Vicary had given lectures at the barber-surgeons' guild house every Tuesday; Clowes did the same. Subsequently, the tradition was continued by Alexander Read, another very adept surgeon. Read described different ways of closing a wound—he discussed, for instance, "consecutive" and "separate" suture techniques. He also discovered a new method which is reminiscent of the recently introduced "wire stitcher" and "surgical tape". A further example of his shrewdness was the "hidden ring-knife". He built a spring-loaded knife that was mounted in a ring, small enough to be hidden in the palm of a hand. When he palpated a boil or abscess, he suddenly sprang the knife open and cut it, without the patient even having seen the instrument.

Read was not only involved in clinical practice. He had a passion for experiments, and was the first to show that the spleen was unnecessary for survival, contrary to previous opinion. Drawing out the spleen through a small hole, he tied off its blood vessels, and observed it to wither and die—yet the dog in question continued to live happily. Probably ignorant of his work,

A Case of Correct Maltreatment

Mary Stuart, Queen of Scots (1542-87), had stomach trouble even in her youth. As the dauphine of France, she was reported by the Cardinal of Lothringen to have "a fitful appetite and her stomach was often out of order". Clearer signs that she had a stomach ulcer emerged when she was refused safe-conduct to return to Scotland. The disease recurred with typical stubbornness at times of sadness and stress—in connection with a suicide attempt at Perth in 1561, her marriages to Darnley and Bothwell, the murder of her secretary Rizzio and of Darnley, her imprisonment in Lochleven Castle, her escape to England, and repeatedly during her imprisonment there.

This was no simple stomach ulcer. Mary vomited blood on several occasions, and at least twice her life was in danger. The worst bleeding occurred at Jedburgh when she visited Bothwell. The description of her condition is typical of a bled-out stomach-ulcer patient in a state of shock. Fortunately the only doctor available, a certain Arnault, was not familiar with the age's fashion of bloodletting. If he had been, it would probably have resulted in therapeutic murder.

On the contrary, Arnault did the best possible thing in the absence of blood or fluid transfusions. He tied off her extremities with bandages, to decrease peripheral blood circulation and maximize flow to the heart and brain, while adding liquid by forcing her to drink wine. After a month's illness, Mary was able to travel.

Marcello Malpighi repeated the experiment about a century later with the same result. In this case the dog, after the operation, was said to have become more gluttonous as well as lazier. But these effects have never since been confirmed in splenectomied animals or humans.

Better known than Read was his contemporary John Woodall (1556–1643) who consummated the fine surgical traditions at St. Bartholomew's. Once a surgeon of the East India Company, he must have distinguished himself greatly from the average merchant-ship doctors, whose jobs were often the last resort for alcoholic or otherwise incapable physicians. Woodall felt a responsibility for the pitiful medical care on board, and wrote the first handbook for ship doctors, *The Surgeon's Mate*. Two hundred years later, James Lind devised what is usually called the first effective prophylaxis for scurvy. Yet the benefits of juice from green lemons had been mentioned in Woodall's book, and he in turn referred to findings from the 1590s in the Dutch and English fleets. The British name "Limeys" for naval seamen is due to the practice of drinking juice from limes every day on long voyages.

Woodall himself was restrictive with amputations, but he showed that such an operation could be made through the ankle. This had been suggested by his years as a ship's doctor in India, where he saw how the country's criminals, punished by losing a foot, dragged themselves about with a clumsy basket-like prosthesis. This was the second time in the history of surgery that inspiration had been supplied by the rigorous Hindu criminal code. The first had resulted in Susruta's nose plastics.

The finest of British seventeenth-century surgeons was Richard Wiseman (1625–86), known as "the father of English surgery". An incurable royalist, he took part as a doctor in the civil war, followed Charles II into Dutch exile, and returned with the loyal troops during the unlucky campaign that ended at Worcester, where he was captured and put in the Tower of London. In spite of that, he was allowed to prac-

RICHARD Wiseman, the "father of English surgery".

tise medicine at the next best prison, Old Bailey! Nor was he slow to use this freedom for entering a royalist conspiracy. He then had to flee the country, and made his living for three years as a ship's doctor in the Spanish fleet. At the time of the Restoration, he was rewarded by his grateful king and rose to high honour.

Wiseman was a systematic man. He made fluent notes on his more remarkable cases, and had over six hundred of them to analyze when he settled down. Assiduously searching for common factors which yielded success or failure, he represented one of the first truly clinical researchers. His book *Several Chirurgical Treatises* appeared in numerous editions and gained wide use. Many novelties could be found here, such as the brain's own insensibility to pain, the description of "white swellings"—an abscess typical of tuberculosis—and an investigation of the scrofula, or swollen neck glands, which we know are also due to tuberculosis. It was the latter disease that people called "the King's Evil" and, oddly enough, the otherwise rational Wiseman upheld their belief in the king's touch as a cure.

As late as Wiseman's day, the idea of poisoning by gunshot wounds was still around. Ambroise Paré suggested that such wounds be bandaged with raw onions, of whose good effects he was convinced. William Clowes agreed, extending the use of onions to burns, which he treated with a mixture of four ounces of raw onion juice and half an ounce of salt. It must have stung, but results were not bad: the patient healed "without blemish or sign of scars". Wise-

man praised the value of raw onions in wound treatment, and commented on it in his *Appendix to the Treatise of Gunshot Wounds*, specially intended for ship's doctors "who seldom burden their cabin with many books". He was, however, careful to point out that the onion-salt mixture should be applied before burn blisters were formed, and absolutely not after they had broken and the skin cover was lost: "for so you will exasperate the Pain, and increase the Inflammation". The reason for his concern with blisters was that he preferred to treat not only gunshot wounds, but also burns, with heating salves or the cauterizing-iron—as if fire had to be fought with fire!

A Less Fortunate Aneurysm

Peter Lowe (1550-1612), personal physician to King James VI in Scotland, and founder of the medical and surgical faculty at Glasgow, spent thirty years as a surgeon on European battlefields. His book The Whole Art of Chyrurgery *was a fine contribution to the art, and made surgery scientific in Scotland where, until then, it had rested entirely in the hands of bunglers. He gave a drastic picture of what can happen when a patient receives ignorant care:*

"I remember from Paris in 1590 when a famous captain (my good friend Jayle, one of the highest chiefs in the Spanish Regiment) suffered an aneurysm… As the oldest surgeon in the regiment, I was sent for, and found it to be an aneurysm which should not be disturbed. My good friend Andrew Scot, who at the time had a large practice in Paris and was very clever at surgery, considered the same. We prescribed remedies against its growth, and sent to the apothecary. But he had already told the Captain that he did not believe in medicines for apostumet, as he called it, so he sent for a barber who was as

ignorant as himself. The barber swore that he had instruments and other measures for every illness. Thus without further ado, he opened the swelling with a lancet, and blood spewed out so violently that the Captain died some hours later. I do not doubt that many such mistakes of the art are committed by fools in these countries…"

The Royal Touch

The touch of a monarch was once believed to cure scrofula, which was therefore called "the King's Evil". This tradition went back to Edward the Confessor in eleventh-century England, and was practised by all English kings until the early eighteenth century. William of Orange helped to end the superstition, for he is said to have touched only one patient, with the words: "May God grant you better health and more sense!" Even under Queen Anne, the long line of Englishmen who had participated in such sessions was joined by the little Samuel Johnson—destined to become the great remodeller of the nation's language.

ST. Bartholomew's Hospital in London, whose fame grew with doctors like Clowes, Woodall and Harvey.

From the Yearbook of St. Bartholomew's

Revealing incidents like these have been collected, for example, in Courtney Dainton's The Story of England's Hospitals:

1558: The matron was assigned fresh soap for washing her clothes (until then she had to use wood ash).

1571: In November, a man wanted to have his leg amputated, but the directors considered the season unsuitable and sent him to a poorhouse to wait until spring.

1634: The directors decided not to accept the corpse of Sir Martin Lumley, an alderman, because he had not willed anything to the hospital.

1652: A widow received a wooden leg at a cost of three shillings (equivalent to nearly seven pounds today).

1684: A cook was dismissed for refusing to accept the Sacrament according to the Anglican Church ritual.

1704: Elizabeth Bond offered to delouse beds and sick-rooms for six shillings per bed. The directors gave her forty shillings, to include delousing the nurses' quarters.

In 1672, Wiseman's work *A Treatise of Wounds* was published by Royston, who called himself "Bookseller to His Most Sacred Majesty". Here we find a description of one of the first operations ever done on peripheral arteries. It dealt with an aneurysm in the arm of a cooper from Maidenhead. The arm artery had widened at a small place, like a balloon in danger of bursting—which would probably have made the man bleed to death in a few minutes. This case was evidently thought to be fascinating, since two other doctors of the Court took part as well as Wiseman.

The event proved dramatic. While the artery was being exposed, it burst and blood spouted forth. Wiseman kept his head and told an assistant to lay a thumb over the hole. He thus gave breathing space to the onlookers who, according to the detailed report, were eager to see the patient bleed to death. "Gentlemen," he announced, "you will now observe how I insert a sonde under the artery, and without causing any injury." He did so, and tied around the artery, whereupon "Mister Whittle took away his finger and there was no bleeding." As this lively account proceeds, we learn that the other doctors thought the patient was still at risk, and pulled out their amputation tools. Yet Wiseman refused, and during a later session the aneurysm itself was removed, so that the patient—who had fainted several times by then—survived with his arm intact.

Exhaustive treatment

On the whole, it can hardly be said that healing arts were of high quality in the seventeenth century. The worst sinners were the internal doctors, since the surgeons had the advantage of dealing more often with visible ailments. Medicine degenerated into "a Galenism in a state of dissolution, propped up by magic, astrology and religion", according to historian Brian Inglis. People used the weirdest remedies, as rare and expensive as possible—this was believed to increase their effectiveness—or else as offensive as possible, on the principle that "evil must be driven out with evil".

Among the former kind were mummy-powder (which had already been condemned by Paracelsus), milled unicorn-horn and castoreum. The latter sort included an awful-smelling root, asafetida, which was also significantly called "devil's dung". As might be expected, these remedies were meant to be taken under suitable astrological constellations and while pronouncing charms. As Inglis describes, the physician Robert Boyle gave a prescription of pulverized mistletoe against epilepsy: "as much as can be held on a sixpence coin, early in the morning, in black cherry juice, during several days around the full moon".

One of the preceding century's basic attitudes was reflected in 1733 by the great botanist Carl Linnaeus, (1707–78), writing in *Diaeta Naturalis* that "man's secretions are unclean for him" (*immunda homini sunt, quae secreta sunt*). Amazing emphasis was laid on all manner of cleansing and draining—in a word, exhaustive—treatments: sweating, blood-letting, emetics, laxatives and enemas.

The doctrine of blood-letting originated in the ancient idea of four humours. The four body fluids were imagined to hold each other in balance. It was then easy to believe that a sanguine, fat person was pathologically full of blood and would feel better by losing some. As a rule, just half a litre was considered enough, but there is a description of a blood-letter in Yorkshire who deprived his fellows of two litres at a time if they were particularly corpulent. It is obvious that anyone must have felt different after such an experience, but whether better or worse is an open question. In special cases, the doctor went even further. Heinrich Callisen, a Dane, treated a constricted hernia by bleeding *ad animi deliquarium*: until the patient fainted. The aim was to make him so weak and limp that the surgeon had a chance of reducing the hernia through its narrow opening.

Blood-letting was an excellent source of income for seventeenth-century surgeons, who

A King's Death

Seldom has anybody received a more exhaustive treatment than did King Charles II of England during his final illness. For a few days after having suffered a stroke, he was blood-let several times and purged, cupped, and given laxatives, bladder-easing plasters, sneezing-powder, ammonia, bitter-water, emetics, absinthe, thistle-leaves and a couple of dozen other herbs. A drink of sweet almond and licorice, in decocted oats, relaxed him while pigeon-excrement was smeared on his feet.

When not even that did the trick, an ultimate refuge was used: forty drops of extract from a man's skull. Doctor Scarburgh, one of the dozen physicians who were guilty of this torture of a dying human being, justified himself in his memoirs of the noteworthy case, by saying that "nothing was left untried". Including the King's death!

were commonly far from free of economic worries. It was used regularly, even for prevention of illness. Yet many clever doctors were convinced that it did good. Thomas Dover, one of the few physicians who was also an active pirate, bled a hundred and eighty sailors when they were afflicted by a strange epidemic, presumably because they had allowed an excess of Spanish corpses to lie and rot in the sun. It must have been a troublesome disease since, according to the report, at least 100 ounces of blood had to be drained from each man. This amounts to nearly four litres, which may permit us to doubt its wisdom.

The popularity of blood-letting reached to the top of society. We know that "Bloody Mary", the grim English queen, became less full of

TWO rich doctors offer blood-letting and uroscopy to their patients at a clinic, portrayed in a manuscript from Bruges, about 1482.

blood, for her accounts show a number of fees for such treatment. Caesar Hawkins received a thousand pounds per year for regular blood-letting at the English court, and became the first surgeon to be knighted for his services.

Blood-letting was the most powerful form of treatment, but cleansing the bowels was also popular. The enema jug was a necessary part of every household; in some circles, it was considered uncouth not to have regular enemas. Louis XIV of France chalked up more than two hundred enemas, and as many purges, in his last

year. Jean Fernel (1485–1558), personal physician to Catherine de Medici, and a fine clinician as well, devoted a whole volume of his surgical treatise to enema techniques. This work became a standard text, thus spreading the enema doctrine far and wide. Fernel used a dried pig-bladder which was tied round a nozzle. The enema fluid was a soothing solution of salt, honey and herbal decoctions.

Avicenna had already recommended a "victory-bringing drug", from the Indian tree now known as *Croton tiglium*. It yielded the very effective and drastic laxative called croton oil, which is strong enough to cause burn injuries—a single seed produces a skin rash. According to the writer Matts Bergmark, "whoever has once been treated with croton oil never forgets it: the effect seems to recur as soon as he smells the oil, and half a milligram turns the stomach inside out." Another popular laxative was colocynth which, according to Arabic authors, was transplanted to Europe via the Salerno School. Colocynth is thought to have been involved when the Prophet Elijah made his disciples eat a soup of cucumber-like fruits. After the first spoonful, they refused to swallow any more, crying "Death is in the pot, thou man of God!"

Besides the principle of exhaustion, two other brands of medical science flourished during the seventeenth century: *iatrophysics* and *iatrochemistry*. The former regarded the human body largely as a machine, obeying the laws of mathematics and statics. One of its main adherents was the great French philosopher René Descartes

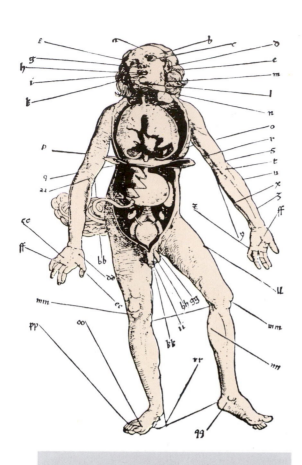

BLOOD-LETTING became such an exact "science" that it was used at particular points to cure various diseases, as shown here from a book by the Dutch doctor Laurentius Phryes (Strasbourg, 1518).

(1596–1650). For good measure, he added that the machine was governed by a soul, which he located in the brain's mysterious pineal gland. His medical views did him little good in the end, as he was summoned to Stockholm by Queen Christina. He put up with the cold, dark climate for some months only to die of pneumonia.

Further prominent iatrophysicists were Giovanni Borelli (1608–79) and Giorgio Baglivi (1668–1707) in Italy. Baglivi distinguished between theory and practice: at the bedside, he forgot his mechanistic thinking and was a good, humane doctor. His words should be heeded by more than one academically inclined physician: "To attend meetings and libraries, to own valuable unread books or publish in every journal, makes not the slightest contribution to the welfare of the ill…"

The iatrochemists, by contrast, believed that life processes were entirely chemical and that the body's function depended on chemical balance. The chief representative was François de la Boë (1614–72), called Sylvius. Not to be confused with his namesake, the irritable Parisian anatomist of the preceding century, he initiated the clinical teaching at Leyden. Still, he stuck firmly to his chemical doctrine and, for example, he classified all diseases as acid or alkaline, to be treated by remedies of opposite nature. Yet even from this doctrine, something useful could emerge, as when Thomas Willis (1621–75), in Oxford, discovered that the urine of a diabetic tastes sweet. Willis was also an adept anatomist and clarified the circulation in the brain, which is termed the *circulus Willisi* to commemorate him. His great book on brain structure was illustrated by none other than Christopher Wren, a professor of astronomy who later became England's leading architect.

The Risks of Blood-Letting

Blood-letting is one of the simplest of all operations. A vein, usually near the elbow, is opened with a lancet or a little spring-knife. In spite of that, nasty things can happen. One operator, on Queen Caroline of Bavaria in the early nineteenth century, confused the blood vessels and opened up the large arm artery, so that she bled to death. Charles IX of France had equally bad luck. The blood-letter damaged a nerve, and it took the king's personal physician, Ambroise Paré, three months to get the thumb back in reasonable working order.

How far the faithful could go in their blood-letting zeal is illustrated by the medical history of Vittorio Emmanuele II. This Italian king caught a bad case of pneumonia. Besides letting his blood for five days in a row, the doctors made sure that nothing was neglected: eighteen relaxed and bloodthirsty leeches were set onto him!

The Continental surgeons

In the midst of such ideas, surgery kept its feet on the ground, preferring facts to speculation. Its champion in early seventeenth-century Germany was Wilhelm Fabry von Hilden (1560–1634), whose name was Latinized to Fabricius Hildanus. Having no formal education beyond primary school, he took the long route as an apprentice and journeyman with barber-surgeons. Luckily, he chose the right spouse, Marie Colinet, who was a renowned midwife and something of a surgeon herself—among the first known women in the profession. She is said to have been the one who first thought of using a magnet to remove metal splinters from an injured eye.

Fabricius Hildanus amassed more than six hundred cases which he published in a series of books. These were collected under the title *Observationen, oder Wahrnehmungen in der Wundartzney*. Many of his recommendations were surprisingly far ahead of his time. For example, he amputated through healthy tissue, whereas his contemporaries still tried to cut as near to it as possible—or under it—with risks that were not worth taking in the long run. Similarly, he tied off the limb above the point of amputation, so as to lessen the bleeding during the operation. On the other hand, he was old-fashioned in post-operative care, making use of "weapon salve". This was a queer mixture of mummy-powder, earthworms, iron oxide, pig brain, and moss from the skull of a man who had been hanged under the sign of Venus. Even more weirdly, the salve was applied not to the wound but to the weapon that caused it!

Fabricius was a genius at inventing instruments and technical aids. One of his best was a tube-shaped device for inserting a ligature wire and tying the base of deep-lying tumours before cutting them out—an improvement on this has hardly been made since. Likewise, his method of correcting a deformed hand with bandages is the same as that of hand-surgeons today. In his case histories, he also speculated about the origins of diseases, with no blind loyalty to Galen or other predecessors. He touched upon the theory of inflammation as we know it, and he understood that foreign bodies, parasites and traumas could influence healing. Thus, with no scientific education at all, he joined the seventeenth century's foremost spokesmen of empirical science in surgery.

While Fabricius was advancing German surgery, the opposite trend occurred—despite Paré—in France, where a setback in medicine was relatively obvious. The paragon of conservatism was Guy Patin (1601–72), professor of medicine and dean of the Paris faculty. He refused to accept Harvey's view of blood circulation because it disagreed with Galen. Nor, in his envy, did he recognize colleagues such as Pierre Bourdelot (1610–85), who was the king's own physician, and Theophraste Renaudot (1586–1653), who had become popular by establishing loan-banks for the poor. Patin's worst hatred was reserved for a Belgian, Jean Baptiste van Helmont (1577–1644) who, like a new Paracelsus, raged against conventional medicine and became a forefather of the iatrochemical school. Patin's remarks about van Helmont are characteristic of the tone of the seventeenth-century academic world:

> "He was a mad Flemish scoundrel who died some months ago, out of his mind. He never achieved anything of value. He believed in only one basis for medicine, built of chemical and empirical secrets. He wrote a great deal on the injuriousness of blood-letting, but it was because he himself got no such treatment that his fury did him in."

And it was doctors of Patin's type that Molière meant by writing:

> "One should never say a person died of fever or pneumonia. What ought to be said is that he died of four doctors and two druggists..."

Nonetheless, some shafts of light penetrated the temporary gloom in France. There were anatom-

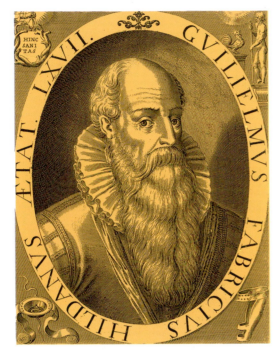

De Gangr. Et Sphacelo Liber;

Quod si nervi ita retracti, & genu adeò in- | tibia verò ita in altum elevanda, ut seamno, eo
curvatum fuerit, ut æger illud extendere non | in loco, quo excavatum est, annecti possit, quem-
possit, in solum conclavis collocandus est æger, | admodum sequens figura indicat,

(ABOVE) Fabricius Hildanus, the "father of German surgery", at age 67. (Right) Hildanus' procedures for leg amputation, presented in an edition of his collected works (Frankfurt, 1646).

ists such as Jean Riolan (1577–1657) who, even though he did not believe in Harvey, contributed to the understanding of circulation by discovering the connections between arteries in different parts of the intestinal mesentery (later called Riolan's anastomoses). Jean Pecquet (1622–74) found the large lymphatic passage in the chest, and the so-called *cisterna chyli*, in 1651—an achievement whose priority he then had to defend against the great Danish anatomist Thomas Bartholin (1616–80).

The ascent from the doldrums of surgery was made possible by the kings, who had realized that things were not as they should be. In 1672, Louis XIV ordained anatomical demonstrations and exemplary operations. He offered quarters in the castle grounds "so that students of surgery might improve themselves in an art

which We have always considered one of the State's most important." The chosen director was Pierre Dionis (d. 1118), a capable surgeon who later published a book about these activities, *Cours d'opérations de chirurgie démontrées au jardin royal*. It went through several editions and translations, used widely for the next fifty years. A further step in rescuing the surgical profession was taken when Louis XIV, after a successful anal-fistula operation, rewarded his surgeon Félix with land, gold and noble rank.

In Italy, the greatest clinician of the age was said to be Giovanni Maria Lancisi (1654-1720). Although an internist and pathologist, he contributed to surgical knowledge by focusing attention on the burst aortic aneurysm, a cause of what was called *Sekundentod* (instantaneous death). Of immediate practical significance,

Louis XIV's Famous Fistula Operation

In 1686, the king was found to be suffering from anal fistulas, which were hardly helped by his many laxatives. First a good conservative treatment was sought. Several patients with similar fistulas were located and sent to various health-resorts. This was set up as a scientifically controlled experiment: four men had to spend a year taking the sulphurous waters at Barèges, and four others the saline waters at Bourbonne-les-Bains. In no case were the results encouraging. The court doctor was then forced to try a fistula-salve invented by a Jacobite monk, who did not even belong to the guild. His annoyance was presumably lessened by the observation that it did not work either.

An operation was the only way out. Charles François Félix, the court surgeon, had never cut a fistula in his life. To begin with, he practised on patients from the poor-hospitals of Paris. Meanwhile, a silver bistoury (since known as bistourie à la Royale), or narrow-bladed knife for making incisions, was constructed—its nearest ancestry being in Galen. At seven in the morning on November 18, the operation took place in the king's bedchamber at Versailles. The only onlookers were Madame de Maintenon, a Minister of War named Louvais, the priest La Chaise, the doctors Daquin, Fagon and Besnières, and four apothecaries who were to hold the patient.

Everything was recorded: Félix cut twice with the bistoury and eight times with scissors. The king never flinched or uttered a sound of pain, and not even his breathing rate changed—according to the protocol. This may be doubted, since the secretary must have expected that the king would read it later and want only a testimony of sublime heroism. An hour after the operation, Louis underwent blood-letting, a likely sign that he was deeply affected. Generally he was quite unwilling to be blood-let, and had not even accepted this "life-saving" procedure some years earlier, when his arm was thrown out of joint.

Next, a courier sped to the Dauphin who, as usual, was away hunting. The crown prince rushed home and entered the bedchamber "too disturbed to speak". In the churches of Paris, faithful crowds gathered to pray. Another messenger told Madame de Montespan at Fontainebleau that she was not welcome at Versailles. We may thus discredit a story that she went to the patient, found her rival Maintenon calmly sewing by his side, and retired to her apartments in a fit of hysteria.

That same evening, Louis insisted on holding a council. On the following day he received the ambassadors, although he was now clearly feeling pain. His suffering was by no means over. Félix did not want the wounds to heal too quickly, and operated again on December 6, 8 and 10. It was on January 11 that the king first promenaded in the Orangerie at Versailles. The people then offered their well-wishes at a public feast with 236 courses.

This operation had a momentous historical outcome. During his convalescence, Louis visited the cloister of Saint-Cyr. To celebrate the occasion, the nuns ordered a cantata entitled Dieu Sauvez le Roi to be composed. An Englishman happened to be present and, enjoying the words and melody, wrote them down. Once home, he translated the text and it has since been known as "God Save the King"…

An Opportunistic Operation

The fashion of fistula operations in seventeenth-century France is not surprising. Given the monarch's central role in society, the people naturally wanted to do as he did. Courtiers defied death by undergoing operations in the hope that the king would deign to inquire about their condition afterward. The surgeons were overrun by individuals who wanted to be cut for the royal ailment. Pierre Dionis, premier chirurgien de Mesdames les Dauphines, was consulted by thirty patients who begged to be operated on. And "the craze was so great that they went out of their minds when he explained that they showed no symptoms", according to a full account of Louis XIV's Anal Fistula by Bengt Lundström.

Too Much Raisin-Paste

Along with blood-letting, laxatives and enemas topped the list of Guy Patin's therapies. They made an appearance in Emile Rostand's masterpiece, Cyrano de Bergerac:

On Saturday the king ate too much raisin-paste,
and caught a feverish colic which he stoutly faced:
then back it came in a new kind of fruit, potato,
which soon was sentenced—for a crime against His State, O!—
by Doctor Guy Patin to eight laxatives and vanished into exile; so the King still lives.

GIOVANNI Lancisi (*left*) and Marco Severino (*right*) added much to surgery in seventeenth-century Italy.

however, was Marco Aurelio Severino (1580–1656), who revived the tracheotomy as an operation for obstructed air-passages. With this, Severino himself saved the lives of numerous patients during a diphtheria epidemic in Naples in 1610. He constructed a tube-like instrument, the trocar, to keep the incised opening free for air passage after the operation.

Blood transfusion makes its entrée

The idea of using blood from a healthy person to transfer youth and vitality to an old or sick one is very ancient. It existed in Egyptian medicine as early as two thousand years before Christ. Similar speculations are found in classical antiquity, as with Ovid:

Draw only the swords
and quick, the changed blood
drains from his body—
I fill his veins with the younger...

We have no definite proof of when the first blood transfusion was made from one human being to another. It was long thought to have happened at Rome in 1492, with Pope Innocent VIII on his deathbed receiving blood from three boys aged ten. The initiative was taken by a Jewish doctor who worked temporarily in the city. All three boys, as well as His Holiness, died. Yet the truth of this tale has been questioned. A particular assertion is that the Pope drank the blood, which is not really how we define a transfusion. Professor Lindenboom of Amsterdam, a researcher in the history of transfusion, considers the entire story a falsification. That some Roman lads were blood-let to death at the same time is credible, but there is no evidence that the Pope was involved.

The potentialities of blood transfusion drew serious attention when Harvey's discovery of circulation opened up a new view of human physiology. Experiments were originally made by using animals. Thus, Francesco Folli succeeded in Florence in 1654 with good results, and this was repeated twelve years later by Richard Lower of Oxford. The latter's experiments, made on dogs, were connected with an important discovery: the dark blood which entered the lungs became bright red after leaving them. This beautiful work was published in London under the resounding title *Tractatus de Core item de Motu & Colore Sanguinis et Chyli in eum Transitu* (1669). Once more, research was followed with interest by the architect Christopher Wren, creator of Saint Paul's Cathedral and some sixty other churches in the city.

Lower did not limit his experiments to animals. In 1667, he gave a patient blood from a lamb. A transfusion of sheep's blood was performed in June of the same year in France, by the mathematician Jean Baptiste Denis at the Sorbonne University. The first recipient was Denis himself, and the second a lad of fifteen, whose doctors had put him in miserable condition with twenty blood-lettings, laxations and enemas. Another of Denis' patients was the Swedish baron Erik Bonde, who became ill during a visit to Paris. As a last resort, this young man was given a transfusion of calf blood on July 24, 1667, but it failed and he died the next day.

After Denis' initial triumphs, blood transfusion quickly became a vogue in Paris. However, a setback was not long in coming. As we now know, human beings cannot receive blood from just any donor at all. If the wrong blood groups are mixed, complications and even death can result, mainly from kidney failure. At that time, and for some centuries, blood groups were unheard of, and many of the transfusions must have had tragic consequences. The first successes were probably due to good luck in using so-called universal donors, whose blood can be given to anyone without risk. But by 1668, the ensuing deaths were so numerous that the government stepped in. An edict by the "Lieutenant Criminel" of Paris decreed that

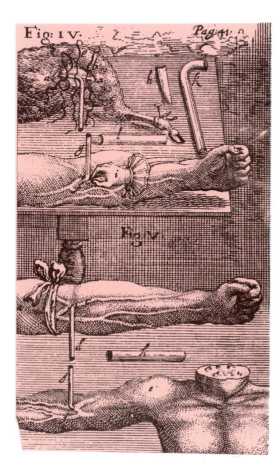

BLOOD transfusion from an animal to a man, and from one man to another, was illustrated in detail as a new technique by Johann Elshotz in a book of 1667.

KARL Landsteiner, the Austrian immunologist and pathologist who discovered blood groups.

transfusions could not be performed in the absence of a member of the medical faculty. This was a virtual death-sentence for transfusions, since the faculty always opposed innovations out of jealousy or other motives.

Here we may look ahead and rejoice that transfusion was to awaken from a century of slumber in the early nineteenth century. The leader of this new era would be the physiologist and obstetrician James Blundell in London. Through animal experiments, he had become convinced that transfusions could save the lives of bled-out patients. His greatest contribution was to build the "impeller", a device that allowed direct blood transfer from human to human. It became the prototype for the "rotanda injector" which was used as late as the 1940s.

Blundell's transfusions were of much help to women in childbirth. He soon had a following, and the method spread beyond the hospitals. There is a description from 1842 of how a ship's doctor, Samuel Hodgkinson, aged twenty-five, saved the life of a woman by giving her blood from a healthy man. In 1868—two centuries after the edict in Paris—a survey was made of all transfusions during the previous half-century. It showed that 100 patients had survived 155 transfusions, an amazing record in ignorance of blood groups as well as of asepsis!

The turning-point in this chronicle was to come, of course, with the discovery of blood groups. In 1901, a modest article by Karl Landsteiner (1868–1943) was published in his native Vienna's *Klinische Wochenschrift*, arguing that human beings had three types of blood, called A, B and 0 (zero). Next year, a group termed AB was added by Decastello. It was proved that blood normally contains antibodies, "agglutinins", which are directed against particular types of blood cells. If a type of blood is given to a person whose agglutinins are directed against it, the red cells clump together, causing complications as in transfusions from animals to man. The risk is avoided by giving blood of the person's own group. It also turned out that type 0 cannot be agglutinated, and can thus be given to anybody. This type may well have been involved in Denis' first experiments.

Besides the AB0 system, further blood-group systems have been found, and are used, for example, in legal cases to identify criminals or establish paternity. But they matter little to blood transfusions, except with the so-called Rh system. It was named after the rhesus monkey, which played a role in its discovery. Incompatibility in the Rh system can also cause problems for pregnancy: babies may be born with serious jaundice, anaemia and other complications, so pregnant women are always given an Rh test. This system was discovered jointly by Alexander Wiener, an American, and Landsteiner. The latter's other contributions to medicine are less familiar—he was the first to describe the "dark field" study of syphilis bacteria, and worked in later years at the Rockefeller Institute in New York, winning the Nobel Prize in 1930.

The new art of childbirth

Delivering children was long the privilege of women. Men were unwelcome and, in many places, forbidden to be present at the event. A doctor named Wertt in Hamburg, fascinated by obstetrics, put on female dress and managed to witness several deliveries before he was exposed and promptly burnt at the stake. There were, of course, communities which allowed physicians to attend, but these were usually too proud to deal with what was regarded as filthy, unqualified labour.

Obstetrics began to develop soon after the Renaissance. The first handbook for midwives was *Der Schwangern Frauwen und Hebamen Roszgarten*, "A Rose Garden for Expectant Women and Earth Mothers" (1513). Its author was Eucharius Rösslin, the city doctor of Worms, who became physician to the Duchess of Braunschweig and Lüneburg. We do not know for sure if he ever actually observed a childbirth, but he was well-read and fluently cited the classical and Arabic medical sources. Moreover, by studying Soranus of Ephesus, he enabled his own readers to learn the ancient method of "turning the foot" in a transverse foetal position. This was actually adopted in the German-speaking countries a few decades before Paré revived it in France.

"Blood is the Vessel of the Soul"

In Leviticus *we find an early claim that the soul resided in the blood, and this has lingered on in popular belief. Some religious sects, such as Jehovah's Witnesses, also use the Bible as a basis for their refusal to take blood transfusions.*

When Samuel Pepys (1633-1703), the great English diarist, heard of blood transfusions, he tactfully wondered what would happen if a Quaker's blood were given to an Anglican archbishop. Perhaps due to similar dark thoughts, a contemporary German doctor tried to patch up marriages by transferring blood between the husband and wife. Queen Christina of Sweden (1626-89) is said to have made it clear that, if she should ever need a transfusion, the blood had to come from a lion!

Much of the advice in *Roszgarten* seems rather rash today, for instance that the birth canal should be lubricated, either by local means or by making the mother drink decoctions. Rösslin also believed that a lengthy delivery could be hurried up if the mother sniffed freshly ground pepper—her sneezing was thought to stimulate uterine contractions. Anyhow, the book went through more than a hundred (!) editions and was eagerly plagiarized. In England, it was published almost verbatim as *Byrth of Mankynde*, credited to a mysterious author named Thomas Raynalde.

In Zürich, too, an unashamed imitation of *Roszgarten* appeared. For some reason, it was called a "gay little book of encouragement"; anything less gay can hardly be imagined. The author was a fanatical theologian, Jacob Rueff, and his sole original contribution was a chapter on monsters. Written with gloomy fascination, it attributed deformed children to the mother's intercourse with the devil. Yet in spite of such works, the books of midwifery had a long life, especially on the Continent. There was little to replace them until 1715, when the chief midwife at the Grand Duchy of Brandenburg's court, Justine Siegemundin, wrote a guide in the form of a catechism.

Ambroise Paré advanced the midwife's profession with the method already mentioned, and perhaps mainly by his own example. If the king's own physician could take up this undervalued branch of medicine, it was good enough for other surgeons as well. He wrote two books on obstetrics. Among other things, he had the courage to initiate a delivery by widening the cervix, and he devised an instrument for this purpose.

The next century saw a decline of quality in French obstetrics just as in surgery. It was again Louis XIV who initiated a comeback, by making his best doctors assist at his own mistresses' deliveries. Some good obstetricians eventually appeared, such as De la Motte and Portal, but primarily François Mauriceau (1637–1709). One of his lasting contributions was the

CHILDBIRTH in the hands of midwives and astrologers: from Jacob Rueff's popular book of 1554. This was an early woodcut by Jost Amman, one of the greatest illustrators of that century.

manoeuvre which is still known as "Mauriceau's turn", allowing a bottom-first baby to be delivered head-first.

The chief Italian advances were in anatomy. Andreas Vesalius did much work on a study of pelvic anatomy, but apprentices went farther than the master. Gabriello Falloppio (1523–63) described the ovaries, and the Fallopian tubes to be named after him. Giulio Cesare Arantius (1530–89) focused attention on pelvic constriction as a hindrance to delivery. Arantius was more of a practising physician than Falloppio, and he observed during protracted deliveries whether the woman's pelvis was normal or narrow. In the former case, "I go gladly to work and, with Almighty God's help, can often bring the situation to a happy conclusion", but in the latter case "I consider it better to run than to fight feebly, and I make myself scarce..."

The advent of forceps

Tongs for extracting a foetus existed as early as the Middle Ages. Normally they were used when the foetus had died in the womb. But the construction of some tongs which have been preserved down to our day indicates that they also made it possible to draw out a living baby. In the sixteenth century, a lithotomist in Zürich described two instruments for aiding delivery. One was called a "duck-bill" and was undoubtedly meant for dead foetuses. But the other, called simply "long, smooth tongs", may have been intended to help with live births.

We do not know how old the use of forceps is. Yet the Belgians and French are certain as to who invented this device. Both countries have statues, commemorative plaques and coins in memory of the Flemish surgeon Jean Palfyn (1650–1730). He became professor of surgery and anatomy at the University of Ghent. Having perfected his instrument, he journeyed on foot—at the age of seventy, lacking enough money for the carriage—to Paris and presented it before the French Academy of Sciences: he himself dared not apply it in practice! It consisted of two spoons, linked with a clamp or a binding, although not crossed with a joint.

Palfyn also sent a specimen of the forceps to the famous Lorenz Heister. The latter tried to use it along with some of his own modifications, but never managed to deliver anyone in this way without injuring the baby. Nor did Palfyn have any success when he eventually got the courage to try the forceps. He died as poor as he had lived, and lies buried at St. Jacob's Church in Ghent, where his later memorial portrays a weeping woman. Palfyn and Heister were the first to publish experiments with forceps. Yet it was to turn out that such instruments had been employed long before them.

On July 3, 1569, one Doctor William Chamberlen fled to England from Huguenot persecution in France. He set up a practice in Southampton, and his son Peter (1560–1631) became established as a physician in London. After anglicizing its name to Chamberlain, the

What Sex will the Child Be?

Francois Mauriceau was both human and wise, as can be seen from his advice to midwives. "If I were a midwife and the parents asked me whether it would be a boy or girl, I would find out what they wanted, then predict the opposite. For if the midwife proved right, they would wonder at her skill—and if she were wrong the parents would pay no heed, but welcome the good fortune that comes unexpectedly."

Bacteriological Warfare

What may be the earliest example of bacteriological warfare was rescued from oblivion by Gabriello Falloppio. He tells how Charles VIII of France, in 1495, besieged Spanish troops who were shut in at Naples, including Falloppio's own father. The new disease from America, which had not yet been named syphilis, raged in the defending army—and considering the unbridled promiscuity of the age, it spread like wildfire. Then someone had a bright idea. The defenders drove their prostitutes, "especially the prettiest", out to the attackers. And the Frenchmen, prompted by lust more than sympathy, received them gladly. Other documents testify that the French troops were afflicted that winter by an unknown illness. Charles VIII had to retreat, and his mercenary force dispersed all over Europe—carrying the syphilis infection!

A Decoct for Operations

Arantius had an apprentice from Venice named Scipione Mercurio, who invented a curious prescription for soaking linen cloths to be used in operations. "Wormwood, agrimony, mint, mallow, pomegranate, dried roses, birthwort, and cat-tail are mixed in sour black wine and added to two pounds of water from a smith's iron-quenching pot…"

WILLIAM Chamberlain, founder of an English line of obstetricians. The forceps which made them famous were probably invented by his son Peter the Elder.

Skill with the Forceps in Literature

Laurence Sterne's picaresque novel Tristram Shandy *tells of a Doctor Slop who lacks three front teeth, which were knocked out when he was using forceps. This figure is a faithful caricature of Doctor John Burton (1710-71) in York, with as high an opinion of his forceps as of himself. In a book on obstetrics, he boasted that he had a midwife measure how quickly he could perform a delivery. Having extracted both the baby and afterbirth in less than half a minute, he could not restrain himself from commenting: "Thus the midwives looked at each other in astonishment..."*

family remained a great medical dynasty for two hundred years and was well-known in the capital city. The Chamberlains went their own way and were often in conflict with the law as well as the British medical societies. There is, in fact, no doubt that their activities in many respects far exceeded the frontier of quackery. One of them ended up in Newgate Prison, but was promptly released when Queen Anne and the Archbishop of Canterbury intervened.

What was the cause of their prosperity, and their ability to gain mighty allies? It was that they jealously guarded a secret which shortened difficult and drawn-out deliveries. This was surrounded by lots of hocus-pocus and camouflage. As a rule, the Chamberlains rented a covered carriage to reach an expectant woman's home. A box was brought in, shrouded with black cloths, and much bigger than necessary so that it would mystify people. The obstetrician shut himself in with the mother, allowing nobody to enter and see what was going on. Since her underparts were hidden by a sheet according to custom, the operation was also obscured and not even the mother could observe it—if she was in any condition to be concerned with more than the quickest possible delivery. When it was all over, the doctor rang a bell to heighten the drama, his instruments were packed into the box, and the family—relieved and intrigued—was admitted to admire the result. One need not add that Doctor Chamberlain took a hefty fee before he and his box left the premises.

The Chamberlain family's secret was the forceps. Their model differed only in details from what we use today. It conferred status and wealth on the doctors, so naturally—although not very ethically—the patent on it was carefully protected. Nor was the business-minded family too proud to advertise, even in an unbusinesslike manner by denouncing their competitors. Peter Hugh Chamberlain, in the fourth English generation, wrote:

"My father and brother and I, but no one else in Europe, have with God's help and our own effort found a means to bring out the child's head when it has met a hindrance or otherwise been unable to emerge, and this without injuring either the mother or the child. All other deliverers must proceed in the usual way, since they do not know our method, and they expose the mother to great danger..."

In the course of years, some of the secret leaked out. One family member moved to Holland and sold at least half of it to an obstetrician named Roonhuysen: that is, he displayed a single blade of the forceps! There is a possibility that Palfyn saw this blade and was inspired by it. But the whole truth was not revealed until 1818. The Chamberlains had invested part of their fortune in a large estate in Essex, where one of them died. The widow, rebuilding the house, built a secret room in the attic and filled it with various relics of her husband. These included a case which contained family items—letters, spectacles, goblets and a copy of the New Testament—as well as three complete forceps. In 1818, the estate was bought by a wine merchant, Mortimer Hall, who found the case and gave it to the Royal Society in London, where it can still be seen.

A forceps delivery requires, to be sure, not only an instrument but also someone who can use it. The Chamberlains had evidently developed a mastery in the art. Apart from that, they were not quite alone with the idea, at least since the early eighteenth century. England's leading obstetrician, William Smellie (1697–1763), had probably heard of Palfyn's so-called *tire-tête* (head-turner) and, in his *Treatise on the Theory and Practice of Midwifery* (1752), he discussed the symptoms calling for a forceps delivery.

Smellie himself contributed a humane detail: he clad the forceps handle with leather, so that its metallic sound would not frighten the mother! But his student William Hunter—whom we shall soon meet—did not believe in forceps. This great surgeon had the habit of exhibiting his rusty tongs to friends as a proof that he had never even used them.

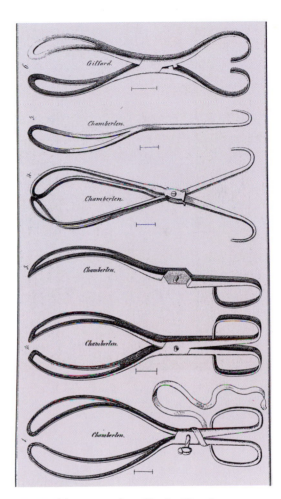

FORCEPS of the type exploited by the Chamberlain family in the later seventeenth century. Their blades curved only in the direction of pressure, fitting the child's head. Other types, soon developed in France, were curved also to fit the pelvis for deeper and easier insertion. The German gynaecologist Hermann Kilian included this picture in his book about such instruments (Bonn, 1856).

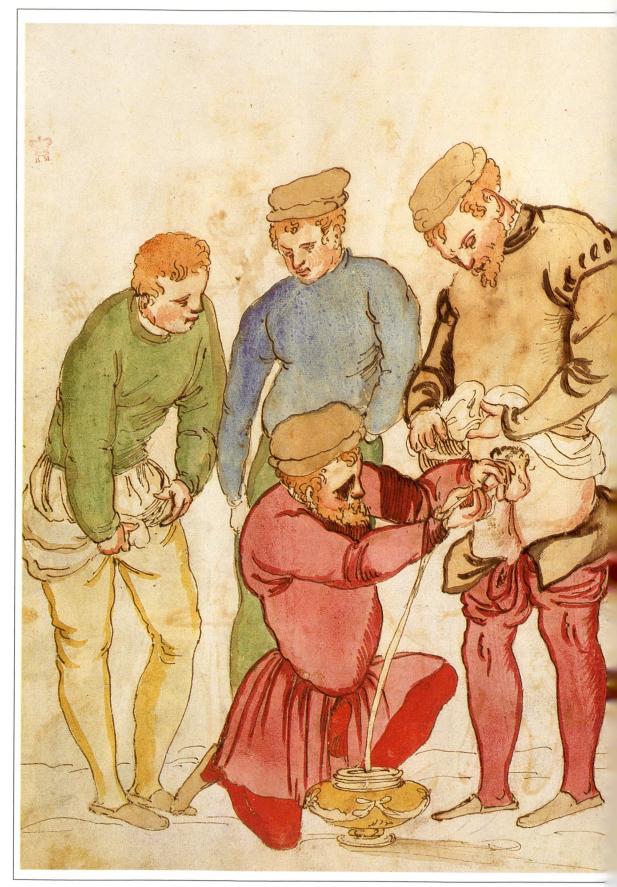

CHAPTER 6

The surgeons of the Enlightenment

During the eighteenth century, statesmen, seamen and colonizers made England into the world's leading nation. She became ever richer while her art, literature, and sciences—not least medicine—bloomed as never before. Yet the "Rule Britannia" spirit of progress arose on foundations that were laid some generations earlier.

One key figure in these developments was Thomas Willis (1621–75) who, as we have seen, discovered the blood supply to the base of the brain, and was the first in Europe to notice that diabetes makes the urine sweet. Even more important was Thomas Sydenham (1624–89), a systematic student of disease symptoms. His careful, correct descriptions paved the way for scientific nosography, which includes the classification of diseases. It was, in fact, the beginning of systematization in medicine as a whole.

Among the nonoperative specialties—to the extent that they already existed—a few were represented very well. William Heberden (1710–1801), a respected London doctor, lectured in 1768 at the Royal College of Physicians on "Some Account of a Disorder of the Breast". This short talk gave, for the first time, a clear and exhaustive picture of *angina pectoris*, a pain due to narrowing of the heart's blood ves-

sels. Another lasting contribution by Heberden was to clarify the diagnostic differences between smallpox and chicken pox.

William Withering (1741–99) was a botanist and physician from Shropshire, practising mainly in Birmingham. On a suggestion from a wise old woman in his home district, he introduced the digitalis plant in 1775 to treat a former master-builder "who was very short of breath, in poor general condition, with a large belly". A decoction of the leaves cured this man's obvious heart ailment. After thoroughly studying the plant's effects for ten years, Withering published *An Account of the Foxglove and Some of its Medical Uses*, stating the same indications for use that we obey today.

Further great doctors were Edward Jenner (1749–1823), the discoverer of vaccination, and John Haslam (1764–1844) who investigated *dementia paralytica* as well as many other mental illnesses. William Cullen (1712–90) and John Brown (1735–88), both Scots, attributed such illnesses to the nervous system, and founded what we call neuropathology. This view was wrong, but it served to hasten the decline of speculative medicine throughout Europe, thus benefiting theoretical science.

William Cheselden

Nor did surgery lag behind internal medicine. The British surgeons suddenly sailed into the world's forefront, and their leader was William Cheselden. Born in 1688 in Leicestershire, he did his apprenticeship with the surgeon James

TYPICAL of eighteenth-century advances in surgery were urinary-stone operations. This portrait of the old catheterization treatment appeared around 1510 in an Italian "medical picture-book" by Henricus Kullmaurer and Albert Meher.

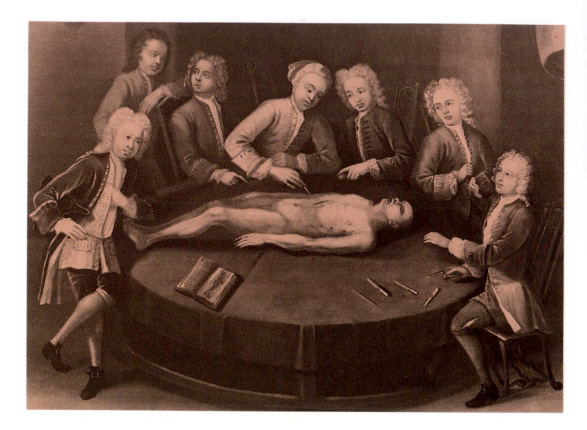

WILLIAM Cheselden dissecting at the Barber-Surgeons' Hall, in a painting from about 1730.

Ferne at St. Thomas's Hospital in London. More significantly, he then learned anatomy from William Cowper (1666–1709), who gave the country's first private lectures on the subject. Cowper was a surgeon of the simpler kind, often derided as "bone-setters". But he had a burning interest in the human body's structure and made new discoveries, such as the small glands at the base of the bladder, still known as Cowper's glands. His enthusiasm infected Cheselden, who took up the torch of lecturing.

Anatomical dissections, a boon not only to future doctors but also to public curiosity, required corpses. These were in limited supply, and when Cheselden bought them for four series of lectures every year, he clashed with the powerful Barber-Surgeons' Society. Its own dissections suffered from a shortage of corpses and the public's shift toward Cheselden. This became a real battle: the Society was right that Cheselden had carelessly exceeded certain rules, and he had to make an open apology. His acquisition of corpses and his public demonstrations were restricted. Yet he continued to dissect on his dining-table, and the incident led to a dislike of the Society. Cheselden opposed it all his life, and finally succeeded in separating the surgeons from the barbers. Surgery was thereby strengthened enormously and the reputation of surgeons rose.

In the latter respect, Cheselden's character was an asset. How he managed to acquire a position in the "establishment" is not fully understood. It may have resulted from his peculiar individuality and broad interests, which embraced such diverse pastimes as architecture, literature, art and—boxing! At the end of his life, he moved easily in the highest circles, even being officially recognized as the personal physician of Queen Caroline.

Cheselden's greatest passion was lithotomy, the removal of stones from the urinary bladder. He held no fewer than three positions as "first lithotomist", namely at his old hospital of St. Thomas, at Westminster Hospital where he displaced his adversary John Douglas, and ultimately at St. George's. This had recently been established on a quiet edge of the city, then known for its pure country air—although today the site, no longer a hospital, is surrounded by heavy traffic. Eye surgery also fascinated him, and he was probably the first to make an artificial pupil. His concern with anatomy found expression in several books. The most beautiful of them, *Osteographia*, was illustrated with his own artistically superb drawings.

Cheselden withdrew in 1737 from the three hospitals where he had worked tirelessly, and took up the sinecure of physician in Chelsea Hospital, more of an old-age home for war veterans. His last fifteen years were occupied with the formation of the new Surgical Society. He must have had a hand in the matter when his son-in-law was chosen as chairman of the Parliamentary commission that investigated the idea. It became a reality in 1745 and Cheselden served as the new society's president until his death in 1752. Above his grave in the cemetery of Chelsea Hospital stands another monument to him, Old Putney Bridge, which he designed!

On Club-Feet

A good example of William Cheselden's instructive style can be found in his book The Anatomy of the Human Body: *"Sometimes children are born with the feet turned inwards so that the sole is oriented upward. In these cases the ankle-joint bones, like the vertebrae of a hunchback, are adapted to the deformity. My first awareness of this ailment came from Mr. Presgrove, an adept bone-setter who then lived in Westminster. To him I sent a patient whom I myself did not know how to treat. His method was to bend the foot as far as possible into its normal position and fix it with sticking plaster. This he repeated several times until the objective was attained. Yet it was not without fault, as the bandage harmed the leg and made the foot's upper part swollen. When I later received another child to treat, I thought of a bandage which I had learned from Mr. Cowper, a bone-setter in Leicester who restored and healed a fracture of my own elbow when I was a schoolboy.*

"According to his method, the foot was restored and fixed with rollers in a mixture of egg-white and wheat flour. They dried stiff and held the foot in place. I can think of no better way to fix fractures, since it holds the extremity in position without the strict bandaging which is the usual cause of poor results. On applying this technique to the club-foot, I wrapped up the whole lower leg from the knee to the toes..."

A Poet's View of Cheselden

In 1736, Alexander Pope wrote to his colleague Jonathan Swift: "I received a very friendly letter from you, which expressed much sympathy for me in my illness which was treated by Mr. Cheselden... I wondered a little over your question as to who Cheselden was. It shows that not even the truest praises spread as far as on the wings of poetry: he is the most renowned and deserving man in the entire surgical profession, and he has saved the lives of thousands with his ability to operate for stones..."

The art of stone-cutting

As the undisputed master lithotomist of all times, Cheselden prompts us to recall the history of this age-old operation. Actually, the earliest known stone ever found in a urinary bladder disappeared in World War II, when London's Museum of the Royal College of Surgeons was bombed in 1941. This stone came from a boy of sixteen who had been buried at El Amarna in Egypt, far back in prehistory.

Ancient surgical literature often mentioned lithotomy and the bladder-stone ailment, which was evidently quite common. It seems to have always affected primitive human beings most. In our day, bladder stones are much more usual among undeveloped tribes than in the civilized world—an unexplained phenomenon. An indication of the ailment's frequency is that it tended to be treated by specially trained experts. Indeed, Hippocrates ordered in his medical oath that bladder stones were not to be dealt with, but left to the capable.

The original method of removing such stones was "perineal lithotomy". Access to a bladder was gained from the perineum, or region between the genitals and rectum. A stone of any real size could generally be located by inserting a finger in the rectum and feeling through the intestinal wall. Susruta, who described this technique long ago as we saw in Chapter 1, gave an excellent account of stone-cutting. Basically the same procedure was known for centuries afterward as "the lesser apparatus", since it was relatively simple and required only a knife and tweezers.

More sophisticated was the "greater apparatus", launched by Franciscus de Romanis, an Italian from Cremona, but published only in 1522 by his apprentice Marianus Sanctus, and subsequently misnamed the "Marian method". It demanded better instruments: a fluted probe was inserted into the urethra, and the surgeon opened a path to the bladder by cutting along the midline toward the probe. Whether this had any advantage over the "lesser" operation is very doubtful. Many patients became incontinent and had to suffer a fistula for the rest of their lives.

The next innovation came from one of the most remarkable figures in surgery's chequered history. Jacques Beaulieu (1651–1714) began his career in the cavalry, but left the army at 21 and became an apprentice to a travelling Italian stone-cutter. In time he called himself Frère Jacques—Brother John—and thus he lives on, not only in the annals of surgery, but in the old children's song:

Are you sleeping, are you sleeping,
Brother John, Brother John?
Ring the bell for matins,
ring the bell for matins,
ding ding dong,
ding ding dong.

Brother John became a qualified stone-cutter at 46, after much trouble. His test operation was made before the college of surgeons at the Hôtel Dieu hospital. He used a new technique of going in from the perineal side, and—correctly in anatomical terms—through the lower pelvic muscles. It went perfectly, but they denied him a license because he had not bothered to prepare the patient with blood-letting and laxatives! Only when he had operated on a royal shoemaker, who recovered in three weeks, did the king, Louis XIV, after attending the event, give him the permit.

His skill does, however, seem to have been variable. All too many deaths occurred during his first work in the Versailles area. Brother John had to leave the capital city and wander about, earning a living by stone-cutting at the market-places. His technique improved steadily and, when he dared to return to Paris in 1701, he performed thirty-eight operations without a single mortality, the best record ever. Then his luck turned again. The distinguished Marshal de Lorges, after prudently watching him operate successfully on twenty-two patients, underwent the treatment—but died soon afterward. So he found himself on foot again, crossing all of

REMOVAL of bladder stones by the "Marian" operation, or *apparatus major*, as illustrated in 1930.

Europe. He left a trail of some 4,500 lithotomies from Amsterdam to Rome, and did more than 2,000 hernias as well. Retiring at 69, he willed his fortune to charities.

The cleverest and quickest stone-cutter who ever lived was certainly William Cheselden, as already noted. When he was gaining interest in this operation, the surgeon John Douglas at Westminster Hospital had just introduced the technique of "high", or suprapubic, lithotomy. A cut was made over the pubic bone joint to enter the bladder. Cheselden was enthusiastic about it at first and, in 1723, wrote his *Treatise on the High Operation for the Stone*, giving Douglas credit. The latter nonetheless became furious, starting a long feud with Cheselden. Their relationship hardly improved when the hospital's directors preferred Cheselden to be their lithotomist.

Cheselden's love of high lithotomy soon soured. Nor could he accept the midline method, or "greater apparatus", which yielded terrible complications and mortality. From

1725 onward, he modified the lateral perineal operation which Frère Jacques had developed in France. Three years later, he could report brilliant results: only 20 of his 213 patients had died, a record unknown until then. It was even better than that, since Cheselden's growing experience had led him to take on patients so old and ill that nobody had thought of treating them. His success was related to his anatomical ability and to his postoperative care for minimizing the bleeding. Discussing the results, he described a patient who had bled afterward:

> "But this occurrence taught me that, if there was bleeding from a vessel which I could not find, I widened the wound with the knife until I found it. Now if Jacques or others, who are said to have done this operation, consciously or otherwise neglected to tie off the blood vessels, it must be that—regardless of their manual skill—many of their child patients, and most of their adult ones, have bled to death."

In an age when narcosis and anaesthesia did not exist, stone-cutting was scarcely a pleasant event for the patient. The surgeon's speed was thus prized all the more highly. On this point, Cheselden could offer good service indeed. On numerous occasions, he completed a lateral lithotomy, from the first incision to stanching of the wound, in forty-five seconds!

The perineal lithotomy was to outlast Cheselden by centuries, and had champions even in the 1920s. But already in his time another method of stone extraction was emerging, the modified suprapubic lithotomy. As stated above, the suprapubic approach is from the front. This was first made in 1561 by a Frenchman named Pierre Franco (1500?–61), desperately trying to save a child of three who had an egg-sized stone. He could not get it out through the perineum as usual, and the child was suffering so much that he dared cut a frontal hole in the bladder. Such a thing had been equated with certain death ever since Hippo-

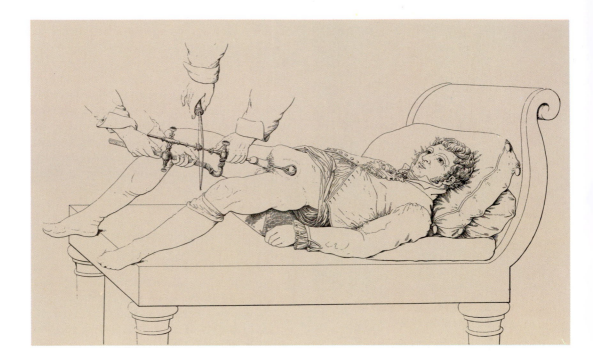

A nineteenth-century instrument for breaking up stones within the bladder, from a textbook of 1847 by its inventor, Jean Civiale.

crates, but Franco succeeded, although he warned his colleagues never to repeat the attempt.

The "Douglassian lithotomy", introduced by John Douglas as we have mentioned, was troublesome. It risked puncturing the peritoneum, or abdominal membrane, and even the intestine. These problems were partly eliminated when Cheselden thought of filling the bladder with oat-water through a catheter, so that it rose over the edge of the pelvic bone joint. Yet there remained difficulties with abdominal-wall rupturing, and with intestinal coalescence in the wound, which was not sewn but left to heal secondarily.

Not until the late nineteenth century would good suprapubic lithotomy become possible with the advance of narcosis and asepsis. Then the bladder—after being drained—and the abdominal wall could both be closed primarily. Today the suprapubic lithotomy is a simple routine operation, whose proud traditions are shown by its conventional name: *sectio alta*, the "high cut".

Pott's four ailments

Cheselden's status as the foremost English surgeon passed to an apprentice. Percivall Pott was born in 1714 on what would become historic ground—the site in Threadneedle Street in London where the Bank of England still stands. When he was only a few months old, his father died, leaving a poor widow. At fifteen, Pott went to study surgery with Edward Nourse of St. Bartholomew's. This prominent doctor charged 200 pounds (equivalent to about 10,000 pounds today) for seven years of instruction. The bill was paid by Pott's distant relative, the Bishop of Rochester.

Surgeons who gave private lessons were usually attached to one of the large hospitals. When Pott received an honour, his "Freedom of the Company of Barber-Surgeons" (this was before the society's division), he started his own private

A Blank Tombstone

It was a consummate method for removing bladder stones that the Franciscan monk known as Frère Jacques demonstrated for the medical faculty in Paris. This institution might have forgiven a failure—but to see its own ability surpassed by someone else was, as the historian Brian Inglis says, simply too much. Persecution followed; after Brother John's death, the story goes that his name was erased from his tombstone and from all the registries, to ensure that nobody honoured his memory.

A Prescription for Bladder Stones

The prominent internal physician Richard Lower (1631-91) was an ingenious experimenter and a leading physiologist of his day. But he apparently went wrong when it came to the effect of fanciful bone-meal water on bladder stones:

"To alleviate a stone-attack and the usually consequent retention of urine, take snailshells and bees in equal quantities, dry them in a moderately hot oven, and grind them to a very fine powder. Take as much of this as a sixpence holds, dissolve it in a quarter-mug of bone-meal water, and give it on an empty stomach, followed by two hours of fasting, every day for three days in a row. It has often been found to break down the stone and drive the urine forth."

Bladder Stones and Legal Milestones

When "justice" was administered after the unhappy Monmouth Rebellion of 1685 in England, the trials were conducted by Lord Jeffreys of Wem, and known as the "bloody assizes". His death-sentences added up to 331, and the worst thing was how they came about. Not a word of self-defence was allowed and the intolerant magistrate drove the prosecution at top speed. Eventually the explanation was revealed: Jeffreys had a bladder stone. Early in the year, he began having trouble urinating, which became ever more painful, forcing him to pass water almost hourly. The trials turned into a martyrdom which he had to get through as fast as possible in order to reach the lavatory!

Hare's Foot Versus Stone-Colic

Samuel Pepys (1633-1703), the famous diarist who recreated the British fleet during Charles II's restoration, was plagued by kidney and bladder stones. When only 22, he was operated on for a stone "as big as a tennis ball" by the leading lithotomist Thomas Hollister of Bart's. This was done in the house of one Mrs. Turner, for better folk avoided the hospitals and stayed with well-placed friends to ensure good aftercare.

Pepys was happy about the operation, but continued to have attacks and often passed "gravel" with his urine. He tried to ward off the attacks by drinking turpentine, which can hardly have been ideal, since it damages the kidneys—in fact he was to die of chronic kidney inflammation and urinary poisoning. As a further safety-measure, he carried a hare's foot. When this did not help, a friend pointed out that it would work only if it included a joint!

Pepys never had children. It has been assumed that his operation, probably made by the lateral perineal cut, rendered him sterile—a frequent complication. On the other hand, it did nothing to inhibit his sexuality, as his diaries eloquently prove.

practice in Fenchurch Street, and also became a doctor at Bart's. He served as its chief physician from 1749 until 1787.

On a cold January morning in 1756, Pott was riding at Southwark. The horse suddenly slipped and threw him off. He received an open fracture of the lower leg, with the bone ends protruding through the skin. Knowing how a fracture could be worsened by bad transport, Pott got himself home, using a detached door as a stretcher, borne by sure-handed men who were accustomed to carrying ladies in sedan-chairs. His surgeon colleagues gathered and agreed that amputation was the only course, since such fractures risked infection and blood poisoning.

The instruments were already laid out when Edward Nourse arrived at a gallop, and advised taking the chance of conservative treatment. Pott was clever enough to keep out of the discussion—a doctor is never objective about his own health or his family's!—and Nourse won the day. The bone was restored and splinted, fortune smiled, and Pott retained a usable leg. Breaks of this kind have since been called "Pott's fracture", which is a rather odd origin for a medical term.

As many as four ailments bear Pott's name. Besides the fracture, there is "Pott's puffy tumour", a swelling in the skull roof due to local inflammation. Insufficient blood supply in the legs is a cause of "Pott's gangrene". And "Pott's disease" is a special condition of the spine resulting from tuberculosis. This last illness was not, of course, discovered by Pott, for the pathology and bacteriology of tuberculosis came to light a century after his time.

Pott devoted the long convalescence from his leg injury to scientific writing. One year after Southwark, *A Treatise on Ruptures* was published. He gave ruptures a very wide definition, including the congenital "rupture" whose anatomy was described quite correctly. Pott was also an enthusiastic advocate of early operations for obstructed hernia, which were adventurous before the invention of antiseptics and narcosis, but are taken for granted today. His ideas about

PERCIVALL Pott, in an engraving from a portrait by the prominent painter Sir Nathaniel Dance.

ruptures were developed in a more detailed treatise, and it led to a bitter academic feud with the Hunter brothers, who demanded priority for tracing the anatomy of congenital ruptures. In truth, neither side was first—the condition had already been described in 1754 by Albrecht von Haller!

Following a book on tear-duct ailments, Pott wrote his great *Observations on the Nature and*

**From Pott's
"Chirurgical Observations"**

Surgery has undergone many great transformations during the past fifty years, and many are to be thanked for their contributions—yet when we think of how many remain to be made, it should rather stimulate our inventiveness than fuel our vanity.

Consequences of Wounds and Contusions of the Head, a systematization of skull-injuries. Another significant work of 1768 dealt with bone fractures and joint dislocations: it reflected his personal experience and, predictably, gave much space to "Pott's fracture". He reported having often seen open lower-leg fractures healed by conservative treatment. In other words, he had repeated his own treatment on other patients.

What made Pott's reputation as a fine clinician and observer, though, was an essay only five pages long, in his *Chirurgical Observations* of 1775. It dealt with cancer among chimney-sweeps. He was the first to see a connection between their smoky working conditions and scrotal cancer. Their own term for this occupational disease was "soot-warts". In Pott's day, such warts were regarded as as a sexual ailment, not least because they often produced sores and could resemble syphilis. But Pott realized that a tumour was involved:

"It is a hard fate that afflicts these people. During their early childhood, they are usually treated with the greatest brutality, freezing and nearly starving to death. They have to squeeze themselves up through narrow and sometimes hot chimneys where they tear and burn themselves, and on reaching puberty they become peculiarly sensitive to a troubling, deadly illness which apparently results from deposits of soot in the skin folds of the scrotum."

This is the world's earliest description of a link between tar products and cancer. It would take until 1915 for Pott's observation to be supported. Then Yamagiwa and Ichikawa in Japan showed that tar from a gasworks, brushed on rabbit ears, caused a typical cancer.

Percivall Pott died of pneumonia in 1788. He lies buried in the little city church of St. Mary's Aldermary, near the place of his life's work. The tomb inscription befits his times, and anything more grandiloquent is hard to imagine—it was written by his son, who became archdeacon at St. Albans. Still, it rings true:

"...while he learned from his predecessors, he also discovered their errors and set them right, pointed out their shortcomings and filled them. Original in thought, quick in judgement, and decisive in action, he put knowledge to its proper use..."

The Hunter brothers

Two of the main representatives of British surgery, the brothers William and John Hunter, came from a poor but frugal and clever Scottish farming family in Long Calderwood, not far from Glasgow. William was born in 1718, ten years before John. He began studies in theology, yet five years at Glasgow University left him with doubts of his own ability as well as of religion. In low spirits, he took a job with William Cullen, then a mere rural doctor.

Cullen had a gift for teaching, recognized the pupil's qualities, and made sure that he went on to study with the oldest of the three famous physicians named Alexander Monro in Edinburgh. After that, William proceeded to London as a student of the obstetrician Smellie, and as assistant to the anatomist James Douglas—brother of Cheselden's antagonist. Later on, Cullen was to display pride and pedagogy as professor of medicine at Edinburgh. Thus William had the luck to be educated by four of Britain's leading doctors and teachers.

James Douglas, best known to posterity through the name of the uterine "Douglassian cavity", died in 1742. His anatomical knowledge and scientific interest had taken root in William Hunter, who afterward started writing with an essay on the blood supply to the knee joint. William then toured the Continent for further studies in anatomy, and opened his own anatomical school in Great Windmill Street in London. The house still stands, although there is now a stage over the place where corpses were buried after dissections.

This school followed the "Paris principle", meaning that each student dissected the whole body on his own. It became a success in both pedagogical and financial terms. At the same time, Hunter was an active surgeon at Middlesex and other hospitals, boasting the curious title "surgeon-man-midwife" The implication is that he came to deal chiefly with obstetrics, and in this capacity he advanced with vast satisfaction to the post of "Physician Extraordinary to the Queen".

William Hunter was elegant and vain, thrifty and careful of his dignity—the opposite of his brother John. As a fashionable child-deliverer, he was the darling of society and had little time for research. His *Anatomy of the Gravid Uterus* was an exquisite book, and embryologically correct: a recent judgement is that it has never been surpassed. Unfortunately, it kindled a long-latent feud between the brothers. William had perhaps exploited John's dissection work, and the latter felt cheated.

The monumental figures of medicine clearly include John Hunter (1728–93). By putting operative surgery on a solid scientific basis, he has earned every bit of the assessment that "he alone made surgeons into gentlemen". In other words, he finalized their elevation from artisans into scientists. To be sure, he was slow off the mark—an unusually difficult child who learned to read several years after his siblings did. Yet his fascination with nature began early. He collected and catalogued birds' eggs, studied insects and other small creatures. As he later wrote, "I plagued folk with questions which no one could answer or even be troubled to know about".

John's development was sluggish and long. Only in his twenties—four to five years after the normal start of a boy's professional career—was he sent, unwillingly, to assist his brother in London. Making anatomical preparations, he quickly showed talent for the medical art. Hundreds of his preparations were destroyed during the Blitz of World War II, but the many which survive exhibit a love of precision, pedagogical presentation and aesthetic appearance. He continued to make them all his life, turning the direct study of nature into colossal knowledge of the structure and development of animals and human beings. It is said that he dissected everything from a bee to a whale. And the whale, towed home by none other than Captain Cook, was prepared with a blubber-axe while moored at a quay in the Thames!

Along with his dissection work, John studied under Cheselden at Chelsea Hospital. He presumably went on to attend Pott's lectures. William tried to put a little polish on this sulky redhaired brother, who even refused to wear a wig, and sent him to Oxford for lessons in decorum and classical languages. It was a lost cause, and John had enough in three months: "They endeavoured to make an old lady of me, and teach me Latin and Greek, but I treated all efforts as one squashes a louse…" He returned to the dissection-hall in London.

For four years he worked day and night, making thousands of preparations, observing and learning. Unhealthy life, and the practical unavoidability of infection in the anatomy room, gave him tuberculosis. After an acute attack, both he and William realized that he had to leave London. William's good connections found him employment as a doctor in the army. He served at the siege of Belle Isle in France, then in Portugal. The work was not hard, but he treated many wounds and laid the basis for his last publication, which is counted among his best: *Treatise on Blood, Inflammation and Gun-Shot Wounds.* Its novelty was to treat shot injuries just like any other wound, there being no reason to enlarge them:

"It is against all the rules of surgery and against what we know of animal economy to make a wound larger, unless one needs to prepare it to do something more—if it is a complicated wound that must be treated in a special way; it should not be opened simply because it is a wound, but because something must be done which cannot be done without

THE Hunter brothers, John (*left*) and William.

making the wound larger. This is ordinary surgery and it should also be war surgery in regard to shot injuries."

With the acceptance of Hunter's doctrine, a conclusive death-blow was dealt to the old "gunpowder poison" controversy.

Two years of open-air life improved his lungs. On coming back to London, John Hunter opened his own anatomical school and surgical practice. His research continued as intensively as before. One of his hypotheses was that two diseases could not exist simultaneously in the same organ: syphilis and gonorrhoea thus ought to be different symptoms of the same sexual illness. To prove it, he injected himself with pus

from a gonorrhoea patient who, unbeknownst to him, also had syphilis. When he contracted the hard canker which is a primary symptom of syphilis, he thought the proof was there.

He then had to undergo the long syphilis cure with silver nitrate and mercury. Experimenting constantly with himself, he took no medicine for considerable periods, to see how the canker reacted. It needed three years to heal finally. He had told his fiancée that she must wait until he fully recovered. The wedding was celebrated in 1771, at eight o'clock on a Sunday morning— the only time of the week when he could spare time for such an irrelevant act. His wife, Anne Home, created a place for herself in history as the author of a song:

"My mother bids me bind my hair
with bands of rosy hue,
to tie up my sleeves with ribbons rare,
and lace my bodice blue."

It was set to music by Haydn, for whose *Creation* she also wrote a libretto, although it was later replaced with a much worse one by Lidley.

Meanwhile, Hunter's *Natural History of the Teeth* had been published. In 1767, he became a member of the Royal Society, which only accepted the authors of important scientific writings. His entrance piece was an article on digestive fluids. Unaware of the fact, he included an acceptable background for the origin of stomach ulcers. His anatomical work proceeded: he had a large house in Leicester Square—where his bust still stands—and a menagerie at Earl's Court, employing fifty people in his household and laboratory! He was now the city's leading surgeon, inspector of all its hospitals, senior physician in the army, and a doctor at St. George's, with a rewarding private practice. Science took everything he earned and, despite enormous income, he lived in poverty and debt.

John Hunter's surgical writings made history. It is safe to say that nobody ever influenced the subject more thoroughly and broadly. His exact observations, practical skill, operative boldness—still based on sound knowledge—and freedom from previous authority were what gave his contributions their special value. He wrote on bleeding and surgical shock, blood coagulation and clots, tissue transplants and sexual illnesses, wounds and arterial inflammation, aneurysms and other inflammations. Mostly published in *Philosophical Transactions*, his works were eventually collected into a book. A further volume, *Venereal Diseases*, partly embodied his self-experimentation.

An instance of his surgical courage is an operation for aneurysm, possibly the most famous ever performed. To begin with, in the spring of 1785, Hunter became interested in the horn-shedding of deer. He found that the horns' blood

supply changed under different conditions: a rich network of blood vessels developed when the crown was in its prime and needed most nourishment, but the vessels decreased in number and size when the horns were shed. Hunter inferred that human beings develop reserve vessels—what we call collateral vessels—if an obstruction occurs in their arteries. Thus, the vascular system is not static but highly dynamic, a function of supply and demand.

In the autumn of that year, a beer-deliverer was admitted to St. George's Hospital with a pulsating tumour in his knee-joint. It may have been caused by long pressure against the coachman's seat while driving on rough streets. The patient could hardly walk, and stopped often to rest the leg. So there was presumably a blood obstruction just under the pulsating aneurysm, which might break at any moment. The common treatment was to amputate, far enough above the spot to avoid knotting up the supply vessel and causing gangrene and blood poisoning. But Hunter's experiments with deer had taught him that a new net of vessels must have developed past the obstruction, or the lower leg would be dead already. Could these vessels be sufficient, if the aneurysm were removed without taking off the leg?

Hunter cut the inner thigh just above the knee—a place known to anatomists as Hunter's channel—and tied under the large thigh artery at four points. The ligature ends were left long and drawn out through the wound, according to custom. Four were used because a single ligature would have to be drawn so tight that it might cut through and cause bleeding. Although a primary healing was intended, the wound formed pus; yet this was cleared up and the beer-deliverer left the hospital without pain, his aneurysm cured and his leg intact. Later, Hunter did four similar operations, and three were successful: the fourth patient bled to death twenty-six days after the operation.

John Hunter's restless activity was remarkable for having been carried out by a sick man, fighting against a lung illness for nearly all of his adult life. Moreover, he soon contracted coronary arteriosclerosis, which gave him angina pectoris. "My life lies in the hands of whoever irritates me," he used to say, meaning that mental disturbances can bring on dangerous attacks. Indeed, he died of acute coronary ischaemia—interruption of blood supply to heart muscles—during a meeting with his hospital staff, the sort of event which has led many subsequent doctors to the point of collapse.

Hunter was buried in the crypt of the parish church, St. Martin in the Fields. Only when his many disciples, Clift, Cline, Abernethy, Jenner, Baillie, Blizard and Astley Cooper, had made it clear to posterity what a giant of surgery he was, did an effort get under way to find his

An Interior View of Hunter's Home

As the wife of the world's most tireless anatomical collector and experimenter, Anne put up with a good deal, and did so gladly. She did not complain when the house overflowed with mummified exotica, embalmed foetuses with double heads, fossils, skeletons, corpses; when students, authors and dissectors ran from room to room, dripping with filth and excrement, bloodied to the elbows. The garden was a Golgotha of bones from animals and humans. A stuffed giraffe was too tall to fit under the roof, but John shortened it by cutting its legs below the knees, and placed it in the hall—a sight that numbed Anne's fastidious guests! This portrait is given by John Kobler in The Reluctant Surgeon.

Remarks by John Hunter

A gentleman commented that he had no wish to lose the reputation he perhaps had as a surgeon by delivering lectures, which at least was modest. In regard to the improvement of surgery, one of its representatives said that he could see no field where it was capable of improvement. The natural conclusion from this utterance is that such a man would not be able to improve it.

The operation is a silent confession of the surgeon's inadequacy.

It is as important to understand the principles of our art as to understand the principles of all other sciences.

(When showing some corpses to Philip Syng Physick's father:) These are the books which your son will be reading under my supervision; others are worth very little.
(In a letter to Edward Jenner:) I believe your solution is right, but why believe? Why not make an experiment?

Hunter's Museum

It took John Hunter thirty years to amass his collection of anatomical, embryological and pathological preparations, at a personal cost of some 70,000 pounds. In the last decade of his life, the collections were arranged by the young surgeon William Bell, to be followed by William Clift and, in 1800 according to Hunter's testament, by the Royal College of Surgeons of England.

A succession of devoted, clever superintendents sorted and catalogued the 65,000 preparations. Most of these were destroyed by a bomb raid in May 1941. The rest, and the preparations which could be restored, have been rearranged for public display in the Royal College of Surgeons in Lincoln's Inn Fields in London. Here we can behold, for example, the skeleton of "the Irish Giant", a huge man who was still alive when Hunter bought his remains. Once the man felt death approaching, he regretted the sale and tried to flee from London, but Hunter's servants shadowed him and eventually brought the body home in triumph!

remains. They were located in a poor-coffin, among thousands of others, in an obscure corner. But then it was moved to the company of great men and kings in Westminster Abbey. The Royal College of Surgeons of England provided an inscription:

"to record admiration of his genius, and as a gifted interpreter of the Divine power and wisdom at work in organic life, and its grateful veneration for his services to mankind as the founder of scientific surgery."

Punching the professors

Surgeons and "learned doctors" were separated by a wider gap in contemporary France than in any other country. One reason was the medical faculties with their inherited pomposity and ingrained immunity to constructive thinking. However, the surgeons' competence really was poor, and most practitioners had a lower social status than anywhere else. Apart from luminaries like Ambroise Paré and some obstetricians of merit, the art was conducted largely as a hobby of the barber-journeymen, with correspondingly poor quality. Even the executioners' assistants earned extra money from minor surgery. These were said to be worth employing because they learned about human anatomy by drawing and quartering their victims!

Attempts to advance the knowledge and social status of surgeons had not been lacking. In 1645, the few surgeons who possessed some academic education merged with the barbers' guild into a college, for support of common interests. This brought an immediate reaction from the university physicians, who soon triumphed: the surgeons were forbidden to bear academic titles, and thus could not even call themselves doctors. Nor was the new organization allowed to term itself a *collège*, which might indicate higher education.

Still, it had money—a signal advantage over the penniless medical faculty. It could build a demonstration-hall for surgical instruction, which it placed next to the *École de Médicine*, annoying the professors. The inauguration was not very peaceful. Led by their dean, the faculty marched to the new edifice for a protest. A general fist-fight resulted, and the professors had to leave the scene with their tails between their legs.

The fresh spirit of surgical education was Georges Maréchal (1658–1736). As personal physician to Louis XIV and Louis XV, he got permission to establish an *Académie Royale de Chirurgie*. The designation "royal" was especially painful to the medical faculty, which drew no comfort from a monarchic decree that the Academy would be totally independent and its members would have the same ranks and rights as the faculty.

The Academy had great importance for the rehabilitation of French surgery. At first, it consisted of the seventy leading "master-surgeons" in Paris. Its initial president was naturally Maréchal. His successors, Germain-Pichaut de la Martinière (1696–1783) and François de Lapeyronie (1678–1747), were no less dedicated to improving surgical education. A new significant step was taken in 1775 when the Academy's own building opened, designed by the king's own architect. An irony of fate is that it now holds the administration of the medical faculty!

Among the most brilliant Academy members was Jean-Louis Petit (1674–1760). As a precocious child, he preferred anatomical dissections to playing with toys. His later teacher was the clever anatomist and surgeon Alexis Littré (1658–1726), who made Jean-Louis an assistant at the age of seven! At eighteen, he became a surgeon in the army and settled in Paris, lecturing and demonstrating in anatomy and surgery. His private courses gained such fame that apprentices came from far outside the country.

Of Petit's significant writings on surgery, most dealt with cancer, skeletal and blood-vessel diseases. He was the first to show how breast cancer spread to a woman's regional lymph glands in the armpit. His surgical work occurred at the

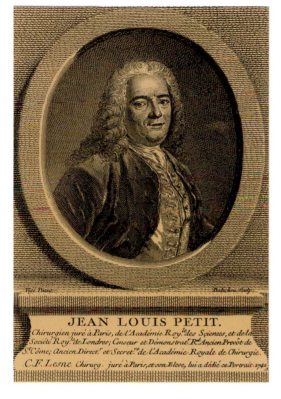

JEAN LOUIS PETIT.

*Chirurgien juré à Paris, de l'Académie Roy.le des Sciences, et de la
Société Roy.le de Londres; Censeur et Démonstrat.r Ancien Prevôt de
S.t Côme; Ancien Direct.r et Secret.re de l'Académie Royale de Chirurgie.*

C.F. Lesne Chirurg. juré à Paris, et son Eleve, lui a dédié ce Portrait 1742.

AN engraving of Petit from about 1765.

The Hangman as Surgeon

*France was not alone in letting the servants of
executioners function as surgeons. As early
as 1579, the hangman Anders Freimut of
Copenhagen received permission to set fractures and treat old wounds. This hobby of
Danish executioners apparently became traditional. King Christian V conferred a salary
on Copenhagen's hangman because he fixed a
broken leg for a court-page. As late as 1732,
Bergen's executioner obtained a royal writ for
the right to practise minor surgery. Frederick I
of Prussia even appointed his favourite hangman as personal physician!*

Well-Armed Well-Wishers

*When the surgeons built themselves a new,
monumental amphitheatre, the medical faculty
members were gripped with envy, as they
had to hold forth in their ramshackle hall from
1617. It was only in 1745 that they too, led
by Jacques-Bénigne Winslow (1669-1760),
were able to inaugurate a new amphitheatre,
"la Rotonde", in the Rue de la Bucherie. This
alone survives of the old faculty's premises.
Begun in 1742, it rescued the members from
an increasing danger of flooding by the Seine
in their original hall. At the inauguration,
Winslow dissected a man's body. The party
invitation stated: "Forbidden to enter with
canes and swords". Such was the fear of
an attack by the surgical students from
St. Côme. For invited surgeons, special ben-
ches were reserved; and between the enemy
camps, police took up cautious positions…
These recollections come from A. Chevalier,
The Medical Faculty of Paris in the
Seventeenth and Eighteenth Centuries.*

Charité Hospital in Paris, where he also gave
practical instruction. Together with Dionis, he
was the founder of modern French surgical education. His memory as an anatomist is honoured
by the name of a muscular gap in the back, the
trigonum Petiti.

Petit was replaced as the country's leading
surgeon by Pierre-Joseph Desault (1744–95),
chief physician at the Hôtel Dieu hospital. He
developed almost equally early and, after only a
few years' study at the Paris faculty, became so
good in anatomy that he began to give private
lectures at the age of twenty-two. It was then
that all teaching outside the faculty was forbidden, and he too received a sharp command to
stop such nonsense. To the credit of certain
faculty members, they took Desault's lectures

under their protection, thus fulfilling the formal requirements. His large audience included not only contemporary students, but even chief doctors at some of the city's hospitals!

Trained as an anatomist, Desault started to think about technical improvements of surgery in, for example, amputation or blood-vessel ligature. But he was not associated with any hospital, and had to let older colleagues try his ideas. Despite the great jealousy among many older doctors, he could not be stopped from joining the Academy, and next from becoming chief physician at the Charité. Six years later, he went to the Hôtel Dieu, regarded as the city's foremost hospital.

Desault's own theoretical instruction offered novelties. Anatomy was to be learned in the dissection-hall, and not limited to the body's structure, which he considered to be dead knowledge unless it was connected with bodily functions. His pedagogical skill became even more evident when he was made a professor at the École Pratique and a chief physician. He abandoned podium lectures and was one of the first surgeons in the world to begin teaching at the bedside. This new, attractive form of instruction drew in students from all over Europe, and many called Desault the Continent's leading surgeon.

His further career was cut short by the French Revolution. The higher institutions of medical learning were closed, and Desault was even arrested—probably through betrayal by one of his numerous rivals. Yet after three days he was released: the new government realized that, especially in these bloody times, the nation's best surgeon could not be dispensed with. He received a fresh job when the medical and surgical faculties were merged into the École de Santé (School of Health). However, his enthusiasm had gone. It would only reappear when he was summoned to the Crown Prince, who had fallen ill in prison. As if to show who had a right to benefit from his art, he gave the patient all his time. Unfortunately he did not get to finish the case, but came down with some infection him-

self and died of blood poisoning, when only fifty-one years old.

The best disciple and friend of Desault was Xavier Bichat (1771–1802). He had been a surgeon's apprentice in the Austrian war, and came to Paris after peace was made, drawn by the already legendary teaching at the Hôtel Dieu. Desault was not slow to see the young student's potential, invited him into his own home, and gave him a job as assistant. He also edited the new *Journal de Chirurgie*, which Desault had initiated but found ever less time to deal with. Not even Bichat's enthusiasm kept it alive—the last two volumes were written entirely by himself! The dearth of writers is a clear sign that Desault and Bichat stood pretty much alone as spokesmen of French scientific surgery in the early revolutionary years.

Bichat died prematurely at 31, due either to typhus or to tubercular cerebral meningitis. The latter cause is a plausible one. It is a strange but common fact that tuberculosis patients show hectic activity before the illness reaches a terminal stage, and Bichat would have been a shining example. He dissected six hundred bodies in a single winter! During his last three years, he produced three thick books including new ideas. He was a forerunner of modern cellular patho-

---

Bichat's Principle

Life is the sum of the functions that resist death.

Alms for the Curer

When Xavier Bichat expired unexpectedly at the age of 31, the surgeon Jean-Nicolas Corvisart wrote to his master Napoleon: "Bichat has just died. Nobody ever did so much in such a short time…but there is not even enough money in the house to pay for the funeral…"

logy, which half a century later was to gain its foremost representative in Rudolf Virchow. He emphasized the tissues, rather than organs, in pathological theory:

"We cannot, therefore, deny that a change in just one of an organ's tissues is frequently enough to disturb the functions in all the others; yet likewise, it is in only one of them that the evil originates."

Indeed, present-day doctors are reminded of his name by one tissue—the fat in the cheeks is called Bichat's fatty body.

Napoleon's surgeon

The state of French surgery, then, was fairly dismal at the outbreak of the revolution in 1789. Field medicine and military hospital organization were not the least confused. Doctors had to work in the wake of the battles, when darkness allowed collection of the wounded who were still able to attract attention. Hygiene was almost totally ignored, and the medics had no interest in prevention of disease or traumatic fever. It might be said that the situation was worse than when the children of Israel wandered through the desert. Certainly hygienic prescriptions in the Old Testament were more rational than those in the French army.

In such circumstances did Dominique-Jean Larrey (1766–1842) of Beaudéan begin his career with the forces of war. It spanned not only the French Revolution, which started when he was just 23, but the entire Napoleonic Age—undoubtedly one of the most lively periods in the history of France. Larrey lost his parents at 13 and was adopted by his uncle Alexis, a senior physician in Toulouse. After more than six years as a surgical apprentice, he was sent to Paris for a better theoretical education, to his uncle's everlasting credit. A grand tour to foreign universities had also been planned, but the war intervened. The nation needed military doctors, and Larrey signed up as a candidate.

DOMINIQUE-JEAN Larrey at the age of 38, as a baron in the newly proclaimed empire of Napoleon.

In contrast to England, whose fleet physicians were usually alcoholic surgeons fit for nothing else, France had naval doctors with good reputations and solid wages, so their jobs were in demand. Larrey passed the tests and was appointed to the frigate *Vigilante*, bound for Newfoundland to help the French fishing fleet. However, he was impatient and went to Brest, well in advance, to prepare himself. Learning what the mission could involve, he inspected the medical equipment, and did something even more unusual for an eighteenth-century doctor: he obtained books on both surgery and the destination of the journey.

The expedition proved a fiasco for him. Continually seasick, he returned to Brest after six months, resigned to leaving the navy. Back in Paris, he was soon performing field surgery on victims from the streets, both at Desault's clinic in the Hôtel Dieu and at Les Invalides. New Year's Day of 1790 found him established as assistant senior surgeon in the latter institution.

When international war broke out in 1792, Larrey became a field doctor, ranking as major with the Rhine army. While it waited at Strasbourg for something to happen, he turned his tireless energy to organizing a military medical association in the city. Once the fighting erupted, he got more than his share of active surgery. Not many battles were needed to convince him that the wounded could only be saved through better organization:

"I now discovered the trouble it took us to move our bandaging stations—our military hospitals. According to the rules, they were supposed to stay about five kilometres from the army. The wounded were left on the field until the battle was over, or gathered at some convenient spot to which the ambulance rushed. But the roads were so choked with waggons, and such delays arose, that most of the victims died before the ambulance arrived. This gave me the idea of building an ambulance that was adequate to help the wounded during the actual battle."

Particularly after a skirmish at Limburg, the conditions were so awful that Larrey wrote to the general with a definite proposal:

"My suggestion was accepted and I received orders to construct a cart which I called the flying ambulance. My first plan was to transport the wounded on a horse-litter, but experience soon made me give it up. The next effort was to make a cart with good suspension, combining speed with safety and comfort."

He described his cart in a report of 1797 from the campaign in Italy. Yet the system comprised much more. For him, an ambulance meant both the means of transport and the personnel who accompanied it. These were a doctor, quartermaster, noncommissioned officer and twenty-four infantrymen, besides a drummer-boy who carried the bandage kit. Also included were twelve light and four heavy dressing-barrows. Larrey thought of the smallest details, such as replacing the saddles' pistol-holsters by courier-bags full of instruments and bandages.

The flying ambulance became a success. Its trial by fire came at Landau, with the seventeen-day attack by Hoche. Despite a leg wound of his own, Larrey went on operating. In April 1793, he was sent back to Paris with orders to arrange flying ambulances for the whole army. His commander had mentioned him in a report, probably the first time such a distinction was conferred on a physician: "His care of the wounded contributed essentially to the cause of humanity and the honour of the fatherland."

Larrey served afterward as senior field doctor in Corsica and Spain. There he had a fine opportunity to study leg amputation, since the Spaniards mined their roads of retreat. The cold in the Spanish highlands taught him how to treat frostbite, which he would encounter often in Russia. He was not above learning from the enemy, whose bandaging techniques were so good that he adopted them as a standard method for his army. With the peace, he briefly became professor of surgery at the military hospital of Val-de-Grace, where his statue still stands. By that time, his skill had been demonstrated in virtually all areas, and Napoleon, when planning the Egyptian campaign, insisted that Larrey should lead the medical corps.

The Middle East was a hard host: its heat, thirst and hunger aggravated the injuries of war. Nor did matters improve when Nelson's fleet captured the ships that brought medical supplies. Only after the Battle of the Pyramids did Larrey get control over his material. The first field hospital was erected at Gizeh, in the shadow of the Sphinx. It was here, and later in Sudan, Syria and Palestine, that Larrey showed his brilliant abilities. Apart from the practical work—at Acre he himself performed seventy amputations and seven trepanations—he adapted his flying ambulances to the desert war, and built camel-litters. Efficiency rose until the wounded were being collected in seldom more than fifteen minutes. He also found time to write down observations about typhus, bubonic plague, leprosy and trachoma. His notes went out to the officers and taught them to take the prophylactic measures known in their day.

LARREY'S *ambulance volante* in a version of about 1802, with a closed litter suspended by leaf-springs on a fast two-wheeled cart. It became the century's standard way of collecting the wounded in war.

When he came home, Larrey was made a baron by Napoleon—and an honorary surgeon of the *Chasseurs de Garde*, who continued to function as the emperor's personal bodyguard in both war and peace. He followed Napoleon in every campaign, including Moscow, Austerlitz and Waterloo, chalking up a total of 25 campaigns, 60 large battles and 400 small ones. In the end he enjoyed well-earned leisure, writing his memoirs. They are not only of medical interest, but have been very valuable to researchers in Napoleonic history because of their factual objectivity. Napoleon, knowing how to treat a personal surgeon, stated in his own testament:

"To the French Army's surgeon general Baron Larrey, I leave a sum of one hundred thousand francs. He is the worthiest man I ever met."

Larrey Condemned

After Waterloo, Larrey was imprisoned by the Prussians and immediately given a death sentence. In the nick of time he was recognized by a German doctor who had once attended his lectures at Val-de-Grace. This man went straight to Marshal Blücher and pleaded for his old teacher's life. It turned out that once, when Blücher's son was wounded in a skirmish and taken by the French, his life had been saved by Larrey. Not surprisingly, the baron was released under oath and, with a Prussian escort, returned to his country.

According to an apocryphal tale from Waterloo, Wellington watched a French doctor going calmly about and bandaging casualties in the thick of battle. The Duke bared his head and said, "I salute such a doctor's honour and loyalty!" Yet Wellington had more to do than gaze at individual healers among the enemy—and hatless sentiments hardly agreed with his stuffy personality.

Three Continental pioneers

The book which had greatest influence on surgery in central Europe during the eighteenth century was entitled, quite simply, *Surgery*. By Lorenz Heister (1683–1758), it appeared in seven German and ten English editions—not to mention French, Italian, Dutch, and three editions in Latin.

Heister, educated in Frankfurt-am-Main, went on to study in Giessen, Leyden and Amsterdam, where he was apprentice to the Dutch anatomists and surgeons Ruysch and Rau. In 1708, he took a doctoral degree at the university of Hardwijk. Surgical handicrafts had occupied him in Ruysch's dissection chamber, and with several clever professionals in the hospitals of Amsterdam, a city which was then one of the centres of surgical education in Europe. Ruysch got him a postgraduate appointment as chief surgeon in the Dutch army—obviously a rapid promotion, which would hardly have been possible without nepotistic backing.

In a book of surgical and anatomical observations, published a couple of years before his death, Heister left some autobiographical notes. Here we can read of the young surgeon's almost incredible inquisitiveness about medicine. If, during his campaigns with the Flemish army, he heard of a surgeon in the vicinity doing anything unusual, he let nothing stop him from paying a visit—even when the operation was in the enemy camp! His interest took root before his medical studies began. He also told how, at the age of seventeen, he had gone to the market in Frankfurt, where travelling quacks operated on hernias, cataracts, gallstones and harelips. Some of them had gradually become quite adept. At the height of his surgical career, he still had deep admiration for a man named Eisenbart who specialized in hernias:

"In the year 1700, at Easter Market, a boy of nine was brought there with hernia. His parents, unable to get any help from Frankfurt's famous physicians, were now begging for an operation on the child. People of that sort do

LORENZ Heister at the peak of his career, with academic titles ranging from London to Berlin.

not try to treat hernia with bandages, since these seldom last longer than the market and can hardly cure a hernia in such a short time. They have another reason as well: a hernia bandage earns them only ten shillings, whereas an operation costs far more... so they always recommend an operation! This migrant doctor took in the patient, gave him a laxative and operated..."

Heister described the process in detail and confirmed that everything went well: after three weeks the wound healed perfectly. His memoirs show profound respect for the travelling quacks, as long as they stuck to their specialties. Among other things, he once watched the same Eisenbart operate successfully upon a woman with a large, malignant tumour on her jawline, presumably in the salivary gland. He also had a chance to see one of the eighteenth century's most famous charlatans in action. This was "Gentleman" John Taylor who, it must be admitted, was exceedingly good at cataract operations.

In the spring of 1710, Heister was invited by the republic of Nuremberg to become professor of anatomy and surgery at the university in Altdorf, which thus acquired a place on the "surgical map". Eleven years later, he moved to Helmstedt in Braunschweig, where he was to stay for thirty-eight years. Under his leadership, this faculty grew into one of Europe's best, a happy situation which ceased at the moment of Heister's death in 1758.

Lorenz Heister constantly preached that an operation ought to be made as elementary as possible. "In every surgical intervention, one should prefer the method which can be used with few and simple instruments, over that which requires a big apparatus difficult to work with: most such tools have been invented out of pomposity rather than utility." This did not prevent him from inventing and testing his own good surgical instruments, perhaps the best-known being an improved trepan and a device for removing tonsils. As mentioned in the last chapter, he was also among the pioneers of forceps.

His other great boost to surgical standards was a systematization of the subject, presented in the book *Chirurgie*. Admirably brief and easy to read, it was illustrated by beautiful copper-etchings of operation methods, step by step, which remind us of modern film-strips and, of course, contributed much to the book's huge popularity.

Heister was a forerunner in many areas. He was among the first to describe appendicitis, and told of a case on which he operated at Altdorf:

An Eighteenth-Century Cataract-Lancer

The braggart's prize certainly goes to Gentleman John Taylor, an eye doctor who was fairly good in his way—with obvious technical skill at, among other things, cataract operations. His swaggering proved too much even for his contemporaries. In his autobiography, he claimed to have cured the kings of England, Poland, Denmark and Sweden, many princes and countless nobles, as well as the Pope. Another of his "feats" was to relieve Johann Sebastian Bach of blindness at the age of 88, which we know is wrong because Bach died blind at 65. Taylor also pretended to have written forty-five scientific works, although whether he included his book The Art of Making Love With Success *is uncertain. In particular, he regarded nuns as far superior to other women in love, wit, vigour and mind, saying that he had visited— naturally in the line of work—every nunnery in Europe. Taylor was appointed "Oculist" by George II, who thus fulfilled an ancestral tradition of finding the most peculiar people for this post.*

Heister on Surgeons (1752)

It is necessary for a surgeon to have complete, or at least very good, knowledge in anatomy as well as in medicine, so that he has enough judgement and understanding to study all the causes and circumstances, and to draw his conclusions from them.

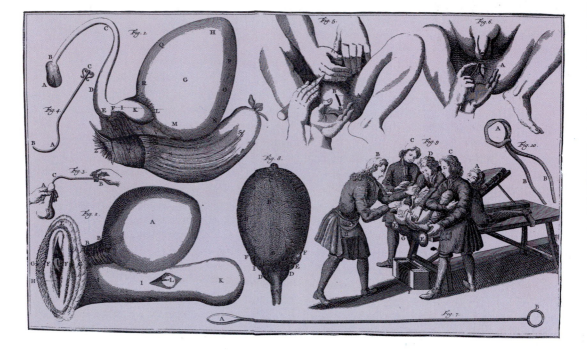

"When I was about to dissect the appendix, I found that this worm-shaped body had darkened too soon and was unusually adherent to the abdominal wall. As I tried to carefully draw it free, its walls burst—though the corpse was quite fresh—and released a few spoonfuls of pus. This proves the possibility of inflammation and pus formation in the appendix just as in other organs, a fact of which I have seen little remark in the literature. We should pay attention to it if, in practice, we find overheating and pain in the organ's vicinity…"

In addition, Heister was one of the first cancer surgeons. He put Eisenbart's lessons to work in 1733 by doing his own operation on a salivary-gland tumour. He developed thyroid operations, and was said to have performed the world's first thyroidectomy in 1752. Probably he was also the first to describe thyroid cancer: in *Chirurgie*, discussing what he called "bronchocele" (struma), he mentioned thyroid destruction "of malignant and cancerous nature which was

LITHOTOMY operations, shown in one of Heister's later books, *Institutiones Chirurgicae* (1739).

scirrhous (hard) and, to some extent, cut off the respiratory and digestive canals". Finally, it was Heister who established the still-valid term "tracheotomy" (for a windpipe incision), which was launched in 1649 by Feyens but had been obscured by the mistaken term "bronchotomy" (such operations are not done on the bronchia).

The name of Scarpa is familiar to modern anatomists and surgeons from many results of its owner's research. No fewer than ten such anatomical ideas have been listed, the best-known being the *fossa Scarpae* in the groin. But Antonio Scarpa (1752–1832) is more of a mystery. Italy's sole contribution to surgery at the end of the eighteenth century has been summed up well by Zimmerman and Weith:

"He was endowed with a brilliant and calculating intellect, enormous energy, boundless ambition, a passion for accuracy and exactness in his research, and a broad range of cultural and artistic interests... Lamentable aspects of his personality brought him hatred and opposition, which could only be held in check by the general fear of his power and ruthlessness..."

Scarpa took his entrance test at the University of Padua when only fifteen. He was instantly fascinated by the famous pathologist Morgagni, whose secretary and assistant he soon became. Five years later he took his degree and, through Morgagni, was made a professor and chief physician in Modena. There he got into an awful fight with the physiology professor, Luigi Galvani, until he shook off the city's dust with a two-year trip to London and Paris. He met both Pott and the Hunter brothers, and was inspired by John Hunter to start a museum for comparative anatomy when he returned home. Moreover, he learned new methods of teaching and introduced them to Italy, later settling in Pavia.

Among the fruits of Scarpa's tireless study was an operation for club-foot, still used in principle today. He described the anatomy of hernias, improved the ways of operating on them, and added to what was known of the eye's anatomy. His own talent in drawing produced some of the best illustrations in medical literature, such as those in his book *Results of Observations and Experience on the Principal Maladies of the Eyes*, published in Venice in 1802. His artistic bent emerged, too, in his collection of old Italian masterworks, bought with the shameless salaries he commanded.

As a faculty head, he ruled with an iron hand. Achille Monti's biography says that "he was cold as death, dreaded like an ancient god who had gone beyond justice; revengeful and merciless; you get the impression that people even quaked at him in his grave." Scarpa was not only the first of the great ruffians of surgery, but possibly the worst. That may have been why nobody wanted to deal with the writings he left behind, and his place in surgical history was unknown until recently.

Scandinavia, except for a few flashes in its darkness, was a medical "third world" until the seventeenth century, when Sweden became an international power. This new political role had to be dressed up in culture, the best example being Queen Christina's importation of the philosopher Descartes (1596–1650). In 1649, he found himself in wintry Stockholm. The odd queen's insistence on having lessons at five in the morning, in her unheated palace, took some months to kill the poor southern scientist with pneumonia. Her own physician—Balthasar Salinus, hired from Danzig—stood lower on the scale of refinement, but he had the apparent distinction of being the first to practise any important surgery in the country.

Salinus was a barber-surgeon, and several colleagues followed him. Simply because internists were almost nonexistent in Sweden, medicine was left to barber-surgeons until well into the

---

Outwitting Kidney-Stones

In J. J. Haartman's book Clear Information for Knowing and Checking the Commonest Diseases (1765), published in Swedish in Åbo, Finland, we read at last how to prevent stones in the kidney tracts:

"He whose body calls for wine, enjoying punch, red or white Portuguese, Madeira, fermented birch-leach, or mead, let him pass to drinking bread-water with wild strawberries, which should be strong as hops... take several trips daily, or each evening take 1/3 quintin (around 1 gram) of good Venetian soap, with 1/6 rhubarb and a little juniper-berry, or with 1/8 burnt shell of mussel, oyster or egg, with juniper-berry and burnt rose-hip, or borax or cress, as well as some pine or fir sap, or with pine ointment which especially helps pale bloated patients, whose bloody urine shows that their tracts are injured by stones..."

ANTONIO Scarpa.

OLOF af Acrel.

eighteenth century. Usually all aspiring doctors started their apprenticeship in that guild. With enough ambition and talent, they could proceed to theoretical studies at one of the two universities, in Uppsala and Lund. Further education was preferably acquired abroad.

The "father of Swedish surgery", however, was Olof Acrel (1717–1806), later ennobled as af Acrel. He reversed the traditional order of study, beginning with two years at Uppsala, where his teachers included Carl Linnaeus and Nils Rosén von Rosenstein. It was Gerhard Boltenhagen, son of a field-surgeon under King Karl XII, who taught him surgery. At twenty-one, he became an assistant to Schützer, the city surgeon of Stockholm, who was so old that Acrel had to do nearly all the work. Schützer appreciated his help and got him a state travel-grant, which he spent sparingly on five years of study in Europe. Indeed, the trip proved far more adventurous than Acrel could have foreseen.

In 1740 we find him at Göttingen, with Albrecht von Haller (1708–1777). Already famous throughout the Continent as a medical genius, Haller was a pioneer of physiology and experimental medicine, the author of nine volumes (*Elementa Physiologiae Corporis Humani*) which were long considered an exhaustive study of the body's functions. As a professor, Haller also covered surgery, but less proficiently than theoretical sciences. Besides, this university town had a serious lack of resources, and Haller's students had to practise by operating on turnips!

Acrel soon continued his apprentice stroll—too poor to ride in carriages—through Switzerland and Italy. In Paris he was supervised by Jean-Louis Petit, and in London he saw Cheselden operate. But his stay in England was shortened by the outbreak of a new European war. Joining the army, he rose on his merit to unexpected posts, such as chief surgeon of a large field-hospital at the fortress of Lauterburg. There he was taken prisoner, but was released when he swore to take no part in campaigns against the Austrians for a year. He returned to Sweden in 1744 and passed his final examination for the College of Surgeons with little trouble. We may, in fact, doubt that the examiners knew as much about surgery as he did.

Together with the physician Abraham Bäck, Acrel established Sweden's first general hospital in 1752, the Royal Seraphim Lazarette in Stockholm. It had two rooms and eight beds—but in 1788 a modern hospital was ready, with 25 rooms having up to 120 beds, "each for one person". The latter advertisement was perhaps inspired by the Hôtel Dieu in Paris, which both Bäck and Acrel had visited: it normally put three or four patients in each bed, and the death of one of them was not always noticed…

Acrel's efforts culminated in a new native school of surgery, mainly due to his treatise *Surgical Events*, written in Swedish and translated into German and Dutch. It was a combined handbook and case-book, describing operations in detail and discussing improved instruments. Here he disagreed with the French school, resembling Heister and preferring simplicity: "arsenals of field weapons are less terrifying than the contents of the Surgical Equipment Chamber". Acrel eventually also became a good eye-surgeon, and published a dissertation comparing the usual methods for cataract operations.

On the whole, Olof Acrel's contributions to Swedish surgery and medicine can hardly be overestimated. He was honoured during his lifetime with a medal from the Swedish Academy of Sciences, and his name endures on the Acrel Medal, which is still fastidiously awarded by the Swedish Surgical Association for significant achievements.

The Seraphim Lazarette in Acrel's Day

Daily life at Stockholm's first hospital was portrayed in Wolfram Kock's book Olof af Acrel:

"*Every one of the city's inhabitants had the right to seek care at the hospital as long as space existed. Without proof of poverty, the monthly charge in advance was two dalers (around £10 today) or six for an extra room. The applicant or his messenger had to be in the reception hall at 10 AM or 4 PM, when the doctors decided his admission. The chief physician or surgeon wrote out an 'admission bill' and a nurse exchanged the patient's clothes for hospital clothing. He could not, of course, receive food from elsewhere, or take strong drinks like wine, schnapps or beer. Smoking was forbidden in the sickrooms. The male patients could shave once a week…*

"*The practical staff consisted of a cook, her servant-girl, a man to saw wood and carry water, a washing-woman and her own servant-girl. The lazarette boys, also meant to deal with wood and water, helped in bathing the patients and in 'bandaging or operating on the externally injured', or when necessary in the sickrooms… Those who worked well for at least twelve years, and reached the age of sixty meanwhile, were entitled to spend the rest of their lives without payment in one of the city's poorhouses!*"

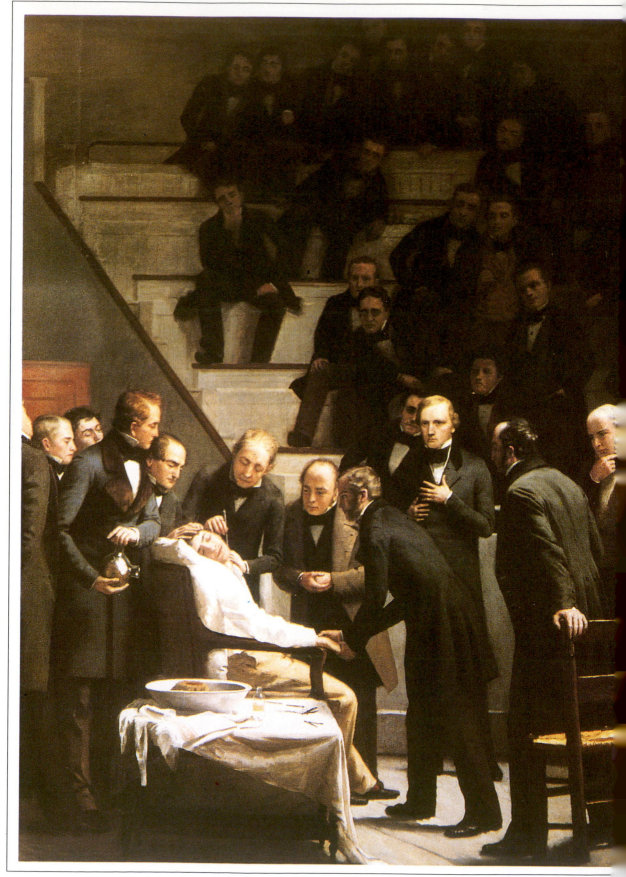

Surgery in the Age of Revolutions

T he late eighteenth and the early nineteenth centuries were a time of enormous innovations in the Western world: from many points of view, our way of life can be said to have begun less than two hundred years ago. Much the same is true of medicine, and we have already followed the careers of some prominent Continental surgeons into this turbulent period. Yet new scientific advances were being made, both in English-speaking lands and during the recurrent wars in Europe, that would lay the foundations for modern surgery.

The great Scots

It has been claimed that the world's medical centre around 1800 was the University of Edinburgh, which has often loomed large in our chronicle. This institution also played an outstanding role in surgery, and would later earn an even greater one with Lord Lister. The surgical teaching and research at Edinburgh began with a remarkable family, first represented by John Monro (1670–1740).

Educated in Leyden—along with Herman Boerhaave (1668–1738), who was to become Europe's leading internist—Monro acquired much experience as an army surgeon in Holland and Ireland. His son eventually told of his skill in sewing together a patient's severed windpipe

and punctured oesophagus, quite a feat even today, though done in about 1715! Monro was interested in administration as well, and took the initiative for Edinburgh's introduction of a complete curriculum in medicine. But his dream was to have his son establish a medical faculty there of the same kind as Leyden's.

Alexander Monro (1697–1767), to be called *primus* (the first) by medical historians, took up this torch by getting the best education available. After working as his father's assistant, he went to London and Paris—then Leyden itself, where Boerhaave had risen to fame and lectured on chemistry, botany and medicine. Among his comrades was Gerhard van Swieten, destined to serve Empress Maria Theresa as personal physician and head of the Austrian medical corps.

In 1726 the dream came true, with a medical faculty at Edinburgh and Alexander as its first professor of anatomy. His showpiece was *The Anatomy of the Human Bones*, to which he subsequently added a long chapter on the nerves. Students flocked around his catheter and dissection-bench, until they caused an acute shortage of corpses. The problem was solved by buying bodies from grave-robbers, but protests forced Alexander to take a stand against this, barely saving his anatomical collection from an angry mob. Still, the grave-robbing continued for a hundred years and, when professionals were lacking, the students did not hesitate to dig up recent burials.

A hospital opened in Edinburgh for six poor patients in 1729. Alexander offered to treat the surgical ailments without pay, but his colleagues

THE demonstration of surgery under anaesthesia at Boston on "Ether Day" in 1846, as painted by Robert Hinckley in 1882.

ALEXANDER Monro *primus*: an engraving (1775) from the painting by Allan Ramsay, one of the great British portraitists.

in the city became so envious that a rotation system was adopted, hardly to the advantage of sick-care. Anyhow, the hospital proved a success and grew into the renowned Royal Infirmary, whose name showed that it already deserved the King's honour. It was installed in a building designed by William Adam, the greatest Scottish architect of the age, whose four sons went even farther in that line.

Alexander Monro's lectures are legendary. He had "brought his science to the highest possible perfection", if we believe Oliver Goldsmith (1728–74), a far better writer than doctor. Since he always related anatomy to practical sick-care, Alexander solidly stimulated the development of Scottish medicine, especially surgery. Although he himself rarely operated—claiming to be afraid of it—he became one of the founders of the British surgical tradition.

The classes grew so large that they had to be

divided, and nobody was more qualified as an assistant teacher than the professor's third son, Alexander Monro *secundus* (1733–1817). He had studied anatomy since the age of thirteen, and became a professor himself at twenty-one. Then he began his clinical education in London under William Hunter, whom his father had taught and often engaged in scientific arguments. Next he went to Berlin and wrote a dissertation on the lymph nodes, studying with Johann Friedrich Meckel (1781–1833). Meckel, whose name has been given to the lower intestinal diverticulum, also belonged to a dynasty of devoted anatomists—his father even ordered that his own skeleton be displayed in the anatomical institute at Halle!

This Monro's professorship was eventually extended to include medicine and surgery. He was a sound anatomist, but seldom operated. His lasting achievement was to publish, in 1783, *Observations on the Structure and Functions of the Nervous System*. There he presented a new discovery, the connection between the heart's ventricles, which is named the *foramen Monroi* after him. Though his knowledge of surgery was only theoretical, he taught it with talent. Several of his students became eminent practitioners—Shippen and Morgan in America, the army surgeon James MacGrigor and, in Ireland, Abraham Colles (1773–1843) who described a typical wrist fracture. Others rose even higher: Charles Bell, as we shall see, founded clinical neurology, and William Withering (1741-99) gained worldwide fame as the discoverer of digitalis, while Benjamin Rush (1746–1813), besides writing America's first textbooks of chemistry and psychiatry, signed its Declaration of Independence.

One of Monro's colleagues at Edinburgh was perhaps the cleverest practical physician then in Britain. William Cullen (1712–90) had begun as a country doctor, not far from the village where the Hunter brothers were born. With no scientific credentials, he entered the faculty as a teacher and held three professorships in a row. Later he got into a notorious debate with a former student, John Brown (1735–88). They were merely philosophizing about the nature of life, although one theory was concrete enough. Brown argued that the size of a dosage meant more than the kind of drug taken—and went on to overdose alcohol as well as narcotics, dying of mental and physical neglect. As for Cullen, he contributed indirectly to surgery by encouraging William Hunter, who came home depressed after failing in theological studies. It was with Cullen's introductory letter, to Scottish friends in London, that Hunter started on a brilliant surgical career.

A generation of Bells

Surgery in Scotland next came to be dominated by the name of Bell. Already in his day, Benjamin Bell (1749–1806) was the country's leading practitioner. No original scientist, he developed techniques in detail, with simpler instruments and a new method of covering amputation stumps. He was the first British surgeon to assemble the knowledge of the time into an encyclopedia, his *System of Surgery* (1784). It reveals his debt to the older Alexander Monro. Thus, he was also the first in Britain to recommend radical operations for breast cancer along

From the Lectures of Alexander Monro

"Of nearly fifty cases of breast cancer which I have seen operated on, only four patients remained free of the disease for two years. It does not always recur in the part of the gland from which it was originally removed, but more often in the vicinity or far away. When it comes back, it is usually more malign and has a more rapid course than in patients who were not operated on." (This observation was later confirmed, and led to radical mastectomy.)

"I do not know of a single patient with a damaged cerebellum who has been cured. On the other hand, one may see patients cured even if large parts of the cerebrum have been destroyed."

Macabre Medical Methods

Careful dissection of human bodies is the best way for a surgeon to acquire his essential knowledge in anatomy. It was also the only way until modern technology introduced models and audiovisual equipment for teaching. Access to bodies was therefore an absolute necessity for medical students of old.

Most bodies came from executed criminals: indeed the phrase "your body shall be given to science" was long included in their death-sentences. Professional morticians cut them down from the gallows— often competing with their pious relatives—and delivered them to the anatomical schools for a small fee. If they ran short, bodies were dug up the night after the funeral—commonly after a battle with relatives who kept watch at the grave.

The most famous of all corpse-suppliers were William Burke and William Hare, a pair of "sack-'em-up men" in Edinburgh during the 1820s. Considering it needless to wait for death, they murdered people. Eight months in 1828 yielded them sixteen victims for sale to the anatomist Robert Knox. They were exposed when one of Knox's students recognized a prostitute whose liveliness he had witnessed some evenings earlier. Hare managed to "turn King's evidence", while Burke was hanged. The magistrate decreed not only that his body be dissected, but that his skeleton be preserved "so that posterity may remember your repulsive crimes". It was done, and Burke's skeleton can still be confronted in the anatomical museum at Edinburgh.

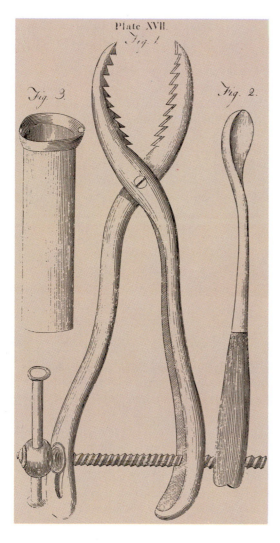

(*LEFT*) Surgical instruments like these were finely illustrated in Benjamin Bell's encyclopedia. (*Above*) Sir Charles Bell, surgeon and neurologist.

the lines which had been launched on the Continent by Petit in Paris. These included removing the lymph nodes in the armpit, from which the cancer initially spreads. Bell had two sons who became surgeons in Edinburgh, and many others descended from them.

The brothers Charles and John Bell belonged to a different family, a poor family in a suburb of Edinburgh. Their father was all the gloomier for being a High Church Jacobite in an overwhelmingly Protestant community. Not least due to their mother's support, the four sons still re-

ceived a good education and sound upbringing.

John Bell (1763-1820) proved to be an adept practical surgeon. He joined the unhappy rotation system at the Edinburgh hospital, and lost the chance to operate at the Royal Infirmary when it was reorganized with a permanent staff. Protesting against this new order, he and his colleagues exchanged fiery letters with the dean, James Gregory—a professor of medicine whose spite and invective were hard to beat. Bell was to find other ways of pursuing his profession, but the fights with the faculty embittered the rest of his life. Indeed, psychologists have guessed that his struggle against official medicine turned him into a general troublemaker.

Be that as it may, Bell forced his colleagues to doubt a number of so-called clinical truths. He showed that a burst aneurysm could be sewn up, and he battled like a hero for the possibility of "primary" healing without pus formation. Yet his greatest gift to the development of surgery was a dogged campaign for good training in surgical anatomy. He himself had experienced the younger Monro's miserable lectures in practical anatomy, "where not even three bodies were dissected in a year unless a lucky heap of horrible murders happened to occur. The fine nerves that must be avoided or divided in our operations were demonstrated on the remains of a corpse which had been fished from the bottom of a whiskey barrel—and this at a distance of a hundred feet!" Bell opened his own anatomy school as a protest against the official one. He well deserves to be called "the father of surgical anatomy".

Charles Bell (1774–1842) was at first his brother's assistant. A sensitive man who always shared his patients' suffering, he did badly in the less attractive tasks of handling human remains. But he became a proficient anatomist while studying other subjects at the faculty. He then got involved in the official quarrels of his brother, who persuaded him to move to London. There he began by publishing *Anatomy of Expression*, a work more of art than of science—for Charles, like John, was an excellent draughtsman. However, he soon proved himself equally scientific with his *System of Operative Surgery* (1807). Two years later, he saw a chance to practise battle surgery: crowds of wounded soldiers arrived in Portsmouth, after the victory at Coruña during the Napoleonic war in Spain. This experience enabled Charles to publish a much-respected book on shot-wounds and their treatment.

Going to Middlesex Hospital as chief surgeon, Charles built up a famous practice, which even drew many patients from the Continent. He also investigated the nervous system, and grew increasingly interested in its diseases. Thus a surgeon became the founder of the branch of internal medicine that we call neurology. In 1829 he was knighted for his services, and in 1835 came

From Surgeon to Sleuth

It was a member of the surgical Bell family who inspired the character Sherlock Holmes. Sir Arthur Conan Doyle, himself a doctor, told of Joseph Bell (1837-1911):

"The most remarkable of those I came to know was Joseph Bell, surgeon at the Edinburgh Infirmary. He was a very peculiar person in both body and soul. He was thin and dark-skinned, with a sharply hewn face and hook nose, piercing grey eyes, high shoulders and an abrupt way of moving…"

In his memoirs, Conan Doyle gave examples of Bell's powers of observation, such as:

"Well, my good man. You have served in the army."

"Yes, sir."

"It is not long since you were discharged."

"No, sir."

"You have been a noncommissioned officer."

"Yes, sir."

"A Highland regiment?"

"Yes, sir."

"And you have been stationed in Barbados?"

"Yes, sir."

"You see, gentlemen," explained Bell, "he was a courteous man, but he didn't take off his hat. One does not do so in the army, but he would have learned civilian habits if he had been discharged long ago. He had obvious authority and he was clearly a Scot. As for Barbados, he was seeking treatment for elephantiasis, and this disease exists in the West Indies, but not in Great Britain."

compensation for the Edinburgh faculty's mental torture of him and his brother: it appointed him professor of surgery.

The value placed on Sir Charles Bell may be judged from a visit he paid to Paris. His notable colleague Philibert Roux cancelled a lecture by presenting him to the students: "Gentlemen, you have seen Bell. That is enough…"

In the wake of Hunter

When John Hunter died in 1793, he left a band of followers whose quality was to be matched by those of only one other surgeon—Theodor Billroth, a century later. English and Scottish surgeons of the early nineteenth century were well-trained in anatomy and pathology. They knew at least elements of physiology, a relatively new science, and were technically refined. Their diagnostics were better than before, not due to new technology or equipment, but simply because all physicians had begun to keep better sick-bed journals, to catalogue these in archives, and thus to learn more from experience. The century's surgery was inspired from England, and its first three quarters were predominantly as British as its last quarter was German.

John Abernethy (1764–1831) worked briefly as Hunter's assistant at the anatomy school, but studied surgery almost entirely at St. Bartholomew's, where he arrived at the height of Pott's career. Despite the sometimes chilly relations between Pott and the Hunter brothers, Abernethy converted to John Hunter's surgical creed, and should be counted among its first apostles. Already before Hunter's death, he had gained a reputation for his lectures and drew students with his spicy language as well as his learning. In 1814 he was made professor of surgery and anatomy at the Royal College of Surgeons of England—and a year later, chief surgeon and professor at his old hospital, remaining there until just before he died.

Abernethy was one of the numerous practising surgeons who have turned into legends during their lifetime. And like many others, he owed this to eccentricity. A rule of his creed was to encourage the patient, which he attempted with a bold bedside manner that often went beyond brusqueness. Usually he succeeded, since patients felt the friendliness and sympathy behind his gruff exterior. He was ready to do anything for those who really needed him—but he had little use for those who complained of imaginary pains, and told them so plainly. By the same token, he was among the most frightening examiners ever known to English surgery students.

Like nearly all Hunter's disciples, Abernethy laid great emphasis on anatomy. The supply of corpses for this purpose had dried up after a long period of abundance. His remedy was typically well-intentioned: the final words of the English funerary ritual, about delivering mortal remains unto the earth, should be replaced by "and thus we dedicate this body to science".

Henry Cline (1750–1827) was a student and admirer of Hunter. "After having heard Mr. Hunter's lectures," he wrote, "I found him so superior to everything else I had learned or heard before that there could be no comparison." Cline became a surgeon at Saint Thomas' Hospital and acquired a solid circle of apprentices. He was so interested in teaching the art that he even lectured on his wedding-day. Perhaps he was trying to copy his mentor who, as we have seen, could hardly spare time from the dissection-room for such an irrelevant ceremony.

The revered Royal College of Surgeons, which still thrives in its magnificent premises at Lincoln's Inn Fields in London, was created in 1800 by Cline, Abernethy, and Sir Everard Home. From the outset it had its own professor of anatomy and surgery, beginning with another of Hunter's followers, William Blizard (1743–1835). He was the first to treat struma by tying off some of its blood supply, and the first who dared to tie off the main blood route to the arm—the subclavian artery—like Hunter's ligature of the thigh artery.

Among other surgeons, one of Hunter's most important students must be mentioned: Edward Jenner (1749–1823). A clergyman's son from Gloucestershire, he came to London for a medical education and became the personal assistant of Hunter, who recognized his qualities. His initial challenge was to arrange the unique zoological collection which Captain Cook had brought back from the first expedition to the South Seas. But all attempts to involve Jenner again in academic medicine failed: he was resolved to be a country doctor, where he could also

EDWARD Jenner in 1800, the year of international triumph for his method of vaccination.

Abernethy Tested

Once the fearsome fool-ferret met his match in a candidate who had aroused his displeasure. He said: "You are a talented young man, so will you kindly tell me which muscles would come into use if I were to kick you down the stairs, as you so richly deserve?" The student replied: "It would be the flexors and extensors in my right arm, for I'd strike back instantly!"

A Laconic Appointment

Nothing was worse to Abernethy than chattering females, as we read in John Timbs' Doctor and Patient. He used to stop them by asking them to open their mouths and saying, "Now shut your mouth and keep it shut!" But one day a woman came to him with a severed finger. The dialogue ran like this:

(First day) Abernethy: Cut off?
Patient: Bitten off.
Abernethy: Dog?
Patient: Parrot.
(Second day) Abernethy: Better?
Patient: Worse.
Abernethy: Change the bandage.
(Third day) Abernethy: Better?
Patient: Well.
Abernethy: You're the cleverest woman I ever met. Goodbye. Out!

indulge his hobbies of ornithology and botany. After getting his degree, he returned home and settled in the tiny town of Berkeley...

Some shaky steps had already been taken towards protection against smallpox. In "variolation", a healthy person was inoculated with pus from a smallpox patient. This brought on the pox, usually in mild form—yet the guarantee was far from full, and several deaths occurred. Jenner noticed that the people in his district gladly let themselves be infected by cowpox: it gave them an ugly outbreak on the hands, but they never caught smallpox. He wrote about it to Hunter, and the answer "Experiment!" was all he needed. On 14 May 1796, he made his classic contribution by injecting from a cowpox pustule into an eight-year-old boy. The boy got slightly ill, but did no worse six weeks later, when Jenner injected him with smallpox. The term "vaccination" was borrowed from the word for a cow in Latin (*vacca*).

Jenner's experiment was criticized as unethical, and he met with strong opposition. Nevertheless, when his report of twenty-three successful vaccinations appeared, he became world-famous. The method was first used on a wide scale in 1800 during a smallpox epidemic in Vienna, and seventy London doctors signed their names to support it. Parliament, too, displayed the nation's gratitude by awarding Jenner 30,000 pounds.

A man of few mistakes

Equally celebrated, at least in his homeland, was the leading surgeon among Hunter's disciples, Astley Paston Cooper (1768–1841). His career resembled the master's. Coming from a large, cultivated, but not very rich clerical family in Norfolk, he took up medicine as a student in Edinburgh. At first he learned little, being more devoted to worldly pleasures. Surgery was considered to be his only hope, since it required less reading than the finer art of internal medicine! This, of course, was before the Hunter brothers made their profession respectable.

But Cooper straightened himself out and went to study in London. He became a surgical aide to Henry Cline at Guy's Hospital—an institution which had been donated by a penitent swindler in the City, and which was already rather well known. On Cline's advice, he then attended Hunter's lectures and grew fascinated by the great man's personality, knowledge and tireless experimenting. When the post of chief surgeon became open at Guy's, he got the job.

Cooper, in contrast to the wilful, sulky, unsophisticated John Hunter, was a charming and agreeable man of the world, looking good and behaving perfectly. Combined with his superb qualifications as a surgeon, these gifts naturally admitted him to the highest circles in England. Summoned to the Court, for example, he took a huge cyst (wen) off the head of George IV, who

Making History

"A three-inch incision skirting the umbilicus was made from the linea alba", wrote Sir Astley Cooper of his historic operation. *"With the finger the peritoneum was scratched through on the left side of the aorta, and worked under the vessel to the right and again through the peritoneum"*. Even today, encircling the aorta can still be difficult and dangerous.

endured the operation only by drinking considerable—though normal for that king—amounts of alcohol. The healthy outcome changed his name to Sir Astley Cooper, Bart.

As a scientific author, Cooper first reported briefly on two patients who had burst both eardrums but, surprisingly, could still hear well. His observations put an end to the old belief that such double perforation led to total deafness. He was also inspired to perforate the eardrums of certain patients, thus relieving many from pain and possibly saving some from deafness.

Cooper's greatest contribution was a *Treatise on Hernia*, in two thick volumes. Based upon years of dissections and operations, it laid the foundation for modern hernia surgery. Curiously, he was the first to understand something which even John Hunter had missed: the role of the abdominal wall's connective tissue layers in the origin and treatment of hernia. Several structures in the groin region still bear his name (such as the *fascia cremasterica Cooperi* and the *ligamentum Cooperi*). So do the tissue threads holding up the mammary glands, for he developed female breast operations as well.

His most famous operation involved a man who was brought to the hospital with abdominal pain. Finding a pulsating tumour inside, he quickly diagnosed an aneurysm—ballooning in one of the large arteries. Cooper was aware that it would soon burst and bleed the man to death in a couple of minutes. Nobody had ever operated under such conditions, so he went to the autopsy room and tested every detail on a cadaver. Then he took his decision and called for the operation. Technically, he succeeded, though the patient suddenly died after forty hours. With courage and skill, Cooper had shown that this kind of operation was possible, and it made an important addition to surgery.

Sir Astley Cooper joined the ranks of England's most honoured surgeons. Even if his knighthood was earned with a minor operation which any novice surgeon could have done, no one thought it inappropriate. He became the king's personal surgeon—remaining so under

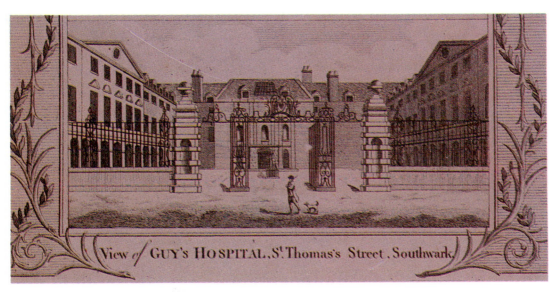

View *of* GUY's HOSPITAL, S.t Thomas's Street, Southwark.

(ABOVE) The famous hospital built in London by, and named after, the investor Thomas Guy in the 1720s.
(*Below*) Astley Paston Cooper: an engraving by the American artist Henry Meyer in 1819.

William IV and Queen Victoria—as well as vice president of the Royal Society. And twice president of the Royal College of Surgeons of England, where we can still see a wonderful portrait of him by the finest painter of his day, Sir Thomas Lawrence.

From the Writings of Sir Astley Cooper

An old Scottish doctor for whom I had great respect, and whom I often met in my work, used to say when we visited a patient together: "Well, Mr. Cooper, there are only two things we need worry about: first to fear God, which is most important for our life after this—and secondly to keep the patient's bowels moving, which is enough for us here."

If you are too interested in new medicines, you will, in the first place, not cure your patients, and in the second place, you will not have any patients to cure.

I have made many mistakes myself—in order to learn the anatomy of the eye, I must say that I had to make a whole hatful. The best surgeon, like the best general, is the one who makes the fewest mistakes."

The Continental pathologists

John Hunter and his school had led the surgical handicraft onto solid ground. Of Cooper, it was said that he elevated surgery from a game of "frightful alternatives or hazardous compromises" to a science. As we have seen, one reason was that surgeons had mastered human anatomy through long, meticulous study.

Yet other aids to the art were being created: pathology and physiology, the knowledge of diseases and body functions. An Italian named Giovanni Battista Morgagni (1682–1771) had founded pathological anatomy with his monumental work *De Sedibus et Causis Morborum* (On the Sources and Causes of Diseases). He taught at Padua for 56 years, which must be a record. Morgagni's greatness lay in his scrupulous combination of case histories with autopsy finds. His book analyzed no fewer than 700 autopsies which he had done, alone or assisting his own teacher Valsalva. Often his description of a disease's clinical course and pathological anatomy is so exact and clear that we can easily diagnose it today.

Morgagni resolved many misunderstandings, such as the idea that a brain abscess was an effect—rather than a cause—of pus formation in the ear, and that paralysis in half of the body was due to an injury in the opposite brain hemisphere. In experimental pathology, too, he was a pioneer. He benefited surgery directly by investigating the results of tying off various blood vessels. Likewise, he described several malignant tumours and gave advice for operating on them, even though he himself never practised surgery.

The chair of anatomy at Padua, which Morgagni held with such distinction, was perhaps the most revered medical professorship in the world. Indeed, his predecessors there had included Vesalius, Colombo, Falloppio and Fabricius ab Aquapendente. He was one of the pioneers in medicine who gained full recognition while still alive. Five foreign academies of science made him an honorary member—and he was a good friend of five Popes in a row, besides

THE pathologist Morgagni.

the King of Sardinia. No less remarkable was his cultivation in languages, writing style, history, art and literature.

After Morgagni, pathology moved from description to theory: what were the basic causes of ailments? The old doctrine of unbalanced body fluids was beginning to die out, as it did not explain phenomena such as tumours and aneurysms. But doctors had to grope in the dark, since they were ignorant of the building-block in the human organism—the cell.

Some researchers already knew a little of this secret. A Dutch apprentice haberdasher and city hall watchman, Antonie van Leeuwenhoek (1632–1723), had seen such tiny structures. He made microscopes for a hobby, and his scientific achievements earned him membership of the Royal Society. Robert Hooke (1635–1703), the all-round naturalist, even noted in his book

THE microscopist Leeuwenhoek.

ern cellular pathology, which was set on course by Rudolf Virchow (1821–1902). A farmer's son from Pomerania, he proved to have an enormous capacity for learning. Before starting medical studies at the renowned Kaiser Wilhelm Institute in Berlin, he had mastered French, English, Hebrew and Italian, as well as the classics and Arabic poetry! Now he met two great teachers, the physiologist Johannes Müller (1801–58) and the clinician who named the disease haemophilia, Johann Schönlein (1793–1864). They persuaded him to enter research, and he graduated in 1843 with a dissertation on rheumatic illnesses.

Only a few years later, Virchow showed that blood clots were due to changes in the blood's flow, composition and vessel walls—known as "Virchow's triad". He took almost a decade to publish the results, which are still valid today. Soon he was one of Berlin's leading academics, but moved to Würzburg for seven years, where he did brilliant work on cells. Unlike Schwann, he realized that "every cell is derived from a pre-existing cell". This explained the growth of tumours and raised the possibility of stopping cancer.

Virchow's scrutiny of the body's microcosm led him into the science which we call microbiology. His special interests were fungi and trichinosis. On the other hand, he was sceptical of bacteriology, which celebrated many a triumph in the late nineteenth century but had committed a lot of mistakes. Sometimes his attitude created scandals by breaking off discussion with prominent researchers. He went very wide of the mark on at least one occasion, Robert Koch's epoch-making presentation in 1882 of the causes of tuberculosis.

The greatness of Rudolf Virchow included his social initiatives. First he was sent to investigate a typhus epidemic in Silesia, and condemned the government for denying its poor Polish population the simplest sanitary and humanitarian facilities. This report made him unpopular, and two years later he took part in the unlucky revolution of 1848, thus losing his job. When he

Micrographia that tissues consisted of "little boxes or cells, distinct from one another".

The real impulse, however, came from botany. In Germany, Matthias Schleiden (1804–81) published an exhaustive account of how plants are built of cells. He inspired similar studies of animal tissue by his friend Theodor Schwann (1810–82), who had won fame by discovering a digestive enzyme, pepsin. Schwann confirmed in 1839 that Schleiden's findings also applied to animals. Among his other contributions, as a professor at Louvain and Liège in Belgium, were the term "metabolism" for chemical changes in living tissue, the principle of embryology that an organism develops from an egg cell, and the fact that nerves are imbedded in an insulating substance—the sheath of "neurilemma", or Schwann cells.

This last observation paved the way for mod-

spread terror, but also affection—as is often the case—and he gladly drank a beer with his students after lectures. Perhaps "the little doctor", as he was called, showed his true personality in caring for patients, with a warmth that brought him esteem. And when his heart failed in 1902, he was given a state funeral in Berlin, an honour granted to very few German physicians. The historian George Bender has summed him up well:

"Although he had many good points, his stubbornness could often impede promising projects. But his positive achievements were much greater than his errors. His courage, energy, diversity, humanity and scientific results made him unique and unforgettable. His work in cellular pathology had far-reaching consequences; they contributed to enormous progress in medicine and surgery, and they showed the way to modern chemotherapy."

One other European giant of pathology in the nineteenth century was Karl von Rokitansky (1804–78) at the General Hospital in Vienna, which became the world's centre of both medical and surgical education during his lifetime. His *Handbook of Pathological Anatomy* built on experience of more than 60,000 autopsies. Among his other additions to the field, he described congenital heart defects, acute yellow atrophy of the liver, and emphysema.

Unfortunately he was born thirty years too early, and clung to the doctrine of humoral pathology in spite of Virchow's cell theory. Criticized for trying to explain various conditions with body-fluid chemistry, he wandered into more bizarre speculation. Still, his opposition warned doctors not to attribute all diseases to the "solid pathology" of body parts such as cells. In fact, Rokitansky was on the track of future developments in serology and endocrinology.

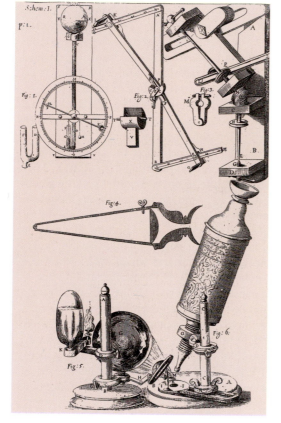

A single-lens microscope, with an optical device to focus light on the sample, was illustrated in *Micrographia* (1665) by Robert Hooke, who had already become a pioneering maker of telescopes.

returned to Berlin as the country's best medical theoretician, he entered politics again and was for a long time a member of Parliament, so progressive that he nearly had to fight a duel with Bismarck, the Iron Chancellor. In addition, he stimulated the study of anthropology and archaeology.

Combining genius with status, Virchow could be arrogant and spiteful. A famous debater, he was considered able to demolish opponents without even raising his voice. As examiner he

RUDOLF Virchow, the founder of cellular pathology.

Physiology crosses frontiers

The founder of experimental physiology is usually said to be Albrecht von Haller (1708–77), already known to us as one of Acrel's teachers. A child prodigy in science, he became professor at Göttingen, then returned to his birthplace, Bern. The connection between the nerves and muscles was what he best clarified, for example by studying why a muscle contracts when stimulated. He collected all the physiology of his day into an eight-volume work, *Elementa Physiologiae Corporis Humana*. It ruled out any new discoveries, since a close reading of it would reveal that Haller had already made them—according to one colleague.

This was François Magendie (1783–1855), a professor of medicine in Paris. He displayed equal humility in his care of patients at the Hôtel Dieu, arguing that a doctor should do as little as possible and let nature take its course—perhaps reacting against the exhaustive therapy inflicted by many of his countrymen. Yet Magendie was a go-getter in research: he bowed to no obstacle and could drive his assistants to despair. Not

least in Haller's own specialty of neurophysiology, he broke important ground, tracing paths of nerve impulses from the spinal cord. He also investigated drugs like morphine, and started work on allergies by proving that egg-white could act as a poison.

A student of his made advances in physiology which were to have deep influence on surgery. Claude Bernard (1813–78) was at first a playwright, but critics persuaded him to try something else. Becoming fascinated with physiology, he began a twenty-year uphill struggle that ended in Magendie's professorial chair. His range grew amazingly: after a dissertation on the

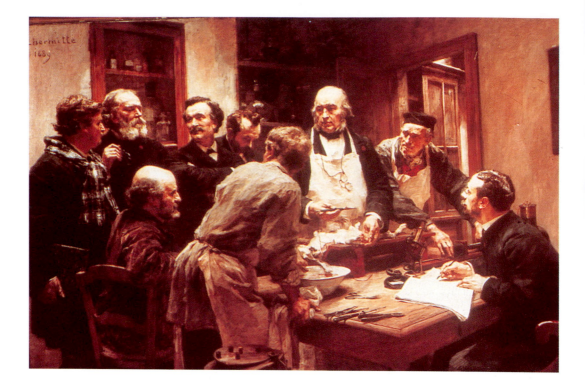

CLAUDE Bernard demonstrates an experiment for the famous chemist Henri Sainte-Claire Deville (seated at left), in a prize-winning painting by Léon Lhermitte (1889).

function of stomach juice, he published a large work on liver physiology, then figured out the role of the pancreas in digestion. Finally he turned philosopher of science, and was the first French scientist to get a national funeral.

Bernard's greatest insight, although surgeons would take long to understand it, was his view of the body's internal environment. In order to function normally, an organ needs a constant environment, which can be regulated by either the organ or the rest of the body. An example is heat regulation: people can go from a hot bath out into cold weather without much change in their internal temperature. The same is true of our inner chemical environment, or "homoeostasis" in later terminology. As Bernard wrote,

"the internal environment's stability is the prime requirement for free, independent existence; and the mechanism providing it is what maintains all the conditions in the internal environment which are essential for life." This teaching revealed the importance of keeping the body's fluids and electrolytes in correct balance—now indispensable for advanced surgery.

Bernard also studied blood vessels and regulation by the vasomotor nerves, a key factor in maintaining the physical environment in the body. Moreover, his work on the liver proved that, besides producing bile, it changed glucose (sugar) into glycogen (starch), which could then be used up as blood sugar. His term for this process was "internal secretion". Eventually, the term was to be given a different meaning: the production of hormones by endocrine glands.

These glands began to be investigated by another leading French physiologist of the century, Charles Édouard Brown-Séquard (1817–94). He was interested in the failure of the adrenal glands during a fatal disease described by, and since named after, Thomas Addison (1793–1860) of England. Experimenting on animals, he removed the adrenal glands and proved that they are necessary for life. But by replacing them elsewhere in an animal, he found that it survived. They must, he decided, be adding something essential to the bloodstream. We now know that this applies to several hormones produced by the adrenal glands.

Both Bernard and Brown-Séquard were touted as pioneers in old age, yet they drew extreme conclusions from their results. Bernard's last years were soured by illness, which he blamed on disturbance of his own internal environment by emotional difficulties. Brown-Séquard went on to clarify some functions of male sex glands, then tried to rejuvenate himself with injections of hormones from the testicles. Announcing that he immediately felt more vital, he aroused a sensation, but was refuted and called a bluffer. That, too, must have been bitter for a man who, nevertheless, had opened scientific doors to endocrinology.

Physiology was sped along its way by the observations and deductions of great clinicians across the Channel. In addition to Addison, there was Robert James Graves (1796–1853) of Dublin, who described the symptoms and bulging eyes (exophthalmus) associated with toxic goitre—a disease named after him and, on the Continent, after Karl Basedow (1799–1854) of Germany. Richard Bright (1789–1858), at Guy's Hospital in London, gave his name to a degeneration of the kidneys, and showed that dropsy can be related either to bad kidneys or a bad heart. Joseph Hodgson (1788–1869), in Birmingham, described symptoms of aneurysm in the heart's aorta. Thomas Hodgkin (1798–1866) wrote a dissertation on diseases of the spleen and lymph nodes, including a cancer that bears his name. (It is odd that Addison, Bright, Hodgkin and even Cooper were all on the staff of Guy's at the same time but there is no record of them ever meeting for a debate or discussion.)

Clinical Observations

A couple of days ago I had my bladder examined by two surgeons. Both washed their hands and instruments. Gosselin did so after the operation, but your pupil Guyon before it…
Claude Bernard (to Louis Pasteur, 1877)

The axiom of medicine is that natural science is its mother.

Karl von Rokitansky

To connect careful and correct observations of the dead with their symptoms during life must, in some measure, advance our noble art… Acute illnesses have to be seen at least once daily in order to learn anything; in many cases, twice daily is not too often.

Richard Bright

Science and Art

Medicine consists of science and art in a certain relationship to each other, yet wholly distinct. Science can be learned by anyone, even the mediocre. Art, however, is a gift from heaven. So you cannot count yourselves among the great doctors by simply acquiring knowledge.

The scientist continually and receptively gathers a vast amount of material, while the artist creates new roads of thought. Knowledge suffocates the scientist, whereas it gives the artist fresh inspiration. Therefore, gentlemen, learn as much as you can—but your learning must be the basis for your art, not an end in itself. A little less science and a little more art, Messieurs!

Armand Trousseau (to his students)

French medicine, however, maintained its drastic traditions well into the nineteenth century. One of its last champions was the wicked Victor Broussais (1772–1838), chief physician at the military hospital of Val de Grâce in Paris. He declared that nearly every disease was rooted in the stomach nerves and could be cured with leeches. This simple-minded notion soon lost scientific favour, but lived surprisingly long. As late as the beginning of our century, an English doctor named Arbuthnot Lane attributed all manner of ailments to trouble in the large intestine, and removed it as often as possible. Even so, Broussais was honoured by having one of the new Paris hospitals named after himself.

His disciple Jean Baptiste Bouillard (1796–1881) went on with leech therapy in another form: a revival of blood-letting. The idea was now that blood-letting had certainly proved dangerous, but because too little blood was let! Bouillard bled his patients time and again—*saigne coup sur coup*—and often took two or three litres from those with pneumonia. As the Swedish historian Acke Renander noted, "this nadir of medicine was reached hardly more than a hundred years ago."

Much more sensible was the country doctor Pierre Bretonneau (1778–1862) of Tours. In 1826 he described diphtheria, naming it after the throat's leathery membranes (called *diphthera* in Greek). He became the first to perform a tracheotomy on a diphtheria patient who was suffocating. This operation was named by his countryman Armand Trousseau (1810–67), who later used it on such patients at the Hôtel Dieu.

The conquest of pain

"That beautiful dream has become a reality: operations can now be performed painlessly." So spoke the adept, popular surgeon Johann Friedrich Dieffenbach (1794–1847), when he experienced the first use of ether in Europe. Undeniably, total relief from pain was to be a prerequisite for the enormous progress made in surgery during the late nineteenth century.

As we have seen, the only important analgesics in antiquity were hashish, mandrake and opium. They were employed into the Middle Ages and beyond, when Paracelsus still ranked opium among a few effective drugs—so effective that he himself probably became an opium addict. The medical role of mandrake was witnessed indirectly by Shakespeare's *Romeo and Juliet*, whose heroine was sent into a deathlike sleep by a decoction of the plant. This, of course, scarcely agrees with its pharmacological properties. Anyone knocked out by mandrake for forty-two hours, like Juliet, would doubtless never have woken up again!

Arab medicine took a heady interest in pain-killing. Rhazes gave various prescriptions for painful illness: mashes, pills, enemas, wines, suppositories, and external remedies such as poultices. What he vaguely called "colic", one of his main concerns, was to be treated with a mixture of quince pips, fennel, camomile and resin from the bdellium shrub—a relative of myrrh. If this worked no wonders, he turned to *falunija*, which was the same as an old Greek panacea, *Philoneion anodynon* (the latter word meant "taking away pain"). An opiatic drug, it survived in the Orient down to our century, and was apparently made from the original formula in Cairo's bazaar as late as World War I, when the authorities banned it. Cairo seems to have been a veritable museum of drug prescriptions: even in 1885, an Arab geographer counted 758 pharmacists in the city.

The Incas of Peru had several herbs for headache and other pains, apart from trepanation and the easier surgical method of blood-letting a patient with a flint-hammer blow between the eyes. They used scopolamine, a poison from the datura plant, as an anaesthetic during operations. Animal substances were also relied on. The Jesuit missionary José de Acosta (1539–1600) wrote that he had felt relief when an aching spot was covered with a piece of bloody meat from the vicuña, a camel-like beast of the Andes. Bones broken by gout were treated with fat from the ñandu, an ostrich-like bird. Shrimp soup was prescribed against stoppage of a mother's milk. Juice from a fried llama kidney was dropped into aching ears.

General narcosis has naturally been the ideal condition in all major operations, for both doctor and patient. The problem is how to tell a therapeutic dose from a lethal one. Opium has been used at times for its anaesthetic properties, but they are limited and it has caused so many deaths as to be forbidden by law. Next came alcohol, whose stages of influence had long been known, and intoxication turned into a medical fashion. Its effectiveness for small wounds is familiar to every surgeon who has sewn up a drunken accident-victim. In the old English navy, an ample dose of rum or whiskey was applied before amputations; and the patient—if still conscious—was given a leather strap to bite on, perhaps mainly so that screams would not unsettle others who awaited the operation. A further method of anaesthesia, used for instance by Ambroise Paré, was to half-suffocate the patient beforehand.

Sir Christopher Wren, the great architect of the Restoration, was more than an enthusiast for medicine, as mentioned earlier. He gave the faculty at Oxford a report on how people might be put to sleep with an intravenous narcotic. The instrument he recommended was a goose-quill attached to a pig-bladder. Robert Boyle, the physicist, was there at the time and, in 1665, published an experiment with this technique, injecting dogs with opium and adding a chemical for comparison:

"The result was that the opium, which immediately circulated to the brain, benumbed the animal without killing it, but that a large dose of *crocus metallorum* (antimony sulphide) made another dog throw up, life and all."

Over a century later, Humphry Davy (1778–1829), a carpenter's son from Cornwall, began his brilliant scientific career as the apprentice of a surgeon and apothecary. Fascinated by a new

idea that nitrogen gas could transmit infections, he experimented with treating wounds on dogs. More or less by chance, he produced and inhaled some nitrous oxide—later called laughing gas—and noted that it was "irritating and moderately depressing, yielded a slow pulse and a tendency to dizziness." Among those who encouraged him was the prominent physician Thomas Beddoes (1760–1808), who was treating diseases by inhalation of gases.

In 1800, Davy published the world's first work on narcosis: *Researches, Chemical and Philosophical, Chiefly Concerning Nitrous Oxide and its Respiration*. Here he reported that the pure gas killed animals, but that a mixture of it with oxygen caused a reversible state of unconsciousness:

A Pleasure for Gentlemen

One of America's oldest newspapers, the Courant in Hartford, Connecticut, was still advertising the same kind of stunt in 1884 which Horace Wells had seen forty years earlier:

"A GREAT EXHIBITION of the effects of inhaling NITROUS OXIDE, LAUGHING GAS! FORTY GALLONS of this gas will be produced and given to everyone in the auditorium who wishes to breathe it. EIGHT STRONG MEN have been engaged and will be in the front row to protect those who may injure themselves or others under the gas's influence. This is a safety measure, since surely no danger exists—probably no one will try to fight. THE GAS'S POWER is to release the urge to laugh, sing, dance, make speeches or fight, depending on individual nature. NOTE: gas will only be made available to gentlemen of the highest respectability!"

"A small guinea-pig was set in a mixture of one part oxygen gas and three parts nitrous oxide. He immediately began to struggle but, after two minutes, lay down on his side and breathed very deeply. Afterwards he made no strong muscular movements, but remained still for nearly fourteen minutes. He then acquired convulsions in the extremities. He was taken out and revived."

The book went on to describe the sensations created by inhaling this mixture. Davy experimented upon famous men as well: the poets Robert Southey, Samuel Taylor Coleridge, William Wordsworth; the inventor of the steam engine, James Watt; one of the porcelain-making Wedgwoods; and a son of Joseph Priestley, who had discovered both nitrous oxide and oxygen in the 1770s. Southey wrote to Davy that "the atmosphere in the highest of all possible heavenly realms must be composed of this gas!" A more factual account of laughing gas was given by Peter Mark Roget, a doctor who compiled the *Thesaurus*.

Davy soon lost interest in his gas, but not surprisingly, as he was no physician and none of his medical friends understood what the discovery meant. Much the same happened eighteen years later, when his assistant Michael Faraday (1791–1867) compared it with the effects of inhaling ether fumes, before he became a pioneer of electricity. Nevertheless, Davy was to be only the first of seven men who are usually regarded as the fathers of anaesthesiology.

The next of these, Henry Hill Hickman (1800–30), was an enthusiastic young country doctor in Shropshire. He experimented rather successfully with partial suffocation by carbon dioxide, and published his findings in a pamphlet in 1824, mainly to attract the Royal Society's attention to the method. Nothing came of it, and he was totally ignored in England. Then he wrote to Charles X of France, who grew curious and passed the letter on to local scientists. The only one who responded was Larrey, but this champion of progress had retired from active surgery. Thus Hickman's work was never put into practice—and perhaps luckily, since carbon dioxide can be too suffocating if used inexpertly. Still, Hickman deserves his status for having made the first planned medical experiments with narcosis.

By that time, laughing gas was proving a marketable pleasure. People paid to step up and sniff it, until they felt giddy and even ready to fight, swinging wildly and falling down, to the delight of crowds. On December 10, 1844, the American dentist Horace Wells (1815–48) visited a fair in Hartford, Connecticut, where laughing gas was being sold by Gardner Colton (1814–98), an inventor. Wells tried the gas, and saw another sniffer suffer self-injury without any pain. The next day, he inhaled a whole bag of Colton's gas, and felt nothing while he had a troublesome tooth pulled out.

Eager to exploit this breakthrough, Wells built an apparatus for inhalation of laughing gas, and demonstrated it in public. It was just a bellows with a wooden tube which he stuck in the patient's mouth, applying a pinch on the nose to keep out air. But when he had to face a test before a sceptical audience of doctors, his subject showed unusual resistance and laughter turned against him. He continued to experiment on himself with anaesthetic gases, and was even hailed as their discoverer by the Paris Medical Society. Yet in New York City, he was jailed and committed suicide.

From gas to poison

As the new work on narcosis proceeded during the 1840s, it became an ever clearer example of how scientific discoveries are often made simultaneously in different places, as if they really do occur "when the time is ripe" for them.

CHARLES Jackson, an American chemist and geologist as well as doctor, was an early self-experimenter with ether, according to this engraving from 1843.

In January 1842, a medical student, William Clarke, gave ether to a friend for a tooth extraction. Two months later, a Mr. Venable was put to sleep for the removal of a cyst on his neck by an American country doctor, Crawford Long (1815–78). Experiments with ether had convinced Long of its analgesic and numbing effects. This first serious use of it was a triumph —he charged the man only 25 cents for it, besides two dollars for the operation.

Long had a modest practice in Danielsville, Georgia. He earned no recognition by helping further patients with ether narcosis. Nor did he bother to publicize it, and he may not have realized its importance. Thus his place in history was to be taken by a former partner, William Thomas Green Morton (1819–68), whom he told about Wells' ill-fated efforts with laughing gas. Morton pursued the hope of finding a better gas, and was introduced to ether by a doctor named Charles Jackson (1805–80).

Morton held a demonstration on October 16, 1846, which is still celebrated as "Ether Day" in the original operation room at Massachusetts General Hospital in Boston, whose founder and chief surgeon was John Collins Warren (1778–1856). The country's first plastic surgeon, he had also presided over Wells' test. He now removed a cyst from the neck of a young man, Gilbert Abbott, anaesthetized by Morton. Actually the patient complained of some pain, so the world's "first" operation with ether narcosis was not entirely successful. But Morton had already gassed thirty-seven customers for a private surgeon, Henry J. Bigelow, who was probably responsible for the demonstration's approval and wrote the first description of the method to reach Europe. This report, too, was the first to mention a preliminary treatment: Morton had found that the ether worked best if a large dose of laudanum (an opium solution) was given initially.

Predictably, Morton's claim to fame was contested by Jackson, Long and Wells, leading to a futile legal battle. Jackson's dark role has been summed up by W. Stanley Sykes:

"All he did was to try and make money from narcosis when it turned out to be a lucky bet. He did not work with it himself, and there is not much proof that he used ether at all, though he wrote a book about it. He did not even take the trouble to watch an ether narcosis until five weeks after Ether Day."

Morton's Fate

William Green Morton capitalized on his ether narcosis by, for example, constructing an inhalator for easier dosage. But the cost of it ruined him, as it did not appeal to doctors. He moved to the countryside, yet spent his last years in New York, still bitterly fighting the authorities for his "rights". In 1868 some doctors, finding him a nervous wreck, advised him to put leeches on his temples and ice on his head. Instead, he ran and tried to cool off in the pond of Central Park. Shortly afterward, he was admitted to hospital and died of collapse, the cause being reported as "apoplexy".

The operation on Ether Day was concluded by Warren with the words: "Gentlemen, this is no humbug." Soon a similar statement came from Robert Liston (1794–1847), perhaps the finest surgeon in England, when he gave the first ether narcosis there: "This Yankee dodge, gentlemen, beats mesmerism..." The latter event was recorded in a painting, which shows a little lamp with an open flame not far from the ether mask. If correct, it means that the operation could have ended with quite a bang. Indeed, one of the students who would have suffered was the future Lord Lister, discoverer of antisepsis.

The explosiveness of ether was not taken very seriously during the early years of narcosis. In 1876, the journal *The Lancet* published an apparatus built by Lawson Tait, which warmed the ether over an alcohol flame before it was applied to the patient. This supposedly helped to prevent bronchitis "which often arises from the intense cold when the ether evaporates". Such devices have apparently all blown themselves up by now. But more reliable narcotics than ether were being sought.

That challenge was met in Edinburgh by the last of our pioneer anaesthetists, James Young Simpson (1811–70). According to tradition, he and his assistants had been testing a series of chemicals when, late one evening, somebody knocked over a bottle of chloroform. His wife brought dinner into the laboratory and found them sleeping peacefully in strange positions. Certain historians, though, say that a Liverpool pharmacist had sent a bottle of chloroform to Simpson, who tried it with good results.

Simpson's services to surgery and anaesthesiology have been called too small to justify the position of his statue, alongside Sir Walter Scott and other luminaries, on Princes Street in Edinburgh. But he certainly made propaganda for narcosis. When religious folk objected to anaesthesia for childbirth ("In pain shalt thou bear offspring"), he pointed out that the Lord had let a deep sleep fall over Adam before removing his rib!

The breakthrough for chloroform came in

(OPPOSITE) James Simpson, the Scottish obstetrician and gynaecologist whose search for a better anaesthetic than ether led him to introduce chloroform.
(*Above*) An apparatus for inhaling the vapour produced by liquid chloroform, illustrated in John Snow's book on anaesthesia (1858).

However, one good thing cannot be denied Jackson—he suggested that a miner's lamp be used if ether operations were performed near the mouth, since an open flame would not suit the gas!

1853: Queen Victoria took it from her doctor, John Snow, for the birth of Prince Leopold. She was evidently satisfied, as she took it again for her next child, and later praised her daughter Vicky's enjoyment of narcosis for the son who would be Kaiser Wilhelm II. James Simpson was knighted, with the pain-conquering motto *Victo dolore* on his coat of arms. Snow became a fashionable superman of medicine, sometimes termed "the world's first anaesthetist"—and he added to his reputation by discovering that cholera germs were transmitted by water.

While painlessness is naturally the patient's main interest, it also enables the surgeon to work with a calm, relaxed subject. Yet there was not much relaxation in the early days of narcosis, and more than one curse has been provoked by sudden body-tension shrinking the operation area to a keyhole. Deep ether narcosis is very relaxing, but requires a skilful anaesthetist, since it brings an increasing risk of respiratory paralysis and other complications. Besides, the body needs time to get rid of a large amount of narcotics, so the patient revives slowly and there can be further problems such as infection and blood clots.

Thus doctors soon began to look for a muscle-relaxing drug which could be given along with the anaesthetic. This was found in the South American arrow-poison *curare*. Some curare had apparently been brought back to Europe in 1595 by Sir Walter Raleigh. But it attracted far less notice than his potatoes and tobacco. Moreover, he gave a misleading description of its effects, and might even have mistaken it for another poison.

The real credit should be given to Charles Waterton, an English squire. His neighbours thought him mad, as he had set up a bird sanctuary on his estate and forbidden shooting; the lake was fished with bow and arrow, to avoid disturbing the birds! However, he was fascinated by all sorts of natural history and made several trips to South America, where he added to his collections and learned more about botany and ornithology. In 1812 he stumbled on curare, then called *wourali*, and returned to experiment with it in England. He found, for example, that an injection of it would kill a donkey after an hour, but could be survived by other animals if they were given artificial respiration with a bellows.

Curare works by blocking the transmission of nerve impulses to the muscles. It is like a false key stuck in a lock that can only be opened by the transmitter substance acetylcholine. With a suitable dose of it, the anaesthetist can inactivate the muscles and relax the patient completely. Yet since some of the muscles control breathing, artificial respiration must be given as long as the drug is working. This was learned by physiologists only in the 1930s. In 1939 curare came into clinical use, though not in anaesthesiology but in psychiatry, to dampen the dangerous contractions of muscles during electrical shock treatment.

A standard form of curare was produced in the early 1940s, making exact dosage possible. Named "Introcostin", it was first used on an anaesthetized patient by H. R. Griffith in the United States, who reported on it in July 1942. A year later, Stuart C. Cullen of Iowa City

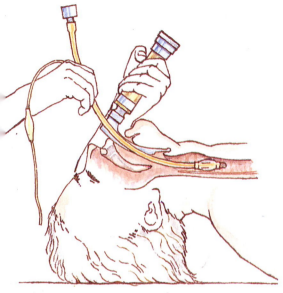

(LEFT) Tracheal intubation—inserting a catheter down the windpipe with the help of a laryngoscope—is performed after giving an intravenous narcotic and a muscle relaxant.

(Right) A modern narcosis system. The central units are a vaporizer, mixer, distributor and electronic ventilator, for supply and exact control of the anaesthetics (such as laughing gas and halothane) and oxygen breathed by the patient. Above these are accessories for measuring the gases in the patient's breath and blood, as well as blood pressure and electrocardiographic impulses.

described two hundred such cases, establishing its value. Today, curare is an important arrow in the anaesthetist's own quiver. We also have a synthetic drug, succinylcholine, with briefer effects of the same kind.

The modern method of inducing unconsciousness is far from poisonous. It begins with a fast-acting intravenous narcotic, usually made from barbituric acid. For longer operations, as on the abdomen, the muscles are relaxed with a drug like those mentioned above. To help the patient breathe, a tube is then inserted in the windpipe using a laryngoscope, and feeds oxygen as well as narcotic gases. This mixture is con-

trolled with a narcosis apparatus. Afterwards, the patient wakes up rather rapidly, but needs supervision for several hours. Most hospitals have intensive-care wards with advanced supervision equipment, such as continuous electrocardiography for registering heart functions. Here the duties are shared by the surgeons and anaesthetists who decide the type and technique of narcosis to be used.

Local anaesthetics

When Baron Larrey amputated the legs of Napoleon's soldiers on the way home from Moscow, he saw that those who were frozen stiff felt almost no pain. Likewise, a modern football coach can relieve a twisted joint by "freezing" it with chlorethyl spray. This technique is still employed by many surgeons for minor incisions, such as for boils. The principle of all local (regional) anaesthesia is to block the nerve terminals which react with pain in a particular area of the body. Various chemicals serve the purpose well.

The earliest of these was cocaine, apparently first used by the Incas, as mentioned in Chapter 1. Cocaine was synthesized from the leaves of the coca shrub in 1858, by Albert Niemann of Göttingen. He described how it "numbs the tongue and takes away both feeling and taste", but he overlooked its value for surgery. This was first realized by a Peruvian army doctor named Moreno y Maiz, who published a report on its pharmacological properties ten years later. It would not be brought into the clinics until 1884, and from a surprising direction.

Sigmund Freud (1856–1939), later the world-famous founder of psychoanalysis, was then an assistant physician in Vienna. He thought that he could cure morphine addicts by converting them to cocaine. The result was only an equally bad addiction, but Freud knew about the local anaesthetic property of cocaine, and got a friend interested in it—the eye doctor Karl Koller (1857–1944). After some experiments on animals, Koller was able to operate on a patient whose eye he soaked in cocaine solution, numbing it totally. Next the method was adopted at the ear clinic by a colleague, Stefan Jellinek, who also used it to numb mucous membranes in the mouth and throat.

Cocaine works very well on thin mucous membranes, but has much more difficulty in getting through thicker skin. To get a local anaesthetic through the outer layers of skin, an "infiltration technique" of injecting cocaine was introduced by Karl Ludwig Schleich (1859–1922) in Germany. The son of an eye doctor, he had presumably heard of Koller's experiences. Schleich possessed many talents and was interested in art and literature: he associated with

August Strindberg and the German authors at Berlin's well-known inn, *Zum Schwarzen Ferkel*, and was called "the last Renaissance man".

Experimenting on himself with various solutions, Schleich decided that half a gramme of cocaine per litre of salt water made an effective anaesthetic. He tried it in thousands of operations, including amputations. Patients crowded to his clinic in Friedrichsstrasse, and hundreds of foreign doctors made their pilgrimage to learn the technique. They had plenty of opportunity, as Schleich and his assistants did a dozen operations every day with local anaesthesia. In April 1892, he reported his results at the German surgical congress in Berlin, adding undiplomatically:

"Having this harmless method, I consider it, for idealistic and moral and legal reasons, no longer justified to use dangerous narcosis when local anaesthesia is adequate…"

His angry colleagues—led by the chairman, a renowned surgeon named Bardeleben—practically threw him out. One suspects that the reaction to Schleich's arrogance was heightened by their envy of the fat fees which he earned.

In America, cocaine was investigated by William Stewart Halsted (1852–1922). He and a friend experimented with it on themselves, so much that they both became addicted and had to be cured during a long boat voyage. But in 1885 they found that a region could be numbed by injecting the anaesthetic around the sensory nerve which supplied just that region. Such "conduction anaesthesia" gained rapid popularity, as it was simple and required less cocaine.

Around the turn of the century, a more effective substance named procaine (Novocaine) was developed by Alfred Einhorn of Germany. Then, too, Heinrich Braun (1862–1934) discovered that local anaesthesia lasts longer if adrenalin is added, as it contracts blood vessels and keeps the anaesthetic in the operation area. Such substances are very reliable today, the two most common being xylocaine and carbocaine, both synthesized in Sweden.

We now have a choice between spinal, conduction and infiltration anaesthesia. The first method eliminates pain and relaxes muscles in, for example, the whole lower body, and was once very common in abdominal operations. Nerve impulses to the spine are blocked by injecting either inside the membranes which surround the cord (spinal anaesthesia) or outside them (epidural anaesthesia). In the latter case, morphine can be used against pain after operations or injuries, or in chronic diseases like cancer where the patient can give it to himself by injection or pump. The conduction method is to inject around the nerves that lead to an arm or leg being operated on, while infiltration means injecting under the skin at a place of minor injury to be sewn up.

Surgery in the United States

The American Revolution created an acute demand for good doctors, especially surgeons. Medical students usually got their surgical training from an older colleague—if any could be found—and went to London, Edinburgh or Paris for further work. The French connection had, of course, been strengthened by that country's aid to the rebels.

One such educated surgeon was Ephraim McDowell (1771–1830), who practised in Danville, Kentucky, near the western frontier of "the white man's civilization". He studied under John Bell in Edinburgh, a great preacher of "sewing together the wound-edges so cleanly, finely and well-joined that they can heal". By chance, McDowell made a pioneering contribution in 1809, when summoned to a woman who was thought to be pregnant. Eventually he realized that her abdomen was, instead, swollen by a huge ovarian cyst, or water-filled tumour.

An operation of this kind had never been done before, but surgery was now the only hope. Leading the patient on horseback to his clinic, he took 25 minutes to remove the cyst, using

The First Ovariotomies

Who invented this operation is still debatable, and probably Ephraim McDowell had a predecessor. In 1701, a woman named Jane Todd Crawford was operated on in Glasgow by the surgeon Robert Houston, for what was called "a tumour in the ovary containing nine quarts of gelatinous substance", which must have been pretty heavy. All we know is that she recovered and that the wound was bandaged with compresses soaked in hot French cognac.

The removal of one or both ovaries was long opposed in France by authorities such as Dupuytren and Velpeau. In Germany it was tried by experts such as Langenbeck, Scanzoni and Bardeleben, but plagued with bad hygiene and technique.

The leading English ovariotomist, Charles Clay in Manchester, had a mortality rate of 44%, and the national average was 86% as late as 1860, due to postoperative infection and bleeding. Ovariotomists were sometimes called murderers and needed great courage to continue.

One of these saw seven out of ten patients die, and said it was unjust to go on. But Thomas Spencer Wells (1818-97) did not give up. By 1862 he had saved 33 out of 50 women, and in 1880 he published a book, 1000 Cases of Ovariotomy, showing that the death rate had sunk to 23%. (In the early 1890s, it was down to 5-7% at several large clinics.)

Apart from cleanliness, Wells' success depended on his skill at stopping bleeding. He devised an artery-clamp, often called the "bulldog", which is still common all over the world. He also used a better cauterizing method developed by his teacher, Baker Brown.

neither anaesthetic nor antiseptic, with just a psalm to comfort her! She lived on for 31 years, and McDowell did some more of these "ovariotomies". Once his sceptical colleagues became convinced of the possibility, they gave him an honorary doctorate.

Some talented Americans were apprenticed to John Hunter in London. Philip Wright Post (1766–1828) investigated human corpses and returned to New York, but had to seek refuge in the city jail while a bigoted mob smashed his anatomical collection. Persisting as a professor of anatomy, physiology, and finally surgery, he founded a museum in the Hunter style.

Trouble also faced William Shippen Jr. (1736–1808), who studied under both of the Hunter brothers and was inspired to establish America's first maternity ward, in Philadelphia. He even created its first faculty for doctors—the Philadelphia Medical College—together with another Hunter disciple, John Morgan (1735–89). But this pair came into conflict. Morgan was outmanoeuvred by Shippen for the post of Army chief physician, and took it so hard that he dropped out of medicine, sank into poverty, and was found dead in an attic. "A man of whom half the world once spoke, he had scarcely enough friends to bury him," said a leading member of that original faculty, Benjamin Rush, who—among other things, as mentioned earlier—opened the first alcoholic ward in the New World.

Philip Syng Physick (1768–1837) was, however, America's leading product of the school of John Hunter, who had noticed his ability and let him do several of the experiments for a book on inflammation, giving him due credit. Physick went on to solve a practical problem in surgery. The threads used for sewing ligatures were not absorbed by the body, but often worked their way out, causing infections and fistulas. Hunter's trick was to leave the thread-ends and pull them out through the wound so that they could be removed later. Physick experimented with threads made of animal tissue or parchment, and discovered a good material, "catgut",

PHILIP Syng Physick.

made of sheep intestines. Back in the USA, Physick introduced a technique of stomach rinsing, which he also used to feed patients: a rubber tube connected to a syringe. It worked much better than an idea Hunter had tried—forcing an eel's skin well down into the stomach! In addition, Physick improved the technique for tonsillectomy, and found new ways of operating on the lens and iris of the eye. He was the first to use a metal-wire sling for removing haemorrhoids, a method basically still usable today.

Physick was regarded as America's best surgeon by far. At his clinic in Philadelphia, he treated the cream of society, right up to the President. He did have some difficulty with Andrew Jackson, who claimed to know more medicine than any doctor and insisted on curing himself with lead sugar and calomel (mercurous chloride, a purgative). Nevertheless, Physick held the country's first professorship in surgery for thirteen years. He became an anatomy professor when he felt too old to operate, but was so famous that people still begged him to do so. Thus, he was nearly forced to remove bladder stones from Chief Justice John Marshall. After his last operation, on an eye, he went to bed and died.

Among other great surgeons at the time, we have already met John Warren, who was well educated in Europe under both Astley Cooper and Dupuytren. James Marion Sims (1813–83), the son of an inn-keeper, studied at Jefferson College in Philadelphia, and launched a promising career in an unhealthy rural part of Alabama. Then he and his family came down with malaria, and he had to move to a better climate in Montgomery. Regaining health, he earned enough money to build a ward with eight beds, and began to operate. His skill soon emerged: patients streamed in for all kinds of surgical ailments, and colleagues took notice when he reported a fine operation for harelip, including a large defect in the upper jaw.

In June 1845, three slave-girls came to Sims, all with fistulas between the bladder, vagina and rectum. This miserable condition was usually caused by poor care in childbirth. Operations on such "vesicovaginal" fistulas had never succeeded; Sims could do nothing. But at the same time he was called to a woman who had fallen from a horse, badly injuring her pelvis. Compelled to act, he tried putting the patient in a bent position to examine the vagina. On the way, he bought a tin spoon to use as a speculum. "I saw everything, as no man had ever seen before… I thought immediately—why should it not be possible to operate on fistulas by this means?" So he started to manufacture special instruments. His first attempt, on the three slave-girls, was a partial failure, yet he succeeded four years later. By then, he had improved the position, which—like those instruments—still bears his name.

A new disease in the South, chronic intestinal infection, made Sims move again. Settling in New York, he collected money with the help of a newspaper magnate, Henry Luther Stuart, and opened America's first gynaecological clinic in 1855. It acquired larger premises—where the Hotel Waldorf Astoria now stands—in 1863,

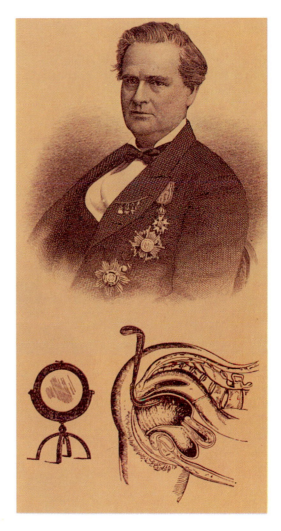

THE gynaecologist James Marion Sims and his "double duck-billed" speculum for inspection of the vagina, aided by light reflected from a mirror.

with Sims leading the staff of younger surgeons. But being a staunch Southerner, he could not stay long, and fled from the Civil War to Europe. There he was warmly welcomed in several cities, and frequently demonstrated his fistula operation. During the Franco-Prussian War, he directed an American ambulance service, with

Sims' Position

In 1854, the New York Medical Gazette carried Marion Sims' report of "two cases of vesico-vaginal fistula cured":

"With the patient placed on the table, left side downward, the thigh bent up towards the abdomen... a speculum could be inserted and the operation field exposed; it went more easily than I expected, but did not show the fistula quite as well as when one has the patient in the regular knee-elbow position. I managed nevertheless to go through the operation's different stages with relative ease. It was done on 12 November 1849, two years after the injury had arisen. Three days after the operation, the catheter slid out by itself, and was not reinserted until four hours later. There was no urine leakage, so the fistula was perfectly closed."

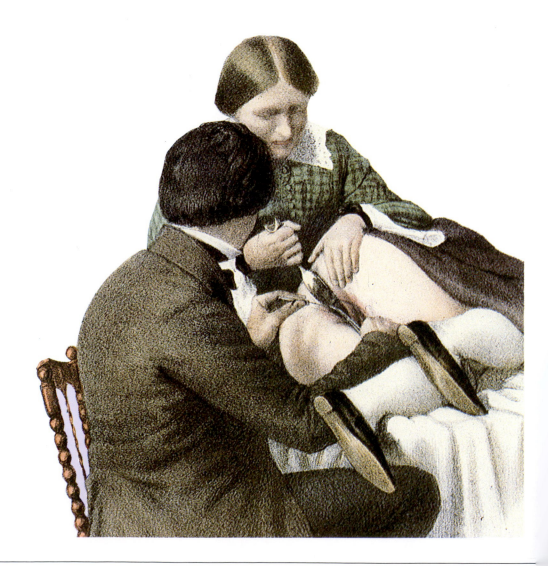

THE hierarchy and the healer: Theodore Roosevelt (*left*) and some congressmen are given a tour of Fort Wright Hospital in Spokane, Washington, about 1909, by the United States Army surgeon E. A. Dean (*right*). The President and the Colonel had other common interests as well—both were advocates of physical exercise, worldwide travellers and diverse intellectuals.

such skill and neutrality that he was awarded a medal by each side.

Marion Sims was the first great gynaecologist, and his fistula operation was only one reason. He also initiated research on menstrual problems, sterility and artificial insemination. Perhaps the simplest sign of his many-sided genius was that he named the operation for removing gallstones—cholecystotomy.

American surgeons would continue to benefit as much from the pioneer tradition and military experience as from urban practice or foreign education. A typically varied career was that of Elmer Anderson Dean (1871–1965). Born on a farm in Tennessee, of English and Danish stock, he showed promise as an opera singer, then worked his way to the University of Pennsylvania Medical School—the country's oldest, having grown out of Shippen's. Graduating in 1898 during the Spanish-American War, he preferred good training to private profit, and joined the army. After marrying his nurse in a yellow-fever camp, he served for twelve years in the Philippine jungles, commanded American hospitals in France during World War I, and finally founded Brooke Hospital in Texas, which became the world centre of burn treatment. Dean supported many improvements such as asepsis, but they made him few political friends, and these were needed to reach the highest post of Surgeon General. In the end, however, his School found that he had been its best student in half a century, and gave him a gold medal.

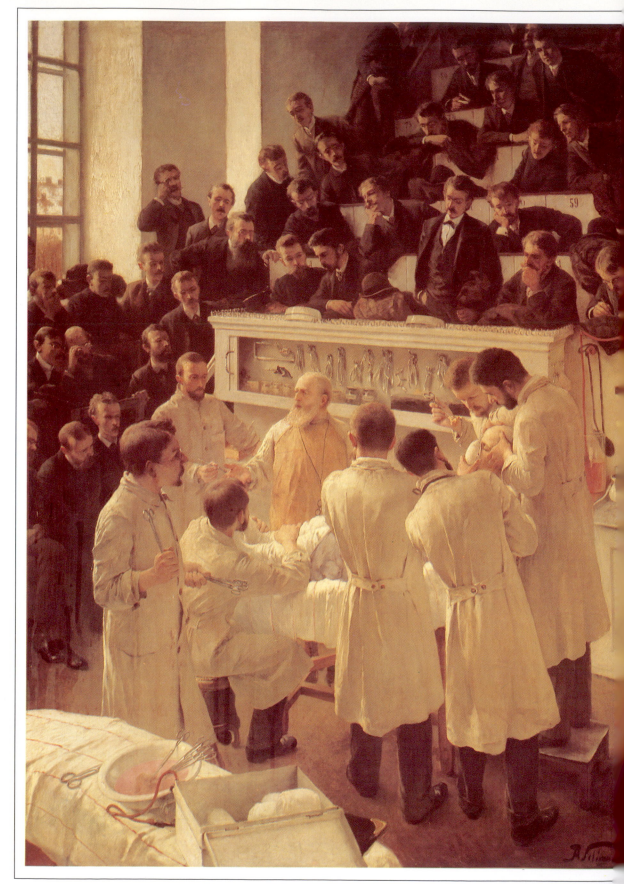

CHAPTER 8

The human face of surgery

Surgery experienced a great upswing in the middle of the nineteenth century. Until then, it had made far more progress in removing the effects of ailments than in dealing with the causes. Doctors still often did more harm than good as a result of basic misunderstandings. But now developments in both the realm of the microscope and the hospital gave medicine a real ability to care for patients, and enabled surgeons to treat them humanely with confidence in their survival.

French expertise

At least in France, theoretical science was surging: its leaders in medicine included Magendie, Bernard, Brown-Séquard, Trousseau and, as we shall see, Louis Pasteur. The country's practitioners continued to improve as well. They eagerly adopted the technique of percussion for diagnosis, which Jean-Nicolas Corvisart (1755–1821), Napoleon's physician, had made known after its invention in Austria by Leopold Auenbrugger (1722–1809). Likewise, the stethoscope had been introduced by René Théophile Hyacinthe Laennec (1781–1826).

Both of these Frenchmen were methodical investigators. They combined records of patients with results of treatment and findings of pathology and anatomy. Their emphasis on bedside observations became the main tool of the new approach in medicine, which flourished especially in England with Addison, Bright, Graves and Hodgkin. Another of their non-operating colleagues was Guillaume Benjamin Arnaud Duchenne (1806–75), the founder of electrotherapy, who also gave his name to an inherited muscular disease. Jean Martin Charcot (1825–93) distinguished "hysteria" from organic nerve ailments and, with his enormous knowledge of the nervous system's physiology, was able to make diagnostic use of muscle and tendon reflexes.

Surgery had gained a new authority with Larrey, yet his wartime service prevented him from refining the art except in traumatology, the study of injuries. Next to him, however, stood one of the strangest figures in surgical history: Guillaume Dupuytren (1777–1835). This son of a lawyer in the village of Pierre-Bouffière began an eventful life by being kidnapped at the age of three—a lady thought him charming and whisked him off in her carriage. At seven, he ran away from home, but was soon brought back and punished. Shortly afterward, a troop of hussars came along, fell under his magic and, surprisingly, got permission to take him with them to Paris.

There, Dupuytren went to a boarding school, but had no fun or success in four years, so he walked home to join the army. His father then ordered him to become a doctor, and sent him to a medical school in Limoges. Resigning himself, he went instead to Paris, and began to perform

THEODOR Billroth operating at the General Hospital of Vienna, painted by A. Seligmann in 1890. With him are notable assistants such as Anton von Eiselsberg (on his left), later a famous surgeon and researcher.

dissections in the anatomical institute. His interest was seized by anatomy and he took up research, including work on the lymph vessels and the inguinal canal. Going to the Hôtel Dieu hospital, he was made assistant physician in 1802, chief physician in 1808, and chief surgeon in 1815. At the same time, he got a professorship in surgery.

The name "Dupuytren's contracture" has been given to a fibrous condition of the palms, often in older men, for which he devised an operation. He was the first to classify burns systematically, using six degrees rather than three as we do. His concern with burns also led to new plastic surgery for repairing skin defects and scars. A better way of handling fractures enabled him to get amazing results: he once reported that 200 of 207 cases of Pott's fracture recovered completely after his extension treatment. In abdominal surgery, he invented an instrument to help in exposing the intestine—a procedure which had been introduced in France in 1793.

Dupuytren was a magnificent teacher, a dazzling technician with wounds, an eloquent lecturer. Bloated with pride and arrogance, he earned the reputation of being "the greatest of surgeons and the smallest of human beings". Although he became a millionaire from private practice, and a baron of France, he was also nicknamed "the brigand of the Hôtel Dieu". Never happy outside his operating theatre—or perhaps inside it either, due to his mania for perfection—he clashed with his colleagues, staff, and the few friends he had. When he died at 57, he had advanced surgery on many frontiers, but nobody mourned him.

A fitting contrast was Paul Broca (1824–80), who might remind us of Sir Charles Bell. Best known as a neurologist, he was professor of surgery in Paris, but contributed most to brain anatomy and anthropology. He described the condition of aphasia, called Broca's aphasia by Continentals—inability to talk because the speech organs do not obey brain signals. Over a dozen anatomical features, including parts of the

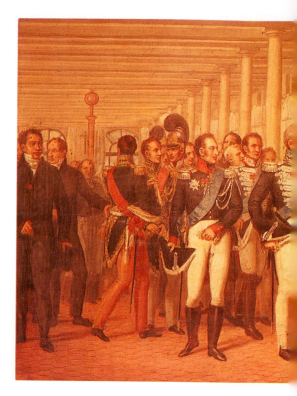

brain governing speech and smell, have made his name familiar to students. Craniometry, the measurement of heads, was perfected by him and has become a classical method of anthropologists.

One of Dupuytren's followers was Auguste Nélaton (1807–73), whose name is immortalized by a urethra catheter. But the leader in urology was Félix Jean Casimir Guyon (1831–1920) at the Necker Hospital. He pioneered prostatic surgery, and was among the first to use the cystoscope, a French development by the medical student Civiale. From the same country came an ingenious blood-clamp, the pean, which is called for by a surgeon every day at any operating theatre in the world. It was named after Jules Péan (1830–98), although some say that one of his assistants invented it. The latter supposedly grew tired of being scolded when the chief got his shirt-cuffs bloodied, since Péan usually operated in evening-dress!

"Nurses were for the most part uninformed and untrained, and more interested in ruining themselves with gin than in rehabilitating or comforting their patients. Many of them behaved like Dickens' character Sairey Gamp. The better nurses worked by day, while at night the patients were turned over to 'watch-women' who knew nothing at all about sick-care and could hardly be counted on to give much attention to their duties for the few pennies they earned with a night's work…"

Actually, ever since the Roman ladies we met in Chapter 2, only monks and nuns had taken care of the sick—that is, of those who were lucky enough to be placed in monasteries and religious hostels. But the medieval method was a matter of spiritual solace—and preparation for death—rather than of physical care. Slightly more specialized were the Beguines, a society of pious women who devoted their lives to sick-care, along with a similar society of men known as Beghards. The first beguinage was established at Liège in 1184 by a priest, Lambert le Bègue. Its few successors were mostly limited to what are now Belgium and Holland. Amsterdam's beautiful "Begijnhof" can still be seen not far from the business centre.

Education for nurses was started in 1836 by Theodore Fliedner (1800-64), a pastor in Kaiserswerth near Dusseldorf. His original aim was to train young women for social work with freed prisoners, but the school—later called an institution for deaconesses—also enabled the local doctor to teach practical sick-care. Having begun with a loan of 2,300 thalers, Fliedner proved a good fund-raiser and even managed to open a branch school.

The most famous student at Kaiserswerth came from England. Florence Nightingale (1820-1910) received her first name from the city of her birth. Dissatisfied with the lazy life of her rich Italophile parents, she was "shy, temperamental, stubborn, introspective, dreamy and indignantly displeased", traits which would last. At seventeen, she had a re-

DUPUYTREN displays the results of a cataract operation to King Charles X at the Hôtel Dieu.

Péan's bad manners nearly equalled those of his predecessor Dupuytren. He was never really accepted by colleagues, and earned no standing in the faculty, despite being the best surgeon in Paris and contributing much to urology and gynaecology. Among other things, he was the first to operate on a bladder diverticulum.

Better medical care

Successful surgery requires more than a good surgeon and thorough preparation. Just as important is the postoperative care, which was at a low level until the mid-nineteenth century. Many patients died because of ignorant or negligent handling after surgery, and the quality of personnel at most hospitals was poor. As the historian Courtney Dainton says:

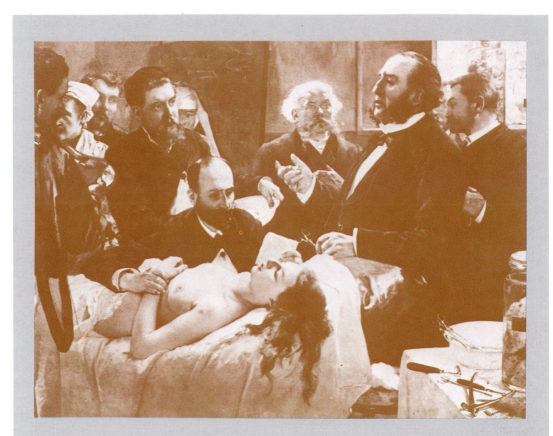

Péan Operates

A chief surgeon at the Royal Seraphim Lazarette in Stockholm, John Berg (1851-1931), gave the following account in his Autobiographical Notes:

"Calm and cold as marble, the surgeon stands in his dinner-jacket, decorated with the Red Button, beside the table where his curt orders clash with the groans of a badly chloroformed patient and other victims. The previous patient is bandaged, and the next is gassed, while the present operation is going on—all in one room to save time. During the operation, Péan pauses briefly to inform the audience in a loud voice of everything he sees and does, keeping a sharp eye and hand on his assistants so that they do not obscure the view. He operates so wonderfully blood-free that hardly a spot reaches his white cuffs. This is explained by his fluent use of the clamp which is named after him, applying it if possible even before he cuts… After the operation, which takes only a few minutes, he makes much of what he has achieved and, unperturbed, receives the usual storm of applause from his packed auditorium."

The Red Button was that of the Legion of Honour. It should be added that, apart from foreign doctors and students, the audience consisted mainly of the best Paris society, who took enormous pleasure in watching operations!

(*OPPOSITE*) Jules Péan delivers a lecture, holding the haemostatic forceps named after him. This work—about 1886—was by Henri Gervex, who started a fashion of painting hospital scenes. (*Right*) Florence Nightingale.

ligious revelation: her mission was to serve mankind. But when she decided to work at a hospital, the family forbade it as socially unthinkable!

Florence got her way. She worked in the slums and helped with operations. In 1851, after much argument, she was allowed to go to Kaiserswerth for training. However, the hard discipline was more suited to German peasant-girls than to her nervous intellect. She stayed three months, returned to become a novice at a convent in Rome, and failed there too. After some months with the sisters of Vincent de Paul, an order in Paris, she was appointed the matron of an institution for "poor persons of rank" in London.

At the same time, the Crimean War had begun. The British base was at Scutari, opposite Constantinople. Hospital conditions there were awful, and a description of them by William Howard Russell, war correspondent of the *Times*, had aroused national indignation. The Secretary for War, Sidney Herbert, was forced to act, and he called for Miss Nightingale. She accepted the mission with joy, and departed with thirty-eight nuns and nursing assistants.

In fact, the conditions were even worse than reported. Florence Nightingale set to work with "obstinate fury", alienating every official she met. But her unquenchable energy, and money collected in England, succeeded in making the medical care acceptable. There is a popular legend of her as "the lady with the lamp", a fair angel who strode among the wounded soldiers, whispering words of comfort and laying a cool hand on their brows. The truth is that she had no time for such gestures. A forceful organizer, she wrote angry letters to ambassadors, generals, chief physicians, and the Secretary for War who,

more than once, regretted having sent her there.

Eventually she became a nervous wreck and sank into depression. Yet coming home ill and tired, she found herself a national heroine. The sum of 44,000 pounds was collected to start a nursing school under her direction, and in June 1860 the first students entered Nightingale School at St. Thomas's Hospital in London. She had proved that nursing was a proper profession for women, although she never regarded it as anything but a calling. All her life, she resisted the licensing of nurses, and whether they got paid for their work did not interest her.

Florence Nightingale created a basic reform in medical care, especially with her two books, *Notes on Hospitals* and *Notes on Nursing*. The main points in her programme were cleanliness and fresh air. Soap, warm water and sunshine, moderate isolation and only one patient to a bed, were her methods. These alone decreased the mortality in hospitals from 40 % to 20 %. Even so, she knew nothing about bacteria, nor

Inside Scutari

According to the dispatches of William Howard Russell from the Crimean War, those who were not already suffering from some epidemic disease when they reached the hospital soon came down with it there, and those with clean wounds were infected to the point of blood-poisoning. Every ward was packed and patients without beds were laid on the floor. The doctors worked "like lions", as one visitor put it, but they were too few. Not uncommonly, a casualty lay for two weeks without being examined. There were no pillows or bed-linen, the sole cover being soldiers' capes. Even instruments were scarce, and no time or opportunity existed for washing hands between operations. The hospital chaplain told that, when he sat on the floor beside the dying to write their last letter home, he had to sweep the fleas off his paper.

Bitter Truths

These remarks by Florence Nightingale are typical of her Notes on Nursing *and* Notes on Hospitals, *respectively:*

"One of the most common observations that can be made at a sick-bed is the comfort experienced by a patient when the skin is cleaned and dried. But it should not be forgotten that this invigoration is not the only benefit. Actually it is a mere sign that the life-force has returned: something which diminished the force has been removed. The nurse should never neglect to attend to the patient's bodily hygiene on the pretext that such measures do little good and are not urgent. This should be, and generally is, observed at all well-managed hospitals, yet it is often neglected by sick-care in homes."

"It may seem superfluous to point out that the first requirement of a hospital is that it should not injure its patients."

did she later believe Lister that they existed. For her, sickness and infection were nature's warning, and medicine needed only to help nature's healing power.

Already during the Crimean War she had shown her poor nerves, and physically she was fragile. The last decades of her life were spent in a wheelchair, despite not being injured or paralyzed. Her state came to be diagnosed as hysteria, and it does seem clear, at no cost to her greatness, that the Angel of Scutari was a hysterical shrew from the age of 37. Nevertheless, in 1907 she received the Order of Merit, one of Great Britain's highest honours, which had never before been awarded to a woman.

Childbed fever

The other side of women's life was notorious rather than famous. At the General Hospital in Vienna, the maternity clinic held two sections. Ward 1 had acquired such a bad reputation over the years that women prayed on their knees not to be admitted there. Childbed (puerperal) fever raged: 10–15 % of the mothers died, and during the particularly difficult month of October 1842, the mortality rate was all of 29.33 %! Things were better in Ward 2, whose rate of around 3 % was normal in other hospitals.

In 1846, the clinic took on an assistant physician from Hungary, named Ignaz Philipp Semmelweis (1818–65). He wondered about the contrast between the two wards. They looked similar, and accepted almost the same kinds of patients. The only difference was that the births were handled by medical students in Ward 1 and by midwifery pupils in Ward 2. As an experiment, these were made to exchange places. This might have caused an "atmospheric-telluric disturbance" in Ward 1, according to the disease theories of the time—but unfortunately, the high mortality rate moved to Ward 2. The section was closed for a while; when it reopened with the medical students still at work, the results were as bad as before.

Semmelweis also noticed that, if a woman arrived too late and had already given birth at

IGNAZ Semmelweis.

should be possible to produce the disease in women by the same cause which produced it in Kolletschka. Consequently I must ask: is dead flesh introduced into the blood of all those whom I have seen die of this disease? And this question must be answered: *yes*."

So the explanation was discovered. What distinguished the two wards was that the medical students came straight from their autopsy exercises in a pathological institution, carrying infections from corpses on their hands. In May 1847, Semmelweis made it obligatory to wash hands with chlorinated water before births. A month later, the mortality in Ward 2 was down to the same level as in Ward 1, and after another year it had sunk to 1 %.

This should have been proof enough. However, Semmelweis' worst enemy was his own chief, Klein, who did everything possible to oppose talented subordinates. A subsequent Swedish colleague, Elis Essen-Möller of Lund, wrote about Klein that "the less said of him, the better—I leave him to the silence and verdict which are unanimous among all authorities." But Semmelweis was supported by two faculty professors, von Hebra and Skoda. Reactions also occurred elsewhere in Europe, although not helped by Semmelweis' tactless way of arguing. He called his greatest opponent outside Austria, the professor and magistrate Friedrich Scanzoni (1821–91) in Würzburg, "a murderer and a Nero of medicine".

Semmelweis was forced to retire to Budapest, where he published a book about infection during childbirth. His unbalanced, difficult temperament turned into mental illness, and he ended in an asylum. Ironically, he died in the same manner as Kolletschka, from blood-poisoning after a cut on his finger.

At about the same time, Oliver Wendell Holmes (1809–94) worked on the problem of childbed fever. In 1843, a few years before Semmelweis' discovery, he gave a lecture in Boston suggesting that the fever was an infectious disease, whose "germs" were transmitted by those

home, or in a carriage, she seldom got childbed fever. It thus seemed that the infection was communicated during actual birth in the clinic. But the real clue appeared when a professor of criminal medicine, Kolletschka, cut his finger during an autopsy and got blood-poisoning. Semmelweis later commented:

"Day and night, the image of Kolletschka's illness pursued me. As we found identical changes in his body and those of the childbed women, it can be concluded that Kolletschka died of the same disease which I have seen so many women die of. But we now know what made Kolletschka ill: the wound he got from the autopsy knife polluted with dead flesh. Not the wound itself, but its pollution, caused his death... Of course, Kolletschka is not the first to die in this way. I must therefore assume that, if the supposition is correct that his disease and the women's are identical, it

A Clue to Childbed Fever

The great botanist Carl Linnaeus, who was also a doctor and had studied under Boerhaave in Leyden, recalled a case of what must have been a retained placenta—in his book Diaeta Naturalis *(1732), written in a jumble of Swedish and Latin:*

"She felt well the first day, was sick and dizzy the second, and died on the third. The doctor ordered an autopsy, and it was found that the midwife's fingernails had scratched the mouth of the uterus when taking out the placenta. An inflammation followed and, when the mouth closed, the infected afterbirth stayed inside."

Chlorine before Semmelweis

At the General Maternity House in Stockholm, the chief physician Pehr Gustaf Cederschjöld (1782-1848) wrote in his Textbook of Care for Women's Family Life *that he had experimented with measures against childbed fever already in 1825. He assumed that it was caused by a miasma, or by contact infection. For the latter, at least, hygiene was useful. He gave every patient a personal sponge and towel for washing her private parts with chlorinated water. Yet he missed the most important thing—the midwife's hands!*

A Doctor and Poet

Oliver Wendell Holmes was equally successful in both of his careers, as doctor and poet. Besides his contribution to anaesthesiology, he created the terms "anaesthesia" and "anaesthetics" for elimination of pain. He became dean of the medical faculty at Harvard University, helping among other things to develop America's first dental college. He also campaigned successfully against quacks and encouraged the medical use of new discoveries in physics and chemistry.

assisting at a birth. A doctor, he said, should wait at least 24 hours between an autopsy and a birth, and should also change clothes as well as washing with chlorinated chalk-water. But a Doctor Meigs in Philadelphia was insulted by the idea that any physician's hands could carry infection, pointing out that childbed fever had even happened to patients of the great Professor Simpson in Edinburgh—and it was absurd to insinuate that Simpson could have dirty hands!

What finally convinced the doubters was an event as late as 1879, thirty-two years after Semmelweis' breakthrough. At a meeting in the medical academy of Paris, a gynaecologist was about to condemn the theory of contact infection in childbirth fever, when a man in the audience interrupted him. The man went up to the podium, drew a row of dots on the blackboard—representing streptococcus bacteria—and said calmly: "Here, Monsieur, is your contagion." The gynaecologist made no reply, for the man was Louis Pasteur.

The dawn of bacteriology

The son of a tanner in southern France, Louis Pasteur (1822–95) became professor of chemistry at the Sorbonne in Paris. It was while working as a chemist in Lille that he grew interested in the process of fermentation. He proved that it was caused by fungi or bacteria. Such microorganisms were already known to exist in the mash, but were believed to arise only during the process. This was the beginning of bacteriology, a science which is essential to safe surgery. It took place during the same half-century as the two other pillars of modern surgery, which likewise created their own special sciences—anaesthesiology and, as we shall see, radiology.

For nearly twenty years, Pasteur grappled with problems close to medicine. He studied wine and beer fermentation, and invented the process of pasteurization, which became most important in the dairy industry. In addition, the government asked him to investigate a silkworm disease that was threatening to ruin the valuable French

PASTEUR in his laboratory (1885): the most
famous painting by the great Finnish artist
Albert Edelfelt.

silk industry. Within a couple of years he found
two different causes, a type of protozoa and what
was probably a virus. Even better, he and his
assistant Duclaux developed a pesticide to control them.

In 1877, Pasteur turned to micro-organisms
that cause disease in humans. Starting with the
anthrax bacillus, whose habits he had charted
for two years, he produced a vaccine against it.
Around this time, he also found a vaccine for
chicken cholera, and is said to have saved the
French chicken industry more money than the
country paid in damages after its war with Prussia

in 1870! Of course, Pasteur was not a doctor—
his interests were in bacterial life and vaccine
development, rather than in individual bacteria
and their connections with disease. But this did
not deter him from explaining their toxic
effects, as well as discovering streptococci and
staphylococci.

His crowning achievement was a vaccine for
rabies, which had been considered incurable.
This work was not without danger for Pasteur
and his assistants: they had to keep a large ken-
nel full of mad dogs that were quite unpredict-
able. Despite having suffered a stroke, Pasteur
never tired (his motto was *"il faut travailler!"*)
and, on one occasion, he even sucked saliva
straight from a dog's mouth. But the result of his
efforts was a serum which cured both humans
and newly infected dogs.

The grateful nation built an institute in Pasteur's honour. It is there that he was buried and that his research in bacteriology is continued. Some years after his death, the French held a referendum to determine who was the greatest man in the country's history, and Pasteur won by a broad margin.

A more practical approach to such research was taken by Robert Koch (1843–1910), who became one of the first professors of hygiene and bacteriology, in Berlin. He got a fine medical education in Göttingen, under the chemist Friedrich Wöhler (1800–82) who was the first to synthesize an organic substance, and under Friedrich Gustav Jacob Henle (1809–85). The latter, a famed anatomist, had written *On Miasmas and Contagions* (1840), advancing the theory that infections consisted of living germ material, although not yet able to prove that they were caused by it. Henle inspired Koch to begin his studies, in a simple laboratory at his surgery as a district doctor in the Polish city of Poznan.

Koch wrote in 1876, to a botanist named Cohn in Breslau, that he had seen rod-shaped anthrax germs through a microscope and noticed two forms. One was an active bacillus; the other, while passive and noninfectious, was very resistant to influence. Koch had developed an apparatus for keeping bacteria alive under the microscope. He showed it to Cohn and to a pathologist, Cohnheim, who realized that he had found something important and helped him to continue. Thus in 1877 he wrote the first work on the origins of wound infections.

Obtaining a post in Berlin, Koch proceeded to invent a new method for culturing bacteria. This opened the way to detailed observation of them. He also revealed that many kinds of bacteria could be killed with bichloride of mercury, which became useful to surgery. But his main discoveries were the bacillae that caused tuberculosis and cholera. He thought that he had found a medicine which could cure tuberculosis, but it proved to be only a diagnostic aid (tuberculin). His work won a Nobel Prize in

ROBERT Koch.

A Forgotten Germ

Bacteriology could have begun three centuries earlier if the ideas of an Italian physician had been accepted. Girolamo Fracastoro (1478-1553), known as Fracastorius, practised in Verona. A true "Renaissance man", he wrote poetry about syphilis, and contributed to Copernicus' famous explanation of the solar system. In 1546 he published a whole book on the spread of diseases by tiny, fast-multiplying bodies.

But this "father of epidemiology" made little impact, and only in 1840 was the germ of his theory revived by Henle, who passed it on to Robert Koch.

1905, and was carried further by others, leading to the BCG vaccine of Albert Calmette (1863–1933) and Alphonse Guerin (1816–95) from France.

Pasteur and Koch launched the first "golden age" of bacteriology, which meant a good deal to surgery and medicine in general. Some of its most important results were the discovery of leprosy bacillae by Armauer Hansen (1841–1912) in Norway, of gonorrhea bacteria by Albert Neisser (1855–1916) in Germany, of basic immunology by Émile Roux (1853–1933) and Alexander Yersin (1863–1943) in France, and—to the great relief of accident victims—of tetanus toxin by Knud Faber (1862–1955) in Denmark.

The baron of antiseptics

One of surgery's outstanding pioneers was Joseph Lister (1827-1912). He came from a rich Quaker home in Yorkshire and his father, a wine merchant, became a member of the Royal Society by building better microscopes. This hobby attracted young Joseph, and if it had not done so, he would probably never have discovered antisepsis—according to a speaker at the Lister Jubileum in 1967.

Lister had considerable talent in art, which he later used to illustrate his scientific writings. At first he thought of it as a profession, to his father's delight, but he decided to study medicine and went to London, since the "finer" universities at Oxford and Cambridge were not yet open to nonconformist religions. As a student he was unhappy, living in the Quaker company of three others and their landlord, a bigot who forbade laughter and called any joke a sin. It encouraged him to read, however, and at the age of 25 he became a Bachelor of Medicine with honours. In the same year he entered the Royal College of Surgeons of England, and his career had begun.

While getting practical experience with some of London's best surgeons, Lister started to do research at the clinic of Walter Walshe.

LORD Lister.

He wrote a study on the eye's ring-muscle, then another on the smooth skin muscles. In both cases he put the microscope to good use, which was unusual in the mid-nineteenth century, especially among surgeons. His lectures on this tool to the medical society must have gladdened his father, with whom he often corresponded. More significantly, he lectured at that time on "hospital gangrene", the serious infection which was to call forth his greatest contributions.

In January 1854, Lister was invited to become first assistant surgeon in Edinburgh—under James Syme (1799–1870), a leader of surgery in Great Britain. He naturally accepted, and the two men became close friends. Lister even married Syme's daughter Agnes, thereby leaving the Quakers, who did not permit alliances with nonmembers. He kept only one Quaker habit, the Biblical use of "thou" instead of "you", due to respect for his father. After six years, he himself got a respectable professorship of surgery in Glasgow, where he took over Male Accident Ward 27 in a newly built hospital.

At that time, the usual explanation for wound infection was that the exposed tissues were chemically affected by oxygen in the air. The remedy was to bandage the wound tightly, using various materials which had no success—such as collodium (a solution of gun-cotton in ether and alcohol), adhesives, and cattle-intestine membranes. But we now know that tight bandages encourage bacterial growth, keeping the right temperature just like a thermostat. Even then, there were others who believed that infection came from a stinking "miasma" in the air. No doubt the sick-wards smelled bad enough, since their own personnel could not bear to stay any longer than necessary. This, however, was due not to a miasma, but to the rotting of wounds.

In any case, nobody tried to prevent miasmas. Certainly the wards had been enlarged, and were sometimes aired out at midday, yet Florence Nightingale's doctrine of fresh air was still science fiction. Facilities did not exist for washing the personnel's hands or the patients' wounds. This was not even thought worthwhile for a surgeon before he went to work. It is strange that the findings of Semmelweis and Oliver Wendell Holmes were not heeded, since the parallel between hospital gangrene and childbed fever is so obvious that cleanliness should have become a watchword.

Lister, after moving to Glasgow, grew interested in a new way of operating on tuberculous changes in the wrist. He had good results as long as the wound was kept free from infection, but six out of sixteen patients got gangrene, and one got blood-poisoning. Thus he turned to the problem of gangrene. Experimenting with frogs, he found that it must be connected with the process of rotting: both involved the "decomposition" of organic material.

Then a chemistry professor, Thomas Anderson, advised him to read a paper in a French journal, by Pasteur—who had won the Royal Society's Rumford Medal. This traditionally long-winded essay showed that rotting and fermentation could occur even without any oxygen, as long as micro-organisms were present. Lister responded with an ingeniously simple experiment. He poured fresh urine into four glass tubes, heated them to drive out air, and sealed three of them. Next morning, the urine was still clear and odourless in the sealed tubes. But it was rotting in the open one, evidently because micro-organisms got in, proving Pasteur right.

If such micro-organisms also caused gangrene, the question was how to kill them. Pasteur had pointed out three ways: to filter them out, heat them up, or expose them to chemical solutions. The first two methods were impossible for living tissues. But Lister had read that the city of Carlisle got rid of a stink in its sewers by pouring carbolic acid down the drains. He borrowed some carbolic acid from Anderson, although in the form of creosote, a smelly tar-like liquid. This was what Lister used to launch the world's first real antiseptic treatment.

At the end of an operation, he cleaned the wound well by hand, removing all tissue remains and blood. The area was then swabbed with creosote, and covered with a linen cloth soaked in it. Tinfoil was laid on to hinder evaporation, and the whole thing was taped. Unfortunately, the raw creosote irritated the skin, and sometimes the bandage caused worse complications than infection. Obviously creosote had to be replaced, but it did decrease the occurrence of gangrene, so Lister knew that he was on the right track. When Anderson gave him purer carbolic acid, side-effects became fewer, and the gangrene almost completely disappeared.

Lister's first report on the treatment was published in *The Lancet* in 1867, which is regarded as the date of birth of antisepsis. He gave clearer statistics a few years later: the death rate after amputations had sunk from 46 % (16 out of 35 cases) to 15 % (6 out of 40 cases). The former rate was comparable to that of other hospitals which did not use antisepsis: 43 % in Edinburgh, and 59 % in Paris. Lister also developed his

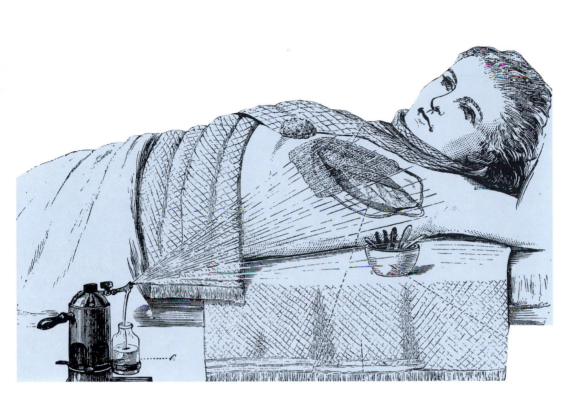

THE proper use of Lister's carbolic spray during operations was extensively illustrated by W. W. Cheyne in a book on "antiseptic surgery" (1882).

technique: surgeons were to wear clean gloves, and wash several times—both before and during operations—with 5% carbolic acid solution. Instruments were washed in the same solution, and assistants sprayed it in the operating theatres.

Many of Lister's colleagues laughed at him, and Hughes Bennett, a professor of medicine in Edinburgh, asked scornfully: "Where are these little beasts? Show them to us, and we shall believe in them. Has anyone seen them yet?" But Lister never bothered to reply, and it is said that he only heaved an occasional sigh at the world's stupidity. Instead, his bacteriological studies led him to the brink of modern antibiotics. In 1877, he found a way to culture a milk-fermenting bacillus, and his microscope revealed a mould which he sketched. This was undoubtedly the same mould that later gave rise to the discovery of penicillin. Another of his achievements was to abandon the technique of long suture-ends and introduce chrome catgut.

Lister left Glasgow in 1869 to succeed Syme at Edinburgh. The articles in *The Lancet* spread his fame round the world, and audiences of 400 or more often came from near and far to hear him lecture in the old auditorium of the Royal Infirmary. Then he moved to King's College in London. Very active, he became the second doctor in England to operate on a brain tumour, developed a new method of repairing kneecaps with metal wire, and improved the technique of mastectomy (breast removal). His discoveries were increasingly praised and brought him much honour—he became Baron Lister of Lyme Regis, and an original member of the Order of Merit.

He retired from practice after his wife Agnes, who had long helped him in research, died in 1893 during one of the first vacations they had ever allowed themselves. Studying and writing lost appeal for him, and he sank into religious melancholy. Yet despite suffering a stroke, he sometimes returned to public life. Edward VII came down with appendicitis two days before being crowned. The doctors did not dare operate before consulting the country's leading surgical authority. What the king told Lister a few days afterward was certainly correct: "I know that if it had not been for you and your work, I wouldn't be sitting here today."

Antiseptics abroad

Lister's first report on carbolic-acid bandages was corroborated in the same year in Germany by Carl Thiersch (1822–95), a pioneer of transplant surgery. The next year, this method was adopted at the prominent hospital of Breslau. And in Copenhagen, it was introduced at the Rigshospital by Matthias Saxtorph (1822–1900), a member of an old Danish medical dynasty, as soon as he had made a visit to Glasgow. A year later, his results inspired a famous letter to Lister, whom he hailed as a benefactor of mankind.

The principle of antisepsis came too late for the Franco-Prussian War of 1870–71. The French amputated some 13,200 extremities, causing 10,000 deaths from surgical fever and gangrene. This almost incredible mortality rate of 76% even included the removal of fingers! However, war has often been a powerful stimulus to progress in medicine. Presumably because of those terrifying figures, surgeons in both France and Germany sent their assistants, immediately after the war, to learn Lister's way of preventing hospital gangrene.

One such surgeon was Johann Nepomuk Ritter von Nussbaum (1829–90), an irascible doctor from Munich. During the early 1870s, the mortality rate at his clinic had risen from 26% to 80% after operations or traumatic injuries. But it dropped like a stone when his assistant Lindpainter returned with the new method. These men became the first to prove statistically the value of antisepsis. Nussbaum exclaimed: "Behold now my wards, which so recently were ravaged by death. I can only say that I, and my assistants and nurses, are overwhelmed with joy and gladly submit to all the trouble this treatment involves."

Another renowned German surgeon, Richard von Volkmann (1830–89) in Halle, had so much gangrene at his hospital—as well as erysipelas, an acute skin inflammation—that he was ready to shut it down until he tried Lister's method. Instantly things improved: he treated 75 open fractures without a single death, and only four out of 139 amputees died, results to be proud of even today. Equally good news appeared elsewhere, and Lister was glorified at the great congress of surgeons in Berlin in 1875. This led to an invitation and, later that year, he made a tour of triumph to Berlin, Munich and Leipzig, also becoming the first honorary member who was admitted to the German surgical association.

The carbolic–acid technique, called "Listerism" as often as "antisepsis", had further champions whom we shall meet—Billroth in Vienna, and Bassini (famous for describing a method of hernia repair which is still used) in Italy. But it was delayed in the United States and Canada, although Marion Sims and William Halsted understood its value quickly. Halsted encountered so much opposition that he had to operate in a tent in the garden of Bellevue Hospital in New York, as his colleagues hated the fumes of carbolic acid. Listerism was also modified by using disinfectants such as iodine instead of carbolic acid.

Among the first to accept Listerism was Ernst von Bergmann (1836–1907). In the Franco-Prussian War, he had experimented with what he called "aseptic" bandages, but he gave them up for carbolic acid. Since this irritated the skin even in pure form, he replaced it with a solution of bichloride of mercury, on the advice of Robert Koch. Then he abandoned this in favour of carefully cleaning the operating theatre, surgeon and patient—as well as sterilizing the instruments in steam. The latter procedure was probably first tried by Lister himself, yet rejected for fear that the "human factor" would find it too complicated!

Thus antisepsis, or defence against bacteria, gave way to asepsis—the complete elimination of bacteria—which is the method we follow. Ironically, the opponents of antisepsis had become its firm advocates, and now opposed asepsis. Lucas-Championnière, Lister's first supporter in France, denounced Bergmann's disciples as a "bandwagon of infidels", citing Lister: "It is safer to use an antiseptic..." Likewise, Americans continue to worship the great man's name in that of a mouthwash, Listerine.

The surgeon's gloves

Surgical gloves were first mentioned in 1758, when a German obstetrician described a hand-cover for his operations. A colleague took up the idea in 1827, emphasizing that gloves were for protecting the surgeon against infection. Josef Jakob Plenck, an expert on dermatology and venereal disease, warned midwives not to insert bare hands in a vagina with sores. Nothing was said about the type of cover: it could have been a horse-bladder or a plain leather glove, both of which have been used by doctors.

Rubber gloves probably made their debut in the 1840s. In 1847, *The Lancet* published a note by Thomas Cattell about a Mr. Potter, who had cut himself while dissecting and died from the infection. Measures for disinfection were advised, along with "the necessity of the use of gloves of vulcanized caoutchouc, or India rubber, which should be kept on finger or hand blocks when not in use…" Next year, the same journal reported a lecture by William Acton to the Royal Medical and Chirurgical Society, on the advantages of caoutchouc and guttapercha (Malayan tree-gum) in protecting the skin from infection—but only in connection with dissections and autopsies, not with surgery.

Surgeons themselves were not yet very concerned. When Listerism arose, they snorted that antiseptics took care of dirt in the wound, and that gloves were needless in the operating theatre. They were right in a way, since (to paraphrase the modern singer Bob Dylan) their clothes were dirty even if their hands were clean! They still usually ran straight from the street to the patient, at most covering their morning-coats with an apron. As Sir Berkeley Moynihan said, when he recalled his education at Leeds in 1888:

"The surgeon arrived and threw off his jacket to avoid getting blood or pus on it. He rolled up his shirt-sleeves and, in the corridor to the operating theatre, took an ancient frock from a cupboard; it bore signs of a chequered past, and was utterly stiff with old blood. One of these coats was worn with special pride, indeed joy, as it had belonged to a retired member of the staff. The cuffs were rolled up to only just above the wrists, and the hands were washed in a sink. Once clean (by conventional standards), they were rinsed in carbolic acid solution."

From Lister to His Father

On 27 May 1866, Lister wrote in a letter: "One of my cases at the hospital would, I think, interest Thee. It was a compound leg fracture with a rather large wound, and with great loss of skin and bleeding in the tissues, which caused much swelling. Though I hardly expected any success, I tried carbolic acid on the wound, to prevent blood decomposition and thus avoid the awful result of pus formation in the leg. Well, it is now eight days since the accident, and the patient has reacted just as if there had been no open wound—as though the fracture had been a simple one. Appetite, sleep, etc. have been good and the leg has gradually decreased in girth without any sign of pus formation. A truly dangerous injury seems to have been robbed of its most perilous element."

Lister on Animals (1897)

There are people who have nothing against eating a lamb cutlet, people who do not even stop at shooting a pheasant despite the great risk of its being only injured and having to die in severe pain—people who still maintain that it is monstrous to inject a few microbes under the skin of a guinea-pig in order to study their effects. These seem to me singularly inconsistent points of view."

It is generally said that gloves for operations were introduced by William Halsted, whom we have already mentioned, at the Johns Hopkins Hospital in Baltimore. He was not exactly the first. In 1878 the *North Carolina Medical Journal* described an ovariotomy by a Doctor Thomas, whose assistants used rubber gloves to protect their hands. But Halsted deserves the honour of popularizing operation gloves, which spread from his clinic around the world.

Halsted's interest in gloves was accidental. His theatre sister had become incapacitated by eczema on her hands, due to the mercury-bichloride solution used to sterilize instruments. Since she was not only a good nurse but also happened to be Halsted's fiancée, he took her complaint seriously and urged her to try rubber gloves. They worked perfectly, and were soon adopted by him and his staff. As the latter remarked, "Venus had come to Aesculapius' aid".

The old hand-washing method, hardly more than a dip of the hands in water and mercury bichloride or carbolic acid, was finally buried by a meeting at Leipzig in 1897. Dr. Bernhard Krönig gave a lecture entitled "Experiments on disinfecting the hands with spirits". He had spread gas-gangrene spores on his surgical colleagues' arms, and applied various disinfectants. Then he took some skin-scrapings and injected them into animals, which died of the same infection. This was not a reliable experiment, as spores are good survivors (and rare in most surroundings today). Yet it made a deep impression, and Krönig was thanked for dealing the audience a "bitter disappointment".

That year, the Polish surgeon Johannes von Mikulicz-Radecki (1850–1905) added to his many achievements, such as being probably the first to use a face-mask during an operation. In an article on the aseptic treatment of wounds, he compared disinfection with alcohol and mercury bichloride—long known as the Fürbringer method—with the wearing of gloves. Not one case of infection in three months had occurred with gloves. However, instead of a material as solid as rubber, he used cheap cotton gloves "of the best quality for servants". They were sterilized with steam and used a dozen times each, being changed during an operation only if they became inconveniently filthy!

A Patent on Rubber Gloves

On 17 April 1878, Thomas Forster of the India Rubber Works in Streatham, Surrey, received British Patent No. 1532 for "improvements in the manufacture of gloves or covers for the hands, to be used for surgical or other operations in which it is essential to protect the hands but still to retain delicate sensitivity."

Nussbaum's Eccentricity

A sketch of Johann Nepomuk Ritter von Nussbaum was given by the Swedish surgeon John Berg in a travel diary of 1879-80, according to the historian Wolfram Kock:

"Nussbaum's whole personality is eccentric. He is so deaf that only a screaming voice can stir him. He is so lame that he needs both a cane and an assistant to make his rounds. And he is quite addicted to morphine. His movements are very lively, his speech reveals an inner fire, but the face is a frozen mask and the eyes, shiny with tiny pupils, bear witness to the drug. He makes no secret of it… He is a bigoted Catholic, great nationalist, kind to the poor, and folksy in manner. To be a busy clinician, an adroit operator, and a warm admirer of Lister, at the same time as he suffers all those oddities, shows a wondrous combination of energy and weakness… When operating, he follows the French custom of dressing in tails (though without decorations)."

Billroth and the Vienna schools

A prouder tradition characterized the General Hospital in Vienna. Its seeds had been sown in this capital city of the Hapsburg dynasty on the Danube by one Heinrich Jasomirgott, who built a pilgrim-hostel in 1158 with a sick-house for both citizens and travellers. By the eighteenth century, several local hospitals existed. Two of the biggest—the Holy Trinity, and the Imperial Royal Spanish Military National—were then merged into one with seventy beds. This soon proved insufficient and, through the personal interest of Kaiser Joseph II, the larger General Hospital was inaugurated in 1784.

Its planner, Dr. Joseph Quarin, was succeeded by an equally brilliant administrator, named Johann Peter Frank (1745–1821). Already famous, he had been a leading opponent of "exhaustive treatment", campaigned for proper nutrition of patients, and done good work in education such as establishing a school for nurses. Under him, the General Hospital became a pace-setter in Europe. Around 1800, the "first Vienna school" included pioneers like Valentin von Hildebrand, an internist; Josef Beer, one of the world's first eye specialists; and the surgeon Vinzenz Ritter von Kern.

Kern laid the foundation for Vienna's renowned surgery. An excellent surgeon, he did over 300 lithotomies with only a few deaths, among the best records of the time. His gift to posterity was the *Operateur-Institut*, opened in 1807 and still active today, though modified. There young doctors were educated for two years in surgical theory and practice. Only when they demonstrated a complete mastery of operations could they leave with a highly valued diploma. This institute delivered, in Kern's day alone, 26 professors and 9 chief surgeons to large clinics outside the university.

The "second Vienna school" became even more famous than the first. Its dominant personality was the pathologist Rokitansky (see Chapter 7). Alongside him, Joseph Skoda (1805–81) compared clinical finds with pathological and anatomical ones, and refined the

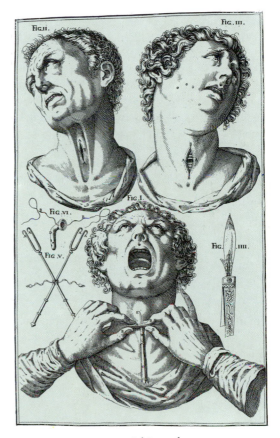

EUROPEAN progress in specialties such as laryngology was built upon studies of the organs involved, often including experiments on animals. This example of a tracheotomy was shown in a book on speech and hearing (1601) by Giulio Casserio, an Italian comparative anatomist and surgeon, who studied under Aquapendente and taught Harvey.

physical methods of diagnostics, though leaving his assistants to carry out treatment. Franz Schuh (1804–65) introduced auscultation and percussion to surgery. Ferdinand Ritter von Hebra (1816–80) broke fresh ground in dermatology, classified skin diseases, and began systematic local therapy.

Other luminaries in the faculty included the chemists Florian Heller—who discovered the albumin reaction—and Ernst Ludwig. A characteristic of the General Hospital was its willingness to develop "daughter sciences": modern medical specialization might almost be said to have started there. For example, it had the world's first clinic for laryngology, founded by Johann Nepomuk Czernak when he obtained a laryngoscope. This instrument was perfected by his successor Ludwig Türck, a neurologist. Next came Leopold Schrötter Ritter von Kristel-li (1837–1908), the first to remove larynx polyps. This interest in diseases of the upper respiratory tract led into otology, and Vienna got the world's first ear clinic in 1873.

It was thus onto a scene of medical science and clinical expertise that Theodor Billroth (1829–94) stepped in 1867, when he succeeded Schuh as chief of the surgical clinic. He was to create one of the finest schools in the history of surgery, and his legacy is still with us. Born in Rügen on the Baltic coast, he liked music more than books. His father, a clergyman, died when he was five, and his mother persuaded him to study medicine. But he kept music as a hobby all his life, wrote reviews and became a good friend of Vienna's musicians, such as Johannes

Opera's Gift to Medicine

The laryngoscope, which revealed the inside of the "voice box" and vocal cords in a living person, was invented by the Spanish singer and teacher Manuel Garcia (1805-1906), who recalled:

"I had often thought of using a mirror to observe the larynx from within while singing, but I had always considered it impossible. In September 1854, on a visit to Paris, I decided to see whether it could be done. I went to the famous instrument-maker Charrière, and asked if he had a thin mirror with a long shaft that could be used to inspect the throat. He had a small tooth-mirror, sent to the London exhibition in 1851, which nobody wanted. I bought it and took it to my sister's, with another little pocket-mirror, impatient to begin my experiment. I warmed the mirror in hot water, dried it carefully, and placed it against the tongue. When I cast in light with the pocket-mirror against it, I saw the larynx wide open before me!"

Charrière's own name was immortalized on the measuring scale of catheters and urethral probes.

MANUEL Garcia

Brahms. The city's reputation in music attracted him as much as its hospital, and at an early stage he set himself the goal of a professorship there.

Educated in Göttingen and Berlin, he chose the latter to start a private practice after graduating. It was a fiasco: not a single patient came in two months! He was saved by stumbling on a job as assistant to the greatest German surgeon of the day, Bernhard von Langenbeck (1810–87) at the Charité Hospital, long known as the founder of *Archiv für Klinische Chirurgie* ("Langenbeck's Archive"). This enabled him to begin scientific research, using a microscope like Lister. He raced through the clinic's large collection of operated tumours and, classifying them, wrote a dissertation.

Billroth was made an associate professor of surgery and histology in 1856. Four years later, his scientific and clinical skills were renowned throughout German-speaking lands, and he became a professor in Zürich. Interested mainly in infection and healing of wounds, he was the first to use regular temperature measurement for post-operative control, and to show that a rise in temperature is often the initial sign of complications. Such measurement was a novelty, introduced in Leipzig by Carl August Wunderlich, who published *The Relation of Body Heat to Illness* in 1868.

When Schuh retired in Vienna, the next professor was obvious to both the faculty and Billroth. He made advances in anaesthesiology, and gathered a circle of assistants who regarded him as a father. The students worked independently in the laboratory, and collaborated with teachers to apply new results in the operation room. Billroth performed the first total larynx removal for cancer, using experimental work by Vinzenz von Czerny (1842–1916) who later became professor at Heidelberg. Most importantly, Billroth's boldness and technique made him the great pioneer in abdominal surgery (see Chapter 9). He was the first to do well with gastric resections, to remove the whole oesophagus, and to create detours around acute or chronic intestinal obstructions by providing "anastomoses" between parts of the digestive tract. Resection of the stomach and intestines was to be developed further by his successor, Carl Gussenbauer (1842–1903).

Billroth was restless at the beginning of his long career in Vienna. New methods and untrained personnel cost the lives of many patients. But he stuck to the task of refining his initiatives, and the mortality rate decreased with better post-operative care. When publishing such work, he and his colleagues set a high standard: no failures were hushed up, and

From Patient to Assistant

The flexibility of medical education in Vienna can be judged from this tale in John Berg's Autobiographical Notes:

"In Schrötter's courses for the past ten years, the demonstrations had been carried out on an old woman from the poorhouse. She had thus learned every detail of the larynx's anatomy and pathology, besides how to use the laryngoscope. For years she had served the students with her throat, advice, information, instruments and charts. I heard this by chance, and now take a private lesson every afternoon from the same crone."

The Conservative Approach

Carl Gussenbauer, coming after Billroth in Vienna, once asked a colleague in private practice why he did not open a patient's abscess. "I prefer the conservative approach," was the reply. "Ah," said Gussenbauer, "but you're supposed to be conserving patients, not abscesses!"

THEODOR Billroth

Billroth on Doctors

A person may have learned a good deal and still be a bad doctor who earns no trust from patients. The way to deal with patients is to win their confidence, listen to them— patients are more eager to talk than to listen—and help them, console them, get them to understand serious matters: none of this can be read in books. A student can learn it only through intimate contact with his teacher, whom he will unconsciously imitate… The patient longs for the doctor's visit; his thoughts and feelings circle around that event. The doctor may do whatever is necessary with speed and precision—but he should never give the impression of being in a hurry, or of having other things on his mind…

scientific discussion was pervaded with sympathy for the patient.

In general, Billroth had a fascinating personality. All writings about him are complimentary. John Berg, the Swedish surgeon, was equally impressed by a visit to the clinic in 1879:

"His entire attitude, like his speech, bore witness to a scientific genius and to one of Europe's admittedly best and most trusted surgeons… While it may be said that he was aware of his superior gift, I saw no sign of haughtiness, and often admired his tolerance towards the younger trainees…"

Powder-blasted stumps

A more gradual, but no less palpable, step towards humane treatment in the nineteenth century was taken by surgeons who did amputations: they learned to save more of the patient than his life. This must be seen against the grim historical background of such operations, which we have mentioned already. Amputation has been practised since time immemorial. Our forefathers knew from bitter experience that it was the only way to save a life in certain circumstances. Saws made of flint and bone have been found which, at least, made it a fairly quick operation. Researchers have found that a limb could be removed in seven minutes with Stone Age instruments.

Already in Susruta's day, Indian techniques of amputation were well-tried. His writings gave exact instructions for it, and his equipment included bone tongs of elegant, sensible design. Celsus, too, provided a detailed description and showed that, even in the first century AD, the Romans saw the value of skin-covering:

"Thus one cuts with the knife down to the bone, in the soft area between the sound and the sick parts, being mindful that no joint is cut, and that it is better to cut away some of the sound part than to leave anything of the

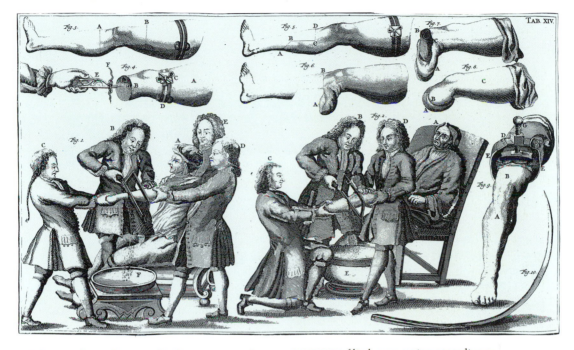

METHODS of limb amputation according to
Lorenz Heister in his *Institutiones Chirurgicae*
(1739).

sick part. Once down to the bone, one pushes
back the healthy tissues and cuts around to
expose the bone on all sides. Then the bone is
cut with a little saw as close as possible to
the soft parts. The roughened bone end is
smoothed, and the skin-cover is pulled forth:
it should be ample in such operations, so that
it can cover the bone on all sides."

The fear of hitting a joint was to last for
centuries, but otherwise Celsus' account is
worth following today.

Later advances in amputation technique were
slow to come (see Chapters 4–6). After the
great Paré's breakthrough in 1536, a long time
elapsed until surgeons dared to defy authority
and stop cauterizing the stump. Even in the
eighteenth century, the British Navy had a practice of exploding a charge of gunpowder on the
stump! The first known thigh-bone amputation
was done by Fabricius Hildanus, and the first
hip-joint amputation by Dominique-Jean Larrey
in 1803. Much of the latter's fame depended on
his skill in amputating, and he is said to have

done as many as 200 amputations after
Napoleon's battle at Borodino in 1812. The
Russian campaign also taught him to diminish
the pain by packing the stump in ice and snow.

As for amputating through a joint, doctors
knew that joints were especially prone to infection, even if they did not call it that. One surgical saying is that "you can spit in a lung, or vomit
into a stomach, but you can't so much as breathe
on a joint!" Until the mid-seventeenth century,
most leg amputations were therefore done in the
middle of the thigh or shin. It was John Woodall
who realized that the patient's mobility could be
improved by saving more of the leg. When he
went against all authority by daring to amputate
feet through the ankle, his results were no worse,
though bad enough: "not more than four out of
twenty lived till they had healed."

(ABOVE) A portable kit of typical nineteenth-century amputation tools, including a screw tourniquet.

(*Opposite*) One of the "screw tourniquets" which were introduced by Jean-Louis Petit in the early eighteenth century, to minimize bleeding after amputation. Allowing steady and adjustable compression, they were among the most important developments in surgery before anaesthesia.

Radical progress was made by those ingenious Scots, Robert Liston and James Syme, both educated in Edinburgh before 1820. At first good friends, they became bitter enemies for some reason, and turned their brilliant surgical practices into a competition, which actually benefited their patients. Liston, with his legendary skill, seldom took more than three minutes to amputate at the thigh. This, of course, was also because anaesthetics were not in use—until he himself, as we have seen, introduced ether into England for an amputation.

Syme's methods have stood the test of time better. Unlike Liston, who amputated with the slightest excuse, Syme preached moderation. He tried to keep as much as possible of the limb without risking the patient's life, and refined the operation through the ankle, which is named after him. Such restraint gave rise to the comment: "He never wasted a word, a splash of ink or a drop of blood."

Today, amputations belong to the specialty of orthopaedics (see Chapter 10). Nearly all amputations are done on the lower limbs and, as a rule, on the lower leg to preserve the knee. They are usually due to arteriosclerosis in older patients and diabetics, whose poor circulation causes gangrene. Only about one such amputation in ten is required by accidents—mainly to young people—while amputations on the upper limbs are mostly for men injured at work. A few amputations are treatments for tumour diseases or chronic infections.

In general, modern prosthetic devices are made of light metal and plastic, enabling the

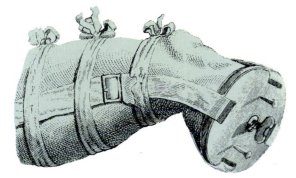

patient to move almost normally, and can have an artificial knee when fixed on the thigh. Arm prostheses are either "active" (with a hand-control) or "passive" (cosmetic), and are now becoming electrically controllable by muscles. Combined with rehabilitation, all of these are miracles compared to the wooden props which once were the only substitute for a lost arm or leg.

Arab Amputations

The old Arab doctors sometimes amputated to prevent gangrene, but disliked the operation—presumably because it could not be done solely with the cauterizing-iron, which they had learned to rely on in all situations, even for many internal illnesses!

Albucasis wrote of a patient with gangrene spreading up the leg from the foot. When the doctors refused to amputate, he calmly laid his foot on a chopping-block and cut off the foot with his sword. Soon he got gangrene in one hand, and turned to Albucasis, who also refused for fear that the man could not bear the operation. So again he drew his scimitar and performed it on himself.

This report invites speculation. Gangrene is usually caused by arteriosclerosis—but few Arabs then had that disease, it seldom produces gangrene in an arm, and the patient in question was fairly young. One suspects that the cause was ergot poisoning, by no means rare in those days.

Nelson's Arm

One of the most famous amputations in history was done on Lord Horatio Nelson, the night before 24 July 1797. He was hit just over the right elbow by a musket ball during an attack on Santa Cruz, Teneriffe. It bled profusely and his life was probably saved by his stepson, Lieutenant Josiah Nisbeth, who

had the presence of mind to constrict the artery above the wound. Confusion followed, as Nelson refused to be carried aboard the frigate Seahorse, since he did not want to make its captain—who had his bride on board—move out of the cabin. Two hours later, the great man was taken onto his flag-ship, the Theseus. A cadet wrote home:

"He helped himself over the rail and, with a calmness that surprised everyone, ordered the doctor to prepare the instruments, for he knew that he must lose the arm, and the sooner the better. He went through the amputation with the same decisive courage which has always distinguished him."

Exactly who did the operation is uncertain. Most facts point to the regular ship's doctor, Thomas Eshelby, but some sources credit a French doctor named Remonier, who was also on board. Indeed, Nelson's veins were tied with silk, which was a French habit—the English preferred waxed thread.

Nelson's stump eventually suffered infection, fistulas and pain, forcing him to give up his command and return to England. Experts—including William Cruikshank, perhaps the country's leading surgeon at that time—realized that the infection was due to the ligature thread. But they did not dare to pull it out and risk bleeding. Nearly four months later, it came out by itself, and the stump healed.

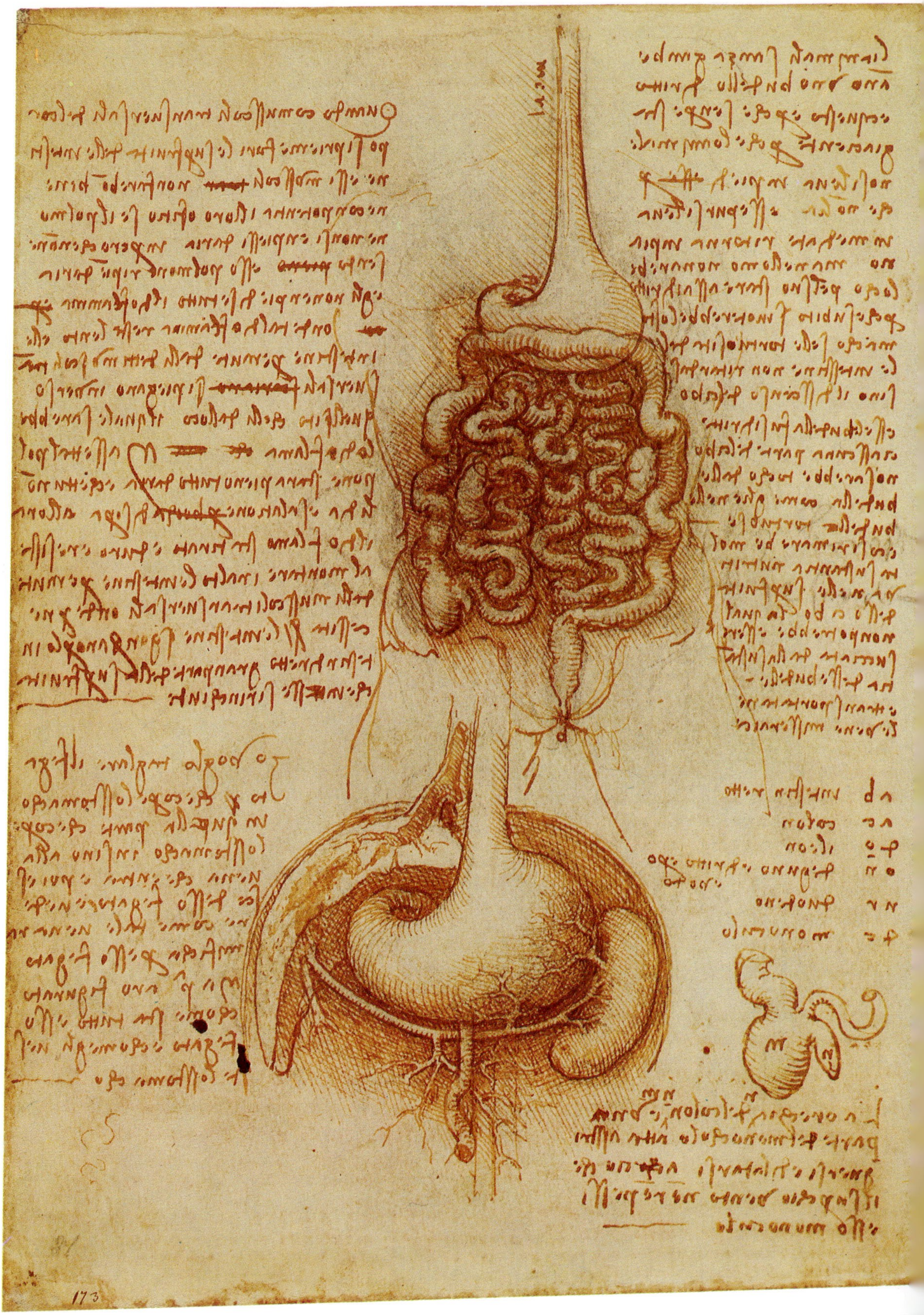

The triumph of complex operations

With the first decades of the twentieth century, we reach a period of explosive development in surgery. It was not greeted without scepticism about the limits of the art. As late as 1874, London's revered professor, Sir John Erichsen (1818-96), wrote that "the abdomen, chest and brain will forever be closed to operations by a wise and humane surgeon." Billroth himself declared that "an operation on the heart would be a prostitution of surgery."

Yet as we have seen, he and his disciples made the breakthrough in digestive-tract operations which replaced the old emphasis on hernias and inflammations, fractures and amputations. Treatment of further organs, including several important glands, was to be the next step in the profession's progress. Ever more numerous and serious ailments now became daily work for surgeons, leading to increasing specialization.

The gastrointestinal tract

Our internal food-processing system has many components whose diseases are handled with gastrointestinal surgery. They range from the oesophagus to the rectum, and include special organs like the pancreas, liver and biliary tract. Peptic ulcers, gallstones, cancer, bowel inflam-

DRAWINGS of the gastrointestinal tract by Leonardo da Vinci, including his theoretical notes and the first known picture of the appendix (*lower right*).

mations, haemorrhoids and hernias are among their commonest ailments. Often a sudden attack causes an "acute abdomen", as is illustrated by appendicitis and intestinal obstructions. The same kind of surgery deals with abdominal traumas, varying from multiple injuries to isolated wounds—frequently due to knives and gunshots—which must be diagnosed quickly for internal bleeding and perforation of organs. At present, however, we shall look at some of the more typical diseases with peculiar histories of abdominal surgery.

Acute appendicitis

People have suffered for centuries from inflammation of the worm-shaped appendage to the upper part of the large intestine. But the first record of what may have been appendicitis was made by Aretaios, around the third century AD. His patient had pus in the right side of the abdomen, which he successfully drained. The appendix was not named, for he knew little of anatomy. Not until 1521 was it described by an Italian anatomist, Berengario da Carpi. It also appeared in the anatomical drawings of Leonardo da Vinci from 1492, as well as in Vesalius' famous book of 1543. Lorenz Heister was familiar with it (see Chapter 6), and used its name *appendix vermicularis* in his *Compendium Anatomicum* (1715).

Another early case was published in 1554 by Jean Fernel, the court physician under Henry II of France (see Chapter 5). A seven-year-old girl had severe abdominal pains and signs of pus formation:

"When the body was opened, the appendix was found to be constricted. A quince fruit was stuck inside, filling it so that the intestinal contents could move neither up nor down… They had flowed over and taken an unusual detour into the abdominal cavity, just above the obstruction."

This sounds more like an acute ileus with perforation. But there is no doubt of the inflamed appendix described by Heister in his public autopsy of a criminal at Altdorf in 1711, already cited. His diagnosis was, to be sure, better than his remedy for the ailment: an enema with softening and dissolving herbs such as mallow and camomile.

Appendicitis in a living person was first diagnosed in 1734 by Wilhelm Ballonius, a doctor in Geneva. The need to treat it by operation, however, was recognized only in the 1880s. Of course, some surgeons have been ahead of their time. Shakespeare's *Coriolanus* (1607) made an odd reference to a "scar from an appendectomy"—although the poet's language has suggested that the word "appendix" here meant the colon's lobes of fat (epiploic appendices) which may have protruded from a hernial opening.

In 1736, the appendix was mentioned by Claudius Amyand, physician to Queen Anne and other rulers of England. He rightly insisted on surgery for a boy of eleven who had a hernia with a fistula passage from the rectum. Finding the appendix lying in the hernia cavity, he removed it: "an operation which was as painful for the patient as it was tiring for me". This took more than half an hour, testifying to the boy's courage!

Not much progress was made during the next century. In 1812, one of John Hunter's students, James Parkinson (1755–1824), correctly described inflammation of the appendix as a prelude to that of the whole abdomen (peritonitis), yet no operation was attempted. In 1836, just a hundred years after Amyand's article, James Burne emphasized that pain and tenderness in the lower right abdomen were typical signs of an inflamed appendix. But he prescribed only blood-letting, leeches and enemas, unless an abscess developed and the pus had to be drained out.

Nineteenth-century doctors variously termed this ailment (para-, peri-)typhlitis. The name "appendicitis" gained acceptance after a lecture by Reginald Heber Fitz (1843–1913) at the Boston Medical Society in June 1886. Having observed many cases and charted the nature, development and symptoms of the ailment, he concluded:

"One cannot ignore the enormous importance of early detection of an appendix which may burst. In most cases the diagnosis is easy. Strong symptoms call for immediate exploration of the appendix after stopping the shock, and for treatment of the inflammation according to surgical principles."

There has been debate as to who did the first appendectomy for acute appendicitis. The American surgeon Carl With (1826–98) was credited by Fitz, but whether he performed the operation before that lecture is uncertain. At least one pioneer, in 1885, was Ulrich Rudolf Krönlein (1847–1910), a student of Langenbeck in Berlin, who succeeded Billroth as professor in Zürich. On another occasion, he operated on a patient's abdomen, and rinsed it for over an hour to stop peritonitis, but could not find the appendix at all! Krönlein, like the great Mikulicz, was among the few European surgeons who soon adopted the operation to treat such "typhlitis". In Scandinavia, it was apparently initiated at Uppsala by Karl Gustaf Lennander, who left a detailed narrative of his first case in 1889.

Improvements came faster in America, due largely to Fitz' contributions, and next to those of Henry Sands and Willard Parker. The latter is said to have made the operation so popular that it became a fashion to have one's appendix extracted. In England, the first to perform a proper appendectomy was probably Robert Lawson Tait

THE first well-documented operation on the abdomen (laparotomy) was a gynaecological one in 1549, when Viennese surgeons saved a woman from a four-year extrauterine pregnancy—without anaesthesia! Her "strange tale" was reported the next year by Mathias Cornax, a professor of medicine, with this woodcut.

(1845–99) in 1880 (reported 1890). Technically adept, he used a method (double invagination of the stump) which has survived to our day. But the British were long conservative, preferring to wait until the inflammation died down before taking out the appendix. Some surgeons even hesitated to remove the whole appendix, one being Frederick Treves (1853-1923). Yet time made him more radical and, by the beginning of the twentieth century, he was one of Europe's leading experts on appendicitis.

Despite acceptance that appendicitis had to be treated by an early operation, mortality was high—about 20% until the 1940s—mainly from a burst appendix and diffuse peritonitis. But most such deaths occur in older people; a greater understanding of its pathophysiology and the replacement of fluids and electrolytes, together with antibiotic therapy which was developed in the 1940s and 1950s, have reduced the overall mortality to below 0.2%.

Gallstones

Observations of human gallstones go back to an Egyptian priestess at Thebes, around 1500 BC. Her mummy, when given to the Royal College of Surgeons Museum in London, was seen to contain a well–preserved gall bladder with thirty stones; unfortunately it was destroyed during the German bombing of World War II. The earliest known description of such stones was made by Alexander of Tralles, the Byzantine physician.

Much later, gallstones were reported in Italy from autopsies, following 1341 when Gentilis da Foligno began to do these at the University of

Padua. Vesalius wrote about gallstones, as did his successor Realdo Colombo in 1559. But the first account of their clinical symptoms came from Jean Fernel. His book *Universa Medicina* (1558) described the colourless excrement, the reddish urine—sometimes so thick that it was dark—and the spread of bile in the blood until the patient turned yellow. He guessed at a relationship to pus formation in the gall bladder:

> "Sometimes there is so much surplus bile that the bladder is stretched to enormous size. If disease sets in, there arise pressure, pain and difficulty of breathing; even vomiting, thirst, hotness and restlessness; after a while, pus formation and intermittent fever. Then the disease becomes serious."

The idea of trying to dissolve gallstones had naturally been thought of. Francis Glisson (1597–1677), an English anatomist, was interested in them, having himself been a victim. He only suggested that fresh grass contained something which dissolved gallstones, since he had seen them in the intestines of oxen after eating winter hay and straw, not after grazing. Likewise, one of Morgagni's students found that turpentine could dissolve some stones, though obviously it could not be given to patients.

In 1743, Jean-Louis Petit reported three cases where the gall bladder had been opened by mistake, while incising abscesses in the upper abdomen. One patient survived briefly, and the autopsies revealed that this was due to adhesions between the gall bladder and the abdominal wall. Petit thus recommended that gallstones should be removed by opening the bladder if such adhesions seemed to exist.

Contemporary knowledge of ailments in the gall system (biliary tract) was collected as early as 1708 by Michael Ettmüller. He mentioned a young student at Leyden, named Teckof, who had found that a dog did not turn yellow when its gall bladder was removed. Moreover, he showed that gallstones can be quite harmless and cause no jaundice. Yet the fact that jaundice occurs

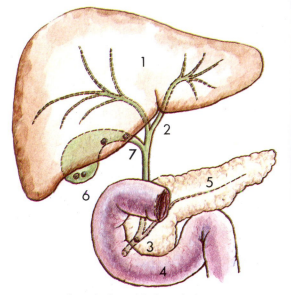

BILE coming from the liver (*1*) through the hepatic duct (*2*) may be obstructed by a stone in the common duct (*3*) before reaching the duodenum (*4*)—which also receives juice from the pancreas (*5*). Stones formed in the gall bladder which stores bile (*6*) may cause an inflammation in it, or produce a biliary colic by temporarily blocking its cystic duct (*7*).

only when a stone gets stuck in the common bile duct, blocking the flow of bile to the intestine, was to be realized only in 1877 by the great neurologist Charcot (see Chapter 8).

Diseases like inflammation of the gall bladder—cholecystitis—were very frequent in the early nineteenth century, calling for sound treatment. One proposal, based on that of Petit, was to sew the gall bladder to the abdominal wall, making it safe later to open the bladder and extract the stones—a cholecystotomy. This was championed by Robert Graves in Dublin (see Chapter 7), but Guilielmus Michael Richter proved the abdominal-wall adherence to be needless. The alternative, a free cholecystotomy, was first performed in 1867 by John S. Bobbs in America. Operating on a thirty-year-old woman for an ovarian cyst, he found instead that her gall bladder was swollen with stones.

Removal of the human gall bladder itself—a cholecystectomy—had indeed been suggested for treating gallstones, as long ago as 1767, by a Frenchman named Herlin who experimented on dogs and cats. The method became a reality in 1882, due to Carl Johan August Langenbuch (1846–1901) of Berlin. In 1884, J. Knowsley Thornton (1845–1904) conquered the old fear of damaging the common bile duct. Noticing two big stones inside it, he crushed them without even opening it, using a gentle rubber-jawed pincer which was normally meant for nose-polyps. His patient stayed yellow for eight days, but recovered when the stone fragments passed

Parkinson's Disease

Parkinson's short report on appendicitis was a mere footnote to that ailment's history, and to his own. He earned fame in medicine with an Essay on Shaking Palsy, describing the disease which now bears his name. The mask-like facial expression, a typical symptom, was all he really missed. A convinced political activist during the American Revolution, Parkinson drew suspicion from some of his patients, by writing a popular pamphlet entitled Revolution without Bloodshed— or Reformation Preferable to Revolt.

A Royal Appendix

Only two weeks before his coronation in 1901, Edward VII of England got stomach pains at Aldershot. His physician, Sir Alfred Fripp, was about to come by special train from London, when a telegram announced that the king felt better. During the next days, the king experienced shivers and nausea, but travelled to Windsor in a slow carriage—still the most comfortable of vehicles. On the fifth day his temperature went up, and the suspicion arose of something more serious than one of the fat, gluttonous monarch's usual belly-aches.

Sir Frederick Treves was summoned, found a tender swelling in the lower right abdomen, and diagnosed "perityphlitis". Having just begun his appendectomic career,

he chose to wait. Again the king improved, and even managed to reach London. The press, tired of rumours, turned to his private secretary and got the laconic reply: "Not a word of truth in reports. Knollys."

That evening a relapse set in, but the swelling was gone, so the wait continued. But three days later—the day before the scheduled coronation—a crisis was at hand. Lord Lister and another famous surgeon, Sir Thomas Smith, were brought in and advised an immediate operation. Edward flatly refused, saying that he could not disappoint his people and had to be at Westminster Abbey next day. Lister's answer was characteristic: "In that case, Your Majesty, it will be as a corpse..."

Obese, middle-aged, and not very healthy of heart, Edward was a poor risk for an operation. As soon as Dr. Frederick Hewitt started to anaesthetize him, his face turned blue-black. Realizing that his windpipe was blocked, Hewitt freed it with a sharp pull on the royal beard. Treves made a cut and, finding a large pus formation, drained it through two thick rubber tubes, then filled it with iodoform gas.

Few complications followed, and after two days the king was reported to be sitting up in bed, smoking cigars. He never again had abdominal trouble, and died eight years later of pneumonia. Sir Frederick Treves was richly rewarded, becoming a baronet with the British lion on his crest.

into the intestine. Two months after that, Thornton dared to open the duct of another patient and take out gallstones. This, the world's first choledocholithotomy, was done at about the same time in America by Robert Abbe.

Of these methods, cholecystotomy long remained the most popular, especially in England and America. But cholecystectomy soon won favour in Germany and Switzerland, due to Langenbuch and, after 1890, to Ludwig Courvoisier. It was introduced into America by Justus van Ohage (Minnesota, 1886), and into Sweden by Hugo von Unge (Norrköping, 1889). After 1910, it became standard in the United States, for example with William James Mayo (1861–1939), the second in the country's most famous family of surgeons.

As biliary surgery developed, a serious complication emerged: "cholemic bleeding" after operations on patients with jaundice owing to stones in the bile duct. In most cases, an operation was delayed, and was done reluctantly if the jaundice persisted. That the bleeding was due to deficiency of a blood protein (prothrombin), and could be stopped by giving Vitamin K, was proved in 1935 by Henrik Dam (1895–1976) of Denmark, earning him a Nobel Prize in 1943 jointly with another biochemist, Edward Doisy of America. Their discoveries were applied with success as early as the 1930s, making such operations so safe that jaundice became a reason for early surgery, rather than against it.

Until about 1930, just sixty years ago, only a quarter of all gallstone patients were operated on, namely those who showed absolute indications—acute cholecystitis, or duct stones and jaundice. Eventually, surgery was also recommended even for relative indications—attacks of pain. Biliary disease began to be considered a "surgical complaint", and operations rose in frequency. Yet during the past decade, they have decreased (in, for example, Sweden by 50% to some 12,500 per year), although not necessarily because we have fewer gallstones.

The mortality rate after cholecystectomy has sunk, due to the possibility of fighting bacterial complications with antibiotics, and bleeding with Vitamin K, as well as to improved anaesthesia and to effective pre- and post-operative care. In people whose only symptom is pain, the rate is extremely low. But older patients are still a risk group, especially when operating for acute cholecystitis and duct stones. Mortality is then 2–4%, mostly of those over age 60 with cardiac disease. This rate, however, is lowered by extracting duct stones through endoscopy (see Chapter 10) instead of opening the abdomen—a growing practice mainly for older patients.

A recent treatment is to dissolve cholesterol stones with "bile salts". Yet since they usually recur afterwards, this is not a good alternative to surgery. Gallstones are also beginning to be fragmented by the shock-wave method which, as we shall see, has come into use for kidney stones.

Gastroduodenal ulcers

The mucous membrane of the stomach, and the upper duodenum at the top of the small intestine, are well known to suffer "peptic" ulcers. Most common are chronic ones, which mainly result in pain but can be complicated by perforation and bleeding. Acute ulcers, accompanying stress and sometimes serious burn injuries, also tend to produce bleeding. It is not yet known what causes such ulcers, though an important chronic factor is the secretion of very acid gastric juice or as a German doctor, Karl Schwartz, said in 1910, "no acid, no ulcer!" The basic research in this field was done by an American and a Russian during the nineteenth century.

William Beaumont (1785-1853), a United States Army doctor, made his contribution by chance, which he exploited to the utmost. Despite the primitive conditions at frontier-forts, he spent eight years observing an extraordinary patient. This was a Canadian named Alexis St. Martin, who had been wounded at close range on 6 June 1822 by a shot in the stomach and left side. Beaumont barely saved his life, and he took nearly two years to recover. His abdominal wall was left with a hole through which a large area of

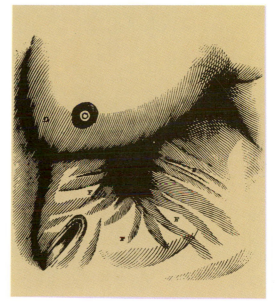

WILLIAM Beaumont (*above*), and his illustration in 1838 (*right*) of the stomach as seen through the hole in his patient's abdomen.

the stomach's mucous membrane could be seen. Giving him various kinds of food, Beaumont studied how the membrane reacted, and kept detailed notes.

Beaumont was so assiduous that the patient ran away. But destiny reunited them a couple of years later, and the studies continued. The outcome was an epoch-making book, *Experiments and Observations on the Gastric Juice and the Physiology of Digestion* (1833). Among other things, it established the juice's composition (including hydrochloric acid), the need for food in the stomach to start the juice's secretion, and the influence of the patient's state of mind. When the patient got angry, increased blood supply turned his mucous membrane bright red!

St. Martin returned to Canada and died a few years after Beaumont's book was published. His relatives, afraid that Beaumont would dissect his body, buried him privately. Not until 1960 did a grandchild reveal the grave's location, and a monument now stands over one of the most remarkable helpmates in the history of surgery.

Further work was done by the Russian physiologist Ivan Pavlov (1849–1936), famous as the father of behavioural psychology. He won the 1904 Nobel Prize in Medicine for discovering that the gastric juice is released by stimuli of sight, smell or taste, which are carried from the brain by the "vagus" nerves. Later it was found that another stimulus, a hormone named gastrin, is produced in the lower stomach. But if the vagus nerves are cut—a "vagotomy"—less hydrochloric acid is secreted, so that ulcers may heal. This was tried in the 1920s and, after research in the 1940s by Lester Dragstedt in America, "truncal" vagotomy was introduced for duodenal ulcers.

Surgery for chronic ulcers was initiated to cure constrictions in the lower stomach—due to scars from ulceration—by connecting the stomach with the small intestine (a gastroenterostomy). Such an operation for cancer was described in 1881 by one of Billroth's assistants, Anton Wölfler (1850–1917), and it was originally performed for full-fledged duodenal ulcers in 1892 by Eugene Doyen (1859–1916) in Paris.

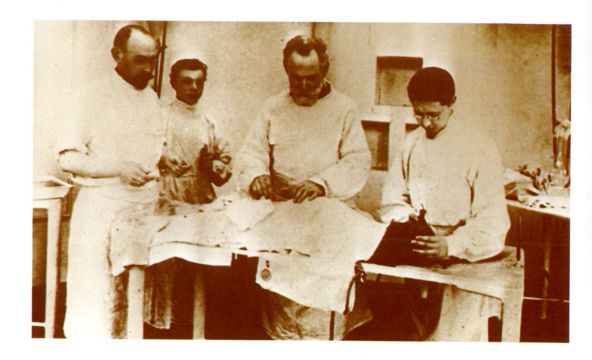

IVAN Pavlov (*centre*), who did important
research on gastric processes, experiments here
on a dog.

Once accepted, it was given up during the
1920s, as nearly a third of the patients got new
ulcers in the small intestine.

The alternative was to remove much of the
stomach with a partial gastrectomy (gastric
resection), reducing the area of cells that secrete
hydrochloric acid. Gastric resection—for cancer
—had begun with Péan in 1879, and again in
1880 with Ludwig Rydigier (1850–1920) in
Chelmno, Poland, but their patients did not
survive it. Theodor Billroth succeeded on 29
January 1881 in Vienna, taking an hour and a
half. His method, connecting the resected stomach with the duodenum, became known as
"Billroth I". Yet the tumour spread, and his
female patient, aged 43, died four months later.

As early as 21 November 1881, Rydigier became the first to do an operation like "Billroth I"
for gastric ulcers. "And hopefully the last," com-

mented a leading surgeon who edited his article
about it in 1882! Luckily, fate decreed otherwise. The patient, a woman of 30, had suffered
for three years with bleeding. She soon went
home cured and, after bearing five children, was
still healthy a quarter of a century later.

On 15 January 1885, Billroth eliminated
another cancer with "Billroth II": closing the
top of the duodenum and connecting the resected stomach with the jejunum. Billroth's
methods would prove to be the most popular
resections for stomach cancer—as well as for
ulcers in the stomach and duodenum. In 1897,
Carl Schlatter (1864–1934) of Zürich even introduced a total gastrectomy, or removal of the
stomach, for cancer. He connected the oesophagus to the upper small intestine, with good
results though the tumour spread, and the
patient lived just a year.

Partial gastric resections for ulcers do have
complications. The stomach may empty too
quickly, causing a "dumping syndrome", with
fatigue, sweating, palpitations and diarrhoea
after eating.

A Stony Saint

Realdo Colombo, the discoverer of lung circulation, had become the Pope's surgeon by the time he helped to dissect Ignatius of Loyola (1491-1556), founder of the Jesuit order. In the fifteenth volume of his great textbook on anatomy, dealing with "things which are seldom encountered", he told how he had plucked stones from the ureter, urinary bladder, large intestine, portal vein, and gall bladder of the man who was made a saint 66 years later.

Ignatius, whose own religious career had begun during surgery for a battle-wound, must have had a tendency to form urinary stones—perhaps due to a tumour in the parathyroid glands. The stone in the portal vein sounds peculiar, though also mentioned in Maffei's biography of Ignatius. Probably Colombo confused the portal vein with the common bile duct, next to it.

The First Cholecystectomy

Carl Langenbuch's achievement involved a 43-year-old man who had suffered from biliary colic for sixteen years, had lost much weight, and was a hopeless morphine addict. The operation occurred on 15 July 1882, after five days of preliminary enemas. Langenbuch removed the gall bladder easily, and found two cholesterol stones. Next day the patient had no fever or pain, and smoked a cigar. He got up on the twelfth day and went home six weeks later, having gained weight. Today, such a patient sits up in the evening after the operation, stands up the next day, and usually leaves the hospital on the fourth or fifth day.

On Perforated Ulcers

Much good advice for identifying acute abdominal ailments was given by an English doctor named Edwards Crisp. About 1842, he fully described a perforated stomach ulcer, concluding: "The symptoms are so typical, I hardly believe it possible that anyone can fail to make the correct diagnosis." But he was pessimistic concerning the treatment: "Once the perforation has occurred, the case must be considered hopeless... In surgery's present state, the idea of cutting open the abdomen and closing the opening would be too quixotic to mention..."

A Surgical Sovereign

Johann von Mikulicz-Radecki crowned his career as professor of surgery in Breslau. The historian Jürgen Thorwald has portrayed him as follows:

"He was a splendid surgeon, a fine teacher, and a friend to his patients, but I never saw a more absolute ruler over his clinic—a more ruthless master to his collaborators. As I later found, none of them were truly happy. What kept them in Breslau was the awareness that they could learn more from Mikulicz than from other German and Austrian surgeons. He was the very king of his realm.

"Mikulicz' domain stretched at that time from Breslau far into Russia. He might be called to Kharkov, St. Petersburg, or Moscow for an appendix or a gallstone. In Kharkov, the Russian governors covered the streets with hay, half a metre thick, to stop the noise of carriages passing the houses where he operated. The most elegant rooms in the best hotels were at his disposal... Mikulicz' private clinic, on Tauntzienstrasse in Breslau, attracted patients from many countries, while his palatial residence was the city's social centre. The team of roans which he raced through the streets was legion; more than once, the police charged him with dangerous driving..."

Similar symptoms may occur after vagotomy. For most patients, a "Billroth I" gastrectomy would be recommended for gastric ulcers, and a proximal gastric vagotomy for duodenal ulcers. This operation denervates only the stomach, not the other abdominal organs. But surgery is not needed if medical treatment succeeds.

Chronic ulcers have long been treated mainly with drugs that neutralize or decrease the secretion of hydrochloric acid. Those used today ("histamine-receptor antagonists") have made operations less frequent.

Real danger is presented by an acute perforated ulcer. Gastric juice running into

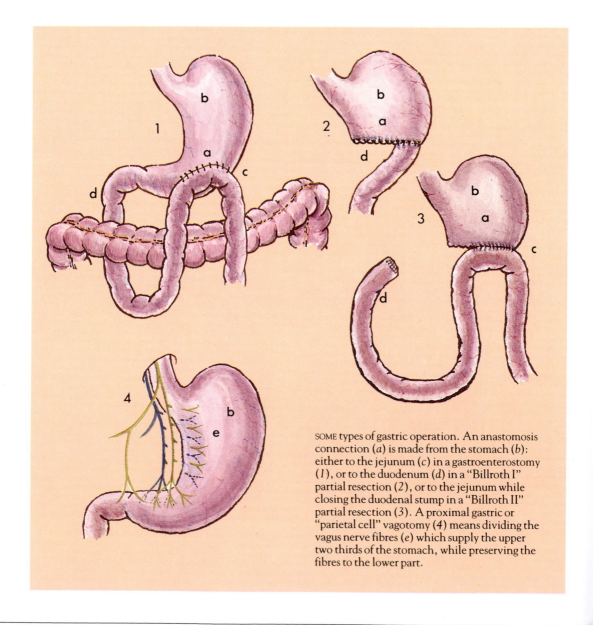

SOME types of gastric operation. An anastomosis connection (a) is made from the stomach (b): either to the jejunum (c) in a gastroenterostomy (1), or to the duodenum (d) in a "Billroth I" partial resection (2), or to the jejunum while closing the duodenal stump in a "Billroth II" partial resection (3). A proximal gastric or "parietal cell" vagotomy (4) means dividing the vagus nerve fibres (e) which supply the upper two thirds of the stomach, while preserving the fibres to the lower part.

the abdomen irritates its membrane, causing pain with some shock, and the hole must be sutured to prevent fatal peritonitis. Mikulicz-Radecki (see Chapter 8), a student of Billroth, wrote in 1884: "Every doctor, faced with a perforated ulcer of the stomach or intestine, must consider opening the abdomen, sewing up the hole, and averting a possible or actual inflammation by carefully cleansing the abdominal cavity."

Presumably due to this statement, the first such acute operation has been ascribed to Radecki, but wrongly. It was not done until 19 May 1892, and at a by no means famous clinic. In Barmen, now part of Wuppertal, a man aged 41, with a classic history of serious stomach ulcers—pain and nausea for twenty years, with four periods of bleeding—suddenly came down with peritonitis and shock. Ludwig Heusner, a private doctor, was summoned to his home late at night. Realizing that he could not be moved, Heusner accomplished the essential operation with difficulty in two and a half hours. A very similar one was performed the next month by Hastings Gilford in Reading, England.

At the end of the nineteenth century, unlike today, duodenal ulcers were relatively rare. Hence their perforation was unusual, and it took a long time before anyone saved a patient by operating. The first to do so was probably Henry Percy Dean, again in England, his results being published during 1894.

The breasts

Though cancer has nearly always been the reason for amputating breasts (mastectomy), a quite different motive led to the earliest record of this operation, in Babylonian times. Paragraph 194 of Hammurabi's code prescribed that, if a wet-nurse committed a crime, "they shall cut off her breasts"—a double punishment, since she thereby lost her job.

Breast ulcers and tumours were known in ancient Egypt, as shown by the papyri of Ebers and Smith. A successful operation on a "knot of fat" was also mentioned, and the treatment for a breast boil was as firm as it is today:

"If you find a swelling over the breast's surface, clearly defined and round in shape, it is a purulent tumour growing in the flesh. It must be dealt with by the knife."

According to Herodotus, the Greek historian, King Darius of Persia had a wife named Atossa who tried to hide a tumour in her breast. When she could no longer do so, the doctor Democedes was summoned, and cured her. His method is not reported, but he doubtless operated, as no other way existed.

The Amazons supposedly cut off their right breasts to facilitate shooting with bow and arrow. Warrior women from the Caucasus who invaded Asia Minor, they maintained their numbers by mating annually with the men from a neighbouring tribe, while killing boy babies. Nobody knows if the tale is true: it may be a memory of well-armed priestesses who served some goddess, like Artemis, in that region. But their breast operation was accepted by Gerolamo Cardano (1501–76), a great Italian physician and mathematician. He claimed that it was performed at age 18, the blood being stanched by cauterization with hot copper, which was thought better than iron for this purpose.

Breasts were long a symbol of fertility, and women who lost them were not only maimed but regarded as inferior. Such a view was exploited by medieval punishment, which often made one or both breasts the price for actual or suspected crimes. When the "crime" was being an early Christian, several of these martyrs became, not surprisingly, saints. Famous examples are Barbara, Christina, Foya, Apollonia—who turned into the patron saint of dentistry—and primarily Agatha, the protectress of all who suffered from breast diseases.

Operations for breast cancer were done at an early date by Aetius of Amida (see Chapter 2). He emphasized that the knife should cut around a tumour in healthy tissue, and that a cauterizing iron should stanch the blood. His method was followed in late medieval times, occasionally replacing cauterization with etching salves of arsenic and zinc chloride. Vesalius was apparently the first to control the bleeding from the large vessels by using ligatures.

It has long been known, too, that a less than radical operation for breast cancer may not only fail to cure the patient, but also hasten the disease's spread through the body. Despite the lack of good anaesthesia, reliable methods of completely removing a tumour were soon sought. Barthelemy Cabrol, a student of Paré, was the first to take away the large underlying muscle as well as the breast itself. A little later, in the early 1600s, Severino (see Chapter 5) did a radical mastectomy—also removing the lymph nodes in the armpit, which are usually the initial organs to which this cancer spreads.

Angelo Nannoni (1715–90), a Florentine doctor recently rescued from obscurity, published a book in 1746 about the surgical treatment of breast cancer, with ideas amazingly like our own. He recommended immediate operation to remove the tumour by a wide margin, along with the underlying fascia, large muscle and nearby lymph nodes:

> "I assume that many will consider this method dangerous… but I have often seen that the powerful breast muscle is not unlike the other muscles in our body, which indeed can be destroyed without any danger to life."

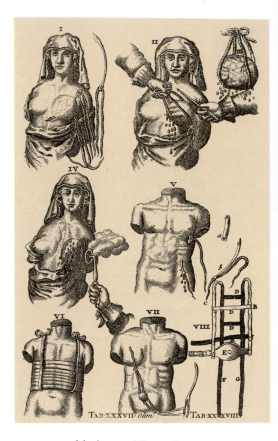

AMPUTATION of the breast, followed by cauterization, as illustrated by Scultetus in his *Armamentarium Chirurgicum* (1741).

But the greatest influence on future breast surgery was that of Jean-Louis Petit (see Chapter 6), first president of the profession's French Academy. While his great *Treatise on Surgical Ailments and Operations* advocated radical removal of the breast muscle and lymph nodes, he left the nipple area alone as a cosmetic measure.

A step backward was taken in the early nineteenth century, with a belief that superficial tumours would wither away if the arteries supplying them were just pressed on. This was refuted in 1818 by John Butter of Edinburgh, who noted that the treatment had cured nobody, that one of his own patients had died after it, and that a woman's health deteriorated during it. By contrast, the radical operation's value was scientifically established by Charles Hewitt Moore (1821–70) at Middlesex Hospital in London.

However, many deaths and complications still resulted. Theodor Billroth's fine clinic in Vienna, then regarded as the world centre of surgery, reported in 1879 that 34 out of 143 women had died from the operation—mostly of infection—and a mere 35 survived it for any length of time. When it was introduced by surgeons like William Halsted in America, the patients usually had advanced tumours which could be removed only by extensive operation.

The beginning of our century brought a wholly new technique for treating tumours: radiotherapy (see Chapter 10). Its use before and/or after a radical mastectomy was the classical treatment for many years, but now it is an individualized post-operative tool. A further development is hormone therapy, since tumour growth was found to be aggravated by the female sex hormone, oestrogen. George Beatson (1848–1933) pioneered it in Scotland from 1896 onward, although he knew nothing about the hormone's effects and simply removed the ovaries. This has been replaced by "medicinal castration", giving anti-oestrogen drugs which block the effects.

Today, examination for breast cancer is combined with X-ray mammography and microscopic study of tumours by puncture cytology or surgical biopsy (tissue removal). If the disease is limited to the breast and the axillary lymph nodes near by, it is considered to be curable—normally by removing them while leaving the muscle (a modified radical mastectomy). If it is suspected to spread farther (metastasis), hormone therapy and/or chemotherapy are used (adjuvant treatment). These, and irradiation, can also help in advanced cases.

Breast cancer makes up a quarter of all cancer in women, and occurs at relatively young ages. Its stage of growth and type of pathology are decisive for the outlook. The survival rate after five years is about 80 % when the cancer is confined to the breast, and 50 % when it involves axillary nodes. Its diagnosis ever earlier with mammography is improving the rates: regular X-rays can detect a very small tumour, requiring only its removal (by segmental resection) and radiotherapy on the rest of the breast. This conservative surgery is far less worrying to the patient. Moreover, post-operative reconstructions of the breast, including silicon prostheses, have become ever more common.

A seventeenth-century engraving of Saint Agatha after removal of her breasts, which an angel carries on a plate. She holds the tongs which were used for the amputation, and the inset picture shows similar tongs from Scultetus' contemporary book.

Saint Agatha's Martyrdom

Agatha was a beautiful girl from Catania in Sicily, during the third century AD when the Romans persecuted Christians. She rejected an amorous consul, who then condemned her to lose both breasts "because she was Christian". The deed was done with red-hot tongs, and she was cast into prison to die, but Saint Peter appeared and restored her breasts as well as her health. So the consul had her fried over a slow fire, and Heaven avenged her by killing his two best friends with an earthquake, which was enough to earn Agatha canonization. Catanians celebrate her memory every year, carrying a triumphant image of her breasts through the streets!

The renaissance of urology

Ailments in the urinary tract were handled by surgeons like Cheselden and Douglas (see Chapter 6) as well as could be done before the advent of narcosis and antisepsis. No technical advances in urology occurred for the next century and a half, but then the tide turned.

Calculus disease

Bladder stones (vesicular calculi) seem to have gone up and down in frequency over the years. One peak was reached around 1800. Surgeons could still cut out such painful pebbles, but they hesitated since the operation often led to infection and fistulas, besides causing quite a few deaths. A safer method was urgently needed: soon came the first attempts at "lithotripsy". A stone could be crushed through the urethra, leaving the fragments to pass out with the urine. An instrument for this purpose was invented in 1822 by Jean Zuléma Amussat (1796–1856). His tongs gripped the stone with two toothed jaws and chewed it up by lever action.

Rapid improvements were made, notably by other Frenchmen. Jean Civiale (1792–1867) had got interested in the problem as a student of Dupuytren. In 1824, at the Hôpital Necker in Paris, he did the first successful lithotripsy with his "trilabium", an elegant device that held a stone with three claws and drilled it to bits. Civiale became the leading urologist in Europe. As a pioneer in describing hypertrophy of the prostate gland, he buried the misconception that it was caused by sexual excess:

"Armchair philosophers have little talent for the pleasures of the flesh, yet it is often they who show prostatic hypertrophy—and so do very abstemious men of other social classes."

Civiale's fame as a practitioner and teacher spread throughout the Continent. In 1858 he was visited by Henry Thompson (1820–1904), already a renowned surgeon, who attended the operations and learned how to use the trilabium. Thompson brought urology back to England,

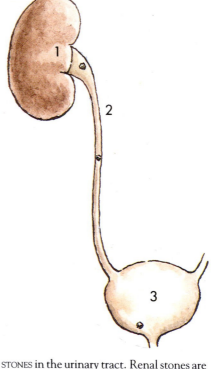

STONES in the urinary tract. Renal stones are formed in the pelvis of the kidney (1) and may cause abrupt pain when they pass down the ureter (2) to the bladder (3), where vesical stones may be formed as well. But about two-thirds of all stones pass out spontaneously with the urine.

and the two friends were to share the honour of curing bladder stones for Leopold I of Belgium. Civiale also had an inventive competitor, Baron Charles Heurteloup (1793–1864), who moved to London—perhaps for the higher fees—and, after obtaining the required permit, did the first English lithotripsy in 1829 on a sailor.

Leopold I was operated on seven times by Civiale. Five months later, he got another stone. His niece, Queen Victoria, enjoyed tampering with her relatives' illnesses, and sent Thompson to treat him in Brussels. Three lithotripsies were performed, and the king made a fast recovery—with no infection in the urinary tract, which had been thought an unavoidable

THE famous doctors at this Victorian dinner-party, painted by the English portraitist Solomon Solomon, included Victor Horsley, Henry Thompson (the host), Thomas Spencer Wells, and Thomas Lauder Brunton (*respectively third, fourth, seventh and tenth from left*).

effect of such operations. Thompson became a national hero in Belgium, receiving the huge fee of three thousand pounds from his patient, and a knighthood from his own queen in 1867, to be followed by a baronetcy in 1899.

Napoleon III, driven to England by the Franco-Prussian war, had previously shown symptoms of bladder stones. Now they grew unbearable: unable to lie down without feeling the pressure of trapped urine, he tied a mattress on his back and leaned against a wall to sleep. In July 1872, Thompson was summoned to him at Chislehurst Castle, and proposed to insert a bladder catheter. The emperor refused until Christmas, but conceded that an operation was

Sir Henry Thompson

One of the most colourful personalities in surgical history, Thompson was educated in London and became professor of surgery at University College and the Royal College of Surgeons. Besides his fine contributions to urology, including several methods of operation, he published scientific works in the field. But not only that: he painted well enough to exhibit at the Royal Academy, collected antique Chinese porcelain, studied astronomy, and was an early supporter of automobiles and of cremation! Also an avid gastronome, he earned a reputation by serving eight-course dinners for eight guests, once a month at his estate outside London.

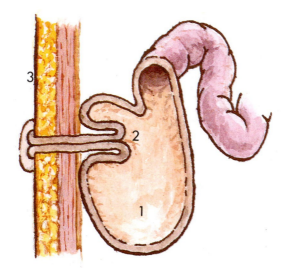

KOCK'S continent ileostomy. The lower end of the small intestine is formed into a reservoir (*1*) which is emptied about three times a day by inserting a catheter into its leakproof nipple valve (*2*) through the abdominal wall (*3*). Such an operation is done after removing the colon and rectum for chronic ulcerative colitis, or as a continent urostomy after implanting the ureters into the isolated intestinal segment. A more recent development is the pelvic reservoir, connected by "ileoanal anastomosis".

inevitable. In two sessions, stone fragments were removed with a lithotrite. Yet when the third was about to begin, he suddenly died of a heart attack. The autopsy revealed that his kidneys were virtually destroyed by the long infection which complicated the disease.

During the twentieth century, calculus disease in the urinary tract, including kidney (renal) stones, was apparently much more frequent, though varying between countries. It is estimated that about 10% of all men, and 4% of women, suffer such stones at some time, half of these undergoing recurrences. In the 1980s, two novel kinds of treatment came to light: percutaneous surgery (removal of stones by endoscopy) and ultrasonic lithotripsy (fragmenting stones with shock waves from outside the body). The older methods of "open surgery" will thus be replaced.

Urinary-tract tumours

Operations on the kidney were once rare, and limited to a "pyelotomy" of its pelvis to take out very painful stones. Thus, in 1700, the English consul at Venice underwent surgery for a kidney stone, and again the next day to stop bleeding—yet the kidney was kept. In fact, the kidney is a

paired organ: one of the two should be safely removable. But such a "nephrectomy" was not even recommended by the brave Theodor Billroth, except for cancer.

The first known nephrectomy was done in 1861, by E. B. Wolcott of Milwaukee, due to a large tumour in the kidney. His patient survived it, but died two weeks later, probably from a related infection or from blood poisoning. Successful results began in 1870 with a German surgeon, Gustav Simon (1824–76). The mortality rate was quite high initially—half the patients died before the era of antiseptics. Still, nephrectomy meant progress, since nearly all kidney tumours are malignant and would, sooner or later, prove fatal.

Tumours of the urinary tract may occur in the kidney, the ureters and, most often, the bladder. Usually shown by blood in the urine, they are now studied with kidney X-ray (urography), ultrasound and cystoscopy. The treatment for kidney cancer is nephrectomy, but that for a bladder tumour depends on its stage, and varies from transurethral resection to removing the bladder (total cystectomy), combined with "urinary deviation" in the latter case.

This deviation can be done through a conduit from the ileum of the small intestine. An ileum reservoir, with a "continent urostomy" operation, is advantageous for the patient and safe for the kidneys. It has been developed recently in Gothenburg, Sweden, from a "continent ileostomy" introduced by Nils Kock in 1964. His low-pressure reservoir pouch, made of the small intestine, is even more valuable as an improvement on the conventional ileostomy after intestinal surgery (proctocolectomy).

Prostate diseases

The male prostate gland, around the urethra where it leaves the bladder, commonly acquires tumours—especially benign adenomas—and the resultant hypertrophy can squeeze the urethra so that urination becomes difficult or impossible. These symptoms have long been known, and attributed to some anatomical obstacle. There are records of desperate patients and doctors trying to overcome the barrier through the urethra, generally causing not a cure but bleeding. The gland itself was described only in 1536, by Nicolo Massa (1499?–1569). Even he did not call it the prostate, which in ancient Greek meant "standing before (the bladder)".

The time-honoured method was to insert a tube into the bladder, unless the obstacle was total. Many such catheters were designed in various shapes and materials, from fish-skin or leather to the gold, silver, or "at least bronze" recommended by Andrea della Croce (d. 1575). His countryman Fabricius ab Aquapendente suggested horn, adding cleverly that it should be softened in hot water before use. More practical catheters were invented by two prominent surgeons, William Hey (1736–1819) and Auguste Nélaton (see Chapter 8).

A total blockage of urine, too, could lead the best of doctors to attempt a "forced" catheterization, pressing the tube right through the prostatic adenoma. Georges de la Faye (1698–1781) did this to his colleague Jean Astruc (1684–1766), but succeeded only by cutting through, with a lancet inside the catheter. He withdrew the lancet, leaving the tube in place for two weeks—and Astruc resumed urinating, with no trouble for his last ten years of life!

Other Frenchmen in our story added similar techniques. One came from the pathologist Cruveilhier, together with Dupuytren. Civiale, disliking its complications, preferred to punc-

ture the bladder just above the pubic bone joint. The latter approach was seemingly pioneered by Pierre Franco, who described a "suprapubic cystotomy". In 1832, Amussat regularized the operation, removing not only a bladder stone but also a section of prostate that stuck into the bladder. Five years later, Louis Auguste Mercier (1811–82) invented what has been called the greatest contribution yet to prostatic surgery—a "prostatotome" that could penetrate where the urethra enters the gland. This was done from the perineal wall between the thighs, familiar since the early days of stone-cutting.

Such methods, of course, relieved the disease rather than curing it. Doctors soon realized that the only long-term solution was to remove the part of the prostate which squeezed the urethra. Several surgeons tried to do so, whether by chance or intention, usually for the kind of benign tumour that grows like a fungus into the bladder and blocks the urethral opening. But the first to consciously operate on the prostate was A. F. McGill (1850–90) of Leeds. He went into

Famous Bladder-Stone Patients

Apart from Leopold I and Napoleon III, we have mentioned a number of lofty victims of this disease—including Judge Jeffreys, the saintly Ignatius of Loyola, and the clever Samuel Pepys. Others were the philosopher Francis Bacon, the physicist Isaac Newton, and the author Horace Walpole. Among statesmen, we find Peter the Great of Russia, Louis XIV of France, Oliver Cromwell and the fat George IV of England. Even Thomas Sydenham, the pioneer of internal medicine, had bladder stones. He wrote in his textbook, no doubt from experience and with deep compassion:

"The patient suffers until he is finally consumed by both age and illness, and the poor man is happy to die."

the bladder from above, criticizing the old approaches: "it is undesirable to restrict the opportunity of operating to gentlemen with unnaturally long fingers"! In 1889, he could report 37 prostatectomies with good results.

Further advances were made by William Belfield (1856–1929) in Chicago. He began with the perineal operation, changed to the suprapubic one and, in 1890, reported 80 cases with a mortality of 14%, which was considered excellent at the time. The rate declined rapidly in the following years. Hugh Hampton Young (1870–1945) did 209 operations with only 2.9% deaths, all among the initial 97.

An instrument had been built around 1807 by Philipp Bozzini, an obstetrician in Frankfurt, for seeing into the bladder and rectum with candlelight reflected by mirrors. It was demonstrated to the faculty in Vienna, yet they rejected it as a "magic lantern", and it was apparently never put into practice. However, in 1877 Max Nitze, a urologist in Berlin, produced the first usable cystoscope, with lenses and electric lighting. Originally meant for diagnosis, this was also employed by Young in forced catheterization. Surgeons quickly found it helpful and, after adding a cauterizer to control bleeding, they adopted it extensively in transurethral resections. These are the preferred approach to prostate operation nowadays.

Prostate cancer is the most frequent form of male cancer, and two thirds of men over age 80 have it, as shown by autopsies. It is often curable when limited, but may spread—usually to the pelvic bones—with small chances of survival. Diagnosis is now done by ultrasound and puncture cytology of the prostate, and by X-ray or skeletal scintigraphy for possible spreading. Only some localized cases receive radical prostatectomy. As a rule, treatment is palliative: about 90% of cases are related to hormones, and they can be helped with antiandrogen therapy, meaning castration or giving the female hormone oestrogen. This method won the Nobel Prize in 1966 for a Canadian-American surgeon, Charles Huggins (b. 1901).

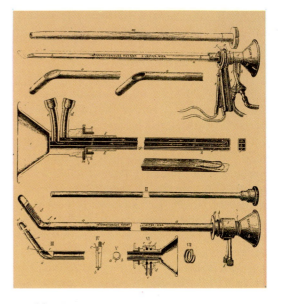

MAX Nitze's cystoscope, patented in Vienna, was published in 1879 as shown here. The thin tube is inserted into the patient's urethra, and an electric lamp at its tip (*bottom left*) illuminates the bladder. Reflections enter a window at the instrument's "knee", are bent by a glass prism, and travel along the tube through a lens system to the doctor's eye.

Endocrine surgery

Endocrinology deals with the functions and ailments of the glands that produce internal secretions, or "hormones" (from the ancient Greek for "excite"), which go directly into the blood, not out through a special duct. These glands often influence each other and control the body's activities. Their main importance for surgery is that the production can suddenly become excessive, because the gland is overactive or else has a tumour that also produces the hormone.

The thyroid and parathyroid glands

As we have seen, the foundations of endocrinology were laid by Bernard and Brown-Séquard in the mid-nineteenth century. The first endocrine organ to be studied was the thyroid gland. Pioneer work was done in Switzerland, as might be expected, since goitre (thyroid enlargement) was unusually frequent there—due to iodine deficiency, as it later emerged. The leaders were two surgeons, Jacques Reverdin (1842–1929) and Theodor Kocher (1841–1917).

Kocher was born and educated in Bern, where he became professor at age 31. His mother belonged to the Moravian sect and left him with a strong sense of religion and duty. Interested only in medicine, even while a student he let nothing distract him from learning and earning high honours. Friends knew his sense of humour as well, but it never entered the clinic or laboratory—only his patients and findings mattered. He died still busy, having gained worldwide respect as a surgeon and, among many other distinctions, the 1909 Nobel Prize.

Bern was the centre of the goitre district. The main problem was that people suffocated from pressure on the windpipe by huge goitres. How these arose, and thus how to avoid or treat them, was unknown when Kocher took over the clinic. One could only remove the thyroid gland, which is in an area full of essential nerves and blood vessels, although Kocher's skill reduced the operation mortality from 13% to under 0.5%. A series of 600 operations, published in 1898, included only one death—from an overdose of chloroform!

After two years of such total "strumectomies", Kocher heard from Reverdin in Geneva that they had tragic consequences. Some patients became sluggish, cold, fat, and even mentally deranged. According to a country doctor, one of Kocher's own cases had ended similarly. Terrified, he traced all the patients he could locate, and 16 out of 18 were suffering from the same swollen condition. He expressed his thoughts to a colleague as follows, in a narrative by the historian Jürgen Thorwald:

"In technical terms we have certainly learned to master the operation for goitre. We can deal with bleeding and prevent loss of speech. Billroth's tetany is so unusual that it has not made us change our methods. But something else has happened… Removal of the thyroid gland has deprived my patients of what gives them human value. I have doomed people with goitre, otherwise healthy, to a vegetative existence. Many of them I have turned to cretins, saved for a life not worth living…"

This mentions three serious complications of total strumectomy: the loss of blood during and after the operation; paralysis of the vocal cords if a nerve to the larynx is damaged; and cramps that arise if the parathyroid glands happen to be removed along with the thyroid. As for cretinism, it is also caused by an inborn thyroid defect, which the Swiss knew well: in their iodine-poor region, even babies could lack the gland functions that are needed for normal physical and mental development. Yet viewing it as an outcome of his operations, Kocher swore never again to remove a complete thyroid gland.

Kocher's discovery would pave the way for an understanding of thyroid regulation—but now he faced an emergency. Rushing to the German surgical congress in Berlin, he warned his colleagues about the effects of total strumectomy. In 1883 the *Archiv für Klinische Chirurgie* published his candid report, taking responsibility for the disaster, and relating it to Rudolf Virchow's finding that the same condition can result from iodine deficiency.

At this time, more thyroid glands had been removed by Billroth in Vienna than anyone else in the world. He had noticed some cases of tetany but, oddly, no cretinism. It was William Halsted in America who guessed the explanation, in a book about the history of thyroid surgery. Whereas Kocher operated with amazing thoroughness, certain to take the whole thyroid and leave the parathyroids, Billroth obeyed his bold temperament, and might take part of the parathyroids while missing some of the thyroid. Modern surgeons also leave a piece of fingertip size to keep the patient normal. And if they do remove the whole thyroid to treat cancer, they can make up for it by administering thyroid hormones.

THEODOR Kocher (*left*) and Jacques Reverdin. Their work in Switzerland included much else besides endocrine surgery, and several kinds of operations and instruments are named after them.

What Kocher operated on at first were "non-toxic" goitres, which do not produce too much hormone or any general effects. But Robert Graves in 1835, and Karl Basedow in 1840, had found that a "toxic" kind of goitre sometimes occurred elsewhere (see Chapter 7), with the opposite symptoms—irritability, weight loss, wild hunger, hyperactivity, warmth and sweating. This disease, named after them in their respective countries, was often exhibited by bulging eyes as well (exophthalmia).

Toxic goitre is related to thyroid overactivity, yet the fact was unknown in 1872, when Sir Patrick Heron Watson first tried to cure the disease by removing a bit of the gland. This proved insufficient, and in 1884 Ludwig Rehn introduced the operation which we now use, a "subtotal" thyroidectomy. Though avoiding

cretinism, it was risky: loss of the overactive gland could make the body respond violently, leading to a fatal "thyrotoxic" crisis. The latter was ultimately prevented with a treatment due to Henry Plummer (1874–1936) in America: calming down the gland by giving the patient iodine for a week or two before the operation.

Iodine cures for goitre were not a new idea. Alexander Manson, a Scot, had some initial success. He fed his patients with burnt sponges and, learning that these contained iodine, replaced them with a pharmacist's standard iodine tincture! But the modern way of eliminating a post-operative crisis is to give "thyrostatic" drugs in advance, impeding the gland's hormone production.

Once endocrine surgery started with work on the thyroid, other such glands were soon charted. In 1880 a Swedish anatomist, Ivar Sandström (1852–89), discovered the four bean-sized parathyroids next to the thyroid. That their removal caused the tetany which had worried Kocher and Billroth was shown by Eugene Gley (1857–1930) in France. And then around 1890, in Breslau, the pathologist

Friedrich von Recklinghausen (1833–1910) described a disease that would be named after him. It decalcified the bones, making them brittle and easily fractured. A common reason for it was eventually realized to be overactivity of the parathyroid glands.

Indeed, a review of Recklinghausen's autopsy notes revealed that he had seen a reddish "lymph knot" behind the thyroid—presumably a parathyroid tumour. In one serious case at the General Hospital of Vienna in 1925, Felix Mandl cleverly diagnosed such a tumour, and found it. Measuring 25 x 15 x 12 millimetres, it was taken out, and the disease vanished. Ironically, the patient had a relapse seven years later, and Mandl operated again. Yet there was no tumour, and none turned up at the autopsy either...

Today we know that the parathyroid glands produce a hormone which regulates the circulation of calcium and phosphorus. Too much of it causes calcium to leave the bones, and often results in kidney stones. While Recklinghausen's disease has become rare, a high level of calcium in the blood usually means hyperparathyroidism, requiring removal of the gland tumour(s).

Abdominal endocrine tumours

The gastrointestinal tract is the body's biggest endocrine organ, to judge from its number of such cells and hormones. An intestinal substance, secretin, was the first to be named a hormone—by the British physiologists William Bayliss (1860–1924) and Ernest Starling (1866–1927) in 1902. Since the 1960s, intestinal hormones have been chemically clarified, and many others identified. But tumours growing from endocrine cells in this tract can also produce active substances.

One example, long familiar, is the carcinoid tumour, usually in the appendix. The most active of the substances it releases is serotonin. Some patients, whose liver is also affected by metastasis, develop a "carcinoid syndrome" with attacks of diarrhoea and facial reddening. Surgeons must take out the primary tumour, and can reduce the tumour mass in the liver by temporarily blocking ("de-arterializing") its blood supply.

Endocrine tumours in the pancreas are the insulinoma and gastrinoma, each producing a hormone. In the first case, this is insulin, causing low blood sugar (hypoglycemia), the opposite of diabetes; such a tumour was described in 1927. In the second case, it is gastrin, making the stomach secrete too much hydrochloric acid, which may lead to ulcers—a syndrome discovered in 1955 by Robert Zollinger (b. 1903) and Edwin Ellison (b. 1918) in America. The tumour must be removed in both cases.

The adrenal gland near each kidney consists of two endocrine systems, the cortex and the medulla. Three hormones come from the cortex. One of these, cortisone, may be excessive due to an overactivity or tumour there—or to influence by a separate hormone, from a tumour in the brain's pituitary gland. The resultant syndrome, with obesity and muscular wasting, was recognized in 1932 by Harvey Cushing (see Chapter 10), and requires removal of that adrenal gland or the pituitary tumour. As for the medulla, it produces hormones such as the well-known adrenaline (epinephrine). Too much of these can cause dangerous episodes of high blood pressure, and the adrenal gland must be removed to get rid of the tumour responsible.

The name of this last instance, a "pheochromocytoma", almost advertises its rarity! Yet seldom-encountered ailments have taught us even more than do ordinary ones about the intricacies of our bodies. And if tumours could spread, so could knowledge in mankind's service. The success of complex operations soon inspired other fields of surgery.

Kocher's Rule

A surgeon is a doctor who can operate and who knows when not to.

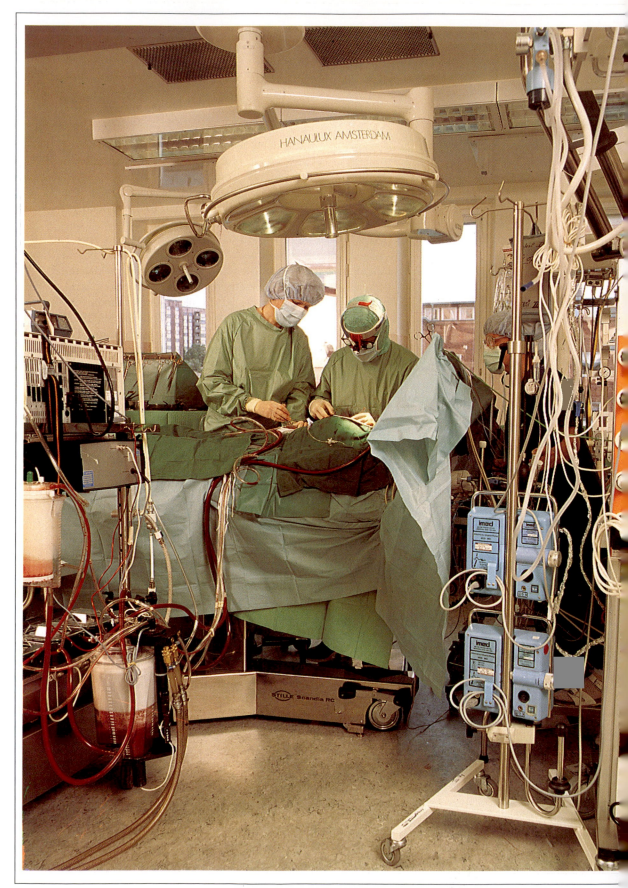

The world of modern surgery

Proceeding through the twentieth century, surgeons at last gained the keys to the rest of the human body. Fresh approaches and revolutionary techniques continued to multiply, while an ancient principle was perfected: treatment by addition rather than subtraction. Instead of just removing sick organs and limbs, we have tried ever harder to repair and restore their normal functions, as with transplants and prostheses.

Specialization also advanced far during the growth of medical expertise. Hospitals expanded, not least at universities, to include individual clinics for urological, neurological, thoracic, orthopaedic, paediatric, plastic and transplantation surgery, besides anaesthesiology and gynaecology. Within many areas, particular kinds of surgeons have established their own fields. But each remains rooted in dramatic achievements of the past.

The central nervous system

For thousands of years, no one dared to operate on the body's "signal network" except by trepanning the head, an old tradition as we have seen. The reason was an almost total ignorance of how the net worked—and consequently, of how to diagnose its illnesses. A science of neurophysiology arose only when David Ferrier

(1843–1928), in Edinburgh and later at King's College in London, began to pinpoint the functions and tumour symptoms of the brain. Greater contributions were made by Charles Scott Sherrington (1857–1952), who won a Nobel Prize in 1932. His book *The Integrative Action of the Nervous System* (1906) has been called the Bible of neurology. It described the reflexes, which are a main clue to the sources of such diseases.

Another giant of brain studies was Ivan Pavlov (see Chapter 9). His name is linked chiefly with "conditioned reflexes", as in the famous experiment with a dog that produced stomach juice at the ring of a dinner-bell. London's neurologist John Hughlings Jackson (1835–1911) devoted himself to epilepsy, discovering connections between limb movements and areas in the brain. While he could not distinguish true epilepsy from the kind that is caused by pressure on the brain cortex, he extended Ferrier's mapping of the motor centres. This provided a way of locating brain tumours.

Soon a clever doctor, Alexander Hughes Bennett, sent a patient to the Hospital for Epilepsy and Paralysis in London, diagnosing a brain tumour. He even stated its position: between the frontal and parietal lobes, in a fissure named after an Italian anatomist who had studied such structures, Luigi Rolando (1773–1831). With hesitation, the patient was operated on, and the walnut-sized tumour was found exactly as predicted! The field of neurosurgery had begun in triumph, although some did call the procedure unethical. The surgeon was Rickman John

AN operating theatre in 1988, with heart surgery in progress, aided by a heart-lung machine (at left).

Godlee (1849–1925), who then became "surgeon-in-ordinary" to two kings, Edward VII and George V. He also wrote the biography of his uncle, Lord Lister, and was likewise knighted.

But the real pioneer was Sir Victor Horsley (1857–1916). An odd man with strong opinions, he had praised abstinence ever since writing a youthful pamphlet against tobacco, and he detested loose talk or loose sexual habits, regarding even the theatre with suspicion. Sports were his pastime, and he wished that he had been an officer instead of a doctor, so that he could concentrate on riding horses. His father, perhaps realizing that such an outlook would have led to frivolity in the Victorian army, forced him to study medicine.

Once committed, Horsley earned every possible honour with training in surgery and pathology. He finally came to neurology, which suited his analytical mind like a hand in a glove. At 28, he took over the surgery in a hospital of neurology at Queen Square in London. This made him the first doctor in the world to deal mainly with neurosurgery. He built up the new specialty's organization and science, writing about injuries and diseases of the pituitary gland, spinal cord and brain.

When he turned fifty, in the midst of a hectic and productive career, Sir Victor caused a sensation by giving up surgery. Leaving his academic posts and hospital jobs, he went into politics with a passion for social reform. But his attacks on alcohol and tobacco, as well as his support for the emancipation of women, were unpopular and he never reached Parliament. During World War I he returned to surgery, as head of field hospitals in India and Mesopotamia, where he suddenly died—presumably of a heat stroke.

The next great figure in neurosurgery, Harvey Cushing (1869–1939), belonged to an American medical dynasty. Able to study at both of the country's richest medical schools, Yale and Harvard, followed by training at Johns Hopkins Hospital in Baltimore, he took full advantage of these opportunities. As apprentice to William Halsted, he got interested in neurosurgery and

THE neurosurgeon Harvey Cushing.

determined to give it better diagnostic methods. Among other things, he was soon one of the first in America to use X-rays.

Cushing became professor of surgery at Harvard in 1912, also serving as surgeon-in-chief at Peter Bent Brigham Hospital in Boston. As the historians Leo Zimmerman and Ilza Veith have written:

"He brought to neurosurgery the ultimate refinements of pre-operative preparation and operative technique. An absolute perfectionist himself, he inculcated subordinates with such a respect for the ritual of brain operation that it resembled a cult. His introduction of silver clips for blood–stanching, in tissues that could not be ligatured or tamponed, was not the least of his innumerable improvements."

Cushing's skill reduced the high mortality rate of brain operations, and it was down to 5% by

1930. Even during the heyday of Victor Horsley, tumour operations had so often been fatal that the British Medical Association considered forbidding them!

In addition, Cushing was a tireless contributor to neurological science. Among his writings, on the pathology and classification of brain tumours, is a long one about "meningioma" tumours that grow from the brain's membranes. Yet his finest work was *The Pituitary Body and Its Disorders* (1912), describing the syndrome which bears his name (see Chapter 9), characterized by "a tomato head on a potato body with four matches as limbs".

A contemporary founder of brain surgery in Europe was Vilhelm Magnus (1871–1929) in Norway. His achievements have been overlooked, possibly since he wrote almost solely in his native language. He first operated on the brain in 1903, to remove a tumour from the cerebrum of an epileptic man aged 47. Some twenty years later, he could report more than a hundred brain-tumour operations with a mortality rate of only 8 %. Just as surprisingly, he did them at poorly equipped private hospitals, lacking the resources of Oslo University.

In neighbouring Sweden was one of the foremost brain surgeons, Herbert Olivecrona (1891–1980), professor of neurosurgery at Stockholm's Karolinska Institute from 1935 until 1960. His advances in treating brain tumours and vascular defects made that clinic a world-famous centre of neurosurgery. His successor, Lars Leksell (1907–85), also earned an international reputation, developing "stereotactic" surgery and the "radiation knife". The first of these is used to operate deep in the brain with mechanical instruments, as when destroying tumours that cannot be seen directly. The second is a cobalt-ray gun that focuses on small benign tumours and deep vascular defects in the brain.

The blood vessels

Little could be done with arteries and veins before 1900, except tying them off to stop bleeding or the flow in a dangerous aneurysm. There was no technique for opening and closing an artery, or for sewing two arterial ends together. Even more distant was the prospect of replacing a damaged blood vessel with a healthy or artificial one.

Aneurysms

Antonio Scarpa (see Chapter 6) wrote a very important book in 1804 about the forms and diagnosis of arterial aneurysms. They then became a primary concern of doctors, and naturally so, as these thin-walled bulges in the blood system are carried with no more comfort than a live grenade. Another Italian surgeon, Giovanni Monteggia (1762–1815), began as early as 1813 to treat aneurysms by injecting a fluid to harden them. Unfortunately, such fluids are swept away in an artery's bloodstream too soon to take effect.

Necessity gave birth to further dubious inventions: wrapping the aneurysm with steel wire, or with tissue taken from the thigh. One curious method was to stick needles into the vessel and pass an electric current between them, hoping to coagulate the blood. This began in 1832, and was still being tried in the 1930s. Even worse, the aneurysm was "reinforced" with steel wire, fed in through a cannula tube. The initiator, Charles Moore in London (see Chapter 9), did not stop until he had filled the aorta with 26 yards of wire—quite a premature Battle of the Bulge! He is said to have got the idea from reinforced concrete, but he started the treatment in 1864, twenty years before that innovation by François Hennebique (1842–1921).

An acceptable technique was developed by a legendary surgeon in New Orleans, Rudolph Matas (1860–1957). "Endoaneurysmorrhaphy" involved holding the swollen vessel between clamps, tying the arterial branches from inside, and strengthening the thin wall with a double row of sutures. Then the possibility of doing something even better—reconstructing arteries—fascinated a young French doctor in Lyons. Alexis Carrel (1873–1948) was to open

HERBERT Olivecrona.

new paths, not only in treating aneurysm, but in the whole field of surgery on the blood vessels and heart.

Just after the turn of the century, Carrel did his first animal experiments. They attracted such attention that he went to America and continued work, in Chicago and then at the Rockefeller Institute in New York City. There he showed that a piece of the aortal wall could be replaced with a piece from another artery or vein, and he found a way of sewing vessels together. In 1910 he wrote an article that can be called the scientific beginning of vascular surgery. It told how to transplant an entire vessel, sewing in the ends with "everted" sutures so that the inside is left free of thread—which might form a blood clot, the worst risk in all vascular surgery.

Carrel had an eccentric character. He well deserved his 1912 Nobel Prize, but did not

ALEXIS Carrel.

into practice. The first operation on an aneurysm with resectioning and vessel sutures, by his countryman Charles Dubost, was done only in 1951.

Since then, the standard method has been to remove the whole aneurysm and insert a substitute. This was originally a freeze-dried vessel from an animal or human. But such vessels tended to dilate and become new aneurysms. It was therefore a relief when the "vessel banks" of the 1950s gave way to artificial prostheses. These artificial vessels were initially made of nylon, and one experimenter created a perfect aorta for a dog from a brassiere, which was donated by his wife!

Today other fibres are used, mainly Dacron, which enables new tissue to grow into its woven meshes. After a few years, the prosthesis can hardly be distinguished from the old vessel. Frequently, too, a Y-shaped "trouser" prosthesis is needed to replace an aortal aneurysm that continues down into the pelvic arteries.

Obstructions

If a clot or a "thrombus" aggregation forms in the blood, it may block the flow—either at the point of formation, or at a point downstream in an artery to which it is swept as an "embolus". Preventing such an obstruction where the surgeon has made sutures is one serious problem, as we have noted.

Thrombosis in a vein occurs especially in the pelvis and legs. It was familiar even to early Chinese doctors like Huang Ti, who wrote: "when the blood coagulates in the foot, this yields pain and freezing." Scientists began to study it during the eighteenth century. In 1718, Giovanni Lancisi (see Chapter 5) demonstrated the obstructions in veins, and shortly afterward it was realized that they often affected patients who stayed for a long time in bed. A breakthrough came in the 1840s when Rudolf Virchow announced his famous "triad" of factors that cause them (see Chapter 7).

bother to mention that his success owed at least as much to Charles Guthrie, a colleague at the Rockefeller Institute. Soon he grew tired of blood vessels, and his final contribution to surgery was the "Carrel-Dakin solution", an antiseptic used in World War I. Turning to philosophy with a book, *Man the Unknown* (1935), he argued that democracy itself should be replaced by a "utopia" where geniuses had the most rights. Three years later, he crowned his long research on tissue culture, keeping organs alive outside the body with a pump built by the aviator Charles Lindbergh (1902–74).

Thus, Carrel was a forefather of innovations like the artificial heart. However, at the end of World War II, he played a suspicious role in French politics, and was accused of helping the Nazis—whose evil doctors had tarnished the reputation of medicine in Germany. As for his suture technique, it faced delay before coming

Several researchers then contributed to treating thrombosis. Jay McLean, a student, published an article in 1916 about how cephalin, an extract from the brain, dissolves thrombi. Three years later, William Henry Howell (1860–1945) and L. E. Holt, at Johns Hopkins Hospital, produced the first study of an even better substance—called heparin, isolated from the liver. Erik Jorpes (1894–1973) in Stockholm revealed its chemical structure in 1935, and persuaded surgeons to put it into practice.

One Swede who did so was Gunnar Bauer (1895–1970), a chief physician in a small-town hospital. He soon became the world authority on preventing and curing blood obstructions. Another was Clarence Crafoord (1899–1984), professor at the Karolinska Institute from 1948 to 1966, a renowned pioneer in heart and lung surgery, such as the first operation for aortal narrowing in 1945.

A blood disease in cattle that eat rotten sweet-clover was noticed in the early 1920s. After twenty years, it was traced to a chemical named dicumarol, which inhibited blood coagulation. This and related "anticoagulants" turned into a worldwide weapon for preventing blood clots. Like heparin, they cannot dissolve existing ones—but we now have an enzyme that can do so, streptokinase. If given in good time, it gets rid of big clots and the blood vessels return to normal. These drugs are also used by the surgeon to prevent thrombosis after most major operations.

An embolus may originate from part of the heart that is narrowed (as in mitral stenosis) or from irregular heartbeat (fibrillation). The clot comes loose, is carried through the aorta by blood, and gets stuck at another narrow point—frequently where the pelvic arteries divide off, or inside one of them or the thigh arteries. To remove such obstructions, the "ballooning catheter" was invented in 1965 by Thomas Fogarty, a young American in Portland, Oregon. The surgeon makes a little cut in the groin, opens a thigh artery, and pushes in the thin tube. It passes the clot, produces a balloon on the other side, and can then be pulled back out, bringing the clot with it.

Chronic insufficiency of blood-flow through the arteries is due primarily to arteriosclerosis, which hardens and narrows them. This occurs sometimes in the abdomen, and more often in the neck or arms—but usually in the legs where it causes pain and fatigue, resulting in an intermittent limp ("window-shopper syndrome"). Apart from physical exercise, several surgical treatments have been developed since the 1940s: to cut out the obstruction with the artery's lining (a thromboendarterectomy), to shunt the blood around it through a transplanted thigh-vein or a synthetic bypass, or to dilate the artery with another "ballooning" device as we shall see.

Varicose veins

Some 10 % of the world's population is estimated to suffer from enlarged veins, most commonly in the lower extremities with symptoms of swelling, heaviness, cramps and, in advanced cases, skin ulcers. The history of these "varices" can be traced far back in antiquity (see Chapter 2).

Hippocrates wrote about varicose veins—sticking needles in them as a cure, probably to no avail—and they were portrayed in sculptures at the temples of Asklepios. The Romans operated on them, apparently by extraction and ligature; one patient was the tyrant Marius who, according to Plutarch's history, thought that they spoiled his beautiful calves! He bravely endured the treatment on one leg, but refused it for the other, saying that the results were not worth the trouble.

The oldest detailed description of such an operation, by Paul of Aegina, rightly stated that the cut must be made in the thigh, since the veins farther down the leg are branched too finely to be treated. His method was a kind of "high ligature", which must have succeeded half the time, as it did when it regained popularity 75 years ago.

The cause of this condition emerged after Fabricius ab Aquapendente discovered the veins' valves in 1574 (see Chapter 5). But only in the early nineteenth century—once industrial machines forced workers to stand still for hours, making the pain worse—did operations on varicose veins resume. The techniques were improved with observations by two English surgeons, Sir Everard Home (1756–1832), an army doctor at St. George's Hospital, and Benjamin Brodie (1783–1862), a personal physician to the future King George IV. Finding that the afflicted veins' size interfered with their valves, Brodie advised closing them as far up as possible, and he alleviated the symptoms by bandaging the leg. As early as 1846, he diagnosed varicose veins by a method which, half a century later, would be named for the German surgeon Friedrich Trendelenburg (1844–1924).

A view of how the disease was regarded in those days is given by a Swede's dissertation, *Varicose Widenings in the Veins of the Lower Limbs*, at Uppsala in 1832. It claimed that they were signs of premature ageing, caused by "debauchery on the path of love"! The best cure was supposedly a mixture of calomel (mercurous chloride), jalap (a Mexican purgative herb), "taraxacum" (dandelions, an old diuretic) and sulphur—evidently in order to drive out the contents of the widened veins. Indeed, diuretic medicines are now used to treat veins that work poorly in the legs, but by eliminating fluid outside the veins (oedema), not inside them.

Modern treatment for varicose veins started around 1890, when Trendelenburg revived the "high ligature" operation—dividing a vein in the thigh. This was later combined with extracting the sick vein, another ancient technique. Now a better instrument, the "stripper", was developed by the surgeon William Wayne Babcock (1872–1963) in Philadelphia. Yet not until the 1940s did doctors learn how swellings, injuries, and eczema in the leg depended on the "perforating veins" in the thigh. These had already figured in the anatomical drawings of Leonardo da Vinci, and were operated on by

a German surgeon, Otto Wilhelm Madelung (1846–1926), in the 1880s. He had to stop because his patients bled badly, some of them fatally.

In the next century, varicose-vein operations competed with "sclerotherapy", which tries to close the veins by injecting an irritant chemical into them. Today, this is acceptable only for small varices and as an aid to surgery. Long studies of patients, mainly in Britain and Scandinavia, have shown that the disease in larger veins must be operated on.

The chest

The problem with an operation—or an injury—that opens up the thorax is air pressure. Normally this is low in the "pleural cavities" around the lungs, to keep them expanded and functioning. But opening the chest lets in air, making one or both lungs collapse, so that breathing is difficult or impossible. As early as the Papyrus Smith (see Chapter 1), the Egyptians described operations for chest wounds. However, these were doubtless superficial, or else holes that were plugged up quickly to let the lungs gradually expand again.

Ambroise Paré may have understood the problem. For shot wounds (see Chapter 4), he recommended that the opening be closed as fast as possible. Whether he ever practised this is

---

Old Light on Varicose Veins

In 1765, a quaint Swedish medical guide by J. J. Haartman (see Chapter 6) offered typical advice for this illness: "Varices are the bags which sometimes occur in the veins. On the feet, they need only blood-letting in due course, besides mild exercise, the feet being kept horizontal and rubbed occasionally upwards. When located in the thighs, they urge thrift in exciting matters and amorous games…"

uncertain, though, and his main concern was the coldness of the air that might rush in. During the sixteenth century, there was little hope for anybody who got a hole in the pleural cavity. Still, at least three such victims in the Napoleonic Wars were saved by Baron Larrey (see Chapter 6).

The lungs

Some isolated incidents of early thoracic surgery exist. In 1499, a doctor named Rolandus simply cut off part of a lung that was protruding from a hernia in the chest wall, presumably after an injury. Milton Antony, an American physician, operated in 1823 on a young man with a large pus formation in the chest. It was attached to a good deal of the lung, which he therefore removed. And in each case, the patient survived.

The possibilities of operating in the thorax were first studied experimentally in Germany, during its surgical "boom" at the end of the nineteenth century. One of the initiatives led to tragedy. M. H. Block, in Danzig, had proved that the lungs of rabbits could be partially removed. To see if it could be done with a human, he used his own cousin, who had tuberculosis in both lungs. When he took out the apex of each lung, the patient died, and Block committed suicide. More successfully, a lung was removed from dogs and rabbits by Themistokles Gluck (1853–1943), an assistant to Langenbeck.

As the true founder of thoracic surgery, we recognize Ernst Ferdinand Sauerbruch (1875–1951). At four, he lost his father to tuberculosis, the "galloping consumption". His mother's father, a shoemaker, imbued him with high social ambitions. Unpromising at school, he wanted to become an officer—the best way to reach the upper class—but he lacked the necessary money and turned to medicine. While his talent for surgery was soon obvious, he preferred research, and went to work on experimental intestinal injuries in Berlin, at the pathological institute.

There his abilities were appreciated by the professor, Paul Langerhans (1847–88), famous as an investigator of the pancreas. He thus became an assistant to none other than Mikulicz-Radecki in Breslau. This great man, as usual, ignored the lowly newcomer for weeks, but at last told him curtly that scientific results were expected of him: how he obtained them was his own business. Fascinated by the idea of doing surgery on the oesophagus and lungs, Sauerbruch decided to solve the problem of lung collapse when the thorax was opened.

He repeated the experiments which were done by physiologists and surgeons on opening the pleural cavities, but found that their pessimism was justified. Next, however, he enclosed the animal's chest in an air-tight cage, decompressed to ten millimetres of mercury. Using gloves built into the cage wall, he could operate while the animal went on breathing! This was uncomfortable and crude, yet the principle was clear. Mikulicz refused to believe his report, and could barely be persuaded to watch a demonstration. As luck would have it, the apparatus then sprang a leak, and the animal died of lung collapse… Enraged at such a waste of time, the professor threw Sauerbruch out of the clinic. We can imagine quite a test of lungs between these self-assured, irascible gentlemen.

A doctor of Mikulicz' calibre always had enemies, and one of them, primarily to irritate him, gave Sauerbruch a place in which to go on working. By 1904, a low-pressure chamber was built with fourteen cubic metres of space, holding a patient and table and a whole operating team. The results were presented in April, at the annual German surgical congress. Mikulicz made amends by praising them, and discussed the future of thoracic surgery, even envisaging operations on the heart.

Once reconciled, the two men remained friends until the following year, when the professor died of stomach cancer—a disease whose surgical treatment he himself had developed along with Billroth. An old colleague from Vienna, Anton von Eiselsberg (1860–1939), came to Breslau to operate on him, but could only say that it was too late to save Mikulicz.

Using the low-pressure chamber, Sauerbruch started to gain experience in thoracic surgery. Even before his work was published, there were suggestions of using high pressure inside the lung, rather than low pressure around it. The solution was to feed an air-tight tube down the windpipe, connected to a closed narcosis system. This method is now often employed even when the chest is not opened.

Sauerbruch eventually became a professor and chief physician at the Charité Hospital in Berlin. Although not active in politics, he allowed the Nazis to use his propaganda value. As an old man, he also failed to realize that arteriosclerosis impaired his judgement. Obsessed with operating, he made mistakes which his assistants— afraid to correct him—had to get up at night to set right. Once deprived of his post, he continued to operate in his kitchen, with grisly consequences.

After that, the most progressive field was tuberculosis surgery. Many patients had chronic lung TB, and were not helped by existing drugs, since these were not effective on the isolated, pus-filled "cavities" in the lungs. An Italian, Carlo Forlanini (1847–1918), introduced a "pneumothorax" treatment, but it went wrong when diseased areas kept the lung stuck to the chest wall. The only way of coping with the illness was to operate, and two methods arose.

First, the "cavity" area could be made to shrink—as Forlanini intended—if the ribs were mostly removed so that the chest wall and the lung collapsed. This is possible even without opening the pleural cavity, and such "thoracoplasty" had been tried earlier by, for example, Jakob August Estlander (1831–81) in Finland. With the low-pressure chamber or high-pressure breathing, one could be still bolder. A radical operation of the kind was launched in 1907 by Paul Leopold Friedrich (1864–1916), and improved by Sauerbruch, who did it hundreds of times. Refinements came from Gravesen in Denmark, Edvard Bull (1845–1925) in Norway, and Einar Key (1872–1954) in Sweden.

ERNST Sauerbruch.

No Sauerkraut for Sauerbruch

Sauerbruch used to begin his operating day by eating half a French pear and drinking a quarter bottle of champagne. Any special guest who happened to be at the clinic was invited to eat the other half of the pear. Never denying himself the pleasures of life, Sauerbruch often had financial problems, in spite of his sky-high fees. This gave rise to the following anecdote.

Manager: "I don't understand how you, with such an income, are constantly overdrawing your account." Sauerbruch: "If you, a bank manager, don't understand it, how do you expect me to?"

Secondly, a yet more radical procedure was to take out part or all of a lung. In spite of many opponents—who feared it would reawaken the latent process of tuberculosis—a "lobectomy" was initiated by S. O. Freedlander of Cleveland in 1935, and has been advanced in America. Both methods of operation became safer, and their mortality rate dropped below 1%, with the arrival of antituberculosis drugs like streptomycin. But these have also made surgery a rare measure for tuberculosis, by preventing the formation of lung cavities.

The main reason for operating on the lung today is lung cancer, very common because of smoking and other factors. Lung resections for cancer were begun in 1933, by Evarts Graham (1883–1957) in Washington. His first patient was a doctor, who outlived him! Besides the lobectomy (removing a lung lobe), segmental resection (removing only a part of a lobe) and pneumonectomy (taking the whole lung) were perfected by Morriston Davies in England, and Richard Overholt in America. A great addition to the safety of such operations is the automatic high–pressure respirator, produced in Sweden by Clarence Crafoord with the otologist Paul Frenckner and an engineer, Emil Anderson.

The heart

As long ago as the time of the Byzantine saint John Chrysostomos (347–407), the heart was called the body's noblest organ. This view took root in the minds of surgeons, who considered the heart "off limits" until a century before our time. A heart injury was a death sentence that could not be challenged even if the chance of sewing up a heart muscle happened to arise.

Morgagni, in 1766, described a condition which came to be known as "cardiac tamponade". If blood leaks from the heart into the pericardium around it, pressure builds up on it, and its pumping activity may stop. The only treatment is to let out blood quickly, and a doctor named Romero reported in 1819 that he had done this for three patients, two of whom lived on—proof of his diagnostic skill as well as

his moral courage. Larrey, too, had succeeded with a man who tried to commit suicide with a stab in the heart. By the mid-1800s, about 400 such cases were recorded, although only some 10 % survived.

But this operation (pericardiocentesis) is not done on the heart itself. Cardiac surgery began in 1897, when a man was found lying in a street in Frankfurt, bleeding from a wound over the heart. Barely alive, he was taken to a hospital, where nobody dared to treat him: the chief was away. Professor Ludwig Rehn (1849–1930), returning the next day, figured that nothing could be lost by operating. In the heart muscle, an injury was found and sewn up, saving the man.

It later emerged that a surgeon named Cappelen in Oslo had performed a similar operation two years earlier, though his patient died. With modern techniques, suturing the heart is easy enough. The outcome of such a procedure depends only on how much blood is lost before the hole can be closed, and about half of the victims survive.

Among acquired heart defects, one of the commonest is mitral stenosis, already mentioned. The valve between the left auricle and ventricle (like a bishop's "mitre" cap) becomes narrowed, slowing down the blood circulation and eventually doing harm. Doctors long wished that a surgical treatment could be found, and this was predicted in 1902 by a famous Scottish pharmacologist, Sir Thomas Lauder Brunton (1844–1916).

Various knives were then tested, to cut through the calcified valve and its supporting ring, while not cutting so much as to cause the opposite defect of mitral "insufficiency"—a flow of blood back into the auricle when the heart muscle contracts. The first operation with such a knife was done in 1923 by Elliott Cutler in Boston. It proved dramatic: the girl's heart nearly stopped, but was revived with adrenaline and hot cloths. She left a little healthier, yet died some years later of the same defect.

In 1925 an Englishman, Henry Souttar, reported that he had operated on a person thought to have mitral stenosis. The diagnosis turned out to be wrong, but he discovered that he could pass his finger through the mitral hole, and suggested that this be done to widen a narrowed valve. Before anyone got a chance to try, however, a new idea occurred to doctors—that the main problem in mitral stenosis was not the valve defect, but its effects on the heart muscle.

Souttar's method was ignored until an American doctor, Dwight Harken, returned to Boston from World War II. He had learned a lot about the heart and its vicinity by removing bullets and grenade fragments. Now he concentrated on mitral stenosis, and fitted his finger with a small knife. On 16 June 1948, he treated a valve by dilating it with his finger as well as cutting its calcified ring. A few months afterward in London, Sir Russell Brock did likewise, with no knife. Their reports spread the method around the world, leading to the "open commissurotomy" operation which is used today.

With mitral stenosis, the surgeon could work on a beating heart, since the main procedure took only a moment. But a long time was needed to correct an inborn heart defect. This is illustrated, most simply, by an opening in the septum (wall) between the auricles. With experience, it could be closed in five to seven minutes—yet the brain could go without blood for only about four minutes.

To increase the allowable operating time, one idea was to cool down the body, because the brain and other organs require much less oxygen at lower temperatures. Experiments on dogs down to around 30°C (86°F) supported this "hypothermia" approach. It was pioneered by William Bigelow in Toronto and by Henry Swan, together with the anaesthesiologist R. W. Virtue, in Denver. Many successful operations on human septum defects were reported by Swan in 1953, and a year later he had treated 100 patients with no mortality.

Hypothermia was not enough for the more serious inborn heart defects—such as the "tetralogy" named after Étienne-Louis Fallot (1850–1911) in "blue babies". These often need

The Surgeon as Musician

Evarts Ambrose Graham was a pioneer not only in lung surgery, but also in X-ray studies of the gall bladder. He described the profession as follows:

"In many respects surgery is like music, which has its great artists and its great composers. The great musical artists are like the great surgeons. They often perform before large audiences with great technical skill, and they have large incomes. But what they accomplish is the work of the composers, the creative men who have made it possible for them to perform and who often have received only modest economic rewards. What our present surgeons need is more men of the composer type!"

Heartfelt Advice

Perhaps the greatest advances in diagnosis of acquired heart defects were made by James Hope (1801-41). He studied in Edinburgh and, after years of training in France, Switzerland and Italy, became chief of internal medicine at St. George's Hospital in London—only to die of lung tuberculosis.

Hope's book Diseases of the Heart and Great Vessels *(1831) described symptoms of valvular heart disease. His observations became a guide to all heart doctors, and paved the way for surgical treatment. Influential, too, were his ethical principles:*

"In the first place, never keep a patient sick when you can do something for him. In the second place, never take a higher fee than what you truly feel you are entitled to. In the third place, always pray for your patients."

a long time to reconstruct anatomy. John Gibbon, Jr. (1903–73), in Philadelphia, devoted nearly all of his surgical career to the problem, and in 1953 he became the first to find a solution: replacing the heart temporarily by a heart-lung machine. This is the basic tool of modern "open-heart" surgery. Among the best-known innovators of related techniques have been his compatriots Michael De Bakey (b. 1908) and Denton Cooley (b. 1920).

The valve between the left ventricle and the aorta can have defects like those of the mitral valves. Surgeons tried to get at them during the 1950s, but did less well than with mitral stenosis. Henry Swan doubted the value of this operation, although in 1959 he performed it on a dozen patients under hypothermia. Cardiologists say that anyone with aortal stenosis, if strong enough to stand the operation, is also healthy enough to go without it. Yet diseased valves must often be replaced with mechanical ones.

Such an artificial heart valve, constructed by Charles Hufnagel in Georgetown, was popular for some time. The first models had a curious complication: as the valve closed, a plastic ball inside it clicked, and the sound proved to be audible when the patient opened his mouth! This irritated at least one man so much that he committed suicide. But prostheses for heart valves have developed rapidly, and those used today contain disks as well as balls.

Angina pectoris

A condition of sharp pain around the heart was first clearly noticed, and named, by William Heberden (see Chapter 6):

"There is one ailment in the chest which has difficult and peculiar symptoms. It should be heeded, as it is neither free of danger nor particularly uncommon... Its localization, the patient's feeling of suffocation, and the anguish accompanying it, give reason for calling it *angina pectoris*."

Its cause was obscure to him, but we now attribute it to poor blood supply in the heart muscle, usually when the heart's own coronary arteries are narrowed or blocked by atherosclerosis.

Even in Heberden's day, there were reports—mainly by English doctors—of victims who also suffered gradual changes in the heart muscle. For example, he received a letter from Edward Jenner (see Chapter 7) about "a kind of hard, fleshy mass which is formed inside the vessel, which itself had irregularly spread bone-like formations", not a bad description of advanced atherosclerosis. Joseph Hodgson (see Chapter 7) pointed out that angina pectoris could be accompanied by changes in the coronary vessels.

The final stage in a serious narrowing of a coronary vessel is a "heart attack", when the muscle gets so little oxygen that it stops working. A good initial description of this was given by Jean Cruveilhier (1791–1874) with a magnificent colour picture in his great work *Anatomie Pathologique du Corps Humain*. However, he did not relate the muscle damage to a narrowed coronary vessel. Not until 1859 was the relationship generally accepted, due to a revealing case published jointly by H. P. Malmsten and G. W. Düben. The short article, originally in their native Swedish, drew such attention that it was reprinted by the medical press in both Germany and England.

As always when a mechanical problem causes a disease, surgeons are implored to come up with a cure for heart attacks. But coronary vessels are hard to liberate: atherosclerosis often covers large areas, and it may be accelerated if these thin vessels are made even narrower when sewn. Fortunately, other vessels can be arranged to supply the heart muscle. Intestinal tissue was sewn to the heart in England by L. O'Shaughnessy, hoping that blood vessels would grow over to the muscle, and this "omentopexy" had some success. A better method, introduced in 1948 by Claude Beck of Cleveland, Ohio, was to make vessels grow over from the pericardium, by simply powdering with talcum to produce an inflammation! In 1950, the Canadian heart surgeon

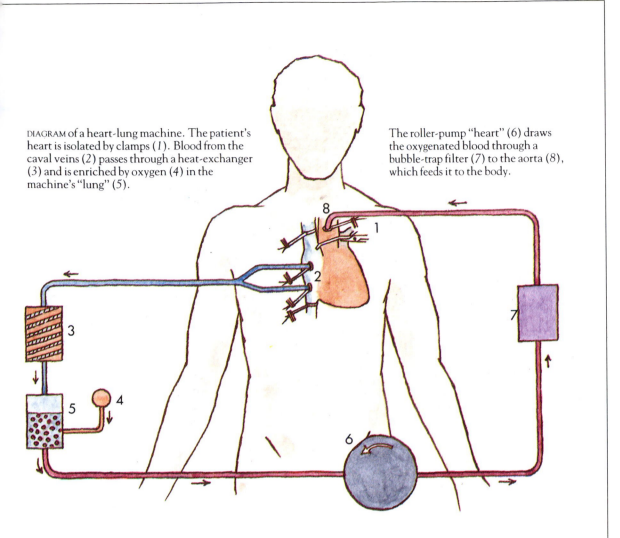

DIAGRAM of a heart-lung machine. The patient's heart is isolated by clamps (*1*). Blood from the caval veins (*2*) passes through a heat-exchanger (*3*) and is enriched by oxygen (*4*) in the machine's "lung" (*5*).

The roller-pump "heart" (*6*) draws the oxygenated blood through a bubble-trap filter (*7*) to the aorta (*8*), which feeds it to the body.

The Heart-Lung Machine

A surgeon can calmly operate inside the heart, or rebuild large vessels to and from the lungs, only if the heart is disconnected. The patient's blood circulation must then be main-tained with a machine to keep supplying oxy-gen to the rest of the body.

The machine has two main parts: a "lung" to oxygenate the blood, and a "heart" pump. Before starting, it is filled with 1.5-2 litres of electrolyte solution. A small dose of anti-coagulant heparin is given to the patient. Then the blood, from two big veins near the heart, is led through tubes into the machine, and spreads as a thin film over a large surface

in the "lung". Oxygen circulating above the blood is absorbed, and carbon dioxide is given out, just as in a real lung. The pump gently feeds the blood back into the patient's aortal artery.

Meanwhile, the real heart is stopped with an electric shock, and clamped off for opera-tion. It is cooled down, and the body tempera-ture is lowered to 28° by hypothermia, so that the tissues need less oxygen. Extra blood can be added through a valve in the machine, which also has a heat-exchanger to control the blood's temperature. Finally the heart starts again, spontaneously or with electrical help.

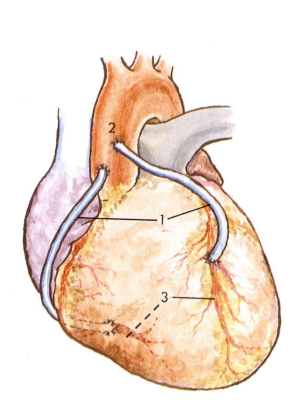

AN example of cardiovascular surgery is this multiple aortocoronary vein by-pass operation, introduced in America during the late 1960s. Vein grafts (*1*) have been sewn in to lead the blood from the aorta (*2*) around stenoses—narrowed areas—in the coronary arteries (*3*).

Arthur Vineberg (b. 1903) created a further technique, connecting one of the chest arteries directly into the heart muscle.

In 1953, the Swedish radiologist Sven Seldinger, with his catheter method, laid the basis for X-ray "angiography", which makes it possible to locate the diseased areas exactly. Such cardiac catheterization had begun in 1929 when Werner Forssmann (1904–79), a surgeon in Berlin, passed a tube through an arm vein into his own heart while watching it on a fluoroscope screen—for which he shared a Nobel Prize in 1956! Since then, the tendency has been to use straightforward coronary-vessel surgery, re-connecting the blood-flow beyond the obstruction.

Today the commonest approach is to implant a "bypass" vein between the coronary vessel and the aorta. A fairly wide connection can be used, and the blood pressure in the aorta is high, so the flow normally stays open—giving the patient great relief from angina pectoris, as regards both the frequency and severity of pain. Such operations certainly prolong the life of people with very poor coronary vessels.

An increasingly popular procedure, begun by Andreas Grüntzig (1978), is to widen narrowed vessels with "balloon dilatation", also called

PTCA (percutaneous transluminal coronary angioplasty). It has the limitation that, in many cases, the vessels are narrowed again. But this may be prevented with an instrument developed by the Swedish thoracic surgeon Åke Senning and the technician Hans Wallstén. Here, ballooning is combined with a spiral-shaped metal "stent", a prosthetic vessel to be placed inside the real vessel, supporting it and keeping the passage open—and eventually growing into it, surrounded by new healthy tissue. The method is, however, still under clinical investigation.

Transplantation and plastic surgery

Substituting a healthy organ for a sick or damaged one has always been a dream of surgeons. Naturally, excellent techniques are needed to unite the transplant with the patient's system of blood vessels. This obstacle seemed to be overcome when Alexis Carrel introduced his suture method. A wave of enthusiasm about transplants followed, but ran into a basic problem—the guest organ could be rejected by the host organism! The body's immunity "defence mechanism" reacted against such foreign cells and killed them.

Some tissues, of skin or bone, can be "autotransplanted" from one place to another in the same patient, with no difficulties of blood supply or immune defence. Even in ancient India, Susruta showed how to move skin when fixing an amputated nose (see Chapter 1). His method was improved by Tagliacozzi (see Chapter 4), who had an assistant—and plagiarizer—in Giovanni Battista Cortesi (1554–1636). They used skin from the upper arm, grafting it gradually onto the face. In all such cases, the skin kept its blood supply from the original site until it had grown onto the new site.

But at Paris in 1869, Félix Jean Casimir Guyon (1831–1920) reported that he had managed to get small pieces of skin to heal on a naked wound, without the original blood supply. In the same year, a more refined description was given by Jacques Reverdin (see Chapter 9). Noticing

A "two-chamber" pacemaker with two heart electrodes which are inserted into the right auricle and ventricle.

The Pacemaker

The heart has its own ingenious system for adjusting its beat frequency according to needs. More body activity calls for more blood to the muscles, so the heart must pump faster and the pulse climbs. This system involves stimuli that travel through nerves in the heart wall and muscles. But as elsewhere in the body, faults can arise in the system, causing "arrhythmic" variations in heartbeat, and sometimes quite dangerous ones.

Since the stimuli are electrical impulses, they can be suppressed by stronger signals from another source. Thus, the heart's rhythm can be guided from outside by a "pacemaker". As a rule, this tiny electronic device is implanted just under the skin with its thin cable running through a vein to the heart's right ventricle. It can work for 5–10 years on a lithium battery which is changed with a simple operation.

The first pacemaker was constructed by Rune Elmqvist and implanted by Åke Senning in Sweden in 1958.

that large wounds healed from small "islands" of skin, not only from the edges, he thought of helping the process by strewing bits of very thin skin on the wound—so that these extra islands also formed new skin.

Reverdin's procedure worked, yet it took time. Due to the great risk of infection, which tends to prevent healing, a method was needed to cover the wound more completely and speed up the healing. Many modifications were tried, with varying success. A big step forward was the graft named after Carl Thiersch (see Chapter 8). He proved that, by first cleaning granulation tissue off the host site, one could lay leaf-thin pieces of skin on its raw surface and make them heal. Unlike Reverdin's millimetre-sized bits, these pieces were as big as postage stamps.

Strong progress in transplanting skin came during World War I. Stimulated by the many burn injuries, it had a leader in Sir Harold Gillies (1882–1960). Better instruments were introduced too. Thiersch's thin double-edged knife or razor blade gave way to the "dermatome", which could be adjusted to cut perfectly even slices of any thickness, and in any size when driven rapidly by an electric motor. A more recent improvement is to run the skin transplant through a little roller with spikes that make fine holes in it, producing a fine net of tissue. Such a "mesh graft" economizes on skin, and heals better because the meshes allow blood and fluid to seep out.

Particularly in battle surgery, and after other bad wounds, it may be necessary to use pieces of bone in, for example, building up a facial skeleton. One can take small pieces of healthy bone from the patient, and chop them into "chips" that serve as the basis for new bones. Even corneas can be transplanted; this "keroplastic" operation—begun by E. Zirm in 1906—has saved the sight of many patients whose corneas have become opaque for various reasons.

As a modern specialty, plastic and reconstructive surgery has a wide range of activity. It includes removing malignant skin tumours and treating birth defects—like cleft lips, jaws and palates—as well as burns and face traumas, urogenital and hand deformities, residues from cancer, and cosmetic operations as on the breast. Due to a discovery called the epidermal growth factor (EGF), large areas of skin can be taken from a burned patient, cultivated and reimplanted to cover the injury, thus avoiding the problem of rejection of "homografts" (allografts) between different individuals.

Operative techniques have also advanced, as in "craniofacial" surgery on the face and skull, requiring collaboration with dentistry and neurosurgery. In "microsurgery", tiny blood vessels and nerves can be sewn back together with the help of a microscope, reattaching a severed hand or foot with no need for a prosthesis.

Organ transplants

The first experimental transfer of a whole organ was done in 1902 by Emerich Ullmann (1861–1937), a Hungarian surgeon in Vienna. He used cannula tubes to supply the organ with blood from the donor. Alexis Carrel, with the new suture technique, "autotransplanted" animal organs like the kidney, heart and spleen, finding that they had a long life. But some unknown biological process seemed to cause the rejection of homografts.

Such immune reactions of the body were studied during the 1940s by Sir Peter Medawar (b. 1915), a biologist at the National Institute for Medical Research in London. He showed that a transplant's life was shorter in a host animal which had previously received a graft from the same donor. The same was true in a host that had been injected with white blood cells from the donor. Evidently these contained antigens which interfered with the transplant. In 1951, Medawar discovered that cortisone could increase the life, thus providing an "immunosuppressive" weapon against rejection. His work, together with Sir Frank Macfarlane Burnet (b. 1899) of Australia, won a Nobel Prize in 1960. An even better immunosuppressor, named azathioprine, was developed by R. Y. Calne in 1959. Moreover, production of antigens

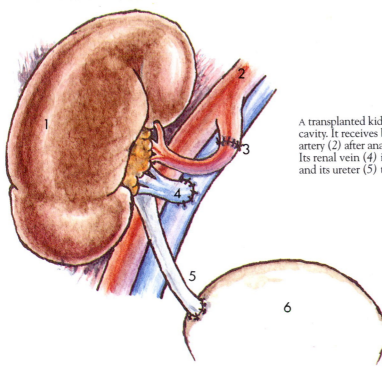

A transplanted kidney (*1*) is placed in the pelvic cavity. It receives blood from the common iliac artery (*2*) after anastomosis of its renal artery (*3*). Its renal vein (*4*) is connected to the iliac vein, and its ureter (*5*) to the bladder (*6*).

turned out to occur mainly in lymphocytes—a kind of white blood cell—and can be inhibited with antilymphocyte globulin (ALG). In 1978, Calne and his colleagues reported the first clinical results of a high-powered immunosuppressor, cyclosporine. Originally an antifungicide, it has been very useful in transplanting organs.

These experiences taught surgeons that the organs have various types of tissue, just as individuals may have different blood types. By determining the tissue types of both donor and host, a transplant is more likely to succeed—yet only identical twins can have identical tissue types. It was on two such twins that the first life-saving human kidney transplantation was done in 1954 in Boston, by Joseph Murray (b. 1919, Nobel Prize 1990) with J. Hartwell Harrison. This was extremely important as it showed that organ transplants could function perfectly in man. They next transplanted a kidney from a cadaver, opening the door to such operations on a large scale.

Up to now, the world has seen about 200,000 kidney transplants, avoiding dialysis treatment for people with chronic kidney damage and terminal uremia. Statistics differ, of course, from country to country. In Sweden, for instance, over 4,000 have been done, starting in 1964. Success depends on the choice of host and donor, being up to 90 % when the donor is a sibling or parent, but lower when the kidney comes from a recent cadaver. After ten years, 85 % of the patients are still able to work.

Human liver transplantation was begun in 1963, by Thomas Starzl in Denver. His progress report in 1981 heightened the interest in this method, and today it is well established—for adults with primary cancer or chronic inflamma-

A Frightening Future?

According to two pioneers, Sir Harold Gillies and Ralph Millard, in their book Principles and Art of Plastic Surgery *(1957), we are not far from science fiction:*

"It is terrifying to think what will happen when the mystery of organ transference has been solved; it can be as revolutionary as the cleaving of the atom. Anybody would be able to go into his local organ bank and, for a not insurmountable sum, trade in a weak heart or a feeble brain for a better one, or a cirrhotic liver for a healthier one. Vacancies after deaths on this planet would be limited to accidents, acts of war, or voyages into space."

ROY Calne, a self-portrait.

tion of the liver, and for children born with narrowed bile ducts and metabolic disturbances. In the United States, some 4,000 livers have been transplanted, lately at a rate of over 600 annually, and in Sweden the estimated need is about 100 each year. With the best modern immunosuppressive drugs, survival after a year is 70 to 80 %.

Diabetes is a chronic illness caused by deficiency of the hormone insulin, produced in islet cells of the pancreas. Young people with "juvenile" diabetes can develop a risk of serious eye and kidney damage. The countermeasure is to transplant a pancreas, usually along with a kidney, leading the pancreas juice out to the small intestine or urinary bladder. This has been done about 1,500 times worldwide, and after one year about 60 % of the patients require no extra insulin. An alternative is to transfer cultivated islet cells from aborted foetuses into the liver or spleen, which may thus start producing insulin—but the few experiments have not yet borne fruit.

The first successful human heart transplantations were done in December 1967 by Christiaan Barnard (b. 1922) in South Africa, and a month later by Norman Shumway (b. 1923) at Stanford University in California, and in May 1968 by Denton Cooley in Houston. By testing constantly for rejection and using cyclosporine to fight it, the survival rate has improved from 20 % after one year to 10 % after ten years. During the past decades, this has become a routine solution to heart failure, and works even in combination with lung transplants.

The number of new hearts grew to about 1,000 by 1977, and to 7,000 by 1987. Today nearly 2,000 more are expected each year in the United States—transplanted at some 100 hospitals, compared with 70 hospitals in Europe. Due to the good results, an ever wider range of patients will probably be accepted, although the supply of donors is a limiting factor. Efforts to develop a good enough artificial heart have met with great difficulty, and are now concentrating on pumps that help a failing left ventricle while awaiting a new heart.

Equally standard, often for children, are bone-marrow transplants, to cure a blood disease like leukemia. Healthy marrow is fed into the patient's blood, after giving chemotherapy and radiation against tumour cells and those that cause rejection. The marrow may have been taken from the patient, then frozen and cleaned of tumour cells, or else it may come from the hip-bone of another person, usually a sibling. Recently the results of these transplants have shown much improvement, reaching a survival rate of about 70%.

Further kinds of transplantation are being studied experimentally. For the small intestine, this work began on animals in the late 1950s, but has yet to solve the problems of rejection. Here the aim is to replace much of the small intestine if it must be removed, for example to stop an inflammation named after the American physician Burrill Crohn (1884–1983). Otherwise, food cannot be absorbed normally and "parenteral" (intravenous) nutrition at home is needed.

For the brain, researchers are transplanting cells from foetuses, to correct a deficiency of "signal substances" that causes brain disturbances. This might cure diseases such as those named after James Parkinson (see Chapter 9) and the German neurologist Alois Alzheimer (1864-1915), although it raises difficult ethical questions.

Handmaidens of surgery

Many other creations of modern science and technology have become invaluable aids to the surgeon. Ranging from chemicals to electronic devices, they were often developed for quite different reasons and delayed in reaching doctors. Yet they eventually inspired the rise of specialized research on "software" for medical purposes, not least in caring for the patient before and after operations.

Radiology

Surgery is least extreme when it is most exact, knowing as much as possible in advance about the ailment's nature, location, and relation to other parts of the body. But exact knowledge requires precise diagnosis, and doctors originally had to rely on their five senses. Only when "X-rays" arrived could they tell for sure whether an operation was necessary and what it would reveal.

Wilhelm Conrad von Röntgen (1845-1923), whose name was given to these rays and became the most familiar name in medicine, actually belonged to the world of physics. Educated in Holland and Switzerland, he held professorships at Strasbourg, Giessen, and Würzburg, studying heat and electricity. Having grown interested in the phosphorescence from metallic salts that are exposed to light, he made a chance observation on 8 November 1895. Experimenting with current through a vacuum in a tube, he noticed a greenish glow from a screen on a nearby shelf. It continued even when he stopped the current, and he found that the screen was painted with a phosphorescent substance. But this could not have been activated by ordinary radiation, since the room was dark.

Obsessed with the invisible rays which his tube seemed to generate, Röntgen proved that they could pass through wood, metal and other materials, unlike light and heat waves. Sometimes he noticed an image of his own hand on the phosphorescent screen. Being an avid photographer, he set up a film before the screen, laid his wife's hand on the plate, and got the world's first X-ray picture, showing both bones and wedding-ring! Weeks later, he sent a report to the scientific academy in Würzburg, On a New Kind of Radiation.

Few discoveries have spread as fast as this one. The world press scooped it up even before his initial lecture on it, at which he asked an anatomist, Rudolf von Kölliker (1817-1905), to place a hand on the film. His picture of the bones, wedding-ring and doctoral ring was welcomed by an ovation. Kölliker proposed that the rays be called "X", and they subsequently received the discoverer's name. Röntgen refused a Bavarian title, but he accepted one of the earliest Nobel Prizes in 1901, and lived on as a professor in Munich.

A Punch at X-rays

In an England which had just sent the poet Oscar Wilde to prison for a homosexual "crime" that no doctor would even call abnormal, poetry was naturally degraded into a weapon against medicine itself, by the magazine Punch in 1896:

O Röntgen, then the news is true,
and not a trick of idle rumour,
that bids us each beware of you,
and of your grim and graveyard humour.

We do not want, like Dr Swift,
to take our flesh off and to pose in
our bones, or show each little rift
and joint for you to poke your nose in.

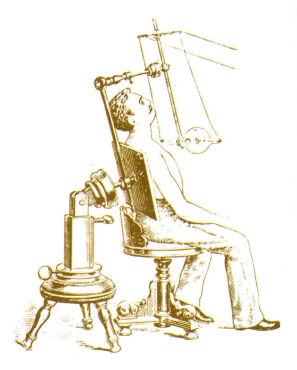

WILHELM von Röntgen—whose basic research gave rise to radiology—and an early apparatus for chest X-rays. The patient sat between the X-ray tube and the film-plate holder. In such a tube, electrons are accelerated by high voltage to strike a tungsten-metal anode and excite its atoms, which relax by emitting X-rays with great penetrating energy.

At first, doctors used X-rays to examine the skeleton, as for fractures—and to locate hard foreign objects. Even during the Spanish-American War in 1898, an X-ray apparatus stood in the front line to look for bullets. However, it was inefficient and needed a long exposure time. One soldier named McKenna had to take twenty minutes of radiation, repeated for some days! His abdomen displayed not only a bullet, but also reddening and slow-healing lesions. Thus the rays were seen to be capable of harming healthy tissue.

These tentative applications marked the beginning of diagnostic radiology. They were promoted by a breakthrough some months after Röntgen's: the discovery of "radioactive" materials that generate rays spontaneously. It earned the 1903 Nobel Prize in physics for Henri Becquerel, and for related studies by Marie and Pierre Curie, all from France.

Many more kinds of rays were gradually recognized, including electromagnetic waves (such as radio, X-ray and gamma-ray photons) as well as particles like electrons and neutrons. In time, rays of varying energy could be produced by sources ranging from low-voltage X-ray tubes to high-voltage linear accelerators or radioactive elements like cobalt. The whole world of atoms and nuclei was brought into the service of medicine.

Diagnostic rays work by being absorbed differently according to the density of organs in the

ONE of the first X-ray pictures taken by Röntgen, demonstrating how the rays were absorbed differently by soft tissue and by denser materials such as bones.

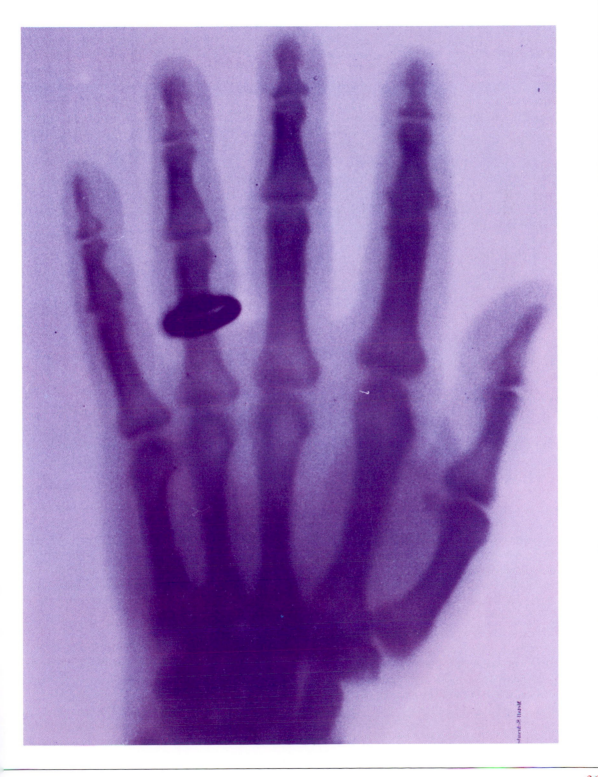

body. The picture shows clear contrast between bones and soft parts—although less contrast between the latter. Soon it was realized that soft organs could be X-rayed clearly by introducing a "contrast material" which absorbs the rays better. This enabled mammography to begin in 1913, when a German surgeon named Salomen injected a fluid into the nipples of amputated breasts, demonstrating how cancer had changed them. Mammography continued during the 1920s in Leipzig, to become accepted after 1962 when Robert Egan proved its value for diagnosing breast cancer. It no longer needs a contrast material.

An iodine contrast material was developed in 1924 by Evarts Graham and Warren Cole in America: for oral or intravenous use with X-rays, it is the oldest means of viewing the biliary and urinary tracts. Such materials can also be given to expose arterial diseases by "angiography". Barium sulphate, taken by mouth or enema, reveals the gastrointestinal tract.

Today the examinations are often done with ultrasound, and with scanning techniques like computerized tomography (CT). Similarly, radioactive and "antimatter" materials are introduced into the body, to give pictures with a gamma-ray camera. A recent innovation, magnetic resonance (MR), shows sections of the body as CT does, but it uses magnetic fields and promises greater development. Even metabolism in particular organs can be observed.

In addition, the harmful possibilities of X-rays suggested that radiation, because of its ionizing effects, could be used to kill diseased tissue. This fact gave rise, early in the twentieth century, to therapeutic radiology—or radiotherapy. Now performed at oncological clinics, it is often combined with surgery. Superficial tumours (as in skin cancer) are treated with low-energy rays, and deep ones with high energy.

Radiotherapy has been increasingly successful due to the invention of equipment with ever higher energy and precision, as well as computers to calculate safer doses. Instead of aiming rays from outside the body, a radioactive source may be placed temporarily inside it to work locally (such as radium for uterine cancer). Diagnostic and therapeutic radiology have also given rise to the new field of "interventional radiology", using special instruments inside the body to treat, for example, kidney stones and narrowed coronary vessels.

A still more powerful role of radiation, as a tool in surgery, began to emerge even in Röntgen's day. Scientists learned that electromagnetic waves heat up the absorbing tissue. The idea of cutting tissue by heating it (also a legacy of the cauterizing-iron!) was to be applied later with a short-wave radio beam, as by brain surgeons. But a great refinement was on the way. In 1917 the famous physicist Albert Einstein (1879–1955) unveiled the principle of the "laser" (light amplification by stimulated emission of radiation). This turned out to be his sole contribution to medicine, once built in America in 1960. Its waves have high energy, can be focused to a microscopic point, are perfectly sterile, and cause minimal bleeding and scarring.

Medical lasers are made mainly of carbon dioxide, argon, or materials like neodymium and YAG (yttrium-aluminium-garnet). They cut tissue rapidly by heating and coagulating it, or by producing photochemical reactions. Some of these optical "knives" or "cauters" are employed in eye surgery, while others penetrate more deeply for tumour treatment. The beam can also be aimed from inside the body with endoscopy (see below). Lasers will never fully replace the mechanical scalpel, but their uses are expanding steadily in all fields of surgery.

Chemotherapy

Dangerous substances in the body have long been fought by adding safe ones to it. No doubt the earliest human beings knew that good food helps against sickness, and the ultimate fruit of this insight is nutritional science. But we have also mentioned the long traditions of treating both external and internal ailments with herbal, animal and other natural medicines. These be-

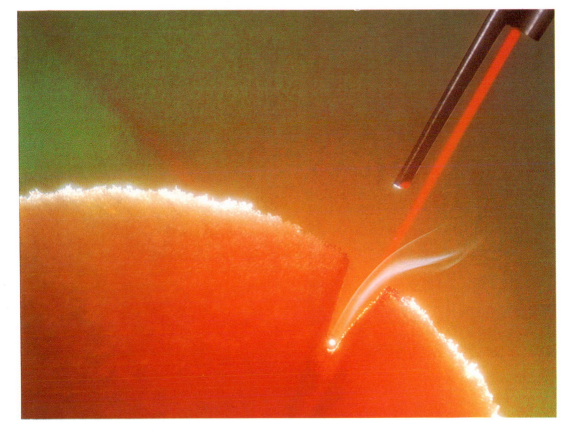

A sample of tissue being cut with a chemical carbon-dioxide laser. Its infrared light beam, less than 1 mm wide, has a power of up to 25 watts and can be sent in pulses up to one second long. This type of laser is portable and has many surgical uses, ranging from dermatology to gynaecology.

gan to be well understood only in the nineteenth century by chemists and biologists, who had the means to seek or invent more such substances.

At the same time, it was becoming clear that the newly discovered causes of infections, micro-organisms, can be combated in two ways. The body's own opposition to them may be strengthened, as by using a vaccine like Edward Jenner's (see Chapter 7). Or else they may be attacked with little or no influence on the body itself: by a "bacteriostatic" substance that prevents their growth, or by a "bactericide" that kills them, in an amount which the body can tolerate. This basic principle of "antimicrobial chemotherapy" was employed first by Paul Ehrlich (1854–1915), a German bacteriologist. He discovered a number of what he called "magic bullets", such as arsenic to treat syphilis, and thus he shared a Nobel Prize in 1908.

The next real progress came in the early 1930s. Gerhard Domagk (1888–1964), director of research at the German company of I. G. Farben in Elberfeld, had been studying the antibacterial action of various dyes. Among the "sulfanilamides", he found a red dye which protected mice from streptococcus bacteria. Rumours of it spread through town—and one day a child lay in the hospital, dying of blood poison-

PAUL Ehrlich.

GERHARD Domagk.

ing from a staphylococcus infection. There was nothing to lose by summoning Domagk, who prescribed some of his dye. The child took on a weird red colour, but revived. More dye tablets were fed, and the illness vanished!

This drug, patented in 1932 under the name of Prontosil, gained fame too quickly for Domagk. He wanted to go on testing it calmly, as was becoming the rule in the drug industry. But its success was speeded up by a new event. At a congress, he had given some of the tablets to a Baltimore doctor, Perrin Long, who used them to save a child in Boston from streptococcus. Much publicity followed—the parents were Eleanor and Franklin D. Roosevelt.

The good results were no coincidence. Prontosil and its rapidly multiplying relatives, known as "sulfa" drugs, proved to be effective against infections in wounds, lungs, the urinary tract

and other organs. Enthusiasm was enormous, and Domagk won a Nobel Prize in 1939—though the Nazis forbade him to accept it and even arrested him, so that he received it only later in 1947. By then, sulfa drugs were revealing some bad effects, such as damage to kidneys and white blood cells, while many bacteria acquired resistance to them. However, recent advances have placed them among our safest weapons against infections.

In 1928, Alexander Fleming (1881–1955) was working as a bacteriologist at St. Mary's Hospital in London. The building, which still exists, was damp and draughty. One day, mould was noticed on a plate where staphylococcus bacteria were being cultured. The story goes that Fleming remarked: "As soon as we open a plate with an old culture, something dreadful happens—it comes out of thin air." Suddenly he

ALEXANDER Fleming.

halted and, after staring for a moment, continued in his quiet voice: "That's strange…" No bacteria were growing at or near the mould spots!

Fleming inferred that the mould, *Penicillium notatum*, contained an antibacterial substance, which he called penicillin. This was to be the world's first identifiable "antibiotic", produced by micro-organisms themselves. He could do nothing with it at the time, but as World War II began in 1939, any medicine against bacteria became worth its weight in gold. A usable antibiotic, tyrothricin, was first found by René DuBos (1901–82), a French-American microbiologist. Then Howard Florey (1898–1968) from Australia, and Ernst Chain (1906–79) from Germany, discovered in England how to obtain useful amounts of penicillin.

Fleming's breakthrough was one of the most important in medical history. Along with Florey and Chain, he was knighted and won a Nobel Prize in 1945. His other honours ranged from a gold medal of the Royal College of Surgeons of England to a *doy-gei-tau* (chieftaincy) of the Kiowa tribe in America, and finally a tomb in St. Paul's Cathedral. Many serious diseases were stopped by penicillin—and it has been followed by various related substances that are even more effective, mostly "specialized" to fight particular kinds of bacteria.

Antibiotics got another boost from Selman Abraham Waksman (1888-1973). Born in the Ukraine, he immigrated to America around 1910, and moved in with a farming cousin. At college, he became fascinated with the microbes everywhere in nature and, by the late 1930s, he was a world authority on those in soil. Fleming's discovery inspired him to look for similar substances, and in 1944 he revealed streptomycin. It not only helped to provide the first real cure for tuberculosis, but also gave surgeons a pre- and post-operative treatment for the disease. He, too, received a Nobel Prize in 1952.

Since then, chemotherapy has made huge strides in fighting both infections and diseases like cancer, as with "cytotoxins" in the latter case. New drugs are produced by mainly synthetic methods, and by "engineering" techniques that change the microscopic structure of known drugs to make them more effective. Yet they cannot improve faster than our basic understanding of how the body itself becomes sick. A tragic illustration is the difficulty of developing an antidote for AIDS ("acquired immune deficiency syndrome"), which emerged as a worldwide epidemic during the 1980s.

Fluid and electrolyte treatment

Another contribution of chemistry to surgery arose from Claude Bernard's principle of homoeostasis, the necessary balance between organs in the body (see Chapter 7). This was found to be true for the mixture of water and charged "electrolyte" elements that regulate the processes in our bodies. Many diseases, injuries and operations cause dangerous imbalance, as the body loses liquid and elements like potassium, magnesium, sodium and chlorine.

The last two make up common salt, which is the oldest medicine used to compensate for such losses and restore the fluid balance. Some patients were injected with salt in the nineteenth century, especially for cholera—and wounded soldiers were given a salt solution during World War I. But this was insufficient, since the solution passed through the body without increasing its amount of blood for long. When much blood has been lost, resulting in "surgical shock", survival depends on having enough blood in circulation. Therefore, an addition of blood is essential, relying on methods of transfusion (see Chapter 5).

Blood transfusion is still the best treatment for this kind of shock. Sometimes, however, time is too short for determining the patient's blood type and getting it from a blood bank. So the next step was to add "plasma", blood from which the cells have been removed, and which need not be typed. Even handier was the invention of plasma substitutes—fluids that behave similarly and stay in the blood system without "leaking" away. The most common of these is dextran, a derivative of sugar, developed in Sweden by Anders Grönwall and Björn Ingelman in 1944.

Today, a veritable arsenal of substitutes is at the disposal of surgeons and anaesthetists. They include nutrients like glycose, amino acids that build proteins, and fats that can go directly into the bloodstream. By analyzing the blood composition, one can decide what is required to get the body in balance. Water, calories and other supplements may be given intravenously before, during, and/or after operation, particularly when the patient cannot eat or drink. In extreme cases, this is continued in an intensive-care ward. Such methods are also used in emergency wards, to save victims of traumatic accidents and shock from multiple-organ failure.

Endoscopy

Whether or not chemicals inside the body can heal it, doctors have long wanted to look inside it, at least when diagnosing ailments. Endoscopy, or internal inspection, began when the ancients inserted tubes in the rectum. Better instruments appeared in the last century, such as the cystoscopes invented by Bozzini and Nitze (see Chapter 9) and Garcia's laryngoscope (Chapter 8). In 1851, a great German physicist and physiologist, Hermann von Helmholtz (1821–94), invented the "ophthalmoscope" to study the interior of the eye itself.

An "oesophagoscope" came in 1868 from John Bevan in England, enabling foreign objects in the oesophagus to be removed. That year, too, the first "gastroscopy" of the stomach was done by an assistant to Adolf Kussmaul (1822–1902), a medical professor in Freiburg. He per-

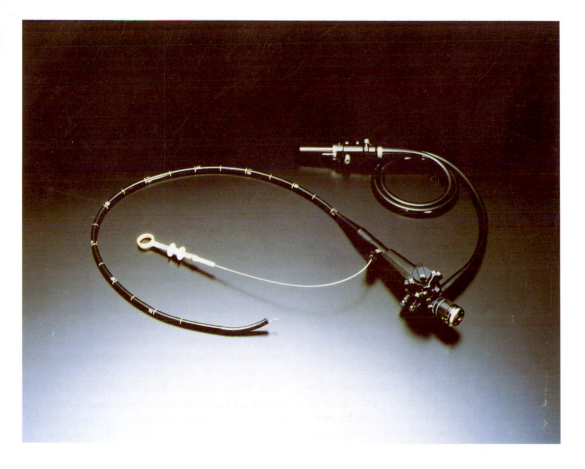

(ABOVE) A "fibrescope" for examining the upper gastrointestinal tract. The flexible insertion tube (at lower left) is over 1 metre long and contains 40,000 light-transmitting fibres. Its tip has two openings for light, and a lens to receive the reflections, which travel back along the tube to the viewing end. There are also an outlet for air or water, and a channel for suction or for insertion of biopsy forceps.

(*Right*) A gastric ulcer in the lower part of the stomach, as seen through the fibrescope.

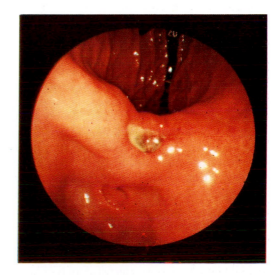

suaded a professional sword-swallower to take in a pipe, nearly half a metre long, equipped with a lamp and lenses! By 1881, the renowned Mikulicz-Radecki (see Chapter 9) provided these kinds of inspection with a practical instrument as well as a classic textbook. At the other end of the food canal, an American surgeon, Howard Kelly (1858–1943), launched a "rectoscope" in 1895 which, with few changes, is still employed today.

At the turn of the century, gynaecologists adopted such instruments for looking into the abdomen, a method generally called "laparoscopy". Similar attention was drawn to the pleural cavity by a "thoracoscope" which Hans Christian Jacobæus (1879–1937), a Swedish physician, constructed in 1911. He used it for tuberculosis therapy, when loosening the adhesions around the lungs. A subsequent innovation is "bronchoscopy", to diagnose and treat, for example, tumours in the bronchi and lungs. Eric Carlens, another Swede, developed the technique of "mediastinoscopy", with which lung cancer has been investigated during the past thirty years.

The early gastroscopes were stiff, and caused the patient much discomfort, if not internal injury. But in 1932, with help from the Berlin instrument-maker Georg Wolf, a bending gastroscope was presented by a German named Rudolf Schindler. He published a remarkable book on the subject in 1923 and, in 1934, would emigrate to work in America as a gastroenterologist. Also in the latter field was Basil Hirschowitz, a South African who moved to Michigan and, in 1958, spearheaded the introduction of a completely flexible gastroscope. This made use of glass-fibre optics, developed in the 1930s for sending light through a tube by total internal reflection.

Many such endoscopic devices have since been created, notably in the United States and Japan. Some include a tiny camera, tongs to take samples for biopsy tests, electrical tools or lasers to coagulate bleeding. The whole digestive tract is open to fibre techniques. Although "entero-scopy" of the small intestine is rather unusual, doctors learned in the late 1960s how to view its upper section by "duodenoscopy", and the large intestine by "coloscopy". In this region, both diagnosis and therapy can be performed on tumours and inflammations, with internal instruments that often avoid extensive surgery.

Thus, methods of looking into the body have led to treating it with the same devices. A further area of use is the liver, biliary tract and pancreas. In 1939, Clarence Crafoord and Paul Frenckner—whom we have already mentioned—showed that a substance can be injected endoscopically to stop varicose bleeding in the oesophagus, caused by cirrhosis of the liver. This procedure has recently experienced a renaissance and is now standard. In 1970 came a Japanese technique called ERCP (endoscopic retrograde colangiopancreaticography) for coping with biliary-tract and pancreas diseases. Likewise, such instruments are commonly used in the urinary tract, as for X-raying the kidneys and ureter (pyelography), or treating tumours and crushing bladder stones (see Chapter 9).

Other specialties

Besides those relatively traditional fields which make up general surgery, several branches of medicine—with their own kinds of operations—have entered our story, and are progressing rapidly today. They deal mainly with women and children, the musculoskeletal structure, and some important parts of our upper bodies: the teeth, eyes, ears, nose and throat.

Obstetrics and gynaecology

Responsibility was long left to midwives (Latin *obstetrix*) for childbirth, and to the woman herself (Greek *gyne*) for healthy female reproductive organs. As we know, ancient and medieval medicine threw some light on these subjects, but obstetrics remained in the hands of family doctors until recently, and gynaecology was at first a separate field for general surgeons. The two specialties began to merge in the wake of pioneers like Semmelweis and Scanzoni, and today both types of in-patient care are practised at women's clinics.

Obstetrics gave up the "wait and see" habit for an active role in the 1950s, when it was realized that the mortality rate of mothers—and of infants, still at least 3%—increased rapidly after twenty-four hours of labour. The rule is now to complete a delivery sooner, leading to more use of Caesarean operations and vaginal techniques. Forceps have become almost needless since the Swedish obstetrician Tage Malmström, in 1957, introduced "vacuum extraction" which is safer for the baby.

Other improvements are pregnancy health care, ultrasound to check foetal development, better anaesthetics during delivery, and devices for keeping watch on the baby. Thus, in advanced countries, mortality has sunk nearly to zero for the mother—and to less than 1% for the baby around the time of birth, which is the special interest of "perinatologists".

Gynaecology involves surgical work to treat, for example, tumours that are usually confined to the uterus and the ovaries. In the cervix, "precancerous" changes can be diagnosed early by health checks, and nearly always cured by local treatment with conization and laser techniques. The five-year survival rate is up to 90% after radical surgery for cancer of the uterus alone, although lower for ovarian cancer since it often spreads farther before being detected. For advanced cancer, radiotherapy and chemotherapy are also employed.

The gynaecologist is equally concerned with genital infections, contraception and infertility, legal abortions, menstrual and climacteric problems. One of the latest developments—for a woman whose Fallopian tubes cannot transport the egg to the uterus—is to take an egg from the ovary, fertilize it with the father's sperm in an artificial environment (*in vitro*), and implant it in the uterus for normal birth.

Paediatric surgery

Medicine for the child (Greek *pais*) has been even more restricted to recent times, and humane places, in which the young are no longer ignored and exploited. A Swedish professor of practical medicine in Uppsala, Nils Rosén von Rosenstein (1706-73), was the "father of paediatrics" who published the world's first text book about it, *Advice on Children's Diseases and Their Remedies* (1765). This earned a wide audience and was translated into most European languages.

Rosén's country established a professorship of child medicine as early as 1845, and began to distinguish surgical ailments from other children's illnesses over a hundred years ago, founding departments of child surgery at Stockholm in 1876 and Gothenburg in 1894. During the twentieth century, paediatric surgery everywhere came to include all operations on people under the age of sixteen. These range from birth defects to general complaints like acute appendicitis, hernias and fractures.

Children differ from adults as regards the causation, progress and pathophysiology of diseases. With cancer, for instance, the types of original cells and affected organs tend to be different in children. One deadly tumour, named after the German surgeon Max Wilms (1867-1918), grows in the kidney from embryo tissue and appears most frequently at the age of two. Yet the commonest malignancy in children, acute lymphoblastic leukemia, can now often be controlled with chemotherapy and bone-marrow transplantation. In children as well as adults, mortality has reduced drastically with use of antibiotics, fluid and electrolyte treatment, for example in acute abdominal diseases. Appendicital peritonitis, once a familiar cause of death in schoolchildren, now claims almost none.

Accidents, too, are of different kinds in children. The skeleton is damaged in characteristic ways, and its growth must be taken into account when repairing bone fractures. About 10% of child accidents are serious and, in countries like the United States, they dominate the death statistics up to age 14.

Some congenital defects are inherited, while others result from environmental factors—such as drugs, alcohol or nicotine which the mother passes to the foetus. Discoveries since the 1950s, as in the science of genetics, have begun to show how defects arise and made it possible to detect and treat many of them at an early stage. In surgery, they often call for special techniques of intensive care which are improving greatly today.

Orthopaedics

The ancient ideal of an erect child (Greek *orthos pais*) was an initial inspiration for correcting problems in the skeletal system and related parts of the body. For example, the writings of Hippocrates described manoeuvres for treating a congenital clubfoot and stretching a scoliotic (curved) spine. But orthopaedics as a specialty was founded and named by Nicolas Andry (1658–1742), a medical professor in Paris. He produced its first basic book in 1741, and symbolized it by a straight pole supporting a bent tree-trunk, which still belongs to its emblem.

The aim was then to relieve such deformities in children with various kinds of bandages and prostheses. Whereas Andry met opposition from surgeons at the time, orthopaedics was becoming closely associated with surgery—also for adults—by the nineteenth century, due to clearer knowledge of bones and muscles, as well as to the need for amputations (see Chapter 8). The old method of "osteosynthesis", rejoining broken bones with mechanical devices, was updated in 1877 by Lister, with metal wire to fix kneecaps. What we now call orthopaedic surgery has a wide range, yet deals mostly with fractures, joint damage, and other problems taken over from general surgery.

Much of the work on fractures is at the femoral neck in the hip joint. Fractures here are increasingly frequent, notably in ageing women with brittle bones (osteoporosis). A flanged nail to unite the bone ends was developed in 1925 by Marius Smith-Petersen (1886–1953) in Boston. Only seven years later, Sven Johansson (1880–

1959) in Gothenburg, Sweden, added a drilling technique to avoid exposing the hip joint, and it soon became a worldwide routine. Seven years after that, a German surgeon, Gerhard Küntscher, invented a nail to be placed inside the bone marrow, for instance in fractures of the leg—something which had apparently already been tried by the Aztecs (see Chapter 1).

Hand surgery grew into a separate field during the early 1940s. Among its main concerns is

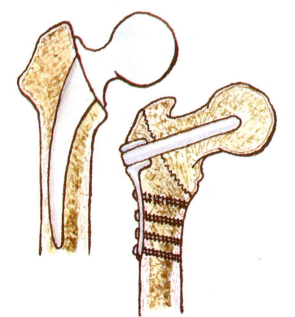

(LEFT) The symbol of orthopaedics, as shown in Nicolas Andry's two-volume *Orthopédie* (1741). (*Above*) Common orthopaedic operations on the hip joint: a prosthesis placed in the top of the femur (at left), and a flanged nail inserted to fix a fracture in the femoral neck (at right).

rheumatoid arthritis, a chronic inflammation which causes pain and distortion in the joints. Degenerative diseases of the hip and knee (arthrosis), especially in old people, have led to "arthroplasty", the partial or total replacement of joints by artificial ones. This began rather unsuccessfully in the 1890s, but prostheses made of plastic, metal and ceramics have improved steadily since the 1950s. As the aged become more numerous in society, we can expect a continuing expansion of such active orthopaedic surgery.

Odontology

That multiple utensil in our jaws, the tooth (Greek *odontos*), has always been exposed to wear, injury, infection and loosening. Clever repairs of teeth were done even in prehistory, ranging from Stone Age Egypt and Denmark to Etruscan Italy—using gold wire, crude drills, bridges, or ivory substitutes. Originally practised by doctors, the dentist's art has gained ever more independent status. Schools of dentistry arose in America from 1840 onward, and in Europe a little later.

Today there are numerous subspecialties, such as oral surgery, periodontics (for loose teeth), orthodontics (straightening the teeth), prosthodontics (false teeth), and paedodontics (children's tooth and mouth diseases). Besides common tooth decay (caries), the oral surgeon may operate on diseases around the teeth or in the jaws, and may help plastic surgeons to remedy lip or palate defects.

Tooth prostheses are constantly being refined with new methods and materials. It was only twenty years ago that a Swedish professor, Per Ingvar Brånemark, launched the use of titanium screws to anchor a bridge on the jawbone. Such implanted attachments have opened the door to extensive reconstruction in dentistry, as well as in other fields such as surgery of the ears, nose and joints.

Ophthalmology

As we have noted in cases of cataract and glaucoma, the eye (Greek *ophthalmos*) is one of surgery's oldest interests. But its functions could not be well understood until the seventeenth century brought discoveries in optics, such as those of the great physicist Isaac Newton (1642–1727). Eye diseases were next put on a scientific basis in France, when Pierre Brisseau explained cataracts by a clouding of the eye's lens (1708), and Jacques Daviel showed how to extract the lens (1752).

A hundred years later, ophthalmology developed into a surgical specialty. Its founder, Albrecht von Graefe (1828–70), was a professor in Berlin. He improved the cataract operation and, in 1856, began to treat glaucoma by "iridectomy", cutting the iris to lower the pressure in the eye. Helmholtz's invention of the ophthalmoscope for diagnosis, and Koller's use

THE traditional cataract operation was one of many detailed illustrations in the first book on eye surgery, *Ophthalmodouleia* (Eye Work) by Georg Bartisch, published in Dresden in 1583.

of cocaine as a local anaesthetic (see Chapter 7), were revolutionary advances. Eye clinics started in the late 1800s on both sides of the Atlantic.

During the 1920s, clouding of the cornea was first treated by transplantation, and the Swiss surgeon Jules Gonin (1870–1935) introduced thermocautery to repair detached retinas, usually in nearsighted people. The latter operation creates an inflammatory adhesion, now with better techniques of extreme cold (cryosurgery) and, as already mentioned, the laser. Since the 1950s, lasers have been widely adopted in ophthalmology—and so has the "operating microscope", with which most work is done today. Cataracts, the leading cause of deteriorating eyesight in the old, can be treated by replacing the lens with a plastic one.

Otorhinolaryngology

The ear, nose and throat (Greek *ous, rhis, larynx*) were initially separate topics in medicine. By the nineteenth century, physicists turned traditional theories about sound, like those of Pythagoras, into the new science of acoustics, which helps to explain how we hear and speak—just as chemistry was coming to grips with our sense of smell. Then physiologists and doctors in France and Great Britain made real progress towards understanding these organs. Along with Garcia's laryngoscope, "otoscopes" for direct examination were invented by ear experts, such as Joseph Toynbee (1815–66) and Emil Siegle (1833–1900).

A combined specialty of otorhinolaryngology thus emerged around 1900. Its first professor in Sweden, Gunnar Holmgren (1875–1954), was a pioneer of the operating microscope in 1923. This development would find other important "microsurgical" applications too, as we have seen. Until the 1940s and 1950s, operations were often needed to treat infections in the ears, throat, nose and sinuses. Ear complications still had a particularly high mortality rate. But with the advent of antibiotics to cure most infections, extensive acute surgery has become rare.

The specialty now includes operations on tumours in such areas as the mouth, tongue, larynx and salivary glands, making up nearly half of the activity at university clinics. Work is done on traumatic face injuries, and on reconstructions as of the middle ear (tympanoplasty). Diseases like otosclerosis (ear-bone hardening), a common reason for deafness in adults, can be treated surgically to restore normal sensations as a rule. The old ear-trumpet has given way to electronic hearing aids, some being implanted in the inner ear. Related fields for preventing and correcting defects are audiology (in hearing) and phoniatrics (in speech).

Surgery in the future

Looking back on all that has happened in the history of surgery, it may seem impossible to predict what will happen soon. Yet one principle is plain enough. Surgery tries to solve problems that depend on the body (our genes and life-style) or on the surroundings (how they can weaken, infect and injure us). Success is a balance between the resources for solution—science, technology, and personnel—and the problems as they change with time. Today we face a potential or certain increase in many such problems, and surgery must develop in order to catch up, or keep up, with them.

In the "advanced" world, apart from cardio-vascular diseases, the main danger is cancer. It accounts for a quarter of all deaths, and up to 40 % of all surgery. About 65 % of cancers occur in people over 65, who—largely due to medical progress itself—are becoming an ever greater fraction of the population. This means more cancer, and other conditions that demand surgery are also more frequent with rising age. Whether adequate care can be provided for the elderly is an important question of geriatrics.

Cancer research is a vast field and often produces fundamental findings, but they are not immediately applicable to large numbers of patients. The commonest kinds of cancer do not exhibit clearly higher survival rates with the methods of treatment already described, including chemotherapy and radiation. More surgery will be needed to reduce the "tumour burden" in those awaiting further treatment.

However, some kinds of cancer have shown much improvement, as in the blood (acute leukemia), testicles, and lymph nodes (Hodgkin's disease). Recent discoveries, like special cancer genes in cells, "monoclonal antibodies" against tumours, and the body's own immunizing processes, hold additional promise. Early diagnosis is essential, and it can be promoted by the "screening" of cancer-risk groups, as with mammography or the observation of occult blood in faeces. The analysis of "tumour marker" substances in the blood is not specific enough for this purpose, though helpful in tracing cancer recurrences after operation.

In sum, the war on cancer may not end with a total breakthrough, but decline with a complex system of self-defence. We now know that much cancer is caused by life-style and environmental factors. It should therefore be reduced through health information, avoidance of tobacco or poor food, and less exposure to radioactivity.

Similar prevention is required for another problem—the abuse of alcohol. This is a huge socioeconomic burden, and an overconsumer of health care, notably in surgery. Alcoholism might lie behind a variety of illnesses, and definitely results in diseases like liver cirrhosis and pancreas inflammation, as well as in serious accidents.

The latter also remind us of the worldwide shortage of emergency facilities for mass disasters, and for epidemics such as AIDS, which usually have social causes. Medical care as a whole is bad or declining in many places, and advanced surgery is still a luxury unknown to most of mankind. Society must provide more money to solve these problems, surprising as they are in the light of our story of past progress.

Among the specialties that will probably go on expanding are oncological, reconstructive, transplantation and trauma surgery. One reason is the growing proportion of old people who need new body parts. Implants and prostheses are increasingly made of "friendly" metal alloys and other materials, due to advancing knowledge of surface chemistry and tissue reactions.

Equally useful to orthopaedic, thoracic, vascular and dental surgeons, these last innovations illustrate how the benefits are spread through close relationships between fields. At the same time, operations in some areas will become ever less "invasive" as they adopt techniques like endoscopy and the laser.

Sophisticated medical equipment is, perhaps, the best sign that surgery—which began as a manual and magical art—has matured into an integral aspect of science and technology. The revelations and inventions of those who seek and apply the truth about nature may have many purposes, ranging from earthbound laboratories to outer space. But they will always affect the ability of surgeons, and indeed all physicians, to maintain and improve the life of mankind.

Recent advances

As we have seen, surgery has evolved over the period of recorded history from the mystical trepanning of skulls to let out evil spirits and the draining of blood to treat all manner of diseases, including anaemia, into a well-developed science-based discipline. Surgery has always been particularly successful in draining pus from abscesses and in removing shattered limbs and painful stones. In modern times the relief of obstruction has saved many lives. Conditions treated include obstruction to flow in the bowel, malfunction of the kidneys, blocked blood vessels, cataracts which obscure the light passing to the retina, wax in the ears, enlarged adenoids and tonsils blocking the airways and interfering with swallowing. In addition, surgery has long been used to remove a foetus by Caesarean section when the normal outlet from the womb is blocked.

Harvey's demonstration of the circulation of the blood was the single most important biological discovery to influence surgery. We can replace lost blood and other tissue fluids, provide nutrition through a vein for a person whose gut is not functioning, and support the lungs, the heart and the kidneys by artificial means. And, although it is unrewarding to make predictions, the current trends point the way in which surgery is moving, and moving very fast. Two of the main branches of current surgical advance are endoscopic procedures and spare parts.

Endoscopic procedures

Minimal Invasive Surgery is the official name for what could also be termed OK surgery—Orifice and Keyhole surgery. New instruments permit the most extraordinary manipulations either via natural orifices, such as the mouth, anus, vagina and urethra, or through very small surgically made incisions. These developments have depended on miniaturisation, on design improvements introducing a bright flexible light source to the area of the operation, and on micro-precision instruments. There needs to be space in which the instrument can be manipulated. This may be natural, such as the vitreous humour of the eye or the synovial fluids of joints. Or it may be artificially expanded, for example, by introducing carbon dioxide gas into the abdominal cavity called a pneumo-peritoneum, providing an artificial cavern in which the light and the instruments can be directed at the site of intervention.

Besides having both light and instruments, a surgeon must be able to see what is happening. This requires a movable telescope connected to a high-resolution colour television monitor. Instead of the traditional surgical approach of feeling and seeing the operation areas directly, a magnified and often beautiful image is projected on the screen, and everybody in the operating-room can see what is happening as a dynamic film show. This can be projected at a distance so that it is possible to teach or obtain advice between widely separated institutions.

There are, however, some disadvantages. At present, the projection is two-dimensional in contrast to normal three-dimensional vision and manipulation. So the surgeon has to learn to use the micro-instruments in the three-dimensional manner but with information that is two-dimensional. This requires special training, and at first it is difficult because normal depth perception is lost. In the past decade there have been advances in microsurgery in all parts of the body, particularly in the eyes and ears but also in the chest, abdomen, and many joints of the body. A surgeon can operate on the retina for a detachment and other damage, the inner ear to restore hearing by insertion of electrodes in the most delicate part of the ear, or the chest to assess the operability of tumours, to clear the air passages and to cut small sympathetic nerves which can relieve arterial spasm.

In the abdomen, gynaecologists have used laparoscopy for many years to examine and operate on the ovaries and the Fallopian tubes, and now to remove ova for ex vivo fertilisation. In 1987, a French gynaecologist named Mouret, skilled in laparoscopy, noted in one of his patients that the gall bladder was full of stones.

He thought it best to remove this and started a revolution in the management of gall bladder disease, which is one of the most common indications for elective abdominal surgery. Today there is no organ in the abdomen that surgeons have not approached laparoscopically. In addition, tumours can be removed through natural orifices and disease can be accurately assessed without the need for exploratory operations.

There is, however, some danger in the enthusiasm for laparoscopic procedures. Cynical critics have said that the very fact that an operation can be done safely and simply by traditional methods is a challenge to the minimal invasive surgeon to do it by techniques that may be expensive and dangerous. This approach is encouraged by instrument-makers who have earned fortunes by devising the new precise and costly equipment. Non-medical popular magazines respond initially with rapturous hyperbole to the new advances, but if complications occur there is a retreat to vicious criticism, so the surgeon must be doubly careful and proceed in a responsible manner.

Surgery has been revolutionised by modern imaging techniques. Normal or diseased anatomy can often be displayed without hurting the patient by scanning techniques, particularly by computerised tomography and magnetic resonance. Design advances in the machines used are occurring with spectacular speed. For many conditions where a clinical diagnosis might be difficult and require great experience and skill, the whole anatomy and pathology can now be shown to the surgeon, providing facilities similar to puzzles which state "cut along the dotted line". Minimal invasive surgery is also moving quickly in terms of radiological techniques, often performed by physicians or radiologists. Bleeding arteries can be plugged from the inside, blocked arteries can be dilated, abscesses in anatomically obscure situations can be drained under visual control using a scanner. A whole new area of procedures that previously could not be done at all, or called for major surgery, can be accomplished on a day-case basis.

Spare-part surgery

Spare parts fall into two categories. One is the inanimate scaffold, often with an important mechanical function, such as an artificial joint. The other is a living organ or tissue needing an essential arterial blood supply and venous drainage.

As we have seen, artificial teeth have been used since pre-Roman times. Now, with modern dental techniques, teeth are preserved as long as possible and then can be replaced with functioning dentures or even direct implantation into the bone of the jaw. The latter procedure is expensive and may be painful, but avoids dentures. Similarly, plastic lenses are used to substitute for opaque cataract lenses when they are removed, and usually the patient no longer needs thick spectacles after this operation. Bone, plastic or metallic implants can be used to repair deformities, both those which occur naturally and those resulting from trauma.

Joint replacement has become one of the most important fields in orthopaedic surgery; as the population gets older, ever more joints will need replacement. The materials used to construct a joint must be strong, and have the right function in terms of movement. Joints also need to be constructed in a way that will permit a close bonding to the patient's own tissues, in some cases with the use of cement. Alternatively they need to allow the patient's own tissues to grow through a porous junctional portion supporting the joint. Hips and knees can be successfully replaced by artificial mechanical joints, and there have been major advances in replacing small joints of the hand for patients crippled by arthritis.

In the ear, replacement of the ossicles that transmit the vibrations has been achieved with artificial ossicles, and electrodes have been introduced into the inner ear which are connected to sound receptors that transmit a signal to the inner ear and then to the brain. It is likely that there will be advances in this type of approach for the treatment of certain forms of blindness, by inserting electrodes directly into the sight-processing part of the brain with a light-sensitive receiver as a substitute for the eye. There will undoubtedly also be advances in artificial limbs giving more control, mobility and power.

Transplantation surgery has developed from nothing to a major sector of surgery in the past thirty years. The first living tissue to be transplanted successfully was the thin epithelium of the cornea, which is remarkably free from rejection. Unfortunately, rejection is the cause of failure of unmodified grafts of skin, bone marrow and organs. Surgical techniques have been successfully developed for the process of transplanting all the vital organs apart from the brain. Even in the brain, certain cells that produce local hormones have been used for treatment of Parkinson's disease. Bone marrow transplant is also a form of cell transplant. The marrow from the donor, injected in a vein of the recipient, homes to the bone marrow area of the recipient like a homing pigeon – always going to the right place, where it rapidly sets up house and produces new red and white blood cells and platelets.

The kidney was the first organ to be transplanted successfully. The surgery is straight forward, joining one artery, one vein, and a draining ureter for the urine. The identical twin transplants (see page 261) show that, if the surgery was done expeditiously, a perfect long-term result should be expected. However, most people do not have the luxury of an identical twin who is healthy and able to give an organ. In all other cases the immune system requires suppression, and all agents used so far are "double-edged swords". Some impairment of the patient's normal protection against infection by bacteria, funghi and viruses is a by-product of suppression of the immune system, if it is to be effective. There is also interference with surveillance against certain tumours developing.

Thus, many patients have to walk along a sharp knife edge between too little immuno-suppression with graft rejection and too much with infection or malignancy. Progress is now being made to broaden that knife edge, by the

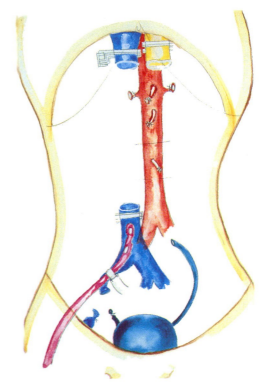

THE empty abdomen after removal of a patient's diseased organs. The oesophagus is divided and clamped; the vena cava has been removed with the liver, as well as the kidney, pancreas and remnants of the small bowel.

use of tissue-typing to produce as good a match between donor and recipient as possible (even if there is no identical twin), and by developing better drugs to stop rejection. To date, immunosuppresive agents have fitted into two categories. First, drugs which interfere with cell division and therefore can have toxic side-effects; and, secondly, antibodies directed against lymphocytes. These antibodies are now becoming more effective and easier to control, but they can only be given for a short period of time before the patient produces antibodies against them.

The complicated biology of tissue transplantation is slowly being unravelled, but it lags far behind the successful surgery of organ grafting. The aim of transplant surgeons is to

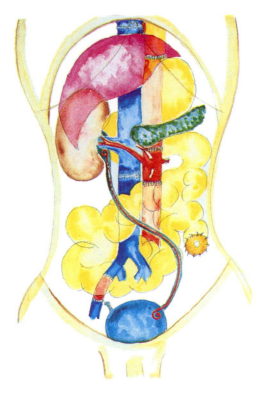

DIAGRAM of the multi-visceral transplant of stomach, duodenum, small intestine, pancreas, kidney and liver.

to be the next major advance in organ transplantation.

The very success of organ transplantation has created a new dilemma: there are not enough organs available for those needing transplants. Although a living, related donor can provide bone marrow, a kidney and, in exceptional cases, a portion of the liver or lung, donors may be of the wrong blood group or a bad tissue type or, for various reasons, may not wish to donate. In most cases there is not a suitable living, related donor. The possibility of using an organ from an unrelated donor has therefore been explored, and it has been felt that donation from husband to wife can be accepted. No doubt lawyers will reap the benefits of subsequent inevitable divorces. New ethical questions arise which are not appropriate for consideration in this book but are very important. For example, the International Transplantation Society considers it unethical to pay donors for organs, or to use organs from executed criminals. Organ donation from cadavers would seem to be ethically far more acceptable, but again there are worries. Organs from most recently deceased people are unsuitable for transplantation, because infection or malignancy could spread to the recipient. Patients who have died from head injuries or brain haemorrhage are the usual sources of organs for donation.

Experienced neurologists and neurosurgeons have described the steps that must be taken to show that the brain stem, which connects the brain to the rest of the body, has been destroyed irreversibly. The patient will have a heartbeat maintained because the lungs are mechanically ventilated, but should be regarded as dead. Artificial ventilation should be stopped, since ventilating a corpse does not benefit the individual and can cause great distress for the relatives and doctors involved. After demonstrating that the brain stem is irreversibly destroyed and that the mechanical ventilation should be stopped, it is necessary to obtain permission from the relatives for organ removal. The requirements for obtaining permission will

overcome rejection in a specific manner, rather analogous to desensitising somebody suffering from an allergy by using small quantities of the allergenic pollen to produce a specific desensitisation. The liver is an organ which seems to be able to do this in some animals and some human patients. A few liver transplant patients have stopped continuous immunosuppression without rejection occurring. This, however, has been exceptional and most patients who have stopped taking their drugs have rejected their grafts. Nevertheless, it may be expected that the production of specific immunological tolerance or "almost tolerance" (whereby the patient would require only a very small non-toxic maintenance dose of the drug) is going

SKETCH of the patient one month after operation, recovering steadily.

THE patient six months after operation, at home eating normally, with all grafted organs functioning well.

depend on the law of the land, and on the general principle of medical ethics that one should not cause distress to bereaved relatives. The unfortunate fact is that there will never be enough human organs for the recipients requiring them, and the shortage will be relatively more severe as the results of organ trans-

plantation improve. Hence there is great interest in the possibility of transplanting organs from animals to man, termed "xenografts". As man is a primate, the nearest relatives to man are other primates. The closest is the chimpanzee, yet this is an endangered species and cannot be used for organ donation. More suitable would be baboons, but they do not grow very large and a baboon's heart, for example, would not be big enough for an adult man. There is also a worry, in all potential grafts from animals to man, that animal infections might be passed on. It is thought that the AIDS virus may have originated in monkeys and spread to man. Similarly, recent concern over bovine spongiform encephalitis (BSE) shows that even species which have been in close contact with man for thousands of years may remain a source of danger. Immunosuppression of the recipient would, in theory, increase the dangers.

From a surgical point of view, the pig would be a very suitable donor. Organs of any size can be obtained; and pigs can be reared in very clean pathogen-free environments. However, the pig and man have been separated evolutionarily for millions of years. Thus, while the organs look quite similar, the structures of pig and human proteins are different – although sometimes the structure is very close between the two species, as in the case of insulin. The normal lifespan of a pig is about fifteen years, and we do not know whether its organs would have a physiological function for longer than that, even if rejection could be avoided. Still, there have been important recent advances in preventing the immediate rejection that occurs because all human blood contains antibodies which fight against pig proteins. It is likely that in the next few years there will be considerable advances in the science of xenografting.

The mismatch between demand and resources

No matter how rich a country is in financial terms, the funds available for health care are not unlimited. All the advances that have been mentioned in this section are expensive, some exceedingly so. Therefore the public and elected governments (in the case of democracies) or ruling powers (in other regimes) will have to decide on priorities, and some form of rationing is inevitable. The idea of rationing is hated by politicians, so there is a tendency to throw the burden of distribution and the arrangement of priorities onto the shoulders of doctors, and then to criticise them for whatever decisions they make. This is a problem on which the views of the whole community should be taken into account, not just those of the medical profession. Surgeons can and should contribute to the decision-making, but should not be made solely responsible for these very serious allocations of resources.

There has been talk of withholding treatment for patients with self-inflicted wounds or diseases. Examples are diseases due to smoking; road traffic accident victims who have been intoxicated, driving recklessly, or involved in criminal activity; and patients with liver disease due to alcohol. A doctor motivated by the Hippocratic ethic should do the best that is possible for a patient who comes for help, irrespective of the place of the patient in society or other personal considerations. It may be difficult to offer the best available treatment to a drunken driver who has killed young children waiting at a school bus stop, or to somebody injured in the course of committing murder. The decision of whom to treat and what type of treatment can be offered should surely be taken by society. The doctor is required by traditional medical ethics to do what is best, with the facilities available, for the patient who has come for help. Society is responsible for making the facilities available.

Surgery through the ages

Many of the leading names in our chronicle are shown here at the times of which they were typical. This generally indicates how medical knowledge has developed and spread in the advanced countries that we know most about.

3000 BC			Imhotep
2000 BC		(Minoans)	
			Hammurabi
			Moses
			Vedas
1000 BC			*Nei Ching*
		Homer	
		Alkmaion	
500 BC		Hippocrates	*Susruta*
		Aristotle	
			Herophilos
			Erasistratos
0		Celsus	Dioscorides
			Soranos
		Galen	Aretaios	Hua To
			Oribasius
		Fabiola	
500			Alexander
			Aetius
			Paul of Aegina
			Hunayn
			Rhazes
1000	Albucasis		Avicenna
		Constantine	
	Avenzoar		

Signs of progress

(see encircled numbers, 1600s—1900s)

1
- Descriptive anatomy
- Blood circulation
- Obstetrical instruments

2
- Development of microscopy
- Beginnings of surgical science
- Vaccination

3
- Scientific bacteriology
- Antiseptic and aseptic surgery
- Anaesthesia

4
- Blood transfusion
- X-rays and radiology
- Antibiotics
- Controlled ventilation
- of the lungs during chest surgery
- Joining of bowel and blood vessels and of nerves
- The heart-lung machine
- Dialysis
- Minimal invasive surgery
- Organ transplantation

Year					
1200					Roger of Salerno
				Lanfranc	
				Mondeville	
				Chauliac	
			John of Arderne		
1400					
		(Aztecs)			Branca
				Pfolspeundt	
		(Incas)			Leoniceno
			Linacre		Benivieni
1500				Paracelsus	
				Gersdorff	
			Vicary	Fernel	Colombo
				Paré	Vesalius
			Chamberlain		Tagliacozzi
1600	①			Hildanus	Aquapendente
			Harvey	Scultetus	
			Willis		Severino
			Wiseman		
			Lower		Lancisi
1700	②			Petit	
			Cheselden	Heister	
			Monro	Haller	Morgagni
			Pott	Acrel	Nannoni
		Shippen	Hunter	Desault	Scarpa
1800	③	Rush	Jenner	Larrey	Monteggia
		McDowell	Abernethy	Laennec	Rolando
		Beaumont	Bell	Dupuytren	
		Physick	Cooper	Langenbeck	
		Holmes	Liston	Rokitansky	
		Warren	Nightingale	Virchow	
		Sims	Syme	Pasteur	
		Fitz	Lister	Billroth	
		Halsted	Treves	Mikulicz	
		Mayo	Horsley	Röntgen	
1900	④	Cushing	Carrel	Kocher	

Bibliography

Books and articles dealing with the history of surgery can be found both separately and within the literature on medical developments as a whole. They include biographies or chronicles of particular doctors, hospitals, specialties, diseases and discoveries; reminiscences and anecdotes from the daily lives of surgeons; and some general accounts of surgery or its place in science and society. The following is a selection from the many sources used for the present book.

W. R. Bett, **A Short History of Nursing**. Faber and Faber, London 1960.

W. J. Bishop, **The Early History of Surgery**. Hale, London 1960.

Z. Cope, **A History of the Acute Abdomen**. Oxford University Press, 1965.

J. Crowlesmith (ed.), **Religion and Medicine**. Epworth, London 1962.

Courtney Dainton, **The Story of England's Hospitals**. Museum Press, London 1961.

Isabelle Elliott, **A Short History of Surgical Dressings**. Pharmaceutical Press, London 1964.

H. Ellis, **A History of Bladder Stones**. Blackwell, Oxford 1969.

Encyclopaedia Britannica, "Medicine", Vol. 23, pages 884–939. Fifteenth edition, 1974.

H. Glaser, **The Road to Modern Surgery**. Butterworth, London 1960.

S. M. Goldie, **I Have Done My Duty: Florence Nightingale in the Crimean War**. Manchester University Press, 1988.

B. L. Gordon, **Medieval and Renaissance Medicine.** New York 1959.

Harvey Graham, **Surgeons All**. Philosophical Library, New York 1957.

D. Hamilton, **The Healers: A History of Medicine in Scotland**. Canongate, 1988.

T. E. Keys, **The History of Surgical Anesthesia**. Schuman, New York 1945.

L. S. King, **The Medical World of the Eighteenth Century**. University of Chicago Press, 1958.

A. S. Lyons and R. J. Petrucelli, **Medicine: An Illustrated History.** Abrams, New York 1978.

F. Mann, **Acupuncture: The Ancient Chinese Art of Healing.** Heinemann, London 1962.

R. H. Meade, **An Introduction to the History of General Surgery**. Saunders, Philadelphia 1968.

Sir William Osler, **The Evolution of Modern Medicine.** Yale University Press, New Haven 1921.

W. Radcliffe, **Milestones in Midwifery**. Wright, Bristol 1967.

Philip Rhodes, **An Outline History of Medicine**. Butterworth, London 1985.

John Scarborough (ed.), **Symposium on Byzantine Medicine**. Dumbarton Oaks, Baltimore 1987.

Henry E. Sigerist, **A History of Medicine.** Oxford University Press, New York 1955.

Jürgen Thorwald, **Science and Secrets of Early Medicine**. Thames and Hudson, London 1962; Harcourt, New York 1963.

Owen and Sarah Wangensteen, **The Rise of Surgery**. University of Minnesota Press, 1978.

R. Woolmer, **The Conquest of Pain**. Cassell, London 1961.

Leo Zimmerman and Ilza Veith, **Great Ideas in the History of Surgery**. Dover, New York 1967.

Illustration sources

Index

Page numbers in bold type indicate illustrations.

Subjects